Books by Michael Mewshaw

MONEY
TO BURN

MONEY TO BURN

The True Story of the Benson
Family Murders

MICHAEL MEWSHAW

NEW YORK Atheneum 1987

SCRIBNER
1230 Avenue of the Americas
New York, NY 10020

SCRIBNER and design are registered trademarks of Macmillan Library Reference USA, Inc. used under license by Simon & Schuster, the publisher of this work.

Designed by Jack Meserole

Manufactured in the United States of America

10 9 8 7 6 5 4 3 2 1

Library of Congress Cataloging-In-Publication Data

Michael, Mewshaw,------------------
Money to Burn

1.   Benson, Steven. 2. Crime and criminals—Florida—Biography. 3. Murder—Floirda—Case Studies. 4. Benson Fanily. I. Title

HV6248.B415M49 1987   364.1'523'0975944   86-48005

ISBN 0-7432-2236-9

Contents

Author's Note

Quotation from written and tape-recorded material appears without the editorial (sic). When it seemed that a word was inadvertently missing, it has been added for the sake of clarity. Mistakes in punctuation, grammar, and spelling have not been corrected because it was felt that retaining an error would help convey the flavor of a document or conversation and the style of the person who had written or spoken it.

For the son treats the father with contempt, the daughter rises up against her mother, the daughter-in-law against her mother-in-law. A man's enemies are the men of his own house.

—MICAH 7:6

BOOK ONE

Public Voices

Chapter 1

Early that steamy summer morning, July 9, 1985, Steven Benson drove inland, away from the Gulf of Mexico, east to the broad white stripe of Interstate 75. Then he turned south toward Naples, Florida, thirty-five miles away. He made the round trip every day, commuting between his home in Fort Myers and his office, temporarily housed in a trailer at the Naples Industrial Park. Given the extent to which Benson's family affairs were intertwined with his business, it seemed fitting that he had set up shop on Domestic Avenue, not on nearby Mercantile, Progress, or Enterprise Avenue.

The beige van he drove was full of bank statements and ledger books, but Steven wasn't headed to the office this Tuesday morning. He was hurrying to his mother's house, where Margaret Benson and the family attorney, Wayne Kerr, were waiting to review the financial records. Mrs. Benson and Kerr were officers in a dozen corporations which Steven had formed with his mother's money.

If Steven was concerned at being called in for an accounting, it would be apparent only to somebody who knew him very well. Quiet and self-contained, he didn't often betray his feelings. He maintained the same bland poker face during heated business deals and domestic crises, and such was his success at concealing his emotions he sometimes came across as cold or arrogant.

Burly and tall—six feet two and a half inches and 230 pounds—he looked a bit like Superman in his disguise as mild-mannered Clark Kent. He had horn-rimmed glasses and smooth pale skin and a small pursed mouth. At the age of thirty-three, he had dark hair that bore a single patch of gray like a silver dollar on the right side of his head. He looked too young to serve as president of so many corporations, and he didn't dress the part either. Usually he wore cheap, out-of-date polyester suits. Today he had on a pair of blue jeans and a short-sleeved shirt. He wasn't just going to his mother's place to deliver business records. He was gong to help stake out a piece of property Mrs. Benson wanted to buy.

Flat and green and wet, this part of Florida seemed to sweep like a river toward the sea. Steven Benson was approaching the edge of the Everglades, which some have described less as a swamp than as a stream six inches deep and eighty miles wide. To build a road or a subdivision here contractors had to dig huge lakes, dredging up sand and shells for foundations, letting the surface water drain into the holes. Soon afterward, according to local lore, fish showed up in these man-made lakes via subterranean channels. Then the alligators and other predators arrived.

Although Steven had more pressing matters in mind, another traveler might have marveled that Naples, now so accessible and the fastest-growing metropolitan area in the United States, had for decades been a tiny hamlet isolated from the rest of the country. Although nineteenth-century land developers had promoted Florida as the "Italy of America," a sunny, healthful, fruit-laden and flower-perfumed peninsula with nascent communities named after European cities, the southwest corner of the state remained shut off, without paved roads or rail lines.

Back then Naples had been connected to Fort Myers by a dirt path that washed away in rainy weather. Miami, on the east coast, was little more than a hundred miles distant, but in terms of time, the journey was immeasurable. As recently as 1923, a group called the Trail Blazers had set off in Model-T Fords to cross the Everglades. Led by Seminole Indian guides, they took eleven days to slog through a jungle of mangrove, cypress, and saw grass to Miami.

In those days, the best way to reach Naples was by boat, preferably a yacht. The rich and the adventurous came down during the winter to hunt, fish, and laze in the sun. The poor came to serve the rich. Those who could afford it lived at the palatial Hotel Naples or in private "cottages." The rest made do in shacks and thatched huts. To caution the have-nots against getting grabby, the first public building put up by the town fathers was a jail. A sturdy structure, it stood until 1954, when it was razed and its stones used to reinforce the seawall.

By 1915, even during high season, Naples could claim a population of no more than two hundred, and until the late 1920s electric power was available only to those who had private generators. Still, the place possessed geographical features that would eventually make it a prime resort. Unlike so many west coast Florida communities, Naples was not simply a narrow strand of beach backed by mangrove swamps. The land between the Gulf and Naples Bay had firm sandy soil and it rose to an elevation of ten feet—a crucial consideration in hurricane country.

At last, in 1928, after thirteen years of work, the Tamiami Trail linked Naples with Tampa to the north and Miami to the east, and a flood tide of tourists rushed in. Since then the history of the town has been written in the language of glossy real estate brochures, Chamber of Commerce news releases, and upbeat feasibility studies. Frequently referred to as the Palm Beach of the Gulf Coast, Naples is said to have the highest percentage of millionaires per capita of any city in America and the second highest percentage of Mercedes Benz owners.

A place of palm-lined streets, zoned neighborhoods where house prices start at half a million dollars, clusters of exclusive shops, luxury hotels and private beach clubs, thirty golf courses, several hundred tennis courts, and gleaming new yacht basins, Naples now appears to have little in common with its crowded, poor, and clamorous sister city in Italy. There is only an occasional incongruous item on a menu—one restaurant features shark *parmiggiano*—and there is crime.

In 1984 the FBI released figures showing that among U.S. metropolitan areas with populations over 100,000, Naples had the tenth highest murder rate, ranking this elite little Eden right up there with Detroit, Los Angeles, and New York. In 1985, the killings increased, and it looked as if Naples might challenge Miami as murder capital of the nation.

The Collier County Sheriff's Department explained that the FBI figures didn't reflect the seasonal influx of tourists, transients, and migrant laborers who swelled the population by almost 40 percent. Sheriff Aubrey Rogers was quoted in the Naples *Daily News* as saying that the value system of migrant farm workers led to violence. "You've got a whole group of people which it's just in their nature to retaliate to get even."

There was also the fact that Naples was an "end of the road" town, a place where drifters and undesirables, following the Interstate, pitched up and caused problems. "Not everybody just wants to retire in the sun," Rogers said.

The police doubted that corpses dumped in Collier County after being murdered in Miami were skewing the body count. They conceded they had a serious homegrown problem. "It's a coastal area so we get a lot of smugglers and that leads to trouble." In their opinion, more drugs passed through Collier County than anywhere else in Florida, which might well mean anywhere in America.

It's not just the long coastline with its thousands of islets and mangrove hummocks, hidden bays and estuaries that make the area attractive to dope dealers. There is the proximity to Central and South America, and there is the terrain east of Naples that's ideal for off-loading drugs.

Out in the Everglades, in an area of failed real estate developments dubbed "the Blocks," thousands of acres of flat land have been paved with a grid of straight roads. Ninety square miles of these roads are unpopulated, and at night small planes swoop down and make drops to delivery men who wait beside the asphalt in airboats and swamp buggies. State, county, and federal agents patrol the area with electronic equipment. But given the speed and efficiency of the smugglers, the police often arrive to find nothing but skid marks left by planes landing and taking off.

Steven Benson slowed his van and exited from I-75, turning onto Immokalee Road. The crime rate, the rising incidence of burglary and murder, meant as much to him—maybe more—as it did to the police. Of his dozen different enterprises, all of which included the name Meridian, the one with the best prospects for success was Meridian Security Network. As described in a full-page ad in the telephone directory, this corporation offered "24 Hour Service and Monitoring" from "Security Specialists Providing Proven, Reliable, State of the Art Technology." Its "Types of Protection" ranged from "Contacts and Traps" to "Motion Detection. Stress, Seismic, Proximity" to "Process Controls, Analog or Digital."

An "electronics whiz," according to everyone who knew him, a fellow who "was daft on wiring things up," Steven aspired to be an executive. But he remained actively involved in servicing the security equipment he installed in the homes and offices of his clients.

From Immokalee Road, Steven crossed over at the rustic sign that marked the entrance to Quail Creek. In the following months this relatively new and unremarkable subdivision—"unremarkable" by Naples standards, at any rate—would be referred to as "posh" and "exclusive," the preserve of rich snobs. But among Neapolitans Quail

Creek prompted more jokes and supercilious comments than it did envy or admiration. Miles from the Gulf and the fashionable beach clubs, and even farther away from the shops of Olde Naples, it was located in a stretch of scruffy pine barrens where imported royal palms struggled for survival, their trunks and fronds supported by struts. It did have two golf courses and thirteen tennis courts. But then so did many real estate developments.

Kinder members of the town's prominent families remarked that Quail Creek was "more for the younger set, more social"—although certainly not in the sense that its residents were socialites. Others laughed at its pretensions and its "early Halloween decor."

The right place to live was Port Royal, an older neighborhood of manicured lawns, broad shady banyan trees, narrow winding lanes, and luxurious homes. Set on seven fingers of land jutting into Naples Bay, Port Royal was where the Bensons had bought a house when they first moved to Florida from Lancaster, Pennsylvania, the family home and business center. But then, after her husband's death, with two of her three children off with their own families, Margaret Benson had decided for reasons best known to herself that she needed an elaborate and much bigger house. The blueprint she submitted for approval was for a strange edifice of over 20,000 square feet that struck the Port Royal Property Owners Association as a cross between Crazy Ludwig's Castle and a motel with garage parking for ten cars.

When the blueprint was rejected as inappropriate, Mrs. Benson was angry enough to consider legal action. She consulted an attorney by the name of Michael McDonnell. But then she left her place in Port Royal, bought a Spanish Provincial home in Quail Creek, and moved in on what she considered a temporary basis. She still wanted to build her dream house, one that had "that million-dollar look."

But she could not make up her mind whether to do massive renovations on the Spanish Provincial, or to purchase three new lots in Quail Creek and start from the ground up. She had given some thought to scooping up the Spanish Provincial, stucco walls, red tile roof, and all, and transporting it to the new property, then expanding its floor space three or four times, so that she would have a 17,000 square foot showcase for her taste and talent. As she mulled over these matters, the architect's fees mounted to $50,000. And still no decision had been reached, no dream house existed except in Margaret Benson's fevered imagination.

By now Steven had reached the guardhouse at the main gate to
Quail Creek. A lot would be said later about the community's security. In some reports it would sound like an armed camp sealed off
against invaders. But Steven had no trouble getting in. The guards
knew him. It wasn't uncommon for him to visit his mother's place.
He also had clients in Quail Creek. Just this past weekend he had
driven over to repair a malfunctioning alarm system. Then he had
gone with Margaret Benson and his sister, Carol Lynn Kendall, to
measure the same lots he was supposed to stake out with string and
sticks this morning.

But one need not have clients or family connections to get past the
security guards and into Quail Creek. The subdivision still had land
for sale, and potential customers could leave their name with the
guards—no identification was demanded—then drive on unaccom-
panied. Since many of the lots were wooded and undeveloped, long
stretches looked no different from the surrounding countryside with
its thick stands of pine and palmetto and scrubby undergrowth.
There was nothing to prevent people on foot from walking out of the
woods and onto the golf cart paths, then making their way to any
address in the community.

Steven proceeded up Valewood Drive, swung left onto Butterfly
Orchid Lane, took another left on White Violet Drive, passed a vacant lot where the bare sandy ground was pale as bone meal, and
arrived at his mother's house: 13002 White Violet Drive stood just off
the third tee of the golf course, close to a water hazard.

Margaret Benson's driveway resembled the showroom of an imported automobile dealership. The family had always had a weak spot
for expensive cars; Margaret's late husband had had to buy a warehouse in Lancaster, Pennsylvania, where they stored their collector's
items, ten antique autos, including a Stutz Bearcat. Here in Florida,
Margaret, at the age of sixty-three, sported around in a metallic
bronze Porsche 928S. Her daughter, Carol Lynn, kept a Datsun
280Z to use whenever she flew down from her home in Boston. And
Scott, Margaret's twenty-one-year-old adopted son, had two red
Lotus Turbos—one out in the drive under a tarpaulin, the other in
the garage.

That was another thing Steven had to take care of today. He had
to talk to Scott about the Lotuses. A mechanic was due to come and
look them over. Neither of the $45,000 sports cars was running right.

This wasn't surprising, since Scott had a habit of pushing them to the limit and then far over the line. He liked to drive on Alligator Alley, out near the Blocks, and really cut loose. In a two-year period he had been hit with six tickets for speeding, reckless driving, and attempting to elude a police officer.

A fifth automobile sat in front of the Benson home, a brown 1978 Chevrolet Suburban. Unlike the two Lotuses and Carol Lynn's Datsun, which had transmission trouble, it was dependable and big enough to accomodate the entire family. The Bensons had ridden it over to the new lots this past Saturday and would do the same today.

There was just one small inconvenience. The air conditioner in the Suburban didn't work. Fortunately, it would be a short trip.

2

Carol Lynn Benson Kendall had been awake since 6 A.M. Bothered by a mosquito, her mother had wakened even earlier. It wasn't unusual for Mrs. Benson to get up at two or three in the morning and begin to fret over her bank statements, computerized accounts, and her "little black book," in which she jotted sums she believed people owed her.

The previous evening, July 8, Carol Lynn and her mother had gone out to dinner with the family attorney, Wayne Kerr, to celebrate Carol Lynn's forty-first birthday. But it hadn't been a terribly festive occasion. They had spend much of the meal discussing money and business matters and Steven's questionable management of the corporations. When they returned home, Mrs. Benson and Kerr had stayed up a while to watch TV, but Carol Lynn had gone to bed, curling up alone on a couch in the living room. Kerr had taken over the guest room. Mrs. Benson would also spend the night on a living room couch. The air conditioning in her bedroom was too cold for her liking.

Shortly after sunrise, the three of them were in the kitchen, at it again—debating what was happening with Margaret Benson's $10 million fortune. Wayne Kerr wore a suit and was ready to head for the Meridian Security Network office as soon as Steven delivered the files. He gobbled a plum for breakfast.

Mrs. Benson meant to go to the office with him. Meanwhile they had a myriad of topics to talk over.

Margaret Benson was a high maintenance client, one whose finances had been complicated by dubious investments, personal whims, and a penchant for impulse purchases coupled with a tendency to procrastinate over practical decisions. Kerr tried to serve as her watchdog and exercise damage control. But he lived in Philadelphia, and the Bensons frequently did things down in Florida without his knowledge or advice.

He was in Naples now not just to audit Steven's accounts. He needed to complete Mrs. Benson's 1984 income tax return, which was months overdue. Never an easy job—Mrs. Benson paid an average of $200,000 in annual taxes—the task was made more difficult this year by the 1984 Tax Reform Act, which had changed some of the provisions governing loans and gifts of the kind that Margaret lavished on her children. Kerr had recommended that she prepare a schedule of what she had given her kids, what she had loaned them, and what sort of interest and repayment terms she had arranged. But his efforts to get her to focus on this had been frustrated. Her mind was preoccupied by the Meridian corporations and by her obsession with building a new house.

Kerr felt that she had to curb her spending. In the last year she had run through $1,500,000. At that rate, she'd run through her entire $10 million in the next seven years.

But Margaret had been rich all her life. Her father, Harry Hitchcock, had made millions with the Lancaster Leaf Tobacco Company, at one point the world's largest supplier of cigar and chewing tobacco. Still hearty at the age of 88, Hitchcock remained a prominent figure in Lancaster, Pa. and had seen his fortune increase five-fold in the last nineteen years. It was impossible for Margaret to imagine there would ever be an end to the money.

She owned four homes and a dozen cars. At the Wiggins Pass Marina, she kept two boats—a thirty-six-foot Carver and a twenty-eight-foot Sea Ray. Just recently she had given her adopted son Scott permission—and a hefty down payment—to have a high performance cigarette boat built to his specifications.

Although the kids had trust funds that brought them each more than $30,000 a year, Margaret continued to shower money upon them. Then she complained that they were wasteful, unappreciative, or worse.

Scott, an aspiring tennis pro, received an allowance of $7,000 a month and private coaching at an annual cost of over $50,000. Carol Lynn, divorced and the mother of two teenage sons, lived in a home Margaret had bought for her in Boston. There she took graduate courses at Boston University, pursuing a master's degree in film production. Her unfinished thesis was a script about international industrial espionage. For her doctorate she hoped to film the script.

While Wayne and her mother discussed finances, Carol Lynn added an occasional comment and gave a glance at the digital clock on the microwave oven. She had asked Steven to be here early. She wanted to start staking out the property by 7:30 A.M. and finish before the sun got unbearably hot. But he was already late; the green numerals on the clock read 7:40.

Carol Lynn rinsed off some dishes and placed them in the dishwasher. Pouring Rice Krispies into a bowl, she put milk and fruit on the cereal, and ate breakfast moving around the room.

She thought of herself as someone who did things very precisely. A stickler for detail, she characterized herself as hardheaded and stubborn. Yet family friends saw her as someone who failed to follow through. Drifting from person to person, project to project, she took up temporary enthusiasms, then dropped them.

Her one marriage lasted less than a year, and long before the divorce was final she had lost track of her husband. She had lived in Texas for a time, entered law school in San Antonio, but quit halfway through.

As a young woman, she had won several beauty contests and in the mid-sixties was second runner-up in the Miss New Jersey pageant, reciting a monologue from *Romeo and Juliet*. Contest organizers remembered her as "an absolute doll. She showed good character." She went on to model gowns at country-club fashion shows. Now at forty-one she was still an attractive woman, with rinsed blond hair, fair skin, and blue eyes that gained an extra shimmer from the contact lenses she wore.

But her mother worried about her and confided to acquaintances that Carol Lynn was unhappy, not taking care of her appearance, and putting on weight, a problem she'd had since adolescence. On visits to Naples she would sit around the house for days in her bathrobe, arguing with Scott or Mrs. Benson. Most of the squabbles were inconsequential, just bickering about Scott's girl friends or wrangles over what sort of tile suited the bathroom. From time to time, however, these conflicts became heated, even violent. Despite almost twenty years difference in their ages, she and her adopted brother showed classic symptoms of sibling rivalry, and although she and her mother were now close, there had been periods when they were estranged. One former employee in Lancaster reported that Mrs. Benson had instructed him not to allow Carol Lynn on her property and to call the police if she refused to leave.

She seemed to do best when she had a specific goal. The graduate program at B.U. had, some people believed, renewed her sense of purpose and self-worth. On this trip to Florida, she was caught up in the debate about the Meridian corporations and the plans for the new house. In addition to measuring the lots, she was drafting sketches for the architects, who, in her opinion, lacked creativity.

At about quarter of eight, when they heard tires crunching on the gravel driveway, Mrs. Benson said, "Carol Lynn, see if that's Steven."

Carol Lynn crossed the kitchen to a door leading to the garage, opened it, and glanced through a window. Steven's van was pulled in facing the house. The rear doors of the van were open, and she could look straight through the windshield and see her brother standing at the back. He had his eyes fixed on the floor of the van and his arms were moving as if he were doing something with his hands.

She returned to the kitchen and told them it was Steven. About five minutes later, he came in and joined the conversation. "Is Scott up?" he asked.

He had told his sister the night before that he wanted Scott to help them stake out the property. But Carol Lynn hadn't spoken to Scott, who usually picked up his girlfriend after work and returned home late. Mrs. Benson went to wake her adopted son.

Carol Lynn moved to a table in the living-dining room to work on her architectural sketches, while Wayne Kerr sat at a desk in the lanai off the kitchen doing Mrs. Benson's taxes. Steven asked Carol Lynn, "Where are the stakes and the stuff we need?"

"Oh, they're underneath there." She indicated a built-in Formica-tipped desk in the kitchen.

He headed to where she had pointed and, Carol Lynn assumed, carried the things to the Suburban.

Then Scott stumbled into the room, wearing a pair of blue shorts. Strongly built and deeply tanned from tennis, he had dark hair cut in a pageboy style. He wasn't happy and demanded to know why he had to get up.

Mrs. Benson told him. "Steven wants to talk to you about the Lotuses."

"I don't know why he wants to talk to me about the Lotuses," the boy complained. "He's already talked to me twice before." But he tottered outside, shoeless, shirtless, moving like a sleepwalker.

Shortly thereafter, Steven reappeared in the kitchen and said to Kerr, who was making a cup of Sanka, "Oh, Wayne, you don't want to drink that instant stuff. I'm going out to get some coffee. In fact, since you're on a diet, I'll bring you back some Danish."

"Why didn't you get it on the way in?" Carol Lynn demanded. She didn't drink coffee. She was watching her weight and didn't want pastry either. Although she said she was eager to get an early start, Kerr later recalled that Carol Lynn and her mother were still in their bathrobes.

Mrs. Benson kept only instant Sanka in the house. She asked her son to bring her some real coffee.

Nobody was happier than Wayne Kerr that Steven was going off to a convenience store. For one thing he detested Sanka. For another, he was a huge, hulking man with an appetite to match his size and a weakness for sweets that was well-known to employees at Meridian Security Network. They always laid in a supply of pastry when he visited the office.

Although they were at odds over Steven's atrocious accounting procedures, Wayne and Steven were good friends. Benson had been best man at Kerr's wedding this past winter. Both were big, fleshy, and seemingly uneasy about their size. They had dark hair, round faces, and horn-rimmed glasses. But Kerr had a mustache and stooped shoulders while Steven had the stiff, straight-backed bearing of a soldier.

When Steven left for the Shop 'N Go, Mrs. Benson and Carol Lynn got dressed and went back to work. Mrs. Benson was in the lanai with her lawyer, reviewing tax information that had been prepared by her secretary, Marty Taylor. Marty herself showed up around 8:30 A.M. and began to organize her day's chores.

With all the confusion around her, all the people coming and going, it was a wonder Carol Lynn could concentrate. The room where she sat sketching house plans was full of distractions and strewn with magazines and newspapers. Foam pads covered the floor as if a carpet were expected but hadn't arrived yet.

Along with a grand piano, lacquered papier-mâché animals crowded the living room like figures from a child's nightmare after a day at the zoo. There was a huge parrot painted in livid colors and an even bigger hippopotamus. In front of the couch, as if guarding the most comfortable seat, lurked an eight-foot-long alligator.

Carol Lynn kept at her sketches until her mother interrupted. "Have you seen Scott? Did he go with Steven?"

"Oh no. I'm sure he didn't. I'm sure he went back to bed."

Wayne Kerr came into the living room, and Carol Lynn and he cracked a few jokes.

Kerr quipped that Steven must have gotten lost.

Marty Taylor said he must have had to grind the beans.

Carol Lynn wisecracked, "The amount of time he's been gone, he could have driven all the way to Fort Myers to get the coffee."

When he came back carrying a cardboard container with three large cups and several cellophane-wrapped packages of pastry, Kerr razzed him for being late. But Steven said he had bumped into a business contact. Kerr didn't press him. The coffee was hot, the Danish was tasty, and that was what mattered to Wayne.

After five or ten minutes of idle chat, Steven asked where Scott was, and Mrs. Benson went to wake him for a second time. Still looking rumpled and grumpy, Scott reappeared. He had put on shoes and a light blue T-shirt with an ad for the Gang Plank, a local nightspot, on his broad chest.

At ten of nine, just as it seemed they were ready to set off, the phone rang. It was Scott's tennis coach trying to schedule a lesson. Scott told him it would have to be later.

Then once that was settled, Steven said, "Oh, Mother, I want you to go too."

Mrs. Benson was surprised. "Why do I need to come along?"

"Well, there are things—things that I want you to see," Steven said.

After remarking that she wasn't wearing the right clothes—she had on a linen blouse and navy blue skirt—and would have to change her heels for a pair of flats, Margaret was at the point of agreeing to go when Marty Taylor reminded her of another appointment. "The pool people are coming this morning."

Though there was some question about the time—were they due at 9 A.M. or 9:30?—there seemed no doubt in Mrs. Benson's mind that men were coming to give an estimate on the cost of installing a swimming pool. She believed a pool would make the Spanish Provincial easier to sell if and when she decided to build a new house. "Someone's got to be here," she said.

"Wayne can get a price on it," Steven said.

"How can Wayne get a price on a pool?" Carol Lynn demanded.

"Just tell them to give us a price on something fifteen feet by thirty feet."

"Steven, that's not going to work." Carol Lynn argued it was like getting a quote on apples when you really wanted to buy oranges. Her mother was in the market for a pool with curved sides and a fountain and special tiles, not a plain fifteen by thirty box.

Steven suggested that when the men showed up Marty should send them over to look at the pool at one of the Ruttenberg model homes. Mrs. Benson felt that that might be all right, but Carol Lynn thought it was ridiculous. That wasn't the kind of pool they wanted.

"Look, we'll do it this way." Carol Lynn insisted that since the new lots were nearby, "when the pool men get here, Marty can take the car and come over and get you, and you can come back and talk with them."

This seemed to satisfy everybody—except perhaps Wayne Kerr, who stood there during all the bickering and debate, scribbling notes about pool dimensions, specifications, and prices, copying down Steven's instructions, then Mrs. Benson's, then Carol Lynn's. In the end, his understanding differed from Carol Lynn's. He assumed the pool should be similar to the Ruttenberg model and if the contractors had any questions they should go look at it.

At last they were ready to leave. Mrs. Benson, Scott, and Steven walked out to the Suburban together. Carol Lynn had to put on her white tennis hat. Then she had to find the dark glasses that she was always setting down and promptly forgetting. Because she wore contact lenses and suffered from allergies, her eyes were sensitive, and she couldn't go outside unless she had the hat and dark glasses.

After pausing at the front door to step into her saddle shoes, she emerged from the house wearing teal blue slacks and a sleeveless pullover with a boat neck collar. Scott sat behind the steering wheel of the Suburban. Mrs. Benson was up front in the other bucket seat. Having just finished swinging his mother's door shut, Steven went and stood beside the right rear passenger seat. That door was open. Because the air conditioner didn't work, the windows were open too.

Carrying the rolled-up plot plan and an insulated plastic glass full of Diet Pepsi, Carol Lynn walked around the driver's side to the seat behind Scott. Both doors on that side were shut. She had to shift the plot plan under her arm and awkwardly open the rear door.

Since the chassis was high off the ground, she couldn't climb in with her hands full. She set the plastic glass and the plot plan on the benchlike backseat. As she did so, her mother asked, "Who's got the keys?"

Steven indicated he had them. "Well, give them to Scott," Mrs. Benson said.

Steven started around the back of the Suburban and reached Carol Lynn as she was climbing in. She had one foot on the ground and one foot inside the car when he put his hand on her behind and boosted her up onto the seat. He moved on to the driver's door and passed the keys through the open window to Scott. Or else—there was some uncertainty about this—he had already handed Scott the keys before coming around to help Carol Lynn.

He turned to go back to his seat, but had a second thought and said, "Just a minute, I forgot something. I'll have to run in the house and get it."

"Fine," said Mrs. Benson.

Carol Lynn left her door open. She didn't like to sit in a closed car on a hot day. From the corner of her eye, she saw Steven proceed past the front end of the Suburban. Then she glanced down to pick up the plastic glass of Pepsi and to pull the plot plan closer to her. When she looked up again, Steven was not in view.

Scott shifted behind the steering wheel, leaning to the right as if to insert the keys in the ignition and start the engine. Carol Lynn thought she heard a *click!* Then abruptly she heard nothing at all and saw only a bright orange enveloping light.

3

Wayne Kerr heard the blast, felt it shake the house and send gravel pelting against the windows. Marty Taylor, sitting nearby at a kitchen counter, heard and felt the blast too. Kerr and she looked at each other. "Oh my God. What was that?"

The lawyer's immediate reaction was that one of the Lotuses had blown up. He lumbered over to a window, but could see nothing. He spun around and headed toward the front door, hurrying his considerable bulk through those confined quarters cluttered with furniture and a menagerie of giant papier-mâché animals.

The door was open and Steven was there screaming, "My God, call an ambulance."

Kerr darted back to the telephone and dialed 911. Marty Taylor rushed over to him. Steven was shaking, his muscles quivering, his

lips moving, but incapable of coherent speech. He could only utter
animallike sounds. When the operator answered, Kerr blurted, "We
have an emergency out at Quail Creek."

"Yes sir, what's the problem?"

"A car blew up."

"A car blew up?"

"Yes."

"Is there anybody in it?"

"Yes, there was." Kerr fought to control his voice. "We need an
ambulance immediately."

"Okay. Are they still in the vehicle?"

"Ah, I can't tell you."

"Where in Quail Creek?"

"13002 White Violet Drive."

"13002 White Water Drive?"

"White Violet!"

"And what's your name?"

"Ah, it's Benson," Kerr said.

In the background, faint voices on sheriff's radios could be heard.
"We're coming. We're coming." Then the emergency operator spoke
to Kerr. "Okay, give me your phone number. They're on their way,
sir. Sir? Hello. Hello, sir?"

But Wayne Kerr was no longer on the line. Marty Taylor had the
receiver. "Hello," she said.

"I need a name, please."

"Benson. B-E-N-S-O-N."

"Give me your phone number."

"598-2955."

"Do you know if they're out of the vehicle yet?"

"I don't know." Marty was in tears.

"Okay, they're on their way."

"It's exploding!" Suddenly there was a second blast and a woman
screamed.

"They're on their way," the operator repeated.

Kerr and Steven stepped out of the house, and the first thing the
lawyer noticed was the gutted shell of the Suburban, its shattered
doors flung wide, its roof peeled back like the top of a sardine can.
Then he saw the bodies and knew he had seen enough. Kerr couldn't
stand the sight of blood; usually he fainted. Since other men were

already tending to the dead and wounded, he decided he could best help by trying to comfort Steven and calm him down. But his friend was by now out of control and in an extreme state of shock.

4

Carol Lynn Kendall wasn't conscious of the second bomb, and didn't remember hearing the first one, didn't remember the Suburban turning into a murderous hive of shrapnel, flying glass, and flaming upholstery. She felt something going through her body, stiffening it, pressing it back into the seat, pulling her down. An orange light surrounded her and seemed to form a tunnel where she was lying down and looking at her own back. With the pain shooting through her, she thought she was being electrocuted. What had she touched to get such a shock?

"I'm being electrocuted. Somebody please help me. I'm being electrocuted," she screamed. Or thought she had.

When no one came, she forced one eye open, her left eye, and saw Scott sprawled on the ground. He didn't appear to be badly injured. There was just a little blood on his mouth. But instinctively she knew. He's dead, she thought.

Suddenly she saw the Suburban was on fire. Flames flickered over the front seats, lapping toward her. Carol Lynn glanced down at her hands and couldn't see them. They weren't there. Oh my God, she thought, my hands are burnt off. How am I going to get out of the car?

But she knew she had to do something to save herself. Leading with her shoulder, she pitched out of the open door. Her brain seemed to be on automatic pilot, and it dictated her body's actions. When you're on fire, her mind told her, you roll on the ground to smother the flames. So she rolled off the gravel driveway and onto the grass.

Still, her shoulder was burning hot. She started to reach up to slap at the flames, but wasn't sure she had hands. If she did have them, she feared they would catch fire too. She grabbed the bottom of her pullover and tore it up over her head and threw it away.

Next thing she knew she was propped on an arm, not so much sitting as leaning at a slant, just like, she thought, the girl in that Andrew Wyeth painting, *Christina's World*. But Carol Lynn wasn't gazing across a field at an ancient clapboard house. She was peering at her brother, Steven, who stood on the walk facing the Suburban.

He looked terrified, looked almost like he was going mad. His expression struck her as one of absolute horror, as if the world had blown up. She called to him. Or thought she did. She was hysterical at that point. She couldn't understand why he wasn't coming to help her.

Suddenly Steven reacted. His eyes opened wider, his jaw dropped, and he exclaimed, "Oh my God, oh my God." Whirling to his left, he ran into the house where he bumped into Wayne Kerr.

"My God, call an ambulance."

A party of golfers on the third tee behind the Benson house heard the blast and saw a billowing column of smoke. One of the men heard Steven holler, "Oh my God. Come quick. Help, somebody."

Three of the golfers scrambled down off the raised tee and galloped to the bomb site. (The fourth man played on through.) Charles Meyer, an older fellow but agile and quick, arrived first, took one look at Mrs. Benson's mangled remains, realized there was no hope there, and raced around the car to where Carol Lynn was curled on her side in a fetal position screaming, "I'm hot. I'm hot."

He grabbed her under the arms and dragged her backwards away from the flames. The Suburban was an inferno. Meyer had never seen such an intense blaze.

He didn't notice his golf partner, Fred Merrill, on the other side of the burning wreckage pulling Mrs. Benson's body away from the fire. Neither man made it more than ten feet before the second bomb erupted and the Chevy burst open like a giant chrysanthemum shedding lethally sharp petals.

Shrapnel shot through Meyer's arm and into his chest. Another piece took off the tip of his nose. He fell and landed on Carol Lynn. Then he struggled to his feet and staggered away, bleeding profusely.

Fred Merrill caught his heel, lost his balance, and was already falling backwards when the second blast hit. That fall may have saved his life. A few metal fragments grazed his chest. One left an abrasion, the other required six stitches.

Carol Lynn wasn't aware of the second explosion or of Charles Meyer saving her life. Her next memory was of people rushing toward her from all directions. She wondered where they came from. The street was usually so quiet, you never saw anybody.

Now there seemed to be men in work clothes everywhere. Two of them stopped at a distance and stared at her. They appeared to be leery of approaching the car. One man was standing up straight; the other crouched down.

"Please, help me," Carol Lynn called.

They hurried to her. "We gotta get you away from this car." Nobody knew when another bomb might blow.

They stood her up and walked her over to a neighbor's lawn. They told her to sit down. But she insisted, "No, if I sit down, I'm gonna die. I won't sit down."

She felt weak and strange, and in her mind she equated standing up with staying alive. As long as she was on her feet, she wasn't dead. But the men kept urging her to sit down and she tried to think of reasons not to. She told them there were bugs in the grass; she didn't want bugs all around her.

Finally they convinced her to sit down, and Carol Lynn asked for ice to cool her burns. Instead, they brought her wet towels. She knew ice was best for burns and again asked them to bring her some.

Steven had come over to see about Carol Lynn. Then he left and she watched him, and he reminded her of those TV newsreels of people caught in wars or in the bloody aftermath of bombings. He could have stepped out of a report from Viet Nam or Beirut, she thought. He was thrashing his arms, throwing his head back and forth, screaming as he circled the burning husk of the car.

Then Steven raced toward the fire, as if to go into the Suburban. Carol Lynn thought maybe their mother was still belted to her seat, trapped in that furnace of jagged metal. Somebody overtook Steven as he reached the right rear corner of the Chevy, grabbed him around the chest, and dragged him away.

A short, shapely blond girl with caramel-colored skin came out of the Benson house. Carol Lynn saw her go to Scott, crouch down, and feel for a heartbeat. Breaking into tears, the girl returned to the house, passing Steven, who was sitting on the porch now with his face in his hands.

Carol Lynn recognized the blond girl. Her name was Kimberly Dawn Beegle, she was twenty, and she worked as a waitress at Port of the Isles, at the edge of the Everglades.

The flames from the Suburban were in danger of igniting the beige van. A trash company employee—a fellow by the name of Brian Nelson, who laughingly referred to himself as a "garbologist"—backed the van out of the driveway and parked it near a neighbor's house. Only afterward did he realize how foolish he'd been. What if the van had been wired? He'd have been hamburger just like the people on the lawn. From the house he fetched blankets and covered their bodies.

By the time Bill Boettcher and Patricia Hedrick of Emergency Medical Service arrived, Carol Lynn was draped in wet towels, but hadn't gotten the ice she'd asked for. She was worried about her contact lenses. She wanted someone to bring her contact lens case. She was afraid she'd lose consciousness with her lenses in.

Patricia Hedrick checked her condition. She had burns and shrapnel wounds on the right side of her face and on her arms, hands, chest, and legs. Her back had been burned on the right side from the shoulder to the base of her spine. Her condition was serious, but not critical.

Ms. Hedrick then crossed toward the bomb site. EMS had received word that a man in the house was hysterical. As Ms. Hedrick got to Scott, she glanced down and kept on going.

Although Carol Lynn's own instinctive reaction had been that her adopted brother was dead, it deeply upset her, even angered her, that the paramedic didn't do more than give him a glance. Weeks later, she would continue to complain that nobody had tried to revive Scott, whom she remembered as hardly having a cut on him.

But this only proved what cruel tricks the eyes can play and how limited is any single point of view. Carol Lynn hadn't seen Scott after he had been rolled onto his stomach. His back was little more than braised, pulverized meat and powder-blackened wounds. A piece of shrapnel had shattered his skull, exposing a pink sliver of brain, and the blast had driven a two-inch wooden splinter into his thorax. His blue shorts were in tatters and a dollar bill in his back pocket was plastered to his buttock.

Mrs. Benson, whom Carol Lynn feared was caught in the car and incinerated, had been blown out of the Suburban, her body badly mutilated, especially on the left side, which looked as though it had been hacked open with a meat cleaver. She had lost almost all of her left hand, both eyes, and much of the flesh from her face.

Patricia Hedrick returned to Carol Lynn and cut off her slacks, socks, and bra, and tended to her second-degree burns and lacerations. She put a compress over the right side of her face, bandaged a bad gash on her right ankle, and rigged up an IV which a construction worker held while Hedrick inserted the needle into Carol Lynn's arm. Then the paramedics swaddled her in sheets, laid her on a gurney, and wheeled her over to the ambulance. Fred Merrill, one of the injured golfers, was a friend of the Benson family. But that day Carol Lynn was as unaware of his presence in the ambulance as she had been of the second bomb and of Charles Meyer rescuing her.

As the paramedics put her into the ambulance, Patricia Hedrick heard her say, "I know my brother has something to do with this. Ask my brother."

She didn't specify which brother.

For the rest of the trip, she kept asking, "Am I going to die? Am I going to die?"

Chapter 2

At Naples Community Hospital, Carol Lynn lay on her back, still hooked to an IV. The tiny room had one wall of glass, looking onto the nurses' station across the hall. But all she saw was the ceiling. A doctor had removed her contact lenses, and she couldn't even say for certain what hospital she was in.

Nurses and doctors bustled through the room. She asked for a priest, and that created confusion. A Catholic priest came. But Carol Lynn was high Episcopalian, and so an Episcopal priest was called.

Then Ruby Caston, the Benson family maid, showed up, and they spoke about Kim Beegle, the girl Scott had slept with last night. According to Ruby's deposition, Carol Lynn then told her, without elaborating, "Kim's brothers killed my mother and my brother."

That afternoon, at four thirty, Thomas Smith entered the room. "I'm a detective from the sheriff's office."

"Where are you?" Carol Lynn asked.

"I'm over here on your left-hand side," Smith said. "I'm wearing a mask here for your own protection at this time. And, just so that you do know, I am tape recording this so I don't have to take so many notes."

"Okay, that's fine."

"Now I understand that you are on medication and so I expect that you're going to be a little groggy and you may be a little bit confused. Okay? But what I have is, I have a couple questions I need to ask of you so that we can attempt to try to get a little better understanding of what has happened."

Officer Smith asked if she understood clearly, and Carol Lynn said, "Yeah, this is like filling out an accident report."

"Kind of—kind of like filling out an accident report then, okay?"

But Carol Lynn wanted to know, "Is this something I should have my attorney here?"

"No. We've already talked to your attorney." Presumably he meant Wayne Kerr.

Officer Smith asked eighteen questions for basic background information. Where were they going and why? Who was seated where? In what order had they entered the Suburban? Were they wearing seat belts? Then he asked, "And where was—uhh—Steven when the explosion occurred?"

"Steven had gone inside."

"He had gone back inside the house?"

"Right."

"Had he—had he come out, or was he still inside when the explosion happened?"

"He was still in the house," Carol Lynn said.

"Do you have any idea what caused the explosion?"

"No way." She gave a gasp. "I—I didn't even know at the time what it was." She described sitting in the car, waiting for Steven, when "maybe there was that kind—*click!*—you know, when you start—start to start a car." She added, "Scott doesn't like to sit without air conditioning, so maybe he was turning it on."

Then she related the sensation of being electrocuted and pulled down and "surrounded by—oh, I don't know, it's hard to describe. But it's like an orangy-red sort of thing, but I don't—I wasn't really conscious.

"It was like I was unconscious, kind of in a way like I am now but not quite." She compared the state to being awake, but not really, to knowing your mind is working, but not being aware of your surroundings or of time. She hadn't become truly conscious until she forced one eye open and saw Scott.

"Okay," Officer Smith interrupted, "let's get away from that for a minute, all right?"

He asked who had been at the house and whether anyone had left. After establishing that Steven didn't live there, but had driven down from Fort Myers this morning, Carol Lynn said, "Yeah, right after he got there, he went out and got coffee and doughnuts for Wayne and my mother."

"Did he come back with coffee and doughnuts?"

"Yeah."

"Which car did he drive?"

"I don't know."

After asking where the coffee and pastry had been purchased, Smith switched the subject to how long Carol Lynn had been in Naples, and this brought on a lengthy account of how Mrs. Benson and Scott had gone to Europe in June so that Scott could play in a series of tennis tournaments. But Mrs. Benson had been ill with pneumonia before, during, and after the trip. "Mother was so sick that they came back early."

While Scott flew on to Florida, arriving around June 17, Mrs. Benson had stayed with her daughter in Boston to be treated at a local hospital. Carol Lynn and Margaret had finally flown to Naples about a week ago.

After several minutes of seeminging aimless talk about Carol Lynn's graduate program, Smith asked, "What about Steve? What was Steve going back into the house for?"

"I don't—I wasn't paying attention. See, he—he had already gotten in the car on the other side, and I told Scott to get in. And Mother said—I—I guess Scott didn't have a key. So he got out of the car, came around and—because I hadn't gotten in yet. So he kind of gave me a boost in. He handed the keys to Scott and started back around the car."

"Who—who gave the keys to Scott?"

"Steven did because Steven had the keys."

"So, wait a minute." Smith performed a tantalizing pirouette around the subject, sliding off to the periphery so that he could slam back to the center. "You—all four of you came out of the house together, you loaded up the car—?"

"Well, kind of," Carol Lynn said. "I mean we didn't walk out the door exactly together, but sort of."

He let her natter on about what had been loaded into the Chevy and when. Then, as if puzzling it out for himself, he said, "So Steve had—Steve—Steve had the keys to the car, and he had come down from Fort Myers. Is it—is—"

"Well—" Carol Lynn cut in, only to have Smith push on through.

"—possible that Steve had driven the car to the store?"

"I wouldn't know," she said. "I don't know. I mean, he—I—I don't know how Steven had—why Steven had the keys. I mean, Mother keeps the keys in the kitchen and, you know, whoever she'll say go get the keys, and somebody'll pick them up. So I don't know."

A moment later Smith asked, "Had there been any problems with anybody? Has there been any family threats?"

"Not that I personally know about."

"Okay, you know, if you look at this, your family is a very prominent name."

"It is?"

"Well, Benson? Aren't you associated with the tobacco Benson?"

"You mean like the Benson & Hedges Benson?"

"Yeah."

"No."

"Somebody advised me that you were."

"My father was in the tobacco business, but we don't have anything to do with Benson & Hedges cigarettes."

Smith was not alone in having been misled about this matter, and he would be far from the last person to link the Bensons to the famous cigarette brand. More than a year later, NBC "Nightly News" would report that Steven and Carol Lynn were heirs to the Benson & Hedges fortune. But by then much more serious journalistic errors had shaped public opinion and several people's fates.

"Well, have you had any family problems?" Smith repeated. "Has there been any family threats? Has there been any rivalries, anybody that would want to hurt Scott, hurt you or your mother or Steven, not maybe all together, but maybe even individually?"

"Nobody would—I mean my mother couldn't possibly have an enemy."

"How about Scott?"

"Scott has some strange friends." But, she assured him, "I haven't met any of them."

"Do you think Scott was involved in any type of illegal activities?"

"No, I don't think Scott was, but—"

"On your way to the hospital, you made a couple different statements about—"

"Well, his—he's got a girl friend who's got some brothers who I understand aren't too reputable."

"Kim Beegle?"

"Right...."

"Do you think that there's any possibility that drugs are involved?"

This subject seemed to fluster Carol Lynn. "With—you—you—mean—"

"With Scott?" Smith said.

"—with her brothers? I mean—I—the only thing I know is hearsay, so I don't know whether—"

"What do you hear for hearsay?"

"Well, I mean, I've heard that they have something to do with drugs."

"Both brothers or just one?"

"I think there's three brothers. I don't know. I've never met them."

But Officer Smith wasn't referring to Kim's brothers. "I meant Scott or Steve. Do you think either Scott or Steve are involved in drugs in any way themselves, personally?"

"I—" Carol Lynn hesitated. "Not that I know of."

"Does Scott or Steve use cocaine or any narcotics?"

"Not that I know of."

"Now it's, you know, important to be truthful, and I'm sure you're being truthful. You see, you need to think real hard. Is there anybody at all that would want to hurt anybody in the family? I mean, it's obvious when you look at this that it appears—well, it appears that it's deliberate."

"Well, I don't know," she said, "how much of these questions I should answer without—answer without the attorney."

"Well, you're not a suspect in any crime."

Carol Lynn explained that she knew only what she had been told, and she couldn't vouch for its accuracy.

"I think it's my job to determine what's accurate," Smith said. "We need to stop these people for your own protection and for Steve's protection."

"Well, let's see, what do I know? I know that Scott sold Kim's brother [David] a boat, and I heard that—I heard, you know, it's like six hands old—"

"Yeah, the rumor."

"—that he's a drug dealer. . . . And then he said—well, he didn't want anything in writing, and he agreed to pay Scott $14,000. And after he'd paid $10,000, he ran it into the mangroves or something and tore out the bottom. And—and he said that he wasn't going to pay Scott any more money, and he was gonna hide the boat so Scott couldn't get it back."

"Okay," Smith pressed her again, "has there ever been any threats made? Did Scott ever say, hey, this guy's threatened us or anything?"

"No, Scott doesn't communicate to me at all."

"Whose vehicle was that?" Smith changed course. "Who drives it all the time?"

"Which vehicle?"

"The one that you were in."

"Well, mostly my mother, but Scott's been using it."

"So who would be the one that used it the most?"

"Oh God, I don't know. I mean, I'm not down here all the time. I mean, lately Scott's been using it because his car is like a lemon, and it kept having stuff wrong with it. So he's been using the Suburban, because he goes down and picks up Kim where she works."

A moment later Smith returned to the prime topic. "So there's nobody that you can think of other than Kim's brothers involved maybe with this boat deal that would have any type of grudge?"

"Not that I know of. I mean, that whole crowd that Scott knows, from what I understand, are kind of shady characters."

"Do you know if he hangs around any place in particular?"

"I have absolutely no idea where he goes at all."

"What about last night? Did Scott go anywhere last night?"

"Well, he left the house at ten thirty, but——we just assume he goes down to pick up Kim."

Smith wanted to know when Scott and Kim came back to the house.

"I don't know," Carol Lynn said. "We were all asleep." She hadn't been aware that Kim had slept there until after the explosions, and she hadn't kept track of Scott's movements this morning any more than she had last night.

"Okay, Carol, as far as you're concerned though, you can't think of anybody—what you're saying to me, as far as you have knowledge, there has been no direct threats, no extortions, no death threats, no—you know—strange letters or anything like that in the recent weeks?"

"Not that I know of. Now, I'm sorry, it's possible that Scott may have had some threats against him—I have in the back of my mind that my mother had said something about the fact that, you know, Kim's brother had threatened him or something. But I can't be sure about that. Maybe Steven would know."

"Okay."

"Or even Wayne might know, because they had sent this brother a letter, a certified letter, but—"

"Okay."

"—as far as I—I don't—I have no knowledge of letters or anything arriving recently. And, as I said, nobody could possibly—I can't imagine anybody having anything against my mother. I mean, she was nice to everybody."

When asked to relate anything else that might be important, Carol Lynn said, "My reaction was it had to be a bomb. I mean, that's after I got out of the car. You know, when I was in there, I didn't think that. But afterwards, because it just was—whatever happened, it was big."

Chapter 3

The Collier County Sheriff's Department agreed with Carol Lynn Kendall. The Benson bomb murders were big. Ultimately it became the county's most extensive and most highly publicized investigation. For forty-four days fifteen local officers worked on the case full time, assisted by twelve investigators from the Bureau of Alcohol, Tobacco and Firearms (ATF), a federal organization whose agents flew into Naples from Miami, Atlanta, and Washington, D.C.

Shortly after 10 A.M., less than an hour after the murders, when Lieutenant Wayne Graham of the Collier County Sheriff's Department arrived at 13002 White Violet Drive, the crime scene had been cordoned off with yellow plastic tape. Firemen from North Naples had extinguished the blaze in the Suburban, popped the hood, and cut the battery cables.

Lieutenant Graham was with SRU, Special Response Unit, the equivalent of a SWAT team. Explosions were one of his responsibilities. He spoke to a few deputies and joined in the search for debris that had blown out of the Suburban. Fragments of metal and glass and dry-cell batteries lay scattered over the driveway, the lawn, and the street out front. The explosion had sent shrapnel scything through the woods across the street, and one jagged scrap had penetrated a Florida Power and Light electrical box.

Graham spotted hunks of human flesh adjacent to a neighbor's driveway. The side panel of the beige van was splashed with blood and bits of skin. The Suburban itself was charred so badly Graham couldn't even guess what color it had been. The body of a white male lay on the left side of the vehicle, the body of a white female lay on the right side.

Graham didn't touch anything. He simply pointed to objects, just as half a dozen other officers were doing. Crime scene experts would later pick up the evidence, label it, enter its location on a schematic chart, and save it for forensic study.

Fifteen or twenty minutes after his arrival, Graham huddled with Lieutenant Harold Young, Supervisor of the Crimes against Persons Division of the Collier County Sheriff's Department. Both men were middle-aged police veterans who had conducted enough investigations to know they needed more personnel. They also agreed that they'd better get someone from the bomb squad to check out the other automobiles at the Benson house.

Although they were too cynical and self-deprecating to make any great claims for themselves, Young and Graham would become central figures in the case. Till the end, they would say there was nothing special about it. It was just another murder, one that was slightly different because the Bensons had money and the media had an insatiable audience to satisfy. This magnified the importance of real or, more often in their view, imagined mistakes by the police. Otherwise, it was a straightforward investigation, with tedious footwork, lots of travel, and the hassle of melding local policemen with ATF agents.

Lieutenant Young appeared to be the administrative type, a desk man given to wearing white shirts and ties. Raised in the coal mining town of McKee, Kentucky, sixty miles south of Lexington, he was short and sturdy and had a full head of dark hair. He drawled his jokes and because of his polite, laconic manner got away with outrageous irreverence. On his desk was a death's head. On his file cabinet stood a painting of a skull.

Yet in more serious moments, when he reflected on all the murder cases he had handled, he said, "Sometimes I think I can't live with this shit. I don't ever want to go to another autopsy of a child."

Wayne Graham spent a lot of time in the field. Sunburnt and ruddy-faced, with receding hair and a trim mustache, he dressed in blue jeans, jogging shoes, and polo shirts. A down-home animated fellow, he managed to make chasing drug dealers sound funny. On the wall of his office hung pictures of the SRU team clad in camouflage uniforms, going through maneuvers in the Everglades. Within easy reach of his desk was an AR-15 semiautomatic .223-caliber assault rifle.

Graham had a thing or two in common with Harold Young besides policework and an iconoclastic sense of humor. He was short, and when it became clear to everybody in Naples that the Benson case was bound to be made into a movie, the secretaries at the Sheriff's Department taunted the diminutive lieutenants that they would be played by Dudley Moore and Mickey Rooney.

Graham also shared Young's dark recognition of the difficulties of their job. It was bad enough being confronted week after week with corpses and with backbreaking, brain-numbing cases. But it was worse, in Graham's opinion, to get an indictment, then go into court and have to fight to present the facts to a jury. "Justice is not just blind," Graham complained. "It's deaf and dumb and has herpes too."

Assisted by Investigator Michael Koors, Lieutenant Youg conducted the first interview with Steven Benson. Koors was a head taller than Harold Young, and where the senior officer dressed and behaved like a cop, Koors looked like an actor in a TV series playing a cop. "Miami Vice" tan and handsome, with long hair and stylish clothes, he was a casting director's and every courthouse groupie's dream.

Koors differed from Young in one other significant respect. They had contrasting reactions to Benson's emotional state. Like so many eyewitnesses who described Steven as hysterical, frantic, and hyperventilating, Koors recalled him as "very violently shaking." He had never seen anybody shake so badly at a crime scene. He couldn't even hold a cigarette.

But Harold Young characterized Benson as quite calm and in good control considering the circumstances.

Whatever his condition, Steven cooperated with the police and, moving into his mother's bedroom, he answered the questions Young and Koors asked. He told them he had driven down from Fort Myers in the beige van, arriving around 7:30 A.M. He had come to stake out the property and, he acknowledged, to deliver the business records he had brought with him. He had gone to the Shop 'N Go in the Suburban because his van was low on gas. He had been delayed at the convenience store when he bumped into somebody from the Sand Castle Construction Company. He said he was so upset he couldn't remember the person's name.

Estimating he had been gone for an hour, Steven said he returned to the house and the family came out to the Suburban to drive to the nearby lots. But he had forgotten something and was going to get it when the first bomb exploded. He claimed he was three steps from the car when that happened.

• • •

Soon after the murders, Marty Taylor made a call to arrange for
Debra Benson, Steven's wife, to be brought down to Quail Creek.
Steven Hawkins, the vice-president of Meridian Marketing in Fort
Myers, went over to pik her up. Hawkins had been to Steven and
Debbie's house for dinner the night before and when he left at 11:30
P.M., Steven was in his robe, headed for bed. After an amiable eve-
ning of social chitchat and an hour of business, death had been the
furthest thing from anybody's mind. Hawkins' instinctive reaction,
like Kerr's, was that one of the Lotuses must have blown up.

Debbie and he started off in Hawkins' car. But then he noticed he
was low on gas, and they switched to Debbie's. It was what Steven
Benson had done earlier that day—use someone else's car and gas.
The way things were going at Meridian Marketing, any small savings
helped. But in Benson's case, investigators immediately assumed he
had more than economy in mind.

A young man with a dark mustache, Hawkins had a deep reso-
nant voice out of keeping with his slim physique. The voice of a news
announcer, a politician, a pastor, it was strong and confident. But
when he arrived at the Benson house, the bodies of Scott and Margaret still lay beside the smoking wreckage of the Suburban, and
Hawkins felt far from strong and confident. He felt sick to his stomach.

Steven came over to let Debbie through the police line. He looked
tired, worn out, but otherwise normal. He said to Hawkins, "Did
you get any money in today?"

"Are you all right?" Hawkins asked.

"Yes," Benson said.

But Hawkins was feeling worse. He went to a neighbor's house
and asked to use the toilet.

Conflicting opinions about Steven Benson's emotional condition
existed even within the same family. When he heard about the bombing, Steve Vaughan, Scott's tennis coach, hurried to the house with
Sheri, his wife. As late as 1 P.M. Sheri thought Steven looked dazed,
confused. He was wandering back and forth, as if he didn't know
what to do with himself.

Her husband, however, saw what he considered troubling behavior. Neither Benson nor Kerr seemed to be handling himself very

well. There was some horseplay with a cigarette, then laughter that left Vaughan feeling uneasy.

He helped with the funeral arrangements and notified relatives. Then he decided they should put out a news release. He had Sheri type it up. She also typed a letter to cancel the purchase of the property where Mrs. Benson had hoped to build her dream house.

Virtually forgotten in the confusion, Kim Beegle sat in the living room and cried as she waited for a friend to come and pick her up. The petite blonde—she was five feet three and weighed 103 pounds —had known Scott since she was fifteen. He had urged her to drop out of high school and she had lived with him off and on for a couple of years, first at the house on Galleon Drive in Port Royal, then here in Quail Creek. They had had to be apart when Scott traveled to tennis tournaments, and when Kim had gone to the West Coast this last winter and won the California Miss Chili Pepper Contest. But she kept her clothes, jewelry, makeup, and hair dryer in Scott's bedroom.

Although Mrs. Benson would later be characterized by the Miami *Herald* as a "Gucci two-shoes," she had let Scott have live-in lovers since his mid-teens. This produced considerable family tension and even legal problems. But Mrs. Benson seemed to have derived vicarious pleasure from the sexual escapades of all her children.

When her ride showed up, Kim Beegle left behind her personal belongings and took just one memento with her: Buck, Scott's dog, a big, bristly-haired mixed breed that was part Bouvier des Flandres, part German shepherd. With the help of several professional trainers, Scott had taught Buck to track people by scent, to protect him and the house, and to attack on command. He had considered teaching Buck to sniff for explosives, but decided that was unnecessary.

Although the Benson house was crawling with policemen, firemen, and strangers, nobody remembered Buck's barking the day of the murders. Much would later be made of the fact that the dog had not barked the night before. Police and prosecutors would point to this as proof that there had been no intruders in the neighborhood. But they had nothing to say, at least not in public, about Buck's silence after the blasts and during the noisy, hectic morning.

When Harold Young suggested the house be checked for explosives, Graham introduced himself to Steven Benson and explained what he wanted to do. Although Graham mentioned nothing about it, it's clear he intended to look not only for bombs, but for anything— remote control devices, triggering mechanisms, fuses, spare batteries —related to the blasts that had already occurred.

Steven approved the search, inviting Graham to come in. Adjacent to Scott's bedroom the officers noticed some radio equipment that aroused their interest But they soon satisfied themselves that it was nothing important.

Scott's room was littered with tennis racquets, shorts, shirts, and shoes. On the floor with them was an empty packet of birth control pills. In the top drawer of the dresser, Graham found a plastic Ziploc bag of marijuana. He left it there. He wasn't looking for drugs, he explained later, just explosives and related material.

Benson and Wayne Kerr tagged along as the officers combed through the rest of the house. Something in the atmosphere felt "weird" to Graham.

Debbie Benson, a short woman with long brown hair, stepped out of the bathroom. Steven introduced her to the officers and explained that they were looking for explosives. This prompted a spate of jokes by Debbie, Kerr, and Steven that set Graham's antennae quivering. Here was half a family lying mangled and dead outside, while the other half laughed about how there could have been a bomb in the commode and Debbie might have been blown up.

Although he himself was a prankster, quick with a quip or a self-mocking remark, Graham didn't see any humor at the moment. He didn't claim to be a psychiatrist; he admitted he wasn't equipped to delve into this odd behavior. It could have been nervousness, their way of releasing tension.

"But I felt in my mind that this doesn't seem right." He started paying closer attention to Kerr and Benson.

By 11:30 A.M. the first agents from Alcohol, Tobacco and Firearms had arrived. Under Title II of the Explosives Control Act of 1970, federal authorities had jurisdiction over bombings. Special Agents George Nowicki, Terry Hopkins, and Tommy Noel, the pilot who had flown the trio in from Miami, set about cataloging the evidence that the Collier County police had located. The guiding principle, as Terry Hopkins enunciated it, was to "look for anything that didn't grow."

Amid the many things that didn't grow—misshapen automobile

parts, scorched wire, splinters from the wooden stakes—were fragments of galvanized pipe and end caps. These went to Agent George Nowicki who marked them, had them photographed, then packaged in Ziploc bags, much like the one that contained the marijuana in the top drawer of Scott's dresser.

Nowicki took a glance at the Suburban and noticed two craters. One was between the front seats where the console had been. The second was under the left side of the rear seat. Both blasts had punctured the floorboard, leaving jagged flanges of metal jutting toward the ground. This suggested the bombs had been inside the car, not attached underneath the chassis.

The Collier County Medical Examiner, Heinrich Schmid, arrived and confirmed that Mrs. Benson and Scott had died of "multiple, overwhelming injuries." A lean man with gold-rimmed glasses, a German accent, and a professional manner, Schmid had been educated at the University of Heidelberg and had performed over four thousand autopsies in his career. After emigrating to Naples, he had been averaging one autopsy every working day. He had little trouble reading the significance of the lacerations, burns, stippling, and streaking on the two corpses.

Since Mrs. Benson's wounds were mostly on the left side of her body and Scott's were on the right side, there was little doubt one bomb exploded between them. A fireball from the blast had scorched the victims and left deposits of spent, as well as unburned, powder. In chemical analysis this residue would reveal the nature of the explosive material. The stippling, or pitting, of the skin showed that burning powder had hit them at close range, and the streaking, or pattern, of the burns indicated that the bomb had erupted near the legs, the force of the blast ripping upward.

Dr. Schmid had the bodies removed to Pittman's Funeral Home where he would perform a complete autopsy.

The bomb disposal unit came down from the Lee County Airport and Officer Gary Beeson asked, and later had to repeat his request, that the search for evidence be suspended while he checked out the other vehicles at the Benson residence. As Beeson rigged up his ropes and pulleys to open doors, hoods and trunks, and start each car from a distance, George Nowicki went into the house. He had been advised that Scott had had some involvement with drugs and had enemies. Debbie Benson had acknowledged that animosity existed between her mother-in-law and her. After more than five years of marriage and three children, she still didn't feel accepted by the Bensons.

In Nowicki's opinion, Steven and Wayne Kerr did not appear at all distressed by what had happened. They were joking and laughing and smiling back and forth.

After Tommy Noel flew a photographer over the crime scene—they snapped pictures from an altitude of 1,500 feet—he joined Nowicki, and the two ATF agents conducted the second interview with Benson. Again he showed no hesitation to answer questions. He told them he had driven the Suburban to a convenience store, then returned and was about to set off with the rest of the family when he realized he had forgotten a tape measure. As he started back to fetch it, he had gone three steps when the first bomb exploded.

Though he said nothing about it to Benson, Tommy Noel had spotted a tape measure outside in the debris. Why, the ATF agent wondered, would he go back to get what was already in the car?

Having heard from other officers that Steven had been three steps from the blast—some interpreted this as three feet, not three yards—Captain Curtis Mills got an idea. He noticed that a mailbox three feet from the Suburban was flecked with blood and slivers of human flesh. Mills felt that Steven's clothes should be spattered with the same substances. So he asked him to surrender his shirt and jeans.

While Steven's story and his composure, as reported by some policemen, prompted suspicions, nobody could quarrel with his cooperation. Asking Mills to bring him some spare work clothes from the beige van, he gave over his shirt and pants.

Late that afternoon, Harold Young climbed into the beige van to check the fuel gauge. Steven said he had driven the Suburban to the Shop 'N Go because his van was low on gas. But Lieutenant Young saw that the gauge indicated a quarter of a tank. Later, Young couldn't say whether it registered precisely quarter full, a little less, or a little more. He just felt the van wasn't low on fuel.

According to the police, Benson was free to leave any time he wanted. But his van had to stay at the scene. Steven explained that it contained business records, and he asked if he could take these with him. ATF agents insisted on searching them first. Steven didn't object. He brought them the cardboard boxes full of papers, files, and pamphlets. Riffling through the records, George Nowicki spotted a toggle switch and two pieces of plastic used as circuit breakers, and on the chance that these had triggered the bombs, he seized them. Steve never knew the difference. He was busy loading boxes of business papers into Debbie's car.

Then while his wife traveled to Fort Myers to pick up the kids—for safety's sake they had decided to spend the night in a motel—Steven set out for the hospital to visit Carol Lynn. Sheri Vaughan drove him there in her car, a Mazda with a noisy, rough-running motor. Steven, normally taciturn, talked a lot on the way, his conversation veering from the deeply personal to the practical. He told Sheri about his father's death five years ago and said he had never recovered from it. Then he remarked that he couldn't believe Sheri drove the Mazda in this condition. "You ought to get it fixed," he said.

Wayne Kerr also visited Carol Lynn that day, and Sheri Vaughan's husband, Steve, drove him to the hospital. The husky tennis pro recalled that Kerr moved off a hundred feet whenever Vaughan started the car.

Standing beside Carol Lynn's bed, looking down from his great height, Kerr spoke to his badly injured client about who should be notified and how Carol Lynn's teenage boys, Kurt and Travis, should be told. He had made arrangements for her to be transported by chartered plane to Massachusetts General Hospital in Boston. Not only did Mass General have one of the nation's best burn centers, Carol Lynn could be close to her kids there.

Kerr had planned to spend the night with Steven and his family at La Playa Hotel on Vanderbilt Beach. They all met—Debbie and the kids, Steven Benson, Wayne, and the Vaughans—in Bonita Springs and bought Chinese food. But then Wayne changed his mind and said he didn't want to stay at La Playa. In that case, Benson said, he wouldn't stay there either. Vaughan called the hotel and canceled the reservations. Kerr went to the Vaughans' home and, as far as anyone knew, Benson, his wife, and three children returned to their home in Fort Myers.

At much the same time, many of the investigating officers gathered for a meeting. According to ATF Agent George Nowicki, Steven Benson was the prime suspect from that night on.

Lieutenant Wayne Graham didn't see it that way. He hadn't gone to the meeting. He grabbed a bite to eat, then doubled back to the Benson house. By now, the Suburban was covered by plastic sheeting, a mobile command post was parked in the driveway, and arrangements had been made for around-the-clock security. Graham stopped at the command post for a while to check that the officers on duty had food and coffee, and that they understood their instructions. They weren't supposed to let anybody pass on White Violet Drive except people who lived farther down the street. As Wayne Graham saw it, they needed to regard "just about everybody in the United States as a suspect."

However flippant that remark might sound, it proved to be nearer the truth than anyone would have predicted. Plenty of suspects would appear before the Benson pipe bomb murder case came to trial. And even then, new names and shadowy faces kept popping up.

Chapter 4

On July 10, Albert Gleason, an ATF explosives specialist, went to work. Having arrived the previous evening from Washington, D.C., he had spoken to some of the investigating officers, but wasn't swayed by their theories and opinions, and he didn't concern himself with victims or possible suspects. His duties pertained to the "what and how" of the explosives, not the "who and why." After twenty years on the New York City Bomb Squad, then thirteen years with the ATF, he knew that to crack a case a cop needed to prove that the suspect had a motive, an opportunity, and the means to commit the crime. Leaving "motive" and "opportunity" to other investigators, he concentrated on "means" and let the debris at the bomb site tell him what had happened.

A heavyset man with horn-rimmed glasses and short gray hair, Gleason had the voice and, occasionally, the irascible manner of a New York cabbie. Having started off as a Navy blaster, he knew his business from both sides of the fence. He had built and detonated bombs, and he had sifted through debris and reconstructed over a thousand bomb sites. Impatient with professional incompetence and with defense lawyers who tried to fudge the facts, he wasn't reluctant to show his temper when necessary.

But he was satisfied with this crime scene. Security seemed tight, and evidence had been correctly processed.

Gleason had no trouble spotting the "seats" of the two bombs. Nobody could miss the crater in the console area and the second crater in the rear.

Then he had to separate vehicle parts from bomb parts. In most cases the choice was obvious, and when in doubt he could always send fragments to the ATF lab in Rockville, Maryland, for microscopic analysis. Many people, including most criminals, mistakenly believe a bomb consumes itself and destroys all evidence. But generally, Gleason managed to identify 90 percent of a bomb's components. On larger pieces of the canister, there was even a possibility of using laser lights and photographing latent fingerprints that remained underneath the scorch marks or soot. When hit by a laser, a fingerprint glowed like a white shirt under a black light.

Studying the scraps of galvanized metal collected by investigators, Gleason estimated that the bombs had been about a foot long, with four-inch end caps screwed on to pipes to seal the explosive. Since the entire inside wafer, or center section, of two end caps and half of a third cap had been found, Gleason knew the manufacturer. One cap bore the letter U for Union Brand, another was stamped G for Grinnell. This might make it possible to trace the seller and, with luck, the buyer.

Still, Gleason asked the police to continue the search for evidence. After the Suburban was moved to a warehouse for further examination, he had them excavate an oval area radiating twenty-five feet in all directions from the bomb site. Digging down to a depth of three inches, the officers worked like archaeologists, shoveling up dirt, sifting it through a wire strainer, pawing through it with magnetized gloves.

Pipe bombs contain three primary components: a canister (in this case the galvanized "nipple" pipe—pipe threaded at both ends), an explosive material, and a detonating device. Gleason would leave it to a chemist to determine whether the pipe contained smokeless or black powder. He focused on the question of how it had been detonated.

Of the various possibilities—a lit fuse, a timer, a remote control device, or a switching device—the last looked most likely. The remains of half a dozen batteries had been found. Some of them came from a flashlight kept in the console. But there were four extra Duracell batteries that seemed to have been very close to the explosion, perhaps close enough to serve as a power source. Gleason figured it took only six volts to detonate the bombs. Four 1.5-volt D-cell batteries would do the job.

In his opinion, electronic-controlled circuitry had initiated the blast. But this wasn't easy to prove. The Suburban had a radio, a CB radio, and a Fuzzbuster or radar detector. By a process of elimination, Gleason had to locate a circuit board that didn't belong in the vehicle. Eventually he found a small part of one which upon microscopic inspection appeared to be different from the others. He also found a manual switch that couldn't be accounted for.

Still, he could not prove with scientific certainty that this was the triggering mechanism. He was left with his hypothesis. The burglar alarm business, Steven Benson's business, was, Gleason pointed out, a switching-control security business. But he would never rule out other possibilities. The bombs could have been triggered by a timer set to go off in minutes, hours, days, or weeks.

Similarly, Albert Gleason could never say for sure whether the fifty-five-second delay between the two bombs was intentional. While his opinion was that the delay had been planned, he couldn't exclude a misfire in which the first bomb burned out the wires running to the second, then the second erupted because of the intense heat generated by the first.

This intense heat raised another question. If Carol Lynn had been inside the Suburban, engulfed in a fireball as she described, how had she scrambled to safety? The first pipe bomb could have contained anywhere from three to six pounds of powder. Even if not much of the twenty pounds of shrapnel had hit her, the combustion would have been an infernal flash of 1600° Fahrenheit. How had she survived?

Gleason explained that the event was evanescent; in an instant the fireball burnt itself out. To do damage, a fire, regardless of how hot, had to endure for a certain period of time. Gleason gave the example of a candle that can burn your hand if you hold it over the flame long enough, but which has no effect on a finger passed quickly through the flame.

As for the pipe bombs in the Benson case, Albert Gleason had seen hundreds of these improvised deals. "I think every adult male at one time or another has fooled around with some form of simplified explosive devices," he explained. "This is just a continuance of a bigger mousetrap."

That same day, July 10, detectives held a second meeting, and Wayne Graham attended this one. Coordinating the efforts of the Collier County Sheriff's Department and ATF, Harold Young and George Nowicki led a discussion of how the investigation should proceed. Nobody pulled rank, nobody created friction. As Graham recalled it, everybody was eager to get to work.

Although Steven Benson might be the primary suspect, everyone at the scene during the murders, anyone connected with the family, came in for scrutiny. Despite the gravity of Carol Lynn's wounds, police didn't exclude the possibility that she had been involved in the bombings. Detectives wanted to talk to her and check her financial situation, her relations with the family, her children, her failed marriage.

Similarly, they decided to take a close look at Wayne Kerr. He claimed to represent every member of the immediate family. But where did his interests lie?

There was also talk about Scott's attitude toward his family. Quite apart from his drug problems—or perhaps as a result of them—he didn't get along with his mother, his brother, or his sister, and judging by what police had picked up in interviews, the boy spent most of his time and money on cars and girls. He had aspirations of becoming a tennis pro, but, as Graham put it, "he wasn't very good."

Impulsive and hot-headed, Scott had been drinking heavily, smoking marijuana, snorting cocaine, and using great quantities of nitrous oxide since his early teens. His wake was littered with expensive broken toys and lots of very angry people. In the past five years he had wrecked a van, ruined the suspension on a Lamborghini, gotten into a barroom brawl and lost a $10,000 wristwatch willed to him by his father, destroyed his mother's dining room table with a belt sander while high on dope, yanked phones out of the wall, fouled up the transmission in his sister's Datsun 280Z, assaulted members of his family, and most recently driven a pickup into a pond, a feat that won him the nickname of "Aqua Man." Mrs. Benson paid $3,077 to have the truck hauled out and repaired.

But the most troubling event in a brief life studded with turbulent behavior had occurred in 1983. Scott Benson had been confined to a mental health unit and forced to undergo psychiatric treatment under the terms of the Baker Act, a Florida statute dealing with people who have demonstrated that they are suicidal, homicidal, or incompetent to care for themselves.

Among those regarded as potential suspects, the name of Guido Dal Molin kept cropping up. An eccentric local figure, Dal Molin, a twenty-year-old high school dropout, had a reputation as an electronics genius. Two years ago, he had customized a Pontiac Trans-Am so that he could drive it by remote control from the backseat, using a joystick to work the brakes, accelerator, and steering wheel.

Naples police ordered him to sit in the front seat or stay off the road.

Embarking on a venture that attempted to channel his talent into more productive directions, Dal Molin went into the home security line, designing his own alarm system. Casually acquainted with Scott, he had also spoken to Steven about business matters.

In 1985, he was back in the news and back in trouble with the police. Caught with the facsimile of a nuclear bomb in the trunk of his car, he was questioned by Collier County deputies and the FBI. Because the eerily accurate replica contained no explosives, investigators didn't file charges. Perhaps they were as befuddled by the incident as were journalists who reported it around the world. Or maybe they were as awed as the expert who said the casing Guido had constructed needed only plutonium to make it a fully functional nuclear device.

Shortly after the murders, a mordant joke began to circulate in Naples. Question: How can we be sure Guido Dal Molin didn't blow up the Bensons? Answer: No mushroom cloud was spotted over Quail Creek.

Lieutenant Harold Young, however, wasn't laughing. He knew that nuclear devices weren't the only weapons in Guido's arsenal. The brooding kid with the black shaggy hair and deep-set, dark-circled eyes—they looked ringed with mascara—had experimented with pipe bombs. Young made a note to call him in for questioning.

But Guido came into the sheriff's office of his own accord and in quick succession satisfied Young that he wasn't involved in the Benson murders, then volunteered to check out the rumor that the killings were related to Scott and his druggie friends. Strapping a microcassette recorder to his ankle, Dal Molin, the story goes, showed up at a party at the house of one of the biggest dope dealers in the county. He mixed with buyers, pushers, middle men, and simple users—kids as young as Guido, businessmen with a sweet tooth for a taste of this or a toke of that, coke whores who'd put out for a toot. The noise in Naples, especially around the marina, was that Scott Benson owed the wrong people a lot of money. Some said he had burned a dealer for $200,000. Others believed that he was trying to get in on the action and finance his habit by selling.

But before Guido could pin down any facts, people at the party heard faint voices wafting up from his foot. It seemed that the Mad Genius had set the microcassette on Play rather than Record. The dealers and dopers laid into him, Dal Molin claimed, beat him badly, and kicked him out of the house. How an electronics whiz could make such a mistake, and why they didn't do worse to a police informer, is anyone's guess.

That was the last time Guido Dal Molin was implicated in the Benson case—until months later when Collier County police charged him with murdering his best friend.

Chapter 5

At first glance, the Naples public housing project provokes stunned disbelief. In a city of such wealth, in a place that prides itself on elegance, where even the Burger King franchise styles itself as "America's Most Beautiful," one simply doesn't expect to run into a mini-slum where blacks sit on the curbside taking long pulls at bottles in paper bags and young bloods boogie to their ghetto-blasters.

Across from the project, in a strip mall, between One Hour Photo and the Child Protection Team Headquarters, Guion De Loach had his law offices. Modest and a bit cluttered, the storefront operation featured a sign on the reception counter saying HAVE YOU MADE YOUR WILL? For thirty-four years, Guion De Loach had specialized in real estate and probate, quietly pursuing his profession. With silvery gray hair and a warm, almost courtly manner, he had no desire to be swept up into the harsh glare of a murder case which would attract lawyers from all over the East Coast and media attention around the world.

But then he heard that Margaret Benson and Scott were dead. While the news shocked him, he was equally surprised by reports of Mrs. Benson's wealth. She was described as a businesswoman, Carol Lynn as a Boston socialite. The national networks referred to a tobacco fortune, and newspapers claimed that Margaret's father, Harry Hitchcock, had a net worth of $400 million.

Although De Loach had known nothing of the family's finances, he did know something which no one else was aware of. Once he revealed it, the news would explode with the force of smokeless powder, and the obscure attorney would be hit by reverberations he had never anticipated.

Late this past January, Margaret Benson had arrived at De Loach's office with Sharon Hester, a lady who worked in the same strip mall. Margaret didn't tell the lawyer much about herself. As De

Loach recalled, "She was very pleasant, very direct, and knew what she wanted." What she wanted was "as simple a will as could possibly be drawn." Upon her death, her estate was to be distributed in equal shares to her three children.

She said she had come to De Loach because she had heard he would do "what she wanted and not give her any flack." He suggested she should consider setting up trusts if there were minor beneficiaries. But she wouldn't say whether her children had children of their own. She repeated that "she wanted a simple, straight-out will and she wanted her three children to share equally in the estate."

When De Loach asked if she already had a will, and could he see it, Margaret insisted that was pointless. Her previous will didn't address her requirements. "She gave me the orders," De Loach said. "I drew up what she wanted."

The result was a single-page document that concluded by saying that Mrs. Benson signed with a "consciousness of the frailties of life and the uncertainties of living." She paid $75. He gave her a copy, keeping the original in his files. Then she dropped from his life as abruptly as she had entered it. Now, less than six months later, she was dead.

Since he had had no further contact with the family and did not know their legal representatives, De Loach decided to let a few days pass before notifying the Bensons. He figured they would need time to grieve. But then he happened to be in the Collier County Probate Court and heard from a secretary that someone was filing a Benson will. De Loach advised her that he too had a Benson will.

On July 11, De Loach was in his office when Jim Elkins, a Naples attorney, telephoned to say he represented Wayne Kerr, who, in turn, represented the Bensons. What was this story about a second will?

De Loach suggested they compare dates.

Elkins said he had a will dated May 23, 1983.

"You lose, Jim," De Loach said, "I've got January 29, 1985." He asked Elkins to have somebody from the Benson family call him.

Shortly thereafter, Wayne Kerr rang and said he wanted to see De Loach right away.

They arranged to meet that afternoon and Kerr arrived at 2 P.M., just after Steven Benson showed up. The two big, bulky men created an instant crowd in De Loach's office. They might have been a pair of football players. But where Steven appeared cool and self-contained, Kerr looked like he had already played a long rough game.

De Loach described him as "perspiring," "quite out of breath and a little agitated."

As he read through the January 1985 will, "Kerr got more upset, started to shake, and he looked over at Steven Benson and said, 'This doesn't look like Margaret's signature.'"

De Loach pointed out that the signature had been witnessed by Sharon Hester, a friend of Mrs. Benson's.

Steven agreed that this was true.

When asked what he intended to do with the will, De Loach said, "I'm going to file it. That's what the law is. I'm going to take it down to the probate court and file it and let the judge handle it."

This seemed to upset Kerr all the more. Steven soothed him and told his friend "to calm down, things will be all right."

Nobody in Naples or Lancaster, Pennsylvania, could fathom why Mrs. Benson had written a secret will and why she had filed it with Guion De Loach. Around the corner, two and a half blocks away, lay the plush law offices of Michael McDonnell, whom Margaret had consulted about her real estate problems in Port Royal.

But while friends and strangers idly speculated what had been on her mind, Wayne Kerr was directly and disastrously affected by her decision. The May 23, 1983, will had delegated him as executor and trustee of the trust funds set up for the beneficiaries. The January 29, 1985, will cut him out of that role, leaving it to Margaret's surviving heirs to serve as co-executors, or to designate that job to someone else. If the De Loach will was ruled valid, Kerr would lose $500,000 to $750,000 in fees.

But the mustachioed lawyer from Philadelphia had no intention of stepping down without a fight. The same day as he filed the '83 will, he also filed a declaration of domicile, claiming that four days earlier he had taken up residence in Florida. He listed his address as 3839 Domestic Avenue, the same place where the Meridian Security Network Office was housed in a trailer. Under state law he needed a Florida domicile to qualify as an executor.

If this concatenation of curious events weren't enough to thrust Wayne Kerr into the forefront of suspects, the attorney's fidgets, nervous tics, and sweaty face would have. Constantly tugging his collar, jabbing his glasses back up the bridge of his nose, mopping his jowls with a handkerchief, he had an unfortunate habit of prefacing sentences with "To be candid with you," or "To be perfectly honest," then explaining that he couldn't comment on Benson family business matters, not even to the police.

That night, a few dozen people gathered at Pittman's Funeral Home, a quasi-colonial structure with four spindly columns, two royal palms, and an American flag flying out front. For all its antebellum airs, Pittman's advertised a "State of the Art Crematory on the Premises."

No minister appeared, nobody gave a eulogy. It was less a memorial service than a last opportunity for friends to view the $7,035 closed caskets and say good-bye to Margaret and Scott before their bodies were flown to Lancaster for burial.

Several Meridian Security Network employees paid a courtesy call, and their conversation inevitably turned toward the murders and what the police were doing to solve them. Some said that investigators had already interviewed them. The police were particularly interested in whether Steven Benson had the technical ability to construct bombs.

There in the funeral parlor, Steven was alleged to have admitted that he had made bombs as a boy.

It is difficult to say whether such an admission, assuming it ever occurred, incriminated Steven or showed that he felt no compulsion to hide anything.

Chapter 6

On Saturday, July 13, Steven Benson, his wife, Debbie, and Wayne Kerr flew to Boston and went to Massachusetts General Hospital to visit Carol Lynn. By all accounts, it was an awkward encounter.

Her right leg, her right arm, and back were charred. Her right ear had been burnt off and the skin on the right side of her face and neck resembled melted wax. At times, medication made her suffering bearable, but it never entirely vanished, and there was always the emotional anguish and horror of what had happened.

Steven asked, "How are you?" and she mumbled a reply.

He said Debbie was in the waiting room and Carol Lynn said, "Oh, I think I'm too tired to talk to her."

The visit limped along for fifteen minutes before Steven left. Later he sent flowers, but Carol Lynn wouldn't allow them in the room. He called Boston on several occasions and spoke to her son Travis. But then Travis told him that his mother wouldn't let him talk to Uncle Steven anymore.

In Naples and Lancaster, Steven's visit prompted a rumor that he had gone there to kill Carol Lynn, to finish the job he had botched with the bombs. When she refused the flowers he sent, a story circulated that were they wired to explode. When he asked Travis if there were security guards at his mother's room this created a red alert. Around-the-clock guards had indeed been hired and paid for by Harry Hitchcock. Now they were notified to be extra vigilant.

Eventually, Steven found himself whipsawed by events, real and imagined. His visits to his sister and his subsequent expressions of concern were seen as insincere at best, murderous at worst. Later the Washington Post claimed that he had never contacted her at all, never even inquired about her health.

Once Steven left the room, Kerr offered his condolences, then asked if she had known about the second will. Carol Lynn said that her mother had discussed it with her a month ago when she returned from Europe.

According to a statement Carol Lynn later gave, Margaret Benson didn't care for trusts or the fees involved in maintaining them. Moreover, she had been extremely unhappy with the lawyer and the bank that had served as co-executors of trusts set up by her late husband.

There was a second reason, Carol Lynn explained, why her mother had Guion De Loach draft a new will. It had to do with a "big problem because of my two brothers." She sighed as she recalled the "big problem." "Scott always gets these really sleazo girl friends who take advantage of him. And Scott doesn't seem to have any—I mean, Scott lets people talk him into things. He doesn't have a great deal of common sense."

Then Mrs. Benson "had the problem of what to do about Steven because not only was there the concern that he would go through his money"—she snapped her fingers—"in twenty-four hours with some big scheme, but there was also the problem of Debbie, because my mother under no circumstances wanted Debbie to get a grain of sand that might have belonged to my mother."

It is unclear how Carol Lynn imagined the De Loach will addressed, much less resolved, the problems she described. If she was worried about Scott's common sense and Steven's headlong, high-rolling business style, why did Mrs. Benson insist on leaving equal shares to her sons? Why did she eliminate the trust provisions which would have moderated Steven and Scott's profligacy? Why did she make them co-administrators of the estate? Far from conveying distrust or displeasure with her sons, the De Loach will showed Mrs. Benson had as much confidence in them as in her daughter.

Furthermore, the De Loach will was scarcely an instrument designed to ensure that Debbie never got hold of Mrs. Benson's money. To the contrary, once Mrs. Benson died and Steven inherited, he was free to pass the wealth along to his wife.

Carol Lynn appeared not to know this. Or perhaps she was preoccupied with another "big problem." Her worry about her sister-in-law went far beyond her fear that Steven's wife would get her mother's money. "Of course, I have always, I have believed for a long time, that Debbie was slowly poisoning Steven."

"Do—do you mean poisoning his mind?" ATF Agent Nowicki asked, "or poisoning his body?"

"I mean poisoning his body, slowly but surely doing away with him so that when it came time that he—he inherited his money she could do the last little bit"—again Carol Lynn snapped her fingers—"and knock him off and collect it all herself, because she has that kind of personality that she has no scruples and no morals. And she is basically an evil person."

After relating these dramatic, if puzzling and unsubstantiated, reasons why Mrs. Benson had gone to Guion De Loach, she delivered another surprising revelation.

"We got talking about the whole situation, because she was really kind of upset about the fact that she had made [the second will] and she thought it was a dumb idea and that she probably shouldn't have done it . . . my mother said that, you know, well she's—the second will—that she was just gonna forget that she had ever even done it. She was gonna go back with the other one."

At the hospital, she told Wayne Kerr that Mrs. Benson definitely didn't intend to stay with the De Loach will.

Buoyed by the news, he announced the following Monday, July 15, that he planned to contest the validity of the second will. In addition to bringing Kerr personal grief and bad publicity, the decision would bring him under sharper scrutiny by the police.

The day of the funeral in Lancaster reminded mourners of afternoons in Naples. The temperature hovered in the nineties and the hazy sky glinted like scoured aluminum. In St. James Episcopal Church, on the tree-shaded corner of Duke and Orange Streets, the Reverend Canon Stanley F. Imboden told a congregation of 250 that the murders of Margaret and Scott Benson were "foolish, ugly, and reprehensible." He compared their deaths to Christ's which "was also calamitous and bewildering."

The Reverend urged the family and friends to seek refuge in the Lord and pray for a prompt solution to the crime. "We cannot undo this tragic story. At the moment, many of the pages are missing, and we can't go back and rewrite them." But he promised mourners,

"Harsh and senseless adversity like the deaths of Margaret and Scott will be redeemed by the hand of God."

At Woodland Hill Cemetery, the Reverend Imboden handed each member of the family a coral-colored rose from the flowers on the caskets, and the next day's newspapers showed Steven with his head bowed, apparently in tears. Debbie wore a dark, broad-brimmed hat, which along with her long straight hair, hid her face. Janet Lee Murphy, Margaret Benson's sister, had her eyes masked by sunglasses. Only Harry Hitchcock, white-haired and ruddy-cheeked, faced the camera with his grief unconcealed. Holding a rose in two hands, he sat with his mouth partially opened, his confusion as obvious as his anguish.

Then the caskets were moved into the Benson-Hitchcock mausoleum, a $60,000 granite structure that dwarfed every other tomb in the cemetery, including the monument on President Buchanan's grave. Laid to rest with Harry's dead wife, Charlotte, and Margaret's husband, Edward, Scott and his adopted mother confronted eternity under the gaze of a stained-glass portrait of Christ praying at Gethsemane. "Not my will, but Thine be done," read the inscription under it.

After the funeral, Steven spoke to his grandfather's attorney, James Adams. Now that his mother was dead and her estate frozen in probate court, neither Steven nor any other Meridian employee would be paid. With a wife and three children to support, he needed money.

Harry Hitchcock agreed to lend him up to $20,000, in exchange for which "Papa" expected Steven to sign a promissory note. Steven accepted the terms and received a check for $4,000.

Later, when this incident was reported in the newspapers from Massachusetts to Florida, they would claim Steven had received the full $20,000 and they would fail to mention that Carol Lynn was also dependent upon her grandfather's generosity. By one of those bizarre quirks that abound in the Benson case, she found herself without medical insurance. Listed as an employee of the Meridian Security Network, she was supposed to be covered by the company's health plan. But the premiums on the policy had not been paid, and she now faced catastrophic expenses.

"Papa" came to the rescue—and he didn't demand a promissory note in return.

Carol Lynn later filed a $400,000 claim against Margaret Benson's estate for her medical treatment and "pain and suffering." According to her personal attorney, the claim was contingent "on the development of information that would lead claimant to conclude Mrs. Benson is liable for claimant's damages."

Carol Lynn would also seek $131,000 for a loan she said was due her from her mother.

Chapter 7

For five days, teams of Collier County police and ATF agents canvassed hardware stores, construction sites, plumbing supply shops, and junkyards asking about four-inch end caps and foot-long sections of galvanized nipple pipe. They specified that the end caps had to be Grinnell or Union brand, and they asked if any such caps had been purchased by Scott Benson, Steven Benson, Carol Lynn Kendall, or Wayne Kerr. They also asked if anybody had recently bought six to twelve pounds of black powder or smokeless powder.

The answers were consistently negative. Few places carried four-inch end caps or four-inch pipe, especially in the uncommonly short length of one foot. Nobody remembered having had any in stock for months.

As for black or smokeless powder, the answers were also negative. The best anybody suggested was that gun freaks, guys who made their own ammunition or collected antique muzzle-loading rifles, sometimes bought shotgun shells, opened the cartridges, and emptied out the powder.

On Monday, July 15, Mike Koors, the tall, handsome detective, called Hughes Supply Inc. on Airport Road in Naples. After checking their files, the folks at Hughes Supply surprised him by saying, yes, they had sold two four-inch end caps on July 5, and two foot-long sections of four-inch galvanized nipple pipe on July 8. Somebody from Del Ray Construction had made both purchases.

Koors told them to hold the receipts, he'd be right there. Along with ATF Agent Terry Hopkins, he sped over to Hughes Supply and interviewed Jeffrey Maynes, the plumbing manager. Maynes remembered the first sale. In fact, he remembered the customer calling and asking for eight caps. Hughes Supply had just two in stock, a couple of U brand caps. The man said he would take them.

Maynes waited on the customer, who came in on July 5 and purchased the caps for $28.05 at 3:25 P.M. To get the corporate discount, the man said he was from Del Ray Construction, then scrawled an illegible signature.

What Maynes couldn't remember was what the guy looked like. He didn't recall a single feature of his face, build, or clothing.

James Link had handled the sale of the pipe, which, according to the receipt, occurred at 4:58 P.M. on July 8. But Link was out now and not expected back until later this afternoon. This gave the investigators a chance to make preparations. When they returned at four o'clock, they brought some evidence-gathering paraphernalia.

James Link was a small, trim man, well into middle age, with silver-rimmed glasses and gray hair. He recalled the transaction quite clearly. It was, after all, an unusual quantity of pipe for Hughes Supply to sell. Generally, they filled large orders.

He described the customer as about six feet tall and 200 pounds. He had a light complexion and wore a black or blue "baseball-type" cap and a pair of sunglasses. Link, who hardly looked like a Beatles' fan, called them "John Lennon glasses," and said they had oval, opaque lenses.

Terry Hopkins showed Link an array of six photographs, one of them a snapshot of Steven Benson. But Link could not identify any of these individuals. The people in the photos all appeared a lot fairer than the customer he remembered. Although investigators had asked whether Wayne Kerr or Scott Benson's names were on the receipt, they didn't show Link pictures of them.

Using a device called an Identikit, Mike Koors had Link help him construct a composite picture of the man who bought the pipe. An Identikit contains isolated facial characteristics in various sizes and shapes and colors. A witness selects those features that best match a suspect's appearance. In this instance, Link could supply only a nose, mouth, chin, and cheeks. The man's eyes had been hidden by dark glasses and his hair covered by a cap.

Koors came up with a picture that bore an uncanny resemblance to Steven Benson. He achieved this effect by inserting details that had not come from James Link. The sunglasses were not oval, wire-rimmed ones like John Lennon wore. The lenses were not opaque. They showed the shape of the suspect's eyes, which Link had never seen. And the composite depicted a man with smooth dark hair and sideburns.

Koors and Hopkins put the receipts into a plastic document case and returned to the Sheriff's office, hoping the lab could lift a set of usable latent fingerprints. They couldn't help noticing that just up Airport Road and around the corner on Domestic Avenue stood the office of Meridian Security Network. Steven Benson could have reached Hughes Supply in a couple of minutes by car and not much longer on foot.

Although the investigators felt they had obtained a valuable lead, they knew the proximity of Benson's office could be seen in a different way. Would a man hellbent on blowing up his family buy end caps and pipes at a store right around the corner? It might be hard to convince a jury he was stupid enough to do that, yet smart enough to construct and detonate two bombs.

Also, they had traced two U brand end caps. But where did the other two, stamped with a G, come from? This question became more puzzling when detectives discovered that Grinnell end caps hadn't been marked with a G in more than eight years. Where had Benson—where had anybody—found caps that old? And where did the murderer get the powder?

At least one witness believed the description James Link gave fit to perfection a person he had reason to suspect. Yet the police seemed indifferent to the information.

For days after the murder, Paul Harvey, captain of Mrs. Benson's yacht, called the Collier County Sheriff's Department. The *Galleon Queen* was a thirty-six-foot Carver that could sleep eight. At Steven's insistence, it was outfitted with an expensive array of electronic equipment. Even the man who sold and installed the gadgetry characterized it as "overkill." But Steven "liked to go first class," and so at a cost of over $30,000 the yacht had radar, automatic pilot, a depth finder, a ship-to-shore telephone, a stereo and intercom system, and an elaborate security system.

When Paul Harvey heard about the murders, he immediately felt they were drug-related. He couldn't believe that the bombs were meant for Mrs. Benson, but he regarded her adopted son as "a very wealthy, spoiled egotist...I can see a lot of reasons why somebody would want to kill Scott Benson."

Harvey had one specific reason in mind when he telephoned the police and urged them to hurry out to the Wiggins Pass Marina and shake down the *Galleon Queen* for bombs. But investigators weren't interested, not even when he recounted an incident that had happened on May 16.

Without any advance notice, Scott had showed up with a few boisterous friends, climbed aboard the *Galleon Queen*, and told Harvey to take them for a cruise. Short and sinewy, with a large droopy mustache, Harvey wasn't much older than these fellows and he didn't mind taking them for a run if they behaved and didn't give him a hard time.

But no sooner had they left the marina than Scott insisted they head for Key West. Already "hopped up, loaded, drunk," in Harvey's opinion, Scott and his friends lit a joint, then started snorting cocaine. They were talking about a deal that had gone down where somebody got burned for big money. As Harvey heard it, these guys had riped somebody off or caused somebody in Everglades City or Chokoloskee to lose $200,000.

Before they reached the pass to the Gulf, Harvey had had enough. He didn't want any part of them or their deals, and he didn't want to have the Coast Guard come aboard, find drugs, and lift his captain's license. He returned to the dock and kicked Scott and his friends off the *Galleon Queen*.

He had vivid recollections of all of them, right down to how they were dressed. He described one fellow as "a tall, heavyset person, probably close to six feet, probably close to two hundred pounds, with dirty blondish hair. The only reason I remember that was because later on they came out with a description in the newspaper of somebody that had been to Hughes Supply, and that seemed to match the person who had been on the boat."

He told the police this, adding that there had been a couple of occasions right around the time of the murders when somebody seemed to have breeched the security and taken the *Galleon Queen* for a run without him. Then he noticed a window was open nd his personal log book was missing.

Wayne Graham, Mike Koors, and two ATF agents responded only when he complained that the yacht might sink if it wasn't maintained, and it couldn't be maintained unless the engines were started and he personally had no intention of doing that until somebody checked for bombs. Once the officers arrived at the marina, Harvey "had to basically force them to open the bilges... and ask them would they please go down and make sure the boat wasn't wired."

Showing little curiosity about the man who matched the description of the customer who bought end caps and pipe at Hughes Supply, the investigators questioned Harvey about Steven Benson. They also collected papers from the *Galleon Queen,* hoping to find Benson's fingerprints and samples of his handwriting.

Before they left, Harvey, dissatisfied with their cursory inspection of the yacht, handed Wayne Graham the keys and said, "If you're not going to check it, the least you can do is turn the engine over."

Harvey didn't stay aboard to see what would happen.

Wayne Graham went to the fly bridge of the thirty-six-foot Carver and stood with the key poised near the ignition. Much later, recalling that moment at Wiggins Pass Marina, the short detective ran a hand through his receding hair, grinned, and said, "I just didn't think the best way to search for bombs was for me to go switching on the motor."

Instead, he hopped off the *Galleon Queen* and handed the keys back to Harvey. Then he and the other officers headed for their cars.

Captain Paul Harvey finally had to persuade an electronics expert to go over the boat inch by inch. He found it was clean. But, in his mind, that didn't change the fact that he'd seen a fellow who matched the description James Link gave the police. When shown the composite picture done by Mike Koors, Harvey was struck again by the resemblance.

Chapter 8

On July 18, an eighteen-year-old woman named Tracy Mullins announced to the newspapers that Scott Benson was the father of her child. It wasn't the first time she had made the claim. At the age of sixteen, shortly after giving birth to Shelby Ann Nicole Benson on April 23, 1983, Tracy had filed a paternity suit. Ordered by the court to take a blood test, Scott had failed to do. Now Tracy said that her baby, currently in the custody of her mother in Valparaiso, Indiana, should inherit Scott's share of the Benson fortune—a share that amounted to more than $3 million.

Besides providing titillation for tabloid readers and adding an exotic twist to an already tangled and flamboyant case, the paternity suit offered insight into the Benson family from a novel perspective —their own opinion of themselves. While Steven remained mostly silent on the matter and Carol Lynn maintained it was "a really tight little unit...we were just an average family," Scott left behind a document that unwittingly revealed just how baroque this "tight little unit" was.

A handwritten draft intended as a response to Tracy Mullins' suit, the eleven-page narrative purported to be Scott's work, but its self-congratulatory tone suggested that Margaret Benson exercised more than passing influence. In fact, some people familiar with her penmanship suspected Mrs. Benson wrote the manuscript.

The style certainly doesn't sound like that of a tennis bum with a taste for drugs, "sleazo girl friends," and sports cars.

"My mother, who had thirty-eight years of marriage to my father, a greatly respected man of the highest character, both in business and in his personal life, is herself a religious person of high integrity and moral values. She, not being blinded by the forces of sexuality, very quickly perceived the true character of Tracy Mullins and was very much opposed to my seeing her."

But this opposition stopped well short of action because Mrs. Benson, for all her high moral values and lengthy marriage, had as little common sense as her adopted son. In the absence of any indication that he had the talent to play in college, much less on the pro circuit, Margaret had let Scott concentrate from the age of sixteen on a "full time tennis career." After financing a year of private lessons in Miami, she allowed him to switch to Harry Hopman's International Tennis Camp at Bardmoor, near St. Petersburg, Florida.

At first, Scott lived in a dormitory room with four or five other boys, training during the day with the former Australian Davis Cup Coach and working out at night in the health club. But soon he moved into a condominium apartment "because my mother wished to spend time with me," or so said the handwritten account. Coincidentally, he had met Tracy Mullins, a tall, thin, green-eyed girl of fourteen, who quit school and lived with him in the apartment, cooking and cleaning for her seventeen-year-old lover "just like we were married," she later told the *Miami Herald*.

The narrative continued: "Since my mother had been recently widowed and had become heir to all the responsibilities of homes in Canada, Atlantic City, New Jersey, Pennsylvania, and Naples, Florida, as well as becoming the new manager of his vast financial complexities [sic], she was forced to travel intermittently." And while she was away, Tracy brought various friends to the condo.

Sympathetic and generous, "because my parents had taught me to be that way," Scott tried to help those less fortunate. He gave Tracy and her friends money and loaned them his mother's Cadillac Seville as well as a Datsun 280Z, which one of them wrecked.

There had been other setbacks in his generous efforts to improve the Mullins kids. When Mrs. Benson's "very nice color TV set" disappeared from the condo, Scott refused to believe Tracy took it. He also wouldn't accept that Tracy was lifting Mrs. Benson's clothes—the fourteen-year-old girl and the fifty-nine-year-old grandmother were the same size—or that she had pocketed "an expensive string of pearls and a pair of earrings that my sister had just left sitting in the bathroom." Much as Mrs. Benson and Carol Lynn complained, Scott wouldn't end the affair.

"My relationship with Tracy was always a very turbulent one. I had never known anyone like this before. I suppose I have a strong sex desire, and Tracy's voluptuous figure, plus her vast sexual knowledge I think from the beginning just overwhelmed me."

For two years, the history of their romance can be traced by police records. Starting with a domestic dispute on September 26, 1981, there was a steady pattern of complaints about fighting, disorderly conduct, and public drunkenness in St. Petersburg, Miami, and Naples.

"Her moods vacillated rapidly," the narrative ran on with scant regard for syntax, "from an extremely aggressive and passionate temptress to a violent raging maniac who hurled any object nearby or dug her fingernails into me or swung at me violently with anything she could hit me with. She did these things if the least little thing displeased her."

Describing humiliation heaped on top of injury, the document makes one wonder if there isn't some slight exaggeration, some faint whiff of paranoia empurpling the prose. At the very least, one wants to ask why Scott took up with her in the first place and why Mrs. Benson paid the bills and provided the couple with a condo at Bardmoor and a room at her home in Port Royal. Since in other instances the Bensons rarely showed any reluctance to take action when somebody crossed them, it is difficult to believe they couldn't have done something to curb Tracy Mullins—if they had wanted to and, one should add, if she bore any resemblance to the person described.

"By the spring of 1982, I had had enough of Tracy's lying and stealing, unreasonable demands for constant attention, her constant jumping in and out of bed with every man she could talk into it, her violent temper tantrums, her complete lack of moral values, her desire for money and her constant nagging to get married which she had started almost from the moment I met her."

Scott and his mother left Bardmoor and moved to Miami, where Scott was trained by a woman tennis pro. But Tracy knew where to find him, and she visited Miami whenever Mrs. Benson was away. Although the narrative alleged "money was her object all along," Scott's own motives seem to have been mixed. Whatever his second thoughts about her, he kept having sex with her.

By August she claimed to be pregnant. But Scott's manuscript said he didn't think he was the father. He wasn't even convinced Tracy was pregnant. She was, he said, "a devious schemer" who might have invented the story to get him back with her.

The document didn't mention, however, that Scott had bought Tracy a diamond ring and taken her to the Planned Parenthood office in Naples which confirmed she was pregnant. He did acknowledge that he saw her again in September, then in October. "I don't know why I went back, except that I guess I was having a hard time getting her out of my system. I told her I wished I could help her, but I didn't think it was my baby." Finally, he broke off the relationship.

Years later, Tracy Mullins still blamed Margaret. "I couldn't believe that his mother had that much control over his life, to break us up like that. She ruined [Scott's] life. He'd still be alive today if he had stayed with me, and we had been married and had a normal family like everyone else." Tracy said Scott wanted to come back to her, but Mrs. Benson threatened that if he did, she would have his dog Buck put to sleep.

Currently participating as an outpatient in a drug rehabilitation program, eighteen-year-old Tracy wanted to concentrate on getting clean, proving Shelby Ann was Scott's baby, and completing high school.

The paternity suit might have remained no more than a gaudy sidebar to the Benson murders if the handwritten document hadn't alleged that Tracy Mullins threatened the Benson family.

"My Miami coach was extremely opposed to her also," Scott's narrative explained, "because of her bad character and the fact that she interfered so much with my career. Tracy often became violent because of this. On one occasion, on the tennis court, she became so violent that she was throwing things and beating up my coach and her husband as well as me. People at the apartment complex witnessed this episode. My coach and her husband feared for their lives because Tracy threatened them and said she would get them if it was the last thing she did. They consulted my mother since they were so afraid for all of us. They knew that Tracy had underworld connections that she lived with on and off. My coach suggested that my mother and I flee to our Pennsylvania home."

But Tracy was said to have tormented the Bensons by telephone. "She constantly resorted to diabolic trickery to harass all of us, such as telephone calls to my mother in the middle of the night saying I was critically injured in an automobile accident. On one accident [sic] she had a friend call my coach while I was in the middle of a tennis match to say that she had been critically injured . . ."

Besides badgering Mrs. Benson with false alarms, Tracy was accused of threatening "my mother and my coach numerous times. My mother feared so for her life that she had her attorney fly down from Philadelphia to help her... Tracy [made] many, many calls to my mother after she thought she was pregnant. She would threaten my mother and say she was going to get a million dollars from my mother. She called so many times in the middle of the night that my mother started taking the phone off the hook.

"Mother was so frightened finally because Tracy told her over the phone that she was having someone do away with me, and that she would get Mother if it was the last thing she did. She had her underworld friends call Mother and threaten her. Mother was hysterical and called the police again. She then hired a private detective firm to patrol her house. She still continued this service. She was so frightened when she had to have her lawyer come to help her that she disguised herself in order to drive at night to the airport to pick him up."

In a sworn deposition given after the murders, Kim Beegle corroborated some of these charges. She said that Tracy Mullins had called and told Margaret that Scott had been in a car wreck. She also stated Tracy had threatened Mrs. Benson, saying, "I'm going to kill you."

Scott had told Kim that he had received death threats—or at any rate, he said he had gone to his mother and gotten money from her with the explanation that his life was in danger. In Kim's words, "he would tell his mom that he was going to get killed by the gangsters because he owed money. If she didn't pay it to them, he would get killed."

Kim claimed that Tracy had contacted Scott in March, just three or four months before his death.

While it is unclear how much Kim knew firsthand and how much had come to her as hearsay, and while it is equally unclear how many of these melodramatic accusations Scott embroidered to serve his purposes, it is apparent that Tracy had run-ins with the police and that the Bensons had complained about her threats. This alone should have led the Collier County Sheriff's Department to check out the story with the same thoroughness as they pursued other leads.

But perhaps the police were too preoccupied with other concerns. Since obtaining the receipts for the galvanized pipe and end caps from Hughes Supply, they had searched everywhere for a set of Steven Benson's fingerprints. But requests to the usual sources proved futile. Benson had never been arrested, never worked for anybody except his family or himself, never served in the armed forces, and thus had never had cause to give a rolled ink impression of his fingers.

By July 18, on the advice of his attorney, Steven refused to answer any further questions from investigators. Police informed the press and emphasized that all other members of the Benson family were continuing their cooperation.

This wasn't, strictly speaking, true. Carol Lynn Kendall also refused to speak with investigators. And Wayne Kerr excluded entire categories of questions from his discussions with law enforcement agents.

If this weren't enough to inflame suspicions against Kerr, the shambling, portly lawyer guaranteed he would stay in the public eye and under police scrutiny when, on July 25, he entered the Naples office of the Dean Witter Reynolds brokerage firm and attempted to take control of more than $1 million worth of stock in Margaret Benson's account. A concerned broker notified the probate court.

The next day Guion De Loach petitioned the court to instruct Kerr to stop acting as administrator of the Benson estate. Although De Loach had no authorization from the Benson family to file such an action, he did so, he explained, out of a sense of duty under the Code of Professional Responsibility, a set of standards for Florida lawyers. De Loach urged that the estate be frozen until the court decided which will was valid.

Within days, both lawyers had hired lawyers. Wayne Kerr was represented by William Blackwell and Guion De Loach was represented by Donald E. Van Koughnet, a former U.S. Attorney who had helped prosecute Alger Hiss in 1950.

The controversy quickened when Van Koughnet charged that Margaret Benson had never properly signed the 1983 will. A sworn statement signed by two employees of Kerr's Philadelphia office was the only evidence of Mrs. Benson's connection to the document.

Beleaguered by investigators and opposing attorneys, Kerr then had the legs cut out from under him by his own client. On July 13, in Massachusetts General Hospital, Carol Lynn Kendall had assured him that her mother had misgivings about the De Loach will and meant to forget it and go back to the May 23, 1983, will.

But on July 30, a Boston attorney publicly announced that Mrs. Kendall now preferred the De Loach will. It was not the first time, and would not be the last, that Carol Lynn reversed directions.

Chapter 9

Digging for clues, investigators had excavated the crime scene at Quail Creek to a depth of three inches, fanning out twenty-five feet in every direction from the bomb site. Ultimately, the search for evidence would force them to dig deeper and extend the radius more than a thousand miles north. On July 22, a team of detectives flew from Naples to Lancaster, Pennsylvania, the Benson family's hometown, the source of its wealth and the origin of its trouble.

Located in the Susquehanna River Valley, Lancaster County boasts in its Association of Commerce and Industry literature "the most productive farmland east of the Mississippi River and the best non-irrigated agricultural land in the nation." Although close to Philadelphia and Baltimore, much of the countryside is still given over to farming. Amish and Mennonite families till the dark earth the same way they have for centuries. Forbidden to use self-propelled vehicles, they pull plows with teams of horses. Then they transport their produce from communities like Blue Ball, Bird-in-the-Hand, and Intercourse to Lancaster Township.

The popular film *Witness* was shot here, and its story of drug-related violence erupting in a peaceful, religious rural Eden presented selective images of the countryside and its people. What the camera overlooked were the highways that crisscross the rolling hills, the real estate developments that border the picturesque farms, and the Hispanic workers who have thronged to the area.

Lancaster Township and its renovated historical center appear prosperous and peaceful. A city of red brick row houses, red brick sidewalks, white church steeples, and ancient trees arching over the streets, it takes pride in its colonial heritage. The Continental Congress met here during the Revolutionary War and George Washington visited on five occasions.

"Principled pragmatism" is, according to *The Heritage of Lancaster*, the town's guiding philosophy. Local patriots participated in the Revolution more often as suppliers of guns and ammunition than as soldiers. Later they took part in the nation's westward expansion, not as explorers or settlers, but by producing Conestoga wagons and Lancaster rifles. Hard workers and sharp traders, they developed a rich, diversified economy.

Today Lancaster ranks as one of the ten safest cities of its size in the United States. (Like Naples, it has a population of approximately 100,000.) But it has known its share of bloodshed. Early on, the Conestoga Indians were an inconvenience. When they weren't on the warpath, they were impeding progress and ruining business.

In 1763 a gang of Scot Presbyterians called the Paxtang Boys decided to settle this problem. They raided a peaceful Conestoga camp and slaughtered anybody who wasn't away at the time peddling baskets. County authorities herded the surviving tribe members into a jail and "placed them in protective custody," according to *The Heritage of Lancaster*.

The following Sunday, when the townspeople and the prison keepers were all conveniently away at church, the Paxtang Boys came back to finish the job. They massacred every man, woman, and child and hung their bodies on hooks. "A Presbyterian minister, Lazarus Stewart, was believed to be the leader of the gang. Despite the widespread expression of revulsion, the Paxtang Boys were never prosecuted. This act of wanton barbarism marked the end of Indian community life in our county."

Far from being an old, blue-blood family, the Bensons arrived in Lancaster from Baltimore after World War II. While they had money and belonged to the right clubs—the Lancaster Country Club and the Hamilton Club downtown—they were not among the richest residents or the most prominent. People said they could have gone further socially, but seemed not to know how. Or perhaps they simply didn't care to. In matters small and large, they flouted local conventions and violated taboos. In a quiet, conservative community, they were ostentatious with their wealth and blind to public opinion. Margaret was never invited to join the Junior League and Carol Lynn did not make her debut.

"They were never central to Lancaster," said one lady who is.

"They were never representative of the town. Not that people here are incapable of wrongdoing. It's just that the Bensons were different."

One member of the extended family who earned a large measure of respect was Harry Hitchcock, Margaret's father, the fount of all the money. True, he lacked something of the low-key, reserved Lancastrian style. He was a glad-hander, a drumbeater. But his warmth and generosity won people over, as did his religious fervor.

Now haloed in white hair, immensely photogenic, and an endless source of good copy, Harry had that larger-than-life quality common to American folk heroes. Born poor in Baltimore in 1897, he had been imbued with enough pluck and luck to fill an entire library with Horatio Alger tales. Some of these stories he wrote up himself and published in the Lancaster newspapers; others he passed on to reporters looking for a human interest piece.

His father, "Baltimore's blind singer professor, Walter T. Hitchcock," opened the Imperial, the city's second nickelodeon, a motion picture theater that charged five cents admission. A life-size portrait of Walter hung in the window, an early example to his son of the values of self-promotion. The show consisted of short subjects and an illustrated song sung by the "blind professor." At the age of seven, Harry provided the sound effects for silent films and sold Smith Brothers Cough Drops during the intermission.

When increasing competition drove the Imperial out of business, the Hitchcocks worked as booking agents for vaudeville acts. But then Harry's mother died and he quit school at the age of twelve to go to work full-time to support the "blind professor" and his younger brothers.

Years later, he regaled a reporter from the Philadelphia *Inquirer* with the story of how he landed a job at the Baltimore Bargain House, a mail order company. "There he met his future wife, Charlotte Brown, and forevermore he would joke that 'she was the best bargain they had.'"

Eventually, Harry went into the tobacco business. Working as a middle man, he bought leaf, processed it, and then delivered it to cigar manufacturers. Traveling up and down the East coast, attending auctions, Harry was on the road three weeks out of every month, logging fifty thousand miles a year.

As he told the Lancaster *New Era*, he knew little about leaf, but a lot about people. "It was true then and continued to be true throughout my experience that I didn't know one kind of tobacco from another. My success came because I made no pretense about being an expert. [I] employed people who did know good tobacco when they saw it."

Ironically, Harry was a lifelong nonsmoker and teetotaler who had taken the Lincoln-Lee pledge in Methodist Sunday school. He had not, however, told his employers that he had sworn off their product. But they found out, and this moment of truth provided Harry with more fodder for the anecdotes with which he entertained journalists and prayer breakfast groups. As printed in the New Era and repeated whenever Harry had the chance, the story ran like this:

"A man from the head office met Hitchcock at a 'big southern hotel' to discuss a job opening in the treasurer's office.

"Young Hitchcock, never before in a dining room that fancy, was 'scared to death' and ordered exactly what the other man did.

"Then 'at the end of the meal,' Hitchcock recalled, the company official 'handed me the biggest, blackest cigar I'd ever seen. He bit off his end and I bit off mine. He lit a match and said smoke up. I said I'm sorry, but I don't smoke.

"'I thought that would be the end of it, but it wasn't.'

"Despite his distaste for tobacco, Hitchcock won a series of promotions that ultimately put him at the top."

Some people, even those who liked Harry, said these uplifting stories glossed over decisive steps in his career. He didn't become a multimillionaire, they claimed, by playing the part of lively yarn spinner and cracker-barrel philosopher. "Harry was a hardheaded businessman," said one Lancastrian, "who found it convenient late in life to embrace Jesus and spend his time going to prayer meetings, eating half-cooked bacon and talking about good fellowship and all that shit."

But the majority view, at least as expressed in public, pretty much matches Harry's. He worked long and hard, displaying his usual combination of pluck and luck, and launched Lancaster Leaf Tobacco, an independent subsidiary of Universal Leaf. It grew into the world's largest trader of dark leaf tobacco, and in the next three decades the company spun off five subsidiaries of its own, including Viroqua Leaf Tobacco in Wisconsin and Lanco Fill Inc. in the Philippines, and it opened operations in Indonesia, Nigeria,

Belgium, Paraguay, and the Dominican Republic. Although the family fortune fell short of the $400 million estimate printed in some newspapers, Harry Hitchcock, his wife and two daughters, Margaret and Janet Lee, had an aggregate wealth of perhaps $40 million.

In 1955, at the age of fifty-eight, Harry suffered two collapses, said to have been caused by physical exhaustion. "I found out the hard way that I was neglecting and sacrificing my family, erroneously feeling I was climbing the road to success."

By chance, just when he needed it most, he went to a prayer breakfast, and it altered the course of his life, allowing him to learn the biblical lesson that it does not profit a man if he gains the whole world but loses his soul. "I had a whole new outlook," Harry said, "I sort of realized that money does not insure happiness. Some of the richest men I know have no money. Some of the most unhappy men I know have a lot of money."

Although he continued to manage Lancaster Leaf, he began to shift some of the responsibilities to his son-in-law, Margaret's husband, Edward "Benny" Benson. A skillful trader, a constant traveler, and a tireless worker, Benson expanded the company's international divisions and branched out from cigars into chewing tobacco.

Meanwhile, Hitchcock quit commuting from Baltimore and settled in Lancaster, in the exclusive residential area of School Lane Hills. He concentrated on charitable and religious activities, serving as a trustee of the YMCA, joining the Gideon Society, the Christian Business Men, and the First United Methodist Church, founding the International Christian Leadership, an interdenominational prayer group, and serving as chairman of the Mayor's Prayer Breakfast. As he approached his seventieth birthday, he cultivated his own gardens figuratively and literally. Planting the acreage around his home with fifty thousand tulips and other flowering bulbs, six hundred azaleas, rhododendrons, hyacinths, and flowering trees, he turned 1510 Center Road into a showplace modeled on Sherwood Gardens in Baltimore and opened it to the public every spring.

"If people don't come and enjoy the beauty of the flowers," Hitchcock said, "it would seem like we gave a big party and no one showed up." He urged visitors to walk the paths through his yard and he thoughtfully planted flowers in front of the house for senior citizens who couldn't get out of their cars. School classes and bus tours arrived on a regular basis, visiting what Hitchcock liked to call "a little bit of Heaven."

Newspapers referred to him as "the garden's own St. Peter" and they printed the poems he wrote and posted on signboards among the tulips:

> Come visit with us in our garden.
> You are welcome to walk on our sod.
> When you commune with our flowers,
> You are getting closer to God.

Punctual as the seasons, honors rained down on Harry. An academic building was named after him at Lancaster Bible College, and then the Hitchcock Arena opened at Messiah College. He had given generously to both institutions, just as he had to the First United Methodist Church. He donated his house to the church, with the proviso that he could go on living there as long as he liked. "The more you give," Harry counseled, "the richer you get."

That certainly seemed to apply in his case. When he stepped down from Lancaster Leaf in 1966, his stock in the company was exchanged for stock in Universal Leaf. In the next nineteen years it quintupled in value.

Still, Harry kept giving things away. Personal possessions meant little to him. His wife and two daughters held his share of the stock. He assumed they would outlive him. But Charlotte died in 1981. Now Margaret was gone too, brutally murdered.

Dreadful as the news was, Harry talked to TV commentators and shared his feelings with the press. He said he had received many letters of condolence, especially from children who had toured his gardens.

"I'm overwhelmed by the love that has been showered on me. It's not just the sympathy and concern. It's the prayers of so many people."

He accepted the tragedy, pointing out that "the Lord has some purpose that has not been revealed to me."

He declared that he felt "no rancor or bitterness. The Lord has forgiven me...I had no choice but to forgive whoever in his sick mind did this act that I can't understand."

He took comfort in his beliefs, drawing strength from the thought that "Jesus Christ is suffering with me. I know the Lord is going through this with me."

If anybody believed these pronouncements presaged Harry's withdrawal from the hurly-burly of the Benson case, they were badly mistaken. He stayed on center stage, quoting verses, speaking in parables, supplementing prayer with the power of his checkbook.

2

It is puzzling that people granted Harry such a pivotal role in the case when he never played that part with the Benson family. He took his son-in-law into the business when Benny came out of the Army Air Corps after World War II, and he supplied money to Margaret and provided discretionary trusts for her three children. But otherwise he exercised little influence, and they ignored the Christian example he set.

Like Harry, the Bensons lived in School Lane Hills. But where Hitchcock's house was modest and its gardens open to the public, the Bensons' seventeen-room gray stone house at 1515 Ridge Road was guarded by an iron gate and an elaborate burglar alarm system. It had an Olympic-sized swimming pool, a cabana, a greenhouse, and a tennis court. The study was mahogany-paneled and decorated with ivory statuary. Mrs. Benson's bedroom had gold doorknobs, and in the bathroom there were gold fixtures and a waterfall.

While Harry had little interest in material possessions, the Bensons were obsessed by them. Whatever they got, they wanted more, and once they had something, they went to extraordinary lengths to hold onto it long after it was of any use to them. Finally, the family had to buy a three-story warehouse for all their excess belongings.

"They had more furniture than Watt & Shand and Gimbel's put together," said Tom West, a family employee. "They were like pack rats, they saved everything." In addition to ten antique cars, the warehouse contained clothes, TVs, snowmobiles, minibikes, furniture, lengths of pipe and other plumbing supplies.

The Bensons not only clung to their possessions, they kept strict accounts of what they had been given. Each Christmas, Benny noted in a ledger every gift the Bensons received, who sent it, and the approximate value. He boasted that he had a record of Christmas gifts for the pasty twenty-four years.

Till the end of her life, Margaret Benson kept similar accounts of what she had given her children. The kids spoke of this as "mother's little black book."

"The greed for money in that family was tremendous," said a close associate. The kids "fought, scrapped, and cursed each other."

Another Lancastrian recalled, "Money was the center of their life. I don't think there was any love. That's why I felt sorry for Carol Lynn. I don't think she ever experienced love or true caring. She was controlled."

As one of Carol Lynn's former boyfriends explained, "Turning the money spigot on and off was the way of control in that family."

Mike Minney, a friend of Steven's from high school, said, "It was carrot and stick from day one . . . the threat was always there that if Steven didn't behave, he would be cut off."

One man who spent a great deal of time at the Benson house felt that Benny needed to dominate everything and everybody. Though he was easygoing when you didn't cross him, he could be autocratic, even ruthless, in business and dictatorial at home.

Margaret Benson submitted to her husband without question. She knew little about financial affairs, and whenever an envelope with a window on it arrived, she handed it over to Benny.

"He gave them things," a family intimate recalled, "but always with strings attached. He picked their cars. He tried to pick their friends and social life. And he expected devotion in return."

Yet while Benny demanded loyalty and professed to value family closeness above all else, he was seldom home. He had to fly around the world buying tobacco.

3

A woman who attended Lancaster County Day School with Carol Lynn remembers her as bright, nice, never mean or vain. She did well in her studies and had a beautiful singing voice. "She had a lot going for her," the classmate recalled, "but it wasn't working. Her parents were always pressuring her."

Not especially pretty in early adolescence, Carol Lynn was overweight, with mousy brown hair and chubby hips and thighs. Margaret, "who always looked like a million dollars," pushed her daughter to do something about her appearance.

Between the ages of twelve and seventeen, Carol Lynn lost weight and changed her shape and her destiny. But this was no fairy tale of an ugly duckling magically metamorphosing into a swan. As her high school yearbook *Challenge*, revealed, she went from a size fourteen to a size seven by dint of willpower and hard work. Her graduation picture showed a smiling, smooth-cheeked girl with sparkling eyes and slightly bouffant hair. Blond hair! She had bleached the mousy brown tresses.

The caption under her snapshot puckishly asked, "Blonde or brunette?" And it gushed "boys, boys, men... Ford Sunliner convertibles do mix with Jaguars."

Proud of their daughter and her hard-won glamour, the Bensons "promoted Carol Lynn, displayed her," said a classmate. "Her parents wanted her to be seductive," and they encouraged her to wear provocative clothes and makeup.

Like other girls at Lancaster Country Day, she became part of the group "cruising the route" around nearby Franklin and Marshall College. She dated fraternity boys and went to their parties at the age of sixteen, giving an impression of greater sophistication and awareness than her contemporaries, many of whom admitted they were in awe of her.

But her former classmate had a different view. "Her parents had created this creature. But then they lost control."

By comparison with his flashy and popular older sister, Steven was quiet and unassuming. He got respectable grades, played a moderately good game of tennis, and was once elected president of his high school home room. But he struck people as straitlaced, never one to argue or fight. As a teenager he got just one traffic ticket, for squealing his tires, and even that charge was dropped.

"He did not have a lot of buddies," recalled Dan Cherry, Jr., who went to McCaskie High School with him.

While most boys in the late sixties wore their hair long and dressed in faded blue denim, Steven always had on a suit coat and tie, and resembled a junior executive. His one touch of dazzle was to drive an MG, then later a Mercedes.

He kept to himself, fiddling with electronic equipment. In grade school he was already building radios and, by the age of ten, he had constructed a Heathkit television set. He worked on chemical experiments in the garage and once burned his hands badly with sulfuric acid.

By the time Carol Lynn had gone off to Goucher College in Baltimore, he started coming under pressure from his parents. Where

Benny and Margaret wanted their daughter to be beautiful and provocative, they wanted him to be as successful as his father and grandfather. He began to suffer migraine headaches.

He confessed to close friends that he "felt rejected, especially by his father. His father didn't have any time to spend with him. He said that he never did some of the things with his father than he wanted to."

Benny didn't care for hunting or fishing or sports. It wasn't just that he was busy and had to spend weeks on the road. He had had polio as a child and avoided strenuous activity.

The one time Benny did take his son hunting, they flew to Florida, to a business associate's property, and went after wild turkey. Spotting a huge bird in a tree, Steven shot it without a second look. As it fell to the ground in a shower of brilliant feathers, he realized it wasn't a turkey. He had killed a peacock.

This incident stands as an example of all the errors Steven committed through eagerness or awkwardness. He was always silent when he should have said something. Or else, at the least appropriate moment, he'd blurt a remark that ruined things for him.

At times, caught up in his own intricate ideas, he threw himself into projects headlong, unable to imagine that other people would not be pleased by the results. At the age of seven, he constructed an elaborate geometrical design in Carol Lynn's bedroom, thumbtacking string from the furniture to the walls to a bulletin board, creating a kind of spider's web. The final thumbtack was jabbed into a picture of her favorite boyfriend. She screamed at Steven, but he couldn't explain why he had done it.

In his early teens, he gave his ID bracelet to Lynn Beyer, a girl he had known since kindergarten. One winter day her family's barn burned down, killing her horse, and Steven made a comment that could be seen as witheringly callous or as another example of his bungling inability to sort through his own emotions and say the right thing.

"Good," he told Lynn, "now that he's dead, you'll have more time for me."

As she recollected many years later, "That ended any type of relationship we had."

Then suddenly, inexplicably, Margaret Benson, verging on menopause, adopted a baby. Confused, Steven started spending more and more time away from the house. Having lived his first seven years in the shadow of a formidable, attractive older sister, he had briefly had his parents to himself. But just as he was emerging as his own man, an adolescent taking his first tentative steps toward independence, a new competitor arrived.

According to most accounts, Steven became Scott's best friend and, after Benny's death, acted as a surrogate father. But Margaret so clearly preferred Scott, who grew up to be all the things Steven was not—handsome, extroverted, and athletic—Steven could not help feeling rejected.

After high school he enrolled as a business student at Franklin and Marshall College and, bankrolled by his father, launched his first venture, Lancaster Landscapers. Investing heavily in equipment— "If there was a right-handed edger we had it," wisecracked a former employee. "If there was a *left-handed* edger we had it"—incurring astronomical start-up costs, he seemed determined to prove himself by spending enormous amounts of money. It was a mistake he would make again—believing that people would take him seriously and that an endeavor would automatically succeed if he sank enough cash into it.

But Lancaster Landscapers never escaped the oceans of red ink Steven roiled up around it. Several times his father had to bail him out with infusions of capital.

Plagued by business problems, he studied very little and dropped out of college before the end of his freshman year. He registered again the next fall, but withdrew after a semester. In 1971, he returned to Franklin and Marshall a third time and managed to complete a year of course work. But the following May, he left college and married Nancy Ferguson. A girl from a working-class family, she came from a part of town called Cabbage Hill. The Bensons had hoped for a match with somebody from a wealthy, prominent family.

Nevertheless, they bought the twenty-year-old newlyweds what real estate agents call a "starter house." It cost $21,900 and was far more modest than the places Steven had lived in. He wired it for stereo and ran a line to a telephone pole, rigging up a bootleg connection for cable television. Working now for Lancaster Leaf, he also struggled to keep his landscaping business alive. But in the summer of 1975 a fertilizer firm filed a complaint for a $3,283 debt. Steven settled out of court.

After the company collapsed, he nominally became a full-time employee of Lancaster Leaf. Some people felt his father was grooming him to take over the business. But Steven tried to start a hardware supply operation; it never got off the ground. He regarded his job at Lancaster Leaf as a sure way to remain second fiddle to his father and third fiddle to his grandfather for the rest of his life.

He "never had a strong interest in the tobacco business," said Claude Marten, who later replaced Benny Benson as head of Lancaster Leaf. "I think Steven wanted to do something that he could say he had done on his own."

Still, he stayed on. "He was in the factory with the customers, trying to learn the business," a company vice-president said. "I'd describe [him] as a management trainee."

Others, less kind, described him simply as the president's son.

Steven smoldered with resentment. Yet he couldn't break away. His family supplemented his salary, then bought Nancy and him a lavish home right across the street from them on Ridge Road.

"When he talked about [computer] equipment and systems, he knew what he was talking about," one business colleague conceded. But he caused the accountants at Lancaster Leaf no end of trouble with his casual spending and bookkeeping.

"I don't think he was well respected," Nancy acknowledged. And this undermined his self-esteem and their marriage.

"Steven's very insecure," she said. He "doesn't love himself, so he needs to have other people all the time reinforce that they love him."

He began to have affairs, some of them blatant enough to prompt gossip at work. He and his young wife went to a marriage counselor. But "he's a very complex person," Nancy said. "I'm not sure he always comes up front with his feelings."

She sensed he wasn't happy, and he admitted she was right. It wasn't just their marriage, Steven explained. He'd never been happy in his whole life.

"Well, what would make you happy?" Nancy asked.

"If I could be a millionaire by the time I'm thirty."

Nancy saw that obsession as his response to pressure from Benny and Margaret. Long past the point where he knew how to please himself, he struggled to please them.

"It's a strange family," Nancy said. "They were always at each other's throats. I mean, it was rare in that family that they weren't arguing."

By March 5, 1977, the couple had separated and Steven filed for divorce, claiming that Nancy "constantly criticized me, the way I dressed, my friends, relatives, just everything."

4

After graduating from Goucher in International Relations, Carol Lynn moved to San Antonio, Texas, and entered St. Mary's Law School. A year and a half later she dropped out and returned to Lancaster with Francis Thomason Kendall, Jr., a former water ski instructor at Cypress Gardens, Florida.

They had been acquainted, according to Carol Lynn, for "nine or ten months." But she was uncertain of his birth date, his birth place, or his profession. She thought he had taken "pre-veterinary medicine" courses at a university, but "it turned out he hadn't even graduated from high school." Only twenty-two, Tom Kendall had been married and divorced before. Carol Lynn, two years his senior, didn't know exactly where or when this divorce occurred—just that it took place sometime prior to their own wedding in St. James Episcopal Church on November 30, 1968.

Almost immediately, the groom and his pregnant bride departed for California, driving a new car. It turned out to be a rough trip, Tom, who had been "nice and considerate before...got really horrible. He would never take any advice about anything," Carol Lynn claimed. They argued whether to use high test or regular gas. Tom thought regular would be all right and told Carol Lynn "to shut my damn mouth" when she disagreed. "This really bothered me because I was raised in a house where my father never used a swear word."

Although Tom said worse things to her, she wouldn't give examples. "I'm not saying things like that." She'd only agree that it was vile and sexually obscene and it upset her and made her cry.

When they reached California, her crying continued. Tom had told her he had a position as assistant manager at Marine World in Redwood City, but it turned out to be a temporary job for three days. After that, he didn't look for work. He slept late, took flying lessons, and paid for everything with "money that my grandparents had given me when I got married."

When asked how she coped, Carol Lynn said, "It was very difficult, but I managed because I had a very good upbringing."

Under the circumstances, with Tom "going through the money like crazy," letting Carol Lynn pay the bills, it seemed best for the honeymooners to return to the East Coast. They lived for a few months at the family summer home on the New Jersey shore. Then the Bensons bought them a house in School Lane Hills. Tom Kendall went to work at Lancaster Leaf and the baby, a son named Kurt, was born that spring, not much more than five months after the wedding.

Because the house at 502 Wilson Drive needed painting, Carol Lynn said she moved with her mother and the baby back to the Jersey shore for the summer. Tom came down on the weekends with her father, but things got no better for the couple. Tom would have nothing to do with the baby and "was really angry because, he told me, it was a boy and he didn't want a boy."

He refused to help Carol Lynn choose a name. He called the baby Spot. "He just didn't pay any attention to him, he didn't act like a normal father and he was really cruel with him."

While she was at the shore, Tom went out with other women and claimed to have slept with Carol Lynn's best friend. Then he accused her of infidelity and "said if he had an idea that I was going out he would kill me." In California, she said, he had threatened to "throw me out of the window of our second floor apartment if I didn't shut up." But this new menace filled her with a deeper dread. "I was afraid not only for my life but for the baby." She thought he might get it into his head that she was unfaithful and "just go and kill me."

He also wasn't nice to her parents. He wouldn't refer to Mrs. Benson by name. He acted as though she didn't have one and ignored her when she spoke. "He knew this bothered her and it bothered me."

At the end of August, Tom stopped going to work at Lancaster Leaf and quit coming to the shore to see Carol Lynn and the baby boy he called Spot. He said he had to finish painting the house. Instead, he overdrew the bank account and left. All this represents Carol Lynn's version of her life with Tom Kendall taken from the transcript of her divorce hearing. Tom Kendall himself never appeared at the proceeding and, to this day, his whereabouts remain a mystery.

While Francis Thomason Kendall wasn't the first, and would not be the last man, to enter and exit her life so abruptly, he at least left Carol Lynn with the name she kept for herself, for Kurt, and for a second son, Travis, born after the divorce became final.

Though she left from time to time to make it on her own, she always returned. A Benson family intimate, speaking of all the children, said, "They didn't really want to break the apron strings. They got everything they wanted." Yet it is unclear whether Carol Lynn got what she wanted.

She had several long relationships, one with a man whom she had known in Texas and who moved to Lancaster to be near her. But fellows who dated her had the impression she didn't really care to let anyone get close. They also described her as demanding. A lawyer in Lancaster compared her to a yacht. "You know the definition of a yacht? A yacht is a hole in the water that you pour money into. Whatever money Carol Lynn gets, she'll run through."

Another fellow remembered that she met him at the front door of her house and announced, "All the other men I go out with feel my time is worth paying the baby-sitter and driving her home."

He agreed to this on the first date, but then figured it was her responsibility or Tom Kendall's to hire somebody to mind Kurt and Travis. She could afford it, he thought.

In fact, Carol Lynn received no alimony or child support and, with two small children at home, she couldn't go off to a job. It was all she could do to keep up with the housework. Neighbors remember the place as a mess.

She lived on her trust fund, but had trouble stretching it to cover expenses. Even after Harry Hitchcock supplemented her income, she had problems making ends meet, especially during those periods when she was at odds with her mother and reportedly wasn't allowed to set foot on the Benson property. At one point she shocked neighbors by asking that Kurt and Travis be given free lunches at Buchanan School. Her income was inadequate, she explained, and she felt her sons qualified for federally subsidized meals.

As always, people admired her looks and her figure. They still tell the tale of the aging Lancastrian with a pacemaker who peered deep into her cleavage and loudly proclaimed that his heart was skipping beats. But men who might have married Carol Lynn didn't care for Mrs. Benson's habit of cornering them and bluntly asking what they were worth.

"I always felt that Carol Lynn had ice in her veins," one bachelor said. "I thought you could strike a match on her. She wasn't a very warm or soft person."

Perhaps if they realized what she endured during those years after Tom Kendall abandoned her and the boys, they would have been less harsh in their judgments. Maybe if they understood the complex relationships within the Benson family, they wouldn't have been surprised by her reluctance to let outsiders get close. If they knew how many matches had already been struck against her cool, enameled veneer, they might have agreed she had no reason to risk making herself vulnerable again.

5

Doted upon by Margaret, receiving little supervision from Benny, Scott grew up spoiled, rash, and given to outbursts of rage that frightened his adopted mother and sister. By his early teens he was drinking and doing drugs and had had minor scrapes with the Lancaster police. It wasn't uncommon for him to drop into the Town Tavern, smart-off with the locals, and get into a brawl.

"Scott was the type of person," said Mark Schelling, one of his closest friends, "that you didn't tell him what to do."

Certainly no one at home tried to. As Schelling observed, "Mrs. Benson was the type of person always to give in to Scott." At first she might put up resistance, but then Scott would badger her, screaming and cursing, until she caved in.

Peggy Miller, a close friend of Harry Hitchcock, remembered Scott's temper tantrums and how he manipulated Margaret. Mrs. Miller regarded his tennis coaches as no better than overpriced babysitters who earned more for minding Scott than some family men made in a year. "More than your prosecutors get," she told one investigator.

"Amen," the man responded.

"When they start out," Mrs. Miller qualified her statement.

"Even when they've been there a while," the investigator told her.

It had crossed Mrs. Miller's mind, just as it had other people's, that the murders might be drug-related. She had heard Scott's cousin, Brenda Murphy, mention that Scott bought and sold drugs.

Although much of the public's, not to mention the police's, attention centered on Scott's use of marijuana and cocaine, his most serious addiction was to nitrous oxide. A greatly misunderstood substance employed by doctors and dentists as an anesthetic, abused by others as a quick, cheap high, nitrous oxide, commonly known as "laughing gas," induces an almost instantaneous feeling of warmth and euphoria. But repeated large doses can lead to confusion, hallucinations, depression, and acute organic brain syndrome. While medical journals do not contend that heavy nitrous oxide ingestion directly produces mental problems, they point out that it may mimic psychotic episodes and release inhibitions against irrational behavior and violence. Studies cite examples of patients prone to maniacal outbursts and suicide. Severe brain damage and deaths have been known to occur. Doctors urge particular caution with adolescents who might take nitrous oxide in combination with other drugs.

Scott Benson had been doing precisely that since junior high school. He started with what kids call "whippets," sniffing nitrous oxide from metal cylinders about the size of large-caliber bullets. Used commercially to aerate whipped cream, these cylinders can be bought in specialty food stores.

Later, as he began consuming the stuff on an industrial scale, he couldn't keep it a secret from his mother. Margaret knew what he was doing and paid for home delivery of tanks of nitrous oxide as if she were paying the milkman. She seemed to be willing to do anything for her adopted son—except get him help.

His aunt, Janet Lee Murphy, thought Scott was a warm, lovable boy, but she didn't understand why her sister let him do whatever he liked, including living with girls in Margaret's house. According to Janet Lee, Margaret didn't approve of this, but she accepted it "because she didn't want to lose him. She wanted him with her. She put up with all his problems. That was the measure of her devotion or obsession or whatever you call it."

For all the family's devotion to him, Scott regarded Margaret with contempt and Benny with indifference. He detested Carol Lynn, whom he considered selfish and shallow. The one relative whose company and approval he sought was Steven. "Scott just emulated Steven. He wanted to be like him," one family associate in Lancaster recalled.

Kim Beegle characterized Steven as Scott's closest friend.

According to Kim, Scott couldn't stand Carol Lynn. "She was just a real bitch. He avoided her whenever possible."

Mrs. Benson could also be "a bitch," Kim said. "It all depended on how she woke up that day . . . She was nice sometimes and then sometimes she was pretty rude, mean. You know, using things against Scott like his car, wouldn't let him drive his car when she was mad at him or threatening to cut him out of the will when she was mad at him."

When crossed, Carol Lynn lashed back at her mother, Kim said. "I've heard her say things to her mom that weren't very nice, things like 'don't worry, Mother, you'll get your pound of flesh,' you know, pretty rude things." At times she sounded almost menacing. "Your day is coming, Mother." It was enough to make Mrs. Benson cry.

After a reconciliation with Nancy, followed by three more separations, Steven filed for divorce a second time in April 1979. It was not an amicable parting.

Having suffered through six years during which Steven and she never had a life independent from his parents, Nancy discovered that the Bensons intended to interfere with the divorce as well. In fact, Nancy had signed a prenuptial agreement at the Bensons' insistence. "That was a setup," she said, "and the Bensons meant to make it stick." They demanded that she leave the marriage with no more than she had brought to it.

According to an attorney knowledgeable about the details, "Given the amount of money involved, I thought Steven was overdoing it. But this didn't seem to be his doing. He was being directed by his family. If the money spent on legal fees had been offered to Nancy, she probably would have been satisfied. But the Bensons always liked to play hardball."

Talking to investigators, Nancy said she had been afraid of Steven, and it wasn't just because he slept with what she thought was a submachine gun under the bed. "I guess it was the power, and because I've learned in my short life that money can do anything and whatever Steven wanted, he was going to get. And I knew he could nail me against the wall if he wanted to."

Yet even after the bitterness and the legal wrangling, after Steven's infidelities and the family's interference, she didn't believe her ex-husband was a murderer. "If I have to pin down a feeling, I have to say I always felt sorry for Steven."

During his separations from Nancy, Steven worked at the Viroqua Leaf Tobacco Company in Wisconsin, one of Lancaster Leaf's subsidiaries. Rather than spend the time polishing his managerial skills, he indulged in his usual doodling, drawing up plans for a new warehouse lighting system and an automatic insecticide device.

He also met a shapely woman with dark hair that hung down her back. Her name was Debra Franks Larson. Daughter of a dairy farmer, she had been married for more than six years to Monte Larson, a bulk fuel oil dealer. When Steven asked her to come east to Pennsylvania, she left Monte and lived with Steven for almost a year before flying down to the Dominican Republic for a quickie divorce. A month later the couple was married in St. James Episcopal Church.

They took up residence at 502 Wilson Drive, in the house recently vacated by Carol Lynn and her sons. Soon afterward, the house on Ridge Road where Steven and Nancy had lived was sold by the Bensons for $156,000—a tidy profit of $77,000 in four years. Then Benny and Margaret sold another $156,000 house they owned in School Lane Hills and purchased a home in Naples, on Galleon Drive in Port Royal. Benny, now age sixty, intended to take early retirement and spend his winters in Florida.

But on the return trip from Naples, Benny fell ill. Tests indicated that he had lung cancer. The prognosis was grim; the disease was terminal.

Carol Lynn and her boys, in the process of moving to Florida themselves, settled in a series of hotels in New York and Pennsylvania to stay near and lend support to Mrs. Benson. Margaret was so distraught over Benny's lung cancer, she would not let anyone smoke in her house for the rest of her life. She held on to her tobacco stocks, however.

Within six weeks, Benny was dead. He had signed a new will bequeathing his personal property to Margaret and placing the rest of his estate in trusts for his wife and for "both natural and adopted children." He wanted to make sure there was no debate about Scott's right to inherit.

Haunted by memories in Lancaster, Margaret decided to make Naples her primary residence. Scott came with her, and so did Carol Lynn, Kurt, and Travis, who lived at the house on Galleon Drive until Scott's allergic reaction to her cats forced Carol Lynn to rent a place on Vanderbilt Beach. With the exception of an abortive move to Texas, Carol Lynn remained near her mother for the next two and a half years, by which time Steven and Debbie had also settled in Naples.

To understand why the Benson children, despite their periodic estrangements, always returned to Margaret, one only has to study the cash flow. Aside from their trusts, their mother was their only steady source of income. Within a month of his father's death, Steven had resigned or been fired from Lancaster Leaf. Scott would never have a job. In her early forties, Carol Lynn was still groping to find a profession.

Seen from one point of view, it appeared that the children exploited Margaret. But looked at from a different perspective, the exploitation may have been mutual.

Early on, Mr. and Mrs. Benson established a pattern guaranteed to produce emotional and financial dependence. While they seemed to be generous, they rarely gave anything to the children outright. Luxury cars and expensive houses were put at their disposal, but always belonged to the parents and could be taken back to remind the kids how helpless they were.

After Mr. Benson's death, Steven began starting up businesses, and his actions took on an irrational edge. On January 5, 1981, he launched a company with the grandiloquent name of United International Industries, Inc. and rented office space where, people remember, he received packages from Singapore, Hong Kong, and elsewhere in the Far East. Describing it as an import-export business, Benson said he dealt in land development and tobacco. He installed a telex to the Philippines and, if the venture had succeeded, he would have competed head-on with Lancaster Leaf.

But he was seldom seen at his office, and no one could confirm that he ever traded tobacco. He did, however, complete one land deal. When he learned that Debra was pregnant, he decided they needed a much larger house and signed a contract to purchase Norwood, a historic mansion and seventeen-acre estate outside Lancaster. It cost $240,000. Steven made what struck the owner as a snap decision and wrote a check for $50,000.

Then he hurried to his mother; he didn't have $50,000. Furious though she was, Mrs. Benson covered the check he had kited.

While this incident underscored the galling insouciance with which Steven spent his mother's money, it also spoke volumes about Mrs. Benson. Much as she might fume, she went on underwriting his expensive pipe dreams, just as she paid for Scott's nitrous oxide and his tennis lessons.

Steven and his pregnant wife moved into the mansion, and although there was talk of developing the land and selling off lots, that never happened. Some say Steven discovered that the terrain was unsuitable for a subdivision. Others maintain he never had any intention of doing more than living there in baronial splendor.

In December of 1981, Debbie gave birth to premature twins. Christopher Logan and Victoria Elizabeth Benson had to remain hospitalized at the Hershey Medical Center until February 1982. By the time they came home, Steven and Debbie were having serious marital problems. Like Nancy before her, Debbie resented the fact that Mrs. Benson always had first call on Steven and expected to run their lives.

In March, Debbie took the twins home to Westby, Wisconsin, and let Steven stew alone in Florida before joining him there. But the separation had solved nothing, and in July she returned to Wisconsin. Later that year, she filed for a divorce, claiming the marriage was "irretrievably broken."

Steven stayed in Florida, occasionally visiting his kids in Wisconsin. He showed little interest in his property in Pennsylvania. He neglected to pay school, county, and township taxes and failed to meet his mortgage for five months straight. The owner repossessed Norwood, and the Bensons forfeited $60,000 in equity.

Yet Steven continued to hatch real estate deals. He considered buying a building in downtown Lancaster and renting out office space. He arranged to have a feasibility study done, but when it indicated the initial costs would be too steep and the potential return too risky, he dropped the plan. He also dropped the firm which performed the feasibility study and he refused to pay the bill. The firm took legal action and accepted half its fee in an out-of-court settlement.

By then, Steven had acquired a Florida real estate license and signed an option on a condominium project at Isle of Capri. Upset that he had once more committed her money without her knowledge, Margaret demanded that he cut his losses and back out of the deal.

This seemed a signal change in Mrs. Benson's attitude, a determination to curb his profligate spending. But before the year was out, she had gone into business with her son, become his corporate partner, hired him as a consultant, and provided access to her accounts. If he can be accused of building castles in the air, she wanted to live in them.

Despite Steven's history of flightiness and financial malfeasance, Margaret was willing to fund the Meridian companies because she dreamed of becoming an entrepreneur and reaping long-range profits. She also liked the tax write-offs and the opportunity to fudge a bit and list her maid, her secretary, her daughter, and some of Scott's friends as corporate employees. She could even defray the cost of maintaining a dozen cars and two yachts by letting Steven set up the shell of a charter business.

By August 1983, when Debbie withdrew her divorce complaint, Steven was more intricately entangled than ever with his mother. Debbie had little choice; she accepted that Steven and Margaret would maintain close contact during the day. But she set down conditions before she returned. She refused to live in the same town as her mother-in-law. She insisted they move to Fort Myers. She also insisted that Mrs. Benson not call them after work.

Steven submitted to her demands. He was eager to have his wife and kids back. When Debbie flew down to join him in Florida, she was pregnant again.

6

During their trips to Lancaster, the Naples police gradually pieced together a picture of the Bensons and their troubled relationships. The family portrait would have been more accurate if they had cast a wider net for information. But from the start the detectives revealed the narrowing focus of their investigation.

When, for instance, they glanced through Lynn Beyer Matthews' high school yearbook, they noticed that Steven had scribbled a message in the margin. "Can't wait for summer so we can bomb around together." In the teenage slang of that era to "bomb around" meant to "drive around," but investigators asked Mrs. Matthews to tell them about Steven Benson's knowledge of explosives. Did he ever set off bombs? Had she seen him detonate them by remote control?

Casting her memory back eighteen or twenty years, she said she recalled going to a creek bed in Lancaster where Steven and other boys set off cherry bombs. He may have had a dry cell battery and ignited the firecrackers from a distance. "It seemed like all the kids loved to fool around with firecrackers, sparklers and things that were going to explode."

But she wasn't positive about any of this. It was possible Steven had stuffed cherry bombs into a toilet roll, lit them, and run. In those days, Mrs. Matthews said, "I was more worried about did my hair look nice."

Despite this disclaimer, the police believed they were on the right track. Questioning Lynn Beyer's younger brother, Robert, currently an attorney in Lancaster, they kept asking about what came to be called Steven Benson's "fascination with explosives."

Like his sister, Bob Beyer remembered that lots of kids set off firecrackers. He recalled a Halloween when a bunch of boys, including Steven, tossed a cherry bomb on the hood of a cop car. The incident Beyer said, was "swept under the suburban carpet"—by which he meant it was minor, insignificant.

But as later reported in newspapers, this childhood prank provided further evidence that Steven had an expertise with explosives. The cherry bomb became a sophisticated device detonated by Benson with a dry cell battery. Beyer was appalled that his statement had been misinterpreted.

Tom West, a mechanic employed by Mrs. Benson to repair her cars, didn't care for Steven. "He was quite an arrogant person to be around." He was tight with his money too. West once asked him for a $20 loan and Steven turned him down. He claimed he had seen Steven take a check from his mother, then whine, "Is this all I get?"

Yet West admitted to police, "I never seen him affiliated with any kind of explosives."

He had, however, gathered that Scott was affiliated with another powdery substance. "I heard that, you know, he liked his candy... Well, he had like, I guess I wouldn't say a nose problem. But I guess he liked his cocaine."

On this subject, West knew whereof he spoke. Six months later he was shot and killed outside a Lancaster bar. The pathologist reported that the blood-alcohol content was twice the level that Pennsylvania law defines as drunkenness, and he had been doing cocaine. The rumor was that he had gotten squeezed in a drug deal or a rip-off.

But from his statement, police gleaned just one shred of information that interested them. Tom West had said Steven Benson "was an electronic gadgetry genius as far as I'm concerned."

· · ·

Determined to find out how great an "electronic gadgetry genius" Steven was and whether his wizardry extended to bomb making, police interviewed Patrick Egan, owner of Commonwealth Security Systems in Lancaster, the firm that had wired the Benson home in School Lane Hills.

Steven, Egan said, had Mrs. Benson "paranoid that the world was going to cave in on her." He estimated that over $20,000 had been spent securing the house. "I mean, we had all the windows contacted. We had motion detectors, we had mats. We had portable panic buttons, radio controlled. We had two complete systems just in case she forgot to turn one on, you know, and flood light controls and, and, and fire detectors and burglar alarm contacts on the pool . . ."

It was ironic that the son who had always insisted on surrounding his mother with security systems was now suspected of murdering her. Had he ordered all these alarms to protect her against his own homicidal impulses? Or was he worried about the threats against Scott and Margaret?

Characterizing Steven as a "wheeler-dealer," Patrick Egan said, "He's a big shot, you know. And he never liked me. He hated me because I was in the alarm business and I—maybe I—maybe I made it on my own, and he never made it for himself. And I don't know what his hang-up was. You know, I didn't drive big Cadillacs. I drive little Datsuns. But it was always 'I'm Steven Benson. Welcome to my house, and I'm in charge.' That's the attitude you got."

Benson liked to fiddle with the system Egan installed, perhaps to teach himself the secrets of the business he would later embark upon. In Florida, he lied about his credentials, claiming to be a member of the Pennsylvania Alarm Association.

"He would dick around with the systems," Egan complained, "and he'd break something. And then he'd call us. And we'd go around and fix it. And he knew everything about everything.

"I saw a lot of gadgets and a workbench in the basement and just garbage stuff. You know, radios tore apart, speakers. He had wires running all over the house. He was a real nut. Ummmm, I mean the capabilities of the guy are there. I mean, he—opinions are like assholes. Everybody has one. He's your man, but you got to pin it to him."

Egan warned the police, "He's very, very intelligent in case you don't known that. You're going to have to put on a hell of a case, because he'll weasel out of it."

But then another Lancaster citizen helped investigators take a crucial step toward making their case. On July 23, Mike Koors interviewed Tom Schelling, a former high school classmate of Steven's who had worked for Mrs. Benson at her house on Ridge Road. In March of 1982, Schelling was on the roof, performing repairs, when he observed Steven pass by down below carrying three copper tubes approximately one inch in diameter. Schelling testified that he couldn't estimate the length of the copper tubes, but he noticed wires protruding from them.

A few moments after Steven disappeared in the direction of the tennis court, Schelling heard three explosions louder than M-80 fireworks. Scrambling off the roof, he rushed to the tennis court, where, he said, he saw Steven holding a small black box about the size of a remote control garage door opener. It had two push-button switches, one red, the other white. Benson was laughing as he walked past Schelling without saying a word. Schelling claimed he looked around the tennis court, but found no sign of damage.

Tom Schelling's account of this incident had enormous impact on the investigation. The police depended on it, and for the next year, the media repeated it as if Schelling's remarks were proven facts.

But "the facts," such as they were, came under sharp scrutiny within weeks of the original statement. Schelling acknowledged that he could not be sure the "small black box" was a remote control device. He admitted he never saw the copper tubes up close, never saw Steven plant a bomb or press a button, hadn't witnessed any explosion, and actually hadn't gone down to the tennis court to search for damage. In short, he could not prove that the alleged bombs were connected with the alleged remote control device or that either was related to the explosion. He had simply heard noises and jumped to conclusions.

Schelling's past had also come under scrutiny. He was an ex-con who had done time for forgery and was on probation for a simple assault conviction when interviewed by Mike Koors.

But this information never appeared in the press or on TV. Instead, the story continued to be cited as evidence that Steven Benson had made and detonated a pipe bomb by remote control just three years before his mother and adopted brother were murdered and his sister was wounded by a similar device.

Chapter 10

I

Richard Cirace, a Boston attorney, came from a close-knit, intensely loyal Italian family. His father had had a law degree but never practiced. He wound up in the wholesale liquor business and became the largest distributor of Italian wines in New England.

There was no question of Rick following him into that line. Mr. Cirace wanted his son to get a degree and practice law. He lived to see Rick finish Suffolk Law School, then set up his own firm. But his son's biggest case started just as Mr. Cirace fell ill with pulmonary fibrosis. In fact it was while Rick was conferring with Carol Lynn Kendall at Massachusetts General Hospital that doctors told him his father's disease was terminal. He died eight months later.

Rick had never heard of Carol Lynn Kendall or the Benson family. But he represented a couple whose child went to school with one of Carol Lynn's boys, and the couple called and said their friend needed a lawyer. The Naples police were flying to Boston to question her.

Some of Rick's ancestors had emigrated from the other Naples, the real Naples, not the retirement resort. In that southern Italian city which haughty northerners call the Calcutta of Europe and the Gateway to the Third World, family vendettas are commonplace, as are gang wars and car bombings. So from the start he sensed eerie associations which, far from making him feel on familiar ground, deepened his tension.

He had his first meeting with Carol Lynn in the Trauma Burn Center. His instinct was to sympathize with her suffering. But he knew he had to question her, not commiserate. He was flying in the dark, coming in late on the case, and he had to hope he could catch up quickly. He also had to hope this badly burned woman was telling the truth. The last thing he needed was to be clobbered from the blind side and learn too late that he was representing not a victim, but a co-conspirator.

For a politician, information is power. For a lawyer, it is survival. Virtually moving his office into her room at Mass General, Rick stressed that she had to tell him everything. She couldn't assume anything was irrelevant or that he knew details which seemed mundane to her. He had to struggle just to keep "the names and players straight."

Gradually, he got what he believed was a comprehensive picture of the Benson family and Carol Lynn's place in it. "Ultimately I was convinced there was absolutely no complicity," Cirace said. He was positive she had played no part in the murders.

Wayne Graham had known and liked George Nowicki for fifteen years. They were based now on opposite sides of the state, with Nowicki in Miami and Graham in Naples, but the Benson case brought them back together and as Graham put it, "We felt that between the two of us we could make the investigation go." Like Harold Young and Mike Koors, they were a Mutt and Jeff combination. Where Graham was short and had a mustache and receding hair, Nowicki was tall with a full head of sandy blond hair.

On July 25, they landed in Boston where an ATF agent took them to a Travelodge. They showered, caught a catnap, then went to the ATF office to make some phone calls. They had arrived with overnight bags. They expected to be back in Florida by the next evening.

But as they say down where Graham hailed from, they got their plows stuck in hard ground before they even started. Rick Cirace informed them he had to be present when they questioned his client. That's how Carol Lynn wanted it and that's how he wanted it. If they didn't agree, Carol Lynn refused to talk.

To put it politely, Wayne Graham had never been fond of the legal profession. Or to put it less politely, in the words he laughingly used after he and Cirace had developed a warmer relationship, "He can be a shit-ass. I mean, he can be an attorney. We're always wary with lawyers. I told Cirace I'd rather have a sister in a whorehouse than a brother as a lawyer." But Graham and Nowicki had little choice except to meet Carol Lynn's demands.

As a courtesy, they thought they should touch base with Ms. Kendall's physicians to tell them what they planned to do and see if there were any medical requirements.

But Mass General had no intention of letting a couple of cops from Florida tell them what they meant to do. The hospital told Graham and Nowicki precisely what they would be permitted to do. First they had to meet with Mass General's attorney, then with the chief of security. Then they had to confer with Carol Lynn's surgeon and the physicians treating her burns.

The doctors told Graham and Nowicki they could speak to Carol Lynn for fifteen minutes, twice a day.

At that rate, the detectives would have to spend the rest of the summer in Boston. Swallowing their distaste for attorneys, they asked Cirace to intercede, and he spoke to the doctors and to his client. Carol Lynn was willing to talk more often, and the doctors agreed that Graham and Nowicki could interview her for fifteen minutes every other hour so long as it didn't impede her treatment.

From the first session, however, Carol Lynn exceeded the limits laid down by the doctors. At times she spoke for over an hour, and her lawyer or the detectives had to interrupt and suggest she take a break. It seemed that the family history had been stewing inside her for a long time, and it poured out, bubbling with grievances, misunderstandings, accusations, and secret iniquities. Once she started, she was reluctant to stop.

Since childhood, Wayne Graham had had an acute fear of fire. Once at a construction site where his dad was working, Wayne had run through a bonfire that singed his hair and blistered his skin. He hadn't been badly hurt; he didn't bear any physical scars. But down deep the experience left its brand, and he remembered the pain and, worse, the smell.

Now at the Trauma Burn Center he was in a place where each room throbbed with torment. Even in the hallway, he heard moans and breathed the odor of charred flesh. By the time Nowicki and he reached Carol Lynn's room, he knew he had better get a grip on himself. "One of the first things you're taught as an investigator," he said, "is that you can't let yourself get emotionally involved with anyone you're questioning."

Carol Lynn had been reduced to burnt meat. That's how she looked to Graham and that's how she smelled. Only her eyes were human as she lay there in bed with her charred right arm and leg up on pillows. Some of her wounds were exposed; others were covered by dressings that nurses periodically changed. The pink shell of her right ear was gone, replaced by little more than a scorch mark. "She had less hair on her head than I do," Graham recalled.

She apologized for her appearance and asked them how bad she looked. They said she looked fine.

Rick Cirace was in the room with them. About the same height as Wayne Graham, he looked shorter because of his burly chest and bull neck. Far darker than either detective from Florida, he kept his color even during the New England winter by going to a tanning center. He had sharp features that might have seemed fierce if he hadn't worn glasses, hadn't smiled so often and been so solicitous of his client.

Before the questioning started, Carol Lynn was already upset and crying. She explained that she didn't want to give a statement, but after speaking with an Episcopal priest, she had decided that she had to go ahead. Still, it troubled her "because I know that I am going to give you facts and things that are going to hurt my brother."

She struck Graham as "a little girl in a woman's body." She had a sweet, thin, quavering voice. But by now, Graham was responding like a pro. He knew he "had to be careful because of the emotional intensity. If we weren't careful, she could manipulate the hell out of us."

Nowicki led off, asking about "the most difficult part" to get it out of the way—July 9, 1985.

She said she would have to backtrack a bit. Steven had surprised her by telephoning the evening of July 8 to volunteer to help her stake out the lots. Stepping further out of character, he had agreed to show up at 7:30 A.M.—"Steven isn't known for early"—and said Scott should come too. She had been so struck by this strange event, she commented to her mother, "You'll never guess who called."

As she described how the family happened to be in the Suburban, headed to the property where her mother hoped to build her dream-house, she displayed such skill as a raconteur, the investigators were swept along and never asked her to resolve contradictions in her story.

She told them "Steven wasn't over at the house very often, certainly never on weekends." Then mentioning a weekend just three days before the murders when he had come to Quail Creek and helped measure the property, she reiterated, "Steven wasn't one to volunteer to do things to help my mother and certainly not early in the morning, although he had been very gung-ho on my mother buying more property."

She also displayed a breezy style that was surprising considering the subject matter. Minutes after she had been crying and upset, she had her listeners laughing loud enough to be heard on tape.

She said how silly it was for Steven to insist on involving Scott. "I can remember thinking at the time, why in the world would he even want to ask Scott to come along. My brother Scott was twenty-one years old and not the kind who ever wanted to do anything to help [laughing]."

Time and again the interview was punctuated by her quips, followed by laughter. No one in the room expressed any disapproval, not even Wayne Graham, who had been so suspicious when Steven, Debbie, and Wayne Kerr had laughed the day of the murders. Tension had produced a kind of giddiness in everybody at Carol Lynn's bedside, and they chuckled at her wisecracks, not because they were indifferent to the seriousness of the situation, but because they needed an emotional release.

From the start, Carol Lynn's version of events differed from what she had told Officer Thomas Smith.

On July 9 Officer Smith asked, "What about last night? Did Scott go anywhere last night?"

"Well, he left the house at 10:30," Carol Lynn said, "but that he goes—we just assume he goes down to pick up Kim, even though he doesn't—"

"Say it?" Smith suggested.

"—he doesn't say he does. And then she—we're sure that's where he goes, down to pick up Kim."

"What time did he come back?"

"I don't know. We were all asleep. You see, she doesn't get off work till 11:30 or something."

Now, on July 26, George Nowicki asked who had slept at the Benson house the night before the murders.

Carol Lynn replied, "Wayne and me and my mother and Scotty and his girl friend."

"That would be—"

"Kim."

"Kimberly Beegle?" Nowicki asked.

"Yeah, I guess that's her full name. I don't know."

"I understand," Nowicki went on, "that Scott would go pick her up from work. What time would he have left to pick her up from work?"

"Well, he usually left—he usually would leave about 10:30 at night."

"Do you think—do—do—" Nowicki rephrased the question. "Were you awake on that particular night? Do you recall if you were awake enough and knew if he left to get her?"

"Oh, boy. I really don't remember. Ummm, whether—whether we all stayed up that late or whether we were tired, I really don't remember. It was my birthday [on July 8]."

"Uh-huh."

"And we had gone out to eat that night. I—I don't think we all stayed up very late. Ummm, but then Scott kind of came and went, and—"

"Okay," Nowicki said.

"—you know, he would just blow in and look all dressed up, looking for the keys, and out he would go."

In contrast to her first statement, she now acknowledged she had no recollection of Scott's leaving. She couldn't even recall if she was awake at ten thirty. She couldn't say with certainty when she went to bed. She only remembered that it was her birthday and they had gone out to a restaurant.

By "they" she didn't mean Scott. He had not gone to her birthday dinner and, according to witnesses, had not been in the house at all that evening. In a statement to the police, Kim Beegle claimed that on July 8 she and Scott had driven in the Suburban to Fort Myers with the dog, Buck, and spent the day and much of the night shopping, hanging out at malls, driving back to Naples, and drifting from restaurants to bars and to clubs. By the time they returned to the Benson house, Kim swore, it was nearly midnight.

As the questions continued, Carol Lynn's replies grew longer and dense with details. She described Steven's arrival on the morning of July 9. When he said he was going for coffee, "Mother said, you know, she'd take some, and Wayne said he'd take some.

"So Steven left to go get coffee and he was gone for an awfully long time."

A nurse knocked at the door. The interview had run ten minutes over the fifteen-minute limit. Nowicki stopped the tape, and they let Carol Lynn have a two-hour break.

When they resumed, Nowicki made a long, halting announcement. Given its puzzling content, one can appreciate why he was tongue-tied. "The time is approximately 2:07 P.M. on—uhh—Friday, July the 26th, and we are continuing the—uhh—with Carolyn [sic] Lynn Benson Kendall. And the same people are present in the room that were present at the inception of the interview. Uhh, at the request of of Mr.—at the request of—uhh—Mr. Richard Cirace—Cirace—umm—I am—uhh—reading into the record that—uhh—Carol Lynn Benson is not the subject of this investigation or any other investigation that we are conducting. Uhh, I'm going to continue if I might—uh—Carol Lynn. Uhh, when we—uhh—I'm going to turn the tape recorder off at 2:08 and will resume in just one minute."

Less than two weeks earlier, Wayne Graham had been canvassing hardware stores and plumbing supply outlets asking if Carol Lynn Kendall had bought galvanized pipe, four inch caps, or smokeless powder. On July 10, at a meeting of investigating officers, Nowicki, Graham, and others had discussed the need to find out about Mrs. Kendall's finances, her children, her marriage, her relations with her mother and brothers. Now, after her initial refusal to talk, they were finally questioning her. But after a single twenty-five minute session, she had been dropped from the list of possible suspects.

It is unclear how Cirace convinced Nowicki to grant this request. It is also unclear whether Nowicki and Graham contacted their superiors during the break. Did Nowicki's announcement reflect the official position of the ATF and the Collier County Sheriff's Department? Did it amount to a grant of immunity? Had some sort of deal been struck in exchange for Carol Lynn's cooperation?

Months later, in a deposition, Wayne Graham would swear that no suspect was eliminated "until after the interview with Carol Lynn." But somehow she got a special exemption at the start.

At 2:09 P.M., Nowicki switched the recorder back on. "Carol Lynn, if you would—uhh—resume for us, please."

She launched into a long monologue. For pages on end, the two investigators listened as she told about Steven's trip to buy coffee and how people in the house joked about how long he was gone. Then she described his sudden insistence that Mrs. Benson come to the property and the debate about what to do with the men who were due to arrive and give an estimate on a swimming pool. Finally Steven, Mrs. Benson, and Scott strolled out to the Suburban while Carol Lynn gathered up her things.

"So by the time I got out there," she said, "Scott is sitting in the driver's seat. And I remember thinking to myself, what in the world is Scott doing in the driver's seat? Only, I guess, because logically in my mind, Steven being my only brother, Steven would do the driving and not Scott do the driving."

Although she said she "logically" assumed "Steven being my only brother, Steven would do the driving," Steven was not her "only brother." If she meant that the natural son got preference over the adopted son, this was something no one else ever noticed. Scott frequently drove the Suburban and had cruised around in it just yesterday for more than twelve hours.

Furthermore, there are disparities between this and her statement to Officer Smith. She had told Smith twice that Scott wasn't in the Suburban even after she climbed in. She said, "I told Scott to get in."

On July 9, she hadn't seen fit to comment on her reaction to where people were seated. Now this seemed quite important to her.

"Mother at this point was sitting in the front seat on the passenger side. And normally I would have sat there because I tend to get carsick, and I was gonna say something to her but I thought oh, heck, she's already in and I—we're not going that far so I'll just go sit in the back." Because Steven had gone to the passenger side, "The only seat left for me was on the other side."

Prosecutors and newspapers would imply there was something sinister about this seating arrangement. But if the devices had exploded simultaneously, anyone sitting anywhere in the Suburban would have been killed.

Once they were all in the car, Mrs. Benson asked, "Who has the keys?" Steven indicated he did, and his mother told him to pass them to Scott.

"Did we clarify," Nowicki asked, "[at] what point he handed Scott the keys?"

"Well, I was trying to remember that," Carol Lynn said, "whether he leaned over the—I mean the logical thing would have been just to lean over the seat and hand him the keys. But he definitely got out of the car. Now whether he had handed Scott the keys already when he was inside of the car, or whether he went around the car and handed the keys in to Scott through the window, I can't say because I really just—my mind wasn't on that at the time."

Later when Graham circled back to the subject, Carol Lynn again conceded, "I'm not even sure at what point Steven gave Scott the keys."

As she discussed the blast, her voice became shaky. She sighed, choked back sobs, then made no further effort to swallow her emotions. She described seeing Scott lying dead on the ground, and realizing she had to save herself from the fire, she tumbled headlong out of the Suburban. She rolled over, smothering the flames, tore off her shirt and threw it away. "And then—uhh—about this time I saw Steven come out of the house and stop on the driveway, and he was —he just looked terrified. And—and it was almost like he was going mad. And he just had—it was—he was—"

The investigators had let her run on long past her limit. She had been speaking for more than three-quarters of an hour. But as she emphasized that Steven appeared to be as horrified and hysterical as she was, Nowicki decided it was time to take a break. On several occasions when Carol Lynn returned to Steven's shock and hysteria, Nowicki interrupted and diverted her to other subjects.

2

In the claustrophobic room, confronted by Carol Lynn's glistening eyes and quavering voice, Graham and Nowicki felt a bond forming between them and the witness. It made them acutely uncomfortable. So they welcomed this break and went and sat in a glassed-in lounge looking out over Boston. Wayne Graham felt he was in a very old city undergoing an altogether new experience. In this business, you didn't bump into many ladies like Carol Lynn. It wasn't just that she was rich, well-educated, and articulate. She took them into her confidence. Whenever they turned off the tape, she discussed her personal life, asking advice on everything from finances to family. She was especially eager to hear their opinions about how to cope with her teenage boys, who were, from what she said, a handful.

"We felt we were being seduced," Graham said later. "We tried to be formal and professional. But she kept turning it into a family affair. We had to regear during every break and try to regain our professional attitude."

Despite their efforts, the interview was unlike any other in the case. Undoubtedly, this was due in part to a peculiar combination of circumstances. The Mass General staff and Rick Cirace called many of the shots, and the severity of Carol Lynn's injuries shielded her from sharp questioning.

But Graham and Nowicki didn't help matters when they brought her desserts which she couldn't get at the hospital and continued to treat her with solicitude even after they realized she was misleading them. On a human level it is understandable that, as Graham explained, "We wanted to be careful to the point of gentleness with how we approached her, especially with some sensitive questions." But on a professional level, it might have been preferable to postpone the interrogation until they could question Carol Lynn with the same detachment as they showed other witnesses.

Instead, they returned at 4:50 P.M. and when Nowicki read into the record the names of those present, Mrs. Kendall chirped up, "And me."

"And, of course," Nowicki said, "Carol Lynn Benson Kendall."

Rather than return to Steven's horrified reaction right after the Suburban blew up, Nowicki asked whether she remembered seeing him "before or after a second explosion, or were you aware of a second explosion?"

The question was of critical importance. If Steven had planted the bombs, possibly with a timed delay, it was implausible that he would have come near after the first blast and risked being caught in the second. All the evidence indicated that Carol Lynn had indeed, seen Steven between the two explosions. But the detectives wanted to double-check. Then they triple- and quadruple-checked.

Carol Lynn, however, could provide no helpful information. She claimed she was aware of the second explosion, but said it occurred four or five minutes after the first explosion. What she described was actually a minor noise, perhaps caused by gas buildup.

According to witnesses, the second blast came about a minute after the first. Carol Lynn had absolutely no memory of this or of being dragged away from the burning wreckage by Charles Meyer, the golfer who was wounded by shrapnel from the second bomb.

Apparently she had been knocked out. She admitted as much herself the day of the murders. Describing the "orangy-red sort of thing" that engulfed her, she told Officer Smith, "I wasn't really conscious." She went on to say to Smith, "I sort of became conscious" when she opened her eyes. But her perceptions remained those of someone in shock. She saw Scott and instinctively knew he was dead, yet felt bewildered and enraged that the paramedics didn't try to revive him.

One has to wonder not only about her recall of events between the two blasts, but her recollection of incidents preceding them. Conceivably the concussion of the bombs scrambled her memory.

"Could I ask you," Nowicki said, "if your mother at any time expressed any fears to you about her own safety in regard to anybody in recent weeks?"

When asked a similar question in her first statement—Did the Bensons have any enemies? Had there been threats against them?—Carol Lynn discussed Scott's "strange friends" and Kim Beegle's brothers. Subsequently, it became public knowledge that Tracy Mullins had filed a paternity suit and there were allegations that she had made death threats. During divorce proceedings, Carol Lynn had claimed that Tom Kendall threatened to kill her. But she mentioned none of that now, and the detectives didn't bring it up.

"Of course, there was always Debbie," she said, "because Debbie hated my mother and made no bones about hating my mother." She claimed that Debbie "told everybody how much she hated my mother and how she wanted everything that was my mother's and did horrible, cruel things to my mother."

"My mother was also afraid of my brother Scott, because Scott sometimes would have [a] wild and violent temper—and—and he would be very great looking in one second and other times there—he would be just kind of off the wall, off the deep end about things. But I mean when he went off the deep end, he was off the deep end, and Mother thought maybe that it—it was because when he was younger he had—had smoked pot and—some—and sniffed that gas stuff."

Given Scott's history of nitrous oxide abuse, his association with suspected drug dealers, the rumor that he'd recently been involved in a rip-off, and the fact that two years ago he'd been confined and forced to undergo psychotherapy because he was a danger to himself and others, Carol Lynn's comments would have seemed ample reason for Graham and Nowicki to explore this subject fully. But they remained silent even when she explained that her adopted brother's frightening behavior wasn't something from the remote past. Mother "told me one time when they had just been in Europe that she was afraid of—of—Scott." This was weeks before the murders.

They let Carol Lynn run on, and she referred to a time when her mother "was in Lancaster," and the two of them were talking. "It wasn't exactly that my mother said that I think Steven would kill me. It wasn't that kind of a thing because we were talking about her—the property that she was thinking of buying. And I—she said something about Steven certainly would prefer it if I didn't because it would—then it would be more money for him if I were dead. I said, Mother, that's ridiculous. What are you talking about?...But she did, I mean, my mother did indicate to me that perhaps she would not put it—it past my brother to do away with her."

The investigators suddenly came alive. There had been a glaring contradiction. This morning Carol Lynn said Steven "had been very gung ho on my mother buying more property." Now she claimed her mother had told her, "Steven certainly would prefer it if I *didn't*" buy more property.

But Nowicki wasn't bothered about that. He asked, "How long ago did she tell you this?"

"When we were in Lancaster about—I'm sorry, in Boston about three weeks ago."

Nowicki didn't press her to make sure she was more positive about the date than she had been about the place. "Three weeks ago" Carol Lynn and her mother were in Naples, not Boston. Neither investigator noticed this.

Instead, they accepted that Mrs. Benson had expressed fear of her natural son shortly after she had been afraid of her adopted son in Europe. Neither Nowicki nor Graham asked what kind of family this was where a mother lived in fear of her children. And they didn't inquire whether Mrs. Benson or Carol Lynn had conveyed this fear to anyone who could provide corrobration.

Unprompted, Carol Lynn added, "I don't think it was like just one thing that precipitated her saying that. It's just that things have been—things have been going on for a while."

"What?"

"Can we go off the record?" Cirace cut in.

"Yeah, sure," Nowicki said. Then when he clicked the cassette back on, he explained, "Carol Lynn was off tape for a few minutes to confer with her attorney."

In his deposition, Wayne Graham later swore that "anything pertinent to the case was on the tape."

"Was there any discussion about the case, her family, or anything of that nature done off tape?"

"No sir." Graham insisted they went off tape only "like to get her something, some juice to drink or something like that."

But the transcript is studded with instances in which Cirace asked to speak off the record during critical conversations, suggesting that they were coaching Carol Lynn or trying to direct her testimony.

"When we stopped," Nowicki reminded Carol Lynn, "you had started a thought concerning—uhh—some concerns that your mother had. Would you continue with that, please?"

"Well, my mother indicated that she wouldn't put it past my brother to possibly do away with her."

"Which brother are you referring to?"

"My brother Steven. I mean I knew she was scared of Scott but that was a different situation. I mean I was scared of Scott."

Again the investigators were content to roll the tape and listen as Carol Lynn caromed from subject to subject, rattling on about how close she and her mother had been. "We didn't have anyone else except each other."

If either detective had heard from sources in Lancaster that Carol Lynn and her mother were not as close as she claimed, they didn't mention it. Graham did later acknowledge that behind Carol Lynn's sweet girlish surface "there's a mean, vicious bitch. As she started in on Steven her voice hardened and her eyes hardened."

"All that seemed to matter lately to Steven was—was using my mother's money and—and he—he wasn't being nice to her." In league with Debbie, he wouldn't let Mrs. Benson see her grandchildren, wouldn't even let her send them birthday cards. Carol Lynn never understood why Steven didn't stand up to Debbie. She asked him about it, "and he got really nasty at me, and he told me to shut up."

He was never reluctant, though, to ask for Mrs. Benson's financial backing.

"Mother didn't have lots of money, but she had enough that she —she could have lived comfortably and not worried about her old age. One thing my mother had a terrible fear of ending up in a—in a nursing home."

Carol Lynn had assured her "she could always come and stay with me. And she said, oh, that she knew she could come stay with me, but she knew she couldn't go with Steven because Steven had already told her that if she ever got sick or anything not to call on him, because he wouldn't take her in. And Scott, he only had his own interests."

Steven "always took advantage of my mother, and he got involved in these really big deals and then at the last minute he—without telling my mother that he'd already committed himself to it, he'd come and he'd get money from my mother. I mean money like $50,000, like large money."

As for the Meridian Company, "When Wayne [Kerr] had come down last year they had found—umm—irregularities. So Steven—umm—and that—I guess one would say embezzlement, but my mother wasn't about to do anything about it at that point and, you know, hoping that Steven would come clean about it all."

The bottom line, Carol Lynn claimed, was that "Steven had gone through about two million, two hundred—two and a half million dollars of my mother's money." So that Mrs. Benson had been afraid "she didn't have enough money left now to even build a house."

This was a serious charge, and a very strange one. Mrs. Benson left an estate of $10 million, more than enough to keep her out of a nursing home and allow her to build a house as extravagant as the one she had in mind. Although there was no doubt she had been reckless about financial matters, and although her children, especially Scott and Steven, had clipped her for large amounts of money in loans and gifts, it was astonishing to think that neither she, her lawyers, her accountants, her bankers, nor her stockbrokers had noticed a two and a half million dollar hemorrhage. What's more, having discovered that a quarter of her gross wealth was missing, Mrs. Benson supposedly told Carol Lynn and no one else. And she hadn't decided to do anything until she learned that Steven bought a house with what she assumed was her money.

"As my mother put it," Carol Lynn said, "it was the straw that broke the camel's back. And she finally was going to do something."

"We would like to go ahead," Nowicki said, "and stop now, and talk about this in detail starting tomorrow." As if offering a preview of coming attractions, he observed that they'd resume "with your mom's visit up here with you in Boston and some of the conclusions she reached and some of the things that she felt had to be done."

But, as it turned out, there was no interview the next day.

3

That evening, Friday night, Wayne Graham and George Nowicki had to reappraise their plans. Although Carol Lynn's statement hadn't progressed as quickly as they hoped, they thought they were getting valuable information.

Only one thing troubled the investigators. She hadn't come clean about a key piece in the Benson family puzzle. While she had supplied unflattering secrets about her brothers, she had held back pertinent facts about herself. And if she misled them in that area, how could they be positive she hadn't done it in others? Graham and Nowicki had to confront Carol Lynn and get her to admit the truth she had been hiding for more than half her life. Otherwise they knew their case would be torn to shreds.

Since they realized they would be in Boston much longer than expected, they decided to switch to a hotel within walking distance of Mass General. Rick Cirace suggested the Parker House, which, he said, was next to the cemetery where Paul Revere was buried. More important to Graham and Nowicki, it was just fifteen blocks from the hospital.

After they changed hotels, Cirace drove them to dinner at Anthony's Pier Four, down on the wharf. The investigators got plenty of fresh seafood in Florida, but, in Graham's opinion, this restaurant was "a real good place." He and Nowicki ordered lobster and although Cirace was picking up the tab, the detectives didn't pull their punches. They told him his client was lying.

The attorney couldn't pretend he wasn't surprised. His dark hair, brushed straight back from his forehead, already gave him a slightly startled appearance. Now he looked stunned.

Throughout the interrogation Carol Lynn referred to Scott as her brother. Well, he wasn't. No, he wasn't her adopted brother either.

He was her son.

As a coed at Goucher College she had gotten pregnant and given birth to Scott in Mercy Hospital in Baltimore on Christmas Day, 1963. Mr. and Mrs. Benson had insisted that the baby be kept. Carol Lynn had had little say in the matter. They brought him home to School Lane Hills and legally adopted him.

This was the thing Cirace had dreaded—being blind-sided. He had begged Carol Lynn to tell him everything. If she held back and then the truth leaked out, it might cast suspicion on her. At the very least, it could undercut her credibility as a witness. He understood why she had not wanted to reveal her secret. Under different circumstances, it wouldn't have been anybody's business that she had had an illegitimate baby. But the pipe bombings hadn't just killed her mother and son; they had thrust her into the headlines and transformed her past into public property. Since she was the sole surviving witness to the crime, everything she said and did was bound to be scrutinized; anything that might impeach her testimony had to be pursued.

Graham and Nowicki didn't need to point out the obvious. Scott's true relationship to Carol Lynn might in some convoluted way have provided the motive for the killings. Had Scott recently discovered who his mother was and resented her for not acknowledging him as her son? Had Carol Lynn feared she was about to be exposed? Was Steven angry that his sister's illegitimate son was the family favorite and stood to inherit an equal share of the fortune, while his own children would receive fractions of his share? Who was the father? Had he harbored a grudge for the past twenty-one years? Had he or anyone else attempted to blackmail the Bensons?

The detectives stressed that if they knew the story, then eventually defense attorneys would find out too. The secret about Scott had not been well kept. Everybody in Lancaster seemed to know it. Even the local newspapers were aware that Carol Lynn was his mother, but had declined to publish the fact. The national press was unlikely to show such restraint. The key to controlling the story was not to try and hide it, but to get ahead of it, take the sting out of it by telling the truth, no matter how painful.

They didn't downplay the possibility that the truth might be uglier and more painful than anybody could predict. One persistent rumor was that Scott was the product of an incestuous relationship. Some claimed that Benny Benson was Scott's father. This had to be checked out.

The next morning, on Saturday, the two investigators and the attorney met at Mass General. While Graham and Nowicki waited in the hospital security office, Cirace went up to his client's room and repeated what he had already said—what he would have to say again in the future. She had to start at the beginning and tell him everything.

Carol Lynn Kendall was upset and angry. She failed to see that her personal affairs were relevant to the case. Although she admitted that Scott was her son, she didn't understand why she had to discuss this with the detectives. As for the rumors about incest, she said they were too vulgar to deserve a reply.

She became so agitated and overwrought her doctors refused to let her be interviewed that day. They would have to wait until tomorrow and see how she felt.

Meanwhile, downstairs in the security office Harry Hitchcock showed up with his daughter, Janet Lee Murphy. About the old man, Wayne Graham later declared, "If George Burns hadn't already gotten the part of God, Harry Hitchcock would have." His daughter was a slender woman in her mid-fifties. She stated flatly, "Steven did it and I want him put in jail."

The investigators closed the door. "Could you tell me why you feel this way?" Graham asked.

She said she just knew it was Steven. No one else could have done it. No one else had a reason to do it.

Eager as Graham and Nowicki were to hear what Hitchcock and his daughter had to say, they were still hoping to question Carol Lynn. So they set up an appointment for that evening with Hitchcock and Murphy. When they learned that doctors wouldn't let them continue the interrogation, they went to Rick Cirace's office and telephoned Florida to give a progress—or no-progress—report. Then they called their wives to say they'd be delayed a couple more days.

Having arrived with overnight bags, both men were running out of clothes. They washed what they could and bought some new things. They were also running low on money. Graham loaned Nowicki $50 because ATF was always notoriously slow about processing funds.

For the rest of the day they toured the city on foot, visiting Bunker Hill and the waterfront, where the USS *Constitution* was docked. Then because George Nowicki was a Celtics fan, they went to the Boston Garden and saw the famous parquet court and all the green championship flags hanging from the rafters.

Willie Nelson was playing on the Common that night. Although Graham had queasy feelings about any man who wore his hair in a pigtail and called himself an Outlaw, he liked country music and they decided to catch the show.

First, however, they met Harry Hitchcock and Janet Lee Murphy at the Holiday Inn.

Since there exists no contemporaneous record of their conversation—Hitchcock and Murphy didn't care to talk on tape—the best one can do is quote subsequent sworn depositions. Wayne Graham was the first to describe the encounter.

QUESTION: What did Harry Hitchcock tell you?

GRAHAM: Well, we discussed the death of his daughter and his grand-children [sic]. We discussed his—his personal feelings as to what had transpired. We talked with him about how he was coping with it at his age, his medical condition. Things like that.

Q. Did you discuss the financial arrangements that Steven had with his mother?

GRAHAM: Yes, sir.

Q. What did Harry Hitchcock tell you?

GRAHAM: He told us that Steven had been spending money of his parents all of his adult life.

Q. Did you ask questions about Carol Lynn's financial relationship with her mother?

GRAHAM: Yes, sir.

Q. What did he tell you about that?

GRAHAM: He also said that Margaret assisted her a great deal, "her" meaning Carol Kendall.

Q. And Scott?

GRAHAM: Scott, he advised that his feelings towards Scott was he was [a] very spoiled young man.

Each of the three children, Hitchcock explained, would have inherited several million dollars on Margaret's death.

When asked what else Harry had had to say, Graham replied: "He stated that he felt that Steven Wayne Benson had killed Margaret. That he had done it."

Q. Did he tell you why he felt that way?

GRAHAM: Yes, sir. He said he felt he had done it because he was taking money from Margaret, that he was using that money and telling lies about what he was doing with the money.

Since this sounded so similar to Carol Lynn's accusations, Graham was asked whether Hitchcock had talked to his granddaughter before speaking to the investigators.

GRAHAM: I'm sure he did, sir. I don't know that.

Q. Do you know if he talked to anyone from law enforcement prior to your talking to him?

GRAHAM: I don't know, sir. I—possibly they did.

In fact, Hitchcock had had an unrecorded conversation in Lancaster with Investigator Mike Koors just four days prior to his untaped conversation with Graham and Nowicki. Whether the eighty-eight-year-old man came to his conclusions about the case independently or had been susceptible to the suspicions and suggestions of Carol Lynn and others, a lot of people claimed later that his attitude shaped theirs.

Graham swore Hitchcock "said that at one point he had called Steven and was going to tell Steven that if he didn't cooperate—he was very angry because Steven refused to cooperate in the investigation. He was very hurt by it. He couldn't understand why his grandson wouldn't do everything in the world to try to find out who did it. So he had called Steven with the full intention of telling Steven that until he cooperated and made a statement, he wasn't going to give him any more money."

Q. How was Harry Hitchcock told that Steven Benson wasn't cooperating?

GRAHAM: I have no—

Q. Do you have any information at that point that Steve Benson was not cooperating?

GRAHAM: Yes, sir.

Q. What was that?

GRAHAM: He wouldn't give a statement.

Q. When was he asked to give a statement?

GRAHAM: I don't know, sir.

Q. Okay, to your knowledge, didn't he give a statement the day of the bombing to law enforcement officials that asked?

GRAHAM: I think he gave them some information, yes, sir.

Q. And I believe the following day after that, didn't he give a statement?

GRAHAM: I don't know about the following day. To the best of my recollection, Mr. Benson refused to talk to us.

Q. Had you given Mr. Hitchcock any information about Steve not cooperating with law enforcement?

GRAHAM: After he made that statement, I answered him that I could understand and appreciate it, that I would find it hard in my soul to understand how one of my children could die and one of my grandchildren would not cooperate with the investigation and I wouldn't blame him if he cut him off.

Q. Did you discuss the trust agreement that Harry Hitchcock had with Steven Benson?

GRAHAM: Yes, sir.

Q. What was that discussion?

GRAHAM: He advised us that from his wife's estate the children received a certain amount of money... and that he was going to cut that off, that he had that right and that he was going to cut it off until Steven cooperated.

What is puzzling about Steven's alleged lack of cooperation and Harry's strategy of cutting him off is that less than forty-eight hours after the meeting with Graham and Nowicki, Hitchcock was back in Lancaster telling a reporter something altogether different than Graham claimed he had told them. On Monday July 29, in the local afternoon newspaper, he announced that Steven had called him to explain that he had refused to talk any further with the police on the advice of his attorney. Hitchcock said, "I think it's fairly common practice to let lawyers do the talking for you. He [Steven] seemed to be in pretty good spirits. He seemed to be composed and inquired about Carol Lynn."

This didn't sound like a man who believed his grandson had cheated his mother out of money all his adult life, then brutally murdered her and his adopted brother. There wasn't any suggestion that Hitchcock intended to force Steven to talk to the police.

Graham swore that Hitchcock went on to enumerate Steven's past failures and financial malfeasances—the abortive property development project, the mismanaged landscape business, the frequent need for Margaret to bail him out.

Q. Did you ask about the details of Carol Lynn's obtaining of the money?

GRAHAM: Yes, we did. We asked if it was the same type of situation or problem with Carol Lynn that Mrs. Benson was having with Steven. And he [Hitchcock] indicated that she was given money to help her with the children and with her furtherance of her education, but he didn't go into great detail as he did with Steven.

Q. Did he describe the relationship between Carol Lynn and Margaret?

GRAHAM: He said that Carol Lynn and Margaret had differences and argued.

Apparently neither investigator pointed out that Carol Lynn now claimed to have been her mother's closest confidant.

What's more, they never asked Hitchcock and Murphy about Scott's relationship with Carol Lynn. Did Scott know the truth? Was it a source of tension among the Bensons? Was it possible Carol Lynn was covering up other secrets?

Harry and Janet Lee later gave depositions in which they were questioned about the July 27 meeting. In contrast to Graham's account, which contended that he had obtained significant information —one can scarcely overestimate the impact of the grandfather and aunt stating bluntly that Steven was guilty—Hitchcock and Murphy couldn't recall anything of great consequence being discussed.

Asked if he had spoken to any law enforcement agents since the funeral, Hitchcock said he had. "I'm not sure of the names. It was right after it happened in Boston that they interrogated me, but I can't remember the names. It was two investigators."

Q. What did the officers ask you, what questions?
HITCHCOCK: Oh, they asked me what—I don't remember the questions and answers now, but they intended to find out what, if anything, I knew about it.
Q. What did you tell them?
HITCHCOCK: Well, I was in such a state of shock that I don't remember now what I said, but I knew very little that I could tell them.

. . . .

Q. Do you have an opinion as to whether or not Steven committed the crime?
HITCHCOCK: I have—no, the answer is no.

. . . .

Q. Did you ever discuss that tragic day with Carol Lynn?
HITCHCOCK: Well, I was up there to see her in the hospital and I was more concerned about her health than I was the background of the crime.
Q. I understand that.
HITCHCOCK: And we probably discussed some of the details, yes.
Q. Can you recall what she told you?
HITCHCOCK: No, I don't. No, I can't recall now what it was.

. . . .

Q. Okay, what did she tell you since she got out of the hospital?
HITCHCOCK: Well, I don't recall.

Since, according to Graham, Harry had accused Steven of spending his mother's money all his adult life, Hitchcock was asked how much he knew about his daughter's finances as they related to her children. The answer turned out to be very little.

Q. There have been allegations that Steven was taking money from Margaret. Do you have any information about that?
HITCHCOCK: I wouldn't have any way of knowing anything about that.
Q. As far as you know, you don't know whether or not he was or he wasn't?
HITCHCOCK: No, I haven't any idea whether it's true or not.
Q. From what you know about the family, was Margaret giving money and material things to all the children?
HITCHCOCK: Well, I don't know just what her—just what she did for the children financially.

It would be hard to imagine a more sweeping refutation of Graham's version of the July 27 interview. While it's possible Harry Hitchcock's memory failed him, it seems unlikely he would forget telling investigators that he believed Steven had killed Margaret and Scott.

Janet Lee Murphy was present during her father's deposition and she didn't dispute anything he said. When it came her turn to be questioned, her recollections—or failures to recall—corroborated his.

Q. What did the investigators talk to you about?
MURPHY: I can't remember.
Q. Do you remember anything?
MURPHY: No.
Q. Do you remember if they asked you any questions about the finances of the family?
MURPHY: I really don't remember. I was very upset at the time.

.   .   .   .

Q. You heard me ask the questions to Mr. Hitchcock concerning money that was given to the children by Margaret. Are you familiar with any of that?
MURPHY: No, I'm really not.
Q. Do you know who owns the house in Boston?
MURPHY: I don't know anything about it.
Q. You don't know anything about that?
MURPHY: No I don't.
Q. Could you describe for me, please, the relationship between Margaret and Carol Lynn?

MURPHY: It was a close relationship. Margaret and Carol Lynn were a loving mother and daughter.

Q. As with most loving mothers and daughters there probably were times when they fought. Are you aware of that?

MURPHY: I really don't know anything about it.

Q. Do you know any times when Carol Lynn was kicked out of the house and told not to come back?

MURPHY: I don't know anything about that.

Q. How about Scott?

MURPHY: No.

Q. Did they have a close relationship, Scott and Margaret?

MURPHY: Yes, I'm sure—yes.

Q. How about Steve and Margaret?

MURPHY: I don't really know.

Q. Do you know if Steven's relationship was any different than it was with the other children?

MURPHY: I don't really know.

Legally, sworn depositions should take precedence over unrecorded conversations. But in the Benson case, police, prosecutors, and the press repeated what was alleged off the record long after it had been denied under oath.

4

On Sunday, July 28, Graham and Nowicki returned to Carol Lynn's room with Rick Cirace. She was still upset and resented the intrusion into her personal life. But her lawyer had persuaded her to tell the truth, the whole truth, not simply that portion she thought was relevant.

She left the investigators in no doubt just how tumultuous her life had been. Although her parents had adopted and raised Scott, there were unresolved problems which were likely to be compounded now that she had to explain to Kurt and Travis that Scott had been their half-brother, not their uncle. She gave Graham an example of how prickly these problems could get. Apparently it convinced them that certain aspects of her private life were too explosive to be revealed. A couple of time bombs were left ticking.

Despite the rumors of incest and the possibility that Scott's father —whoever he might be—could have had a motive to commit murder, the investigators did not press Carol Lynn to name the man.

The untaped conversation continued for more than two hours. Yet in his deposition to the defense attorneys, Wayne Graham swore that "anything pertinent to the case was on the tape" and that there had been no "off tape" discussions of Carol Lynn's family. Again, it is worth wondering whether Carol Lynn was coached or guided by her lawyer or the investigators during the frequent "off-the-record" conversations.

At 12:25 P.M., Nowicki turned the tape recorder on and began by backtracking to the evening of July 8, when Margaret Benson and Wayne Kerr had gone out to dinner with Carol Lynn to celebrate her forty-first birthday. She described her mother and Wayne acting "like two little conspirators . . . it was like the plot thickening."

The family attorney had flown down to Florida, ostensibly to work on Margaret's tax returns, she said. "But that was gonna be sort of the cover for going through all the books and all the checkbooks to try and start to find where all the money had been going to, because Steven had been confronted the year before by Wayne and my mother about the fact that he was embezzling money from my mother. And Wayne had even pointed out to Steven that if his mother wanted to, she could have him sent to jail. And I think the idea was that, you know, I guess to kind of shake him up and maybe he'd break down, because, of course, my mother wouldn't at that point anyway have sent Steven to jail."

Whether it would ever have reached the point where Mrs. Benson would have had her son jailed, Carol Lynn conceded, "I can't say . . . but my mother was intent on making sure that Steven had to sell his house and any automobile and sell any interest that he had in his Meridian Marketing."

Reemphasizing that Steven had misappropriated two and a half million dollars—"I mean we're not talking little teeny, but big big amounts"—she explained that the Meridian corporations were owned and financed entirely by Margaret Benson. "Well, that infuriated Steven . . . So right from the start we figured he had planned that he would get this other company going and little by little had been funneling money up there."

"This other company" was Meridian Marketing, which Steven was said to have started with Margaret's money, but without her knowledge or approval. Or perhaps she did know about Meridian Marketing. Employees of Meridian Security Network surely did, because Meridian Marketing did PR and advertising work gratis for them. But according to Carol Lynn, Steven had lied, or not told the full story to Mrs. Benson.

Still, it was the new house, not the new company, that was "the straw that broke the camel's back." Yet here too there was confusion. Mrs. Benson knew weeks before Wayne Kerr's arrival in Naples that Steven had bought a house, but apparently she had been led to believe he had sold his Datsun 280Z to cover the down payment.

During the day on July 8, Mrs. Benson and Wayne Kerr had driven up to Fort Myers and got a glimpse of the house. They stayed in the car, the millionaire widow at the wheel of her Porsche 928S, the hulking 220-pound lawyer squeezed into the seat beside her, and they stared out at what looked from their vantage point to be "an estate," in Margaret's words. It had a pool and a tennis court and, as Mrs. Benson told her daughter, the wooded lot was so large it made the tennis court seem small. Her own current home had neither a pool nor a tennis court.

But the most galling sight was the blue Datsun 280Z parked in the driveway. If Steven hadn't sold the car, that meant just one thing to his mother. He had used her money to buy the house.

After less than a minute the "two little conspirators" sped off to the Meridian Security Network office in Naples. There they confronted Steven. Margaret asked whether he had sold his Datsun, and he assured her he had, not knowing she had just seen it. When Mrs. Benson demanded, "Then what's that out in front of the house," he tried to pass it off as somebody else's car.

Mrs. Benson wasn't irate, any more than she had been weeks ago when she first heard Steven had a new house. "She was so mild-mannered and ladylike and diplomatic," Carol Lynn said, "irate is not exactly the word that would connect with my mother."

Still, she was extremely distressed, and she told Wayne Kerr what she intended to do to get her money back. She was still telling him that night at the birthday dinner. According to Carol Lynn, her mother meant to put a lien on Steven's house and car, and close down the Meridian corporations.

Throughout her long and digressive statement, Carol Lynn kept reiterating the same point: Margaret Benson had finally decided to do something about her son's lying and stealing.

The conclusion seemed inescapable. Having realized his crimes had been discovered and that his mother planned to crack down,

Steven had killed her to save his failing business empire and grab his inheritance before she cut him off.

But as Carol Lynn continued her loquacious narrative, she brought up matters that undermined the case being built against her brother. After she once more accused him of making $150,000 deals, then saddling Mrs. Benson with the debts, George Nowicki interrupted. "Could—can I ask this question?"

"Why was my mother so stupid to do it?" Carol Lynn joked.

Graham, Nowicki, and Cirace burst into laughter.

Although that wasn't the question Nowicki intended to ask, it deserved an answer. As Carol Lynn conceded, Mrs. Benson "had had no business experience." Still, she yearned to become an entrepreneur and she went about realizing her aspirations in the same dreamy, unrealistic fashion that Scott tried to become a tennis pro and Carol Lynn a film producer. She should have known what to expect from Steven. She had already bought him four houses, backed him in numerous ventures, and had ample reason to realize he was, as Carol Lynn put it, "the kind who was always thinking in terms of grandiose schemes. I mean, if he opened a company, it couldn't be the John Smith Pencil Company. It had to be World Wide Industries."

His mother couldn't have been terribly surprised when he once again proved himself to be a gadget-happy, pie-eyed executive and a bookkeeper whom Wayne Kerr characterized as "a CPA's nightmare." Although she had a right to be angry that he had botched things up, it seemed just as possible she had been victimized by his hare-brained business practices as by criminal behavior.

More important, there was no evidence that Steven knew about his mother's plans, assuming she had any. Since Carol Lynn insisted to the investigators that Margaret and Kerr concealed their intentions—"They were still playing it kind of pretty below the belt"— why would he leap to the conclusion that he had to murder her? Even if he had swindled money from his mother, wouldn't he more likely have reasoned that she would forgive him, just as she had always forgiven her kids their sexual escapades, drug abuse, illegitimate children, and irresponsible spending?

But the investigators were less interested in the inconsistencies of Carol Lynn's statement than in their suspicions about Steven. Nowicki asked, "Is that a normal thing for someone in the family to go out and get coffee and doughnuts?"

After much dithering about Steven's not being there very often— one would have thought it was he, not she, who lived in Boston—

Carol Lynn said, "In a way, I guess it was strange for him to go out and get coffee for us because he could have walked into the kitchen and gotten coffee...as far as the doughnut part, I don't know. I mean, he didn't—it wasn't like there wasn't coffee in the house."

She was wrong. There was no coffee in the house. There was decaffeinated instant Sanka which Wayne Kerr "absolutely detested" and Steven wouldn't drink. Mrs. Benson liked real coffee too and she ordered some the morning of July 9. Kerr was also eager to have doughnuts or Danish.

If Steven's delinquencies constituted the major theme of Carol Lynn's statement, the secondary motif was her complaint that someone was always cheating or taking advantage of or committing crimes against the Bensons. If it wasn't a tennis pro or an architect or a car dealer or one of Scott's "sleazo girl friends," it was a family lawyer or a bank. She charged that one bank had wiped out a trust fund her father had set up. Another had colluded with a family lawyer, violated the wishes of her parents, and billed "huge, huge amounts of money every month to act as executors." This was, she said, why her mother had instructed Guion De Loach to draft a will that eliminated all trusts and made the children co-administrators.

Some of her animadversions were amusing. "If you've looked at wills, it's written in a combination of Cyrillic and Greek and six other languages [laughter]—that nobody understands including the lawyers half the time. So—I'm sorry, love, but that's true."

Other remarks, especially those dealing with Debbie Benson, were unsettling. But before Graham and Nowicki allowed her carte blanche to excoriate her sister-in-law, they double-checked a number of points which would pop up in intriguing new forms during the next year.

Graham asked if she had wanted Scott to come along to stake out the lots, and she said, "I thought it was dumb. I mean Scott doesn't particularly like to help, and Scott doesn't particularly like to have to get up early in the morning if he doesn't have to. And Scott could be a miserable SOB if he's having to do something he doesn't want to do."

In explanation of why Margaret and Scott's trip to Europe was cut short, she said, "Scott got [it] in his head that he was coming home. And so he went and he changed all the reservations." In her statement to Officer Smith, she had said Margaret's illness forced them to return early.

The investigators again pressed her to say when everybody had gone to bed the night before the murders.

CAROL LYNN: I think we all went to bed pretty early.
NOWICKI: Okay.
CAROL LYNN: Because I know I was tired and—umm—I don't think we watched any television. I don't remember.

Then they unleashed her on Debbie Benson and she cut loose with a splenetic outburst of accusations. She had already told them that Debbie was "basically an evil person" who had "no scruples and no morals," who had tried "to beat up my poor little mother for no reason," and who Carol Lynn suspected had been slowly poisoning Steven so that she could finish him off with a fatal drop once he inherited his share of the family fortune. Now she added to the list of her sister-in-law's alleged misdemeanors and felonies. But before she could gain momentum, Rick Cirace broke in. Again one can only speculate about what went on during the frequent off-tape conversations.

CIRACE: Can we go off the record for a minute?
NOWICKI: Certainly. The time is approximately 7:34.
(Tape recorder turned off)
NOWICKI: The time is approximately—uhh—7:44, and we are back on record. And we are discussing Steven Benson and his wife Debra and the overall relationship of the Benson family.
CIRACE: Can you hold one second?
NOWICKI: One minute pause.
(Tape recorder turned off)
NOWICKI: Okay, we're going to continue now. We were off tape for a couple of minutes. Please continue.
CAROL LYNN: Well, Debbie had kidnapped the children and taken them to Wisconsin. And she lived in this little rural county where her family controlled everything, like the chief of police and this judge who pulled a little shenanigan to make it seem as though Debbie had been a resident in Wisconsin even though she hadn't been a resident in Wisconsin, so that they could keep the children away from Steven and make sure that Steven couldn't see them.

This supposedly took place during the time Debbie filed for divorce. Anxious to save the marriage, Steven flew out to visit his kids and estranged wife, but whenever he came east again, he was always sick, deteriorating "little bit by little bit." He had "very curious attacks... almost like heart attacks."

When he had gone to consult a lawyer in Wisconsin, he wound up "in the intensive care of the hospital. And while he was in there Debbie sneaked into the hospital and stole his briefcase and jimmied the locks on the briefcase and took all the papers that were pertinent to the divorce that would be of any advantage to Steven if in any way he wanted to gain custody of his children."

But then Debbie abruptly changed her mind about the divorce. Carol Lynn thought this was because Harry Hitchcock had had health problems, and Debbie believed her husband would soon inherit a sizable sum of money. Before she'd reconcile, however, she insisted on some conditions, including one that Steven "was never permitted ever again to speak to his family."

Since Steven had continued to maintain close contact with his family, especially his mother, this seemed as odd as any of the more sensational allegations Carol Lynn leveled. But if it caused the investigators misgivings, they gave no indication as the witness rambled on and on:

And then, a couple of months later while they're kind of negotiating her terms with which she would be willing to come back, she suddenly just says that she's pregnant. Uhh, now it's—it's very possible that the child is my brother Steven's, but in my opinion I've never been very sure about that, because she was certainly not sitting home alone knitting while she was in Wisconsin. And she had been running around on her first husband when she met Steven. And since she wasn't in love with Steven anyway, it certainly would not have been out of character for her to be with other people.

She said she knew Debbie didn't love her brother because two days before the wedding Debbie had told her so.

I was kind of appalled about it because, you know, this is my brother, and I really love him. And, you know, he's already had one marriage that didn't work which hurt him badly. And—and so I said, "Well, Debbie, if, you know, you're not in love with him you certainly shouldn't marry him."

And she just giggled a little and says, "Oh well, it'll be kind of like a lark." And she says, "Besides, if I don't like it after a couple of months, I can always get a divorce."

There are obvious parallels between Carol Lynn's own life and her accusations against Debbie. Having just admitted that she'd had an illegitimate baby, she questioned the legitimacy of Debbie's third child. Having had a brief marriage to Tom Kendall, a man she scarcely seemed to know, she accused Debbie of entering into a loveless, calculating union with Steven. She would go on to add that Debbie was an indifferent mother and a lazy and slovenly housekeeper—which were precisely the criticisms that neighbors and family employees had leveled at Carol Lynn.

At one point, she said Steven underwent a "gallbladder operation, but he doesn't get well the way he should have gotten well. He just kept lingering and lingering, and he still just kind of never got well."

That's why I was always so suspicious that she was poisoning him on the side so that when my grandfathaer died and the money became available then she could finish him off and it would look like a natural death of some kind because there are poisons like that that you can use that make it look like heart attacks or gallbladder attacks and things.

And Debbie wasn't well educated, but she was street smart and—and very conniving and sneaky. And—and it—it wouldn't have been something that she would not have been capable of figuring out how to do or even to acquire some kind of poison. It could have even been some herbal medicine from the woods in Wisconsin, because they really lived in the back woods. I mean, they grew up in—with sort of like fourteen children in a house without plumbing. So I think they used a lot of, I don't know, herbal things. So it wasn't something that was out of the question.

According to Carol Lynn, Debbie left Margaret Benson no doubt how she felt about her. "She told my mother she hated her. She told my mother that she was jealous of my mother and that she wanted everything that belonged to my mother. And—uhh—there were instances when she exhibited violence towards my mother."

This was all the more offensive because "my mother was about five four and weighed about a hundred and ten pounds and was [a] little Miss Milquetoast, if you ever met one, I mean always diplomatic, always said the right thing because she never wanted to hurt anybody's feelings."

Carol Lynn described an occasion when Debbie started "screaming at my mother that how dare she show up at their house and that she was never permitted ever to show—show her face at their house without having called for an appointment first and started swearing at her and raised her hands and started to strike my mother. And—and I—I stepped in—in between them and pulled my mother back."

If it wasn't awful enough that Debbie had tried to attack Mrs. Benson and was poisoning Steven, she also showed no interest in domesticity.

CAROL LYNN: Steven had to do all his own laundry and—and do the cleaning and everything after he got home from work because she didn't do that kind of stuff. And—

CIRACE: Are you all right?

CAROL LYNN: Yeah, I'm—

CIRACE: Are you feeling okay? I mean I don't mind you talking if you're all right—

CAROL LYNN: I know, I'm all right.

CIRACE: Do you—

CAROL LYNN: Oh, but she was—it was—I—

NOWICKI: Let's—let's just go a little further with it, and then I think we can—

CIRACE: Okay.

CAROL LYNN: All right.

NOWICKI: —can conclude.

CAROL LYNN: Okay, I definitely—I—but I'd had used—you know, you said had I noticed anything strange. I really had noticed that Steven's attitude toward my mother had become—not alienated, perhaps that's not the word, but—but really very cold—cold about things. And my—my mother was very suspicious about what—what Steven was stealing from her—uhh—because he never came over to the house unless like she was—was going away for the weekend. Then suddenly he'd want a key to come in. And he would take things of—of Mother's with —without saying anything or returning them. And it just didn't—it was as though he was—he just didn't seem to—to care anymore.

Carol Lynn caught herself and realized she had blundered off the subject, which was Debbie, not Steven. "But there—there were other, you know, there were other incidents too. I thought—just thought of one, and then I forgot it."

Finally she remembered an episode which she said occurred in

Lancaster when Debbie threw a temper tantrum in front of Harry Hitchcock and Janet Lee Murphy.

CAROL LYNN: So she was constantly teaching the children to—to hate my mother and—and doing anything that—that she could to—to try and—and—and turn Steven against my mother and—and against the family.

CIRACE: Okay—uhh—Carol Lynn, let us just go off tape for a minute.
(Tape recorder turned off)

NOWICKI: Uhh, the time is approximately 8:20 and we were off tape approximately two or three minutes, and we are now concluding the interview with Carol Lynn Benson Kendall on July the 28th, 1985.

More than twenty-five percent of Carol Lynn's 136-page statement consisted of serious allegations about Debra Benson. If there were substance to them, one could understand why the investigators let her run on with her grievances against her sister-in-law. They might have tried to prove Debbie was an accomplice or an accessory to the crime. Just as important, if the charges were manifestly false, the investigators might have used them to put Carol Lynn's comments about Steven into perspective. They provided a context within which to weigh her credibility.

But the Collier County police never attempted to verify these accusations against Debbie, nor did they ever discover evidence that would corroborate other significant points in Carol Lynn's testimony. They were interested exclusively in her statements about Steven. Disregarding everything else in the interview, they professed to believe Carol Lynn completely on two subjects: her brother's financial motives and his actions around the time of the murders.

The taped portion of Graham and Nowicki's contact with Carol Lynn had ended, but the conversation continued. All along she had fretted over what had happened to her mother; she had a horror that Mrs. Benson had been trapped in the Suburban and consumed by flames. She begged the investigators to tell her the truth.

It was, Wayne Graham remembered, another tense and emotional moment. "We told her her mom was blown out of the vehicle and wasn't burned up. We said she never knew what hit her and she hadn't suffered much. When she asked how badly she had been disfigured, we told a white lie."

Carol Lynn rested easier in the thought that her mother hadn't been burnt or mutilated beyond recognition.

"Afterward, George Nowicki said, 'I always knew you were a bull-shitter, Wayne. But I never knew you could bullshit that good.'"

The detectives then did something they had never done before with a witness. They bought a card and a gift and passed them to Rick Cirace to give to Carol Lynn.

Thereafter, Carol Lynn called Graham and Nowicki "my knights in shining armor." They spoke with admiration of her courage, intelligence, and cooperation.

This admiration was not necessarily shared by Graham and Nowicki's colleagues, and it didn't extend to the entire Benson family. While they paid elaborate deference to the Bensons in public, members of the prosecutor's team referred to the family in private as "scumbags with Gucci bags" and "white niggers."

After the interview, Carol Lynn Kendall carried on with her convalescence and by August 10 she had recovered sufficiently to be sent home. Although scheduled to return for treatment as an outpatient, she could at least assume some semblance of normal life with her teenage boys.

Shortly after she returned from a month in the hospital, her son Travis is said to have asked for a large sum of money to go out on the town. When she refused to give it to him, he reportedly knocked her down, took the money and left. When asked to confirm the incident, Carol Lynn's attorney did not hesitate to do so.

Chapter 11

By the end of July, all the Meridian corporations had folded. Steven did not have the credit or the capital to fund the companies on his own.

In fact, he barely had enough cash to support himself. If he had embezzled $2.5 million, he was keeping it well hidden. According to his few close friends and business associates, he never showed any signs of personal extravagance except for the flashy cars his mother gave him. She had bought him a red Lotus Turbo at the same time she bought one for Scott—the titles were, as always, in Margaret's name—but he had given it back. It was too much trouble and expense to maintain. He preferred to drive a van.

His tastes in clothing, food, and entertainment also tended to be down-market. He wore cheap polyester suits or work clothes, and he and Debbie seldom went out and rarely invited people over. Until they moved into the new house on Brynwood Lane, they lived in rented places with rented furniture. Even Carol Lynn conceded her brother didn't drink, gamble, take drugs, or run with a fast crowd.

Rich Rodriguez and his wife, Cherry, met Steven and Debbie in 1982 when Rich began to sell and install the electronic equipment Steven ordered for his mother's boat. A handsome, mustachioed man with dark wavy hair, Rodriguez had started his own business and felt some sympathy for Steven's aspirations. Yet he was objective enough to understand why his friend fell short of his goals. "He had a lot of intelligence, but no common sense. He'd jump into a project and throw money at it. If it didn't work, he'd jump into something else."

From what Rodriguez observed, Mrs. Benson and her son weren't simply in business together. Steven looked after numerous details of his mother's personal life. Unlike Carol Lynn who claimed Steven seldom helped out, Rodriguez remarked, "If Mrs. Benson said come over at 11:35 P.M., Steve would hop in his car and get on over there."

Yet as far as Rodriguez could see, Steven never had much money of his own. Although on constant call, he received just $36,000 a year as a consultant to his mother. This was less than half of Scott's annual allowance.

"Steven was work, work, work," Rodriguez said. "Even at home he was stuck in his room fiddling with his computer." But Scott was "play, play, play," and where Steven was "quiet and polite, Scott was a loud, argumentative, arrogant brat." Rodriguez frequently found marijuana on the *Galleon Queen* after Scott and his friends had partied on the boat.

On the Fourth of July, Steven had invited Rich Rodriguez, Cherry, her parents, and Steven Hawkins and his wife over for a cookout, and it quickly became apparent how delighted Debbie and Steven were to have the new house. For Debbie, after years of renting, it meant she had won; they would stay in Fort Myers and not move to Naples near Mrs. Benson. For Steven it seemed to signal success. In an exclusive neighborhood, at a prestigious address, he could pretend he was the prosperous executive he had always yearned to be.

But as Rich Rodriguez recalled, Steven's house, for all the pride he took in it, "was in horrible condition and needed a lot of work. It was definitely the worst place in the neighborhood." Empty and on the market for years, it was run down, the lanai roof was rotten and needed repairing, and so did the rest of the roof. The electrical system was shot, the air conditioner didn't function, and the tennis court was unplayable. The lines had faded, the net was ripped, and the surface was pockmarked and sprouting grass in the cracks.

The owner had dropped the price to $235,000 and accepted a 10 percent down payment. He agreed to finance it himself and arranged easy interest terms.

Even so, Debbie and Steven couldn't afford to fix it up or buy new furniture. In the dining room they had a card table and a few chairs from a secondhand store. The living room was empty except for cardboard boxes. They had to rent folding chairs for their friends on the Fourth of July. The Bensons slept on water beds that a Fort Myers firm had offered as a trade-off for advertising work done by Meridian Marketing. It is worth wondering whether Mrs. Benson would have been so furious had she realized the house was a handyman's special, not "an estate."

Still, Debbie was happy here. One of ten children, she had grown up on a dairy farm, the daughter of extremely poor parents whom neighbors in Wisconsin referred to as "good people." Leo Robinson, a friend in Fort Myers, described Debbie as still a "farm girl . . . She's a real down-to-earth girl."

Her first husband, Monte Larsen, would not speak ill of her even after she left him for Steven. "Debra's basically a homemaker," Larsen said. "She has her faults like everyone else, but she's basically a good honest person."

Among her faults, according to acquaintances, was a tendency to drink a few beers and become strident and critical of Steven for not standing up to his mother. In the opinion of one fellow, she "seemed to have an attitude problem toward men."

Yet no one contended she was guilty of anything more serious than occasional gauche behavior, and everyone agreed she was a "homebody," "family oriented," "a very modest, quiet-living kind of person." As Rich Rodriguez put it, while Steve was "business, business, business," Debbie was "kids, kids, kids."

Although there was no question that Debbie didn't get along with Margaret, friends felt she didn't keep the grandchildren away from their grandmother out of spite and she didn't refuse Mrs. Benson's Christmas and birthday gifts to insult her. She found Margaret's ostentatiousness offensive. People remembered one Christmas in particular when, despite Debbie's pleas that Margaret show restraint, she arrived with an entire truck full of toys for Victoria, Christopher, and Natalie.

Given the way that wealth wreaked havoc in Steven, Carol Lynn, and Scott's lives, it was difficult to quarrel with Debbie's decision. And given the frequency with which Mrs. Benson interfered in her children's marriages, it was no surprise that Debbie wanted to keep her distance. But after struggling for years against her mother-in-law's domination, she now found Margaret ruling from the grave. The Meridian corporations had collapsed and Steven's consulting fees had stopped. Then Harry Hitchcock cut off his trust fund, and they were left with no income, no way to meet their monthly mortgage payments. If something wasn't done soon, they would lose their house.

On August 5, in separate motions, Steven Benson and Carol Lynn Kendall petitioned the Collier County Probate Court to appoint them co-administrators of their mother's estate. These requests indicated that they had come to accept the January 1985 De Loach will as valid.

2

On August 8, Wayne Kerr, who drafted the May 1983 will, was subpoenaed by state prosecutors Lee Hollander and Jerry Brock. William Blackwell represented Kerr at the proceeding. Lieutenant Harold Young and ATF Agent George Nowicki were also present.

Another attorney entered the room. A powerfully built man with a shock of curly brown hair, a toothy smile, and a strong jaw, he readjusted his rimless glasses, then announced:

"My name is Michael McDonnell, of the firm of McDonnell and Berry of Naples, Florida, and I have been employed to represent Steven Benson.

"I am here today to place on record Mr. Benson's invocation of the attorney-client privilege between himself and his attorney, Wayne Kerr, who is here under subpoena.

"We wish the record to be clear that this invocation of the privilege is being made without reservation."

Saying he would wait outside in case any question arose concerning this matter, McDonnell left, and a moment later William Blackwell instructed Kerr on the immunity provisions of the subpoena.

... you have the right, under the Fifth Amendment of the United States Constitution and also the Florida Constitution, not to be compelled to say anything.

KERR: Right. I understand.
BLACKWELL: To the extent that any of these questions may give rise to something that could conceivably be used against you, I want to discuss with you before you do that.
KERR: Absolutely.

Blackwell informed the prosecutors that Wayne Kerr "has represented various members of the Benson family individually and collectively and as to any and all of these individuals he will claim privilege as to the communications he had with them."

Over the next three hours, Kerr refused to answer forty-eight questions. Unless ordered to do so by the court, he declined to discuss any of his business dealings with the Benson family.

State prosecutor Jerry Brock said, "We disagree with your opinion of the attorney-client privilege, but that is a matter we will hash out with the court."

Yet even when the huge, fidgety lawyer refused to answer, the questions revealed a great deal about the State's presumptions, and in those areas where Kerr felt free to respond, his recollections provided a fascinating counterpoint to Carol Lynn's version of events.

Asked if he had a purpose other than preparing Mrs. Benson's taxes when he flew to Naples from Philadelphia on July 7, Kerr said yes. "It involved looking into business operations."

BROCK: At whose request, if anyone's, were you doing that?

KERR: At Margaret's request.

BROCK: When had Margaret contacted you with respect to making that request?

KERR: To the best of my knowledge—I think it was two weeks before.

.　　.　　.　　.　　.　　.　　.　　.　　.　　.　　.　　.

HOLLANDER: On one of these occasions that you spoke to Lieutenant Harold Young—

KERR: Uh-huh.

HOLLANDER: —do you recall telling him that your doing work on taxes was merely a cover for your real purpose down here?

KERR: I don't believe I said that, specifically.

HOLLANDER: Do you recall the fact that you told [Lt. Young] that the real purpose for your coming down here was to remove Steven from any interest in the alarm company?

KERR: See, I—I mean, that certainly that may be his interpretation, but there were two goals involved and one of the goals, of course, was the tax matters... There was another matter that was of interest. However, I don't think I can express it in those terms.

HOLLANDER: In what terms did you express it to Officer Young?

KERR: I can't really recall at this point.

HOLLANDER: What was your other purpose? Was one of your other purposes in coming down here to remove him, Steve, from the alarm business?

KERR: I consider my purpose as being privileged.

.　　.　　.　　.　　.　　.　　.　　.　　.　　.　　.　　.

HOLLANDER: Do you recall telling Lieutenant Young that your purpose was either to remove Steve from the alarm company or, in the alternative, to shut the alarm company down?

KERR: I believe what I conveyed to Mr. Young was—that there was a—uhh, part of being down here, of course, was to analyze business operations.

HOLLANDER: Did you also convey that—

KERR: But I did not analyze any business operations when I was down here.

HOLLANDER: I thought that was what you were doing on Monday morning [July 8].

KERR: Yes, for one hour. I mean, I couldn't draw any conclusions at that point.

Moments later, Kerr reiterated that "one of the purposes of my stay—my purpose in coming down here was investigatory. Certainly, alternatives were being examined. However, like I said before, the investigation was not to the point where conclusions could be drawn, nor were any alternatives selected at that point."

All of this contrasted with Carol Lynn's statement and the investigators' operating assumptions. They were convinced that Mrs. Benson had made a firm decision and that Steven was aware of it.

After reviewing the events of Sunday evening, July 7, when Kerr stayed at the Benson house with Margaret and Carol Lynn watching "Murder, She Wrote" on TV, the prosecutors turned to July 8. Kerr and Margaret had stopped in the Meridian trailer office on their return trip from Fort Myers, then had gone to Quail Creek. Because it was Carol Lynn's birthday, the three of them squeezed into the Porsche and drove over to Plum's Cafe. He ordered the lasagna special, he remembered, and Margaret picked up the tab, paying with a credit card.

Kerr managed to pin down with reasonable accuracy when they returned from dinner. Unlike Carol Lynn who, in her statement, twice admitted she couldn't recall the time or whether they watched television or when she went to bed, Kerr said, "I remember watching—uh—Katie and Allen, or something like that. Some TV program."

" 'Kate and Allie'?" Hollander asked.

" 'Kate and Allie,' right."

He had it in his mind that Carol Lynn disappeared, presumably for bed, while Margaret and he went on watching the show.

Hollander asked whether Kerr remembered Carol Lynn answering the telephone before they left for Plum's, then announcing, "Guess who called?"

KERR: I don't recall that.
HOLLANDER: You do not.
KERR: No.

Since Carol Lynn had described this incident to Graham and him, George Nowicki spoke up. "You would have been sitting out on the screen[ed in] patio and Carol Lynn would have answered the phone and come over to you and Margaret and said, 'Guess who called?' "

KERR: When was that?
NOWICKI: Before you all went to dinner.
KERR: I mean, it's not—it don't ring a bell, but—I can't recall that statement.
HOLLANDER: (resuming the questioning): Do you recall the statement concerning that Steven had called to make sure Scott was going next morning?
KERR: I can't recall that being said to me. I mean—those statements do not ring—it's not something I heard before.

Jerry Brock took over the interrogation and, in the midst of more questions about the dinner at Plum's, he abruptly changed directions.

BROCK: Did you bring some pipe caps down here from Pittsburgh [sic].
KERR: Pipe caps? No. I don't even know what pipe caps are. But no.
BROCK: You did not bring any?
KERR: No. Absolutely not.
BROCK: Did you see any when you were over at the house?
KERR: What are they? I don't even know what they are.
BROCK: They are caps that screw on the end of galvanized pipe. Did you see any of those in any of the vehicles anywhere at the house?
KERR: No.
BROCK: Did you see any sections of pipe that were about four inches in diameter and twelve inches long?
KERR: No.

.   .   .   .

BROCK: You did not bring any of those down from Pennsylvania?
KERR: No.

.   .   .   .

BROCK: You did not bring any gunpowder down with you or did you purchase any gunpowder at anyone's request?
KERR: No, I did not.

BROCK: Did you see any when you were over at the house or at any of the businesses, or other locations that you went to?

KERR: No.

BROCK: From the time that you arrived until the explosion?

KERR: I mean I wouldn't even—I wouldn't even know what it is contained—I didn't see any. Is gunpowder a white substance? I don't know if I would know it if I saw it.

BROCK: It is your testimony that you did not purchase any at the request of anyone?

KERR: That's correct.

Obviously, it troubled the prosecutors that while they suspected Steven of buying two end caps at Hughes Supply, they still had no idea where he got the eight-year-old Grinnell caps and the smokeless powder.

Lee Hollander focused on the morning of July 9. While dressing in his room, Kerr had noticed Steven pull up in front of the Benson house in a beige van. The lumbering, stoop-shouldered lawyer said he reached the kitchen at approximately 7:30 A.M. His memory was that "Margaret and Carol Lynn were both in their bathrobes, you know, their night clothing."

This was a potentially important point. Carol Lynn had stressed in her statement that she wanted to get an early start to beat the summer heat. She had admitted taking some small delight in the thought that Steven, who "isn't known for early" would have to get up long before his usual rising time.

But from what Kerr recalled, it was Carol Lynn, not Steven, who wasn't ready to go at 7:30 A.M. And Margaret hadn't dressed yet either. Had Steven decided to make a run for coffee and Danish, figuring there was no rush, and this would give Carol Lynn time to change out of her nightclothes?

Kerr's testimony raised other questions about that morning. Carol Lynn said her mother initially resisted Steven's encouragement that she come with them to the new lots. But Kerr had different recollections of this and related incidents.

HOLLANDER: Do you recall Mrs. Benson saying that she didn't want to go to the stakeout?

KERR: What is a "stakeout"?

HOLLANDER: They were supposed to stake out the property, right?

KERR: Yeah. No, I don't recall [Mrs. Benson's not wanting to go].

HOLLANDER: Do you remember a discussion concerning the pool man coming?

KERR: Yes, I do.

. . . .

HOLLANDER: Was there any discussion from any of them that they did not want to go look at these properties, that they wanted to stay there and wait for [the pool man]?

KERR: I don't recall if there was.

A minute later, Hollander returned to the subject.

HOLLANDER: Did Carol Lynn talk to Margaret about staying to talk to the pool man herself, about Margaret staying?

KERR: I wasn't really involved in those discussions. I mean, there could have been discussions happening, but I wasn't involved.

HOLLANDER: Did you hear Steven saying to them how important it was that they go to see these pieces of property?

KERR: I don't recall that specific language.

. . . .

HOLLANDER: Did Scott state that he was not going to go?

KERR: Not in front of me. I didn't hear him making any statement.

HOLLANDER: Did you hear Steven making any statement that Scott had to go?

KERR: No, I don't recall any statement being made to that effect.

None of this proved Kerr's recollections were correct and Carol Lynn's wrong. He conceded he may have missed some discussions while he was working in the lanai. But where she painted a picture of Steven orchestrating the action and going to great lengths to get Margaret and Scott to come along, Kerr depicted a much more subdued scene during which, to his knowledge, Steven never pressured anybody and never did anything out of the ordinary except take a long time to return with the coffee and Danish. In this instance, as in many others, investigators had to depend on Carol Lynn's uncorroborated testimony.

BROCK: Were you instructed by Margaret, during the period of time that you were down here in July of this year, to prepare a new will for her?

KERR: I'm going to have to claim the attorney-client privilege on that question.

BROCK: On behalf of whom?

KERR: Margaret.

. . . .

HOLLANDER: Have you told Lieutenant Young and Investigator Koors and Agent Nowicki that funds were used from Meridian Security to finance Meridian Marketing?

KERR: I can't recall saying that to them.

HOLLANDER: You are not saying that you did not, though?

KERR: I can't recall. They can produce a signed statement that I indicated that?

Hollander changed the subject.

After Kerr repeated that he had flown down to Florida on a "fact gathering" mission, as well as to do Mrs. Benson's 1984 taxes, Jerry Brock tried to establish with whom he shared these "facts." Although Kerr swore he had learned very little before the murders, the prosecutors were anxious to know whether he had conveyed his client's suspicions and plans to Steven.

BROCK: Did you perform any services in furtherance of your attorney-client relationship with Steven that would have conflicted with the furtherance of your attorney-client relationship with Margaret?

KERR: Of course not.

BROCK: Did you reveal any conversation that you had with Mrs. Benson in furtherance of your attorney-client relationship with Steven?

KERR: No.

BROCK: Did you reveal any of the conversation that you had with Mrs. Benson in furtherance of your attorney-client relationship to any other member of the Benson family?

KERR: Absolutely not.

After Jerry Brock took his shot, Lee Hollander tried.

HOLLANDER: Did you at any time advise [Steven] that you were coming down here for the purpose of removing him from the Security System or closing the business, and/or removing him from the will?

KERR: No.

HOLLANDER: You did not?

KERR: No, I did not.

Eventually, Brock came back into the questioning:

BROCK: Was there any discussion that you are aware, either between yourself, Margaret and Steven, relating to removing him from his position in

any of the companies, or excluding or rewriting a will excluding him as
an heir?

KERR: No.

Prosecutors learned little or nothing in this interview that sub-
stantiated Carol Lynn's story on its most important points. But this
didn't appear to bother them. In the next few weeks, they ignored
Kerr's sworn statement and included in court documents and released to the press what were purported to be his unrecorded comments. These, in combination with Carol Lynn's testimony, would
constitute a major portion of their case. Perhaps they believed that
once Kerr was forced by the court to provide full answers about his
dealings with the Bensons, they would get corroboration of Carol
Lynn's account.

Meanwhile, Judge Hugh Hayes ruled, on August 13, that the
1985 De Loach will was valid. He appointed Naples attorney Carl
Westman of the firm of Frost and Jacobs as interim personal representative, or administrator, of the Benson estate. Eventually, under
an agreement acceptable to both Carol Lynn and Steven, the term
"interim" was dropped from Westman's title.

On August 16, Wayne Kerr bowed to the inevitable and dropped
his motion to administer the estate.

3

Frank Kendall—no relation to Carol Lynn Kendall—was an
agent with Alcohol, Tobacco and Firearms, working out of the Atlanta office. Craggy-faced and bearded, with silver hair and a high
forehead laddered with wrinkles, Kendall fit a Hollywood casting
director's idea of an artist or writer. But he was a latent-fingerprint
examiner and in the course of a twenty-three-year career, he had
studied hundreds of thousands of prints.

From the crime scene of the Benson pipe bomb murders he had
been sent several Duracell battery casings and three small pieces of
duct tape. But he wasn't able to lift any prints. Laser light tests on
scraps of galvanized pipe and end caps had also failed to raise anything of value.

At one point, investigators in Naples asked Kendall to process a
letter that Steven Benson had sent to his sister. The agent managed to

lift some finger and palm prints, but didn't have known impressions of Steven's prints for comparison.

On July 30, Kendall received via DHL air courier service two sales tickets from Hughes Supply Inc. Ticket number N.183200 reflected the purchase of two four-inch end caps on July 5. Ticket number N.183451 reflected the purchase of two twelve-inch sections of nipple pipe.

Removing the documents from their plastic covers, Kendall treated them with chemicals and examined them. On the face of each sales ticket he found "a good latent palm print." He referred specifically to "a writer's palm" made by a left-hander. Steven Benson was left-handed.

The sales ticket also revealed some partial fingerprints, at least one of which was complete enough to yield an identifiable print—if, that is, Kendall had some inked impressions for comparison.

The problem was that police still had not located a sample of Steven Benson's fingerprints anywhere in the United States. And it wasn't as if investigators hadn't been industrious and imaginative in their search. Wayne Graham had even called the neighborhood garbage collector and learned what time he picked up Steven's trash. ATF agents showed up on the same schedule, pawing through refuse for papers or other objects likely to retain a print. But they came away with nothing except dirty hands and useless scraps of rubbish.

About the time the Collier County Sheriff's Department began to mull over unorthodox legal measures, Steven Benson was doing the same thing—searching for a loophole in the law. He needed money. By this point, he and his family were dependent on the generosity of friends like Rich and Cherry Rodriguez who bought them food and delivered it to the house on Brynwood Lane so that Debbie didn't have to go out and run the gauntlet of reporters, rubberneckers, and cops.

Benson's financial desperation was lost on the press and, therefore, on the public. Portrayed as the scion of a multimillionairess, he was assumed to be rich in his own right, and this assumption became unshakable once stories started to circulate that he had embezzled $2.5 million.

Although he had had to sign over his car to the law firm of McDonnell and Berry to serve as a retainer, he was perceived as someone who could hire the best legal minds in America. While not charged with anything yet, he was compared to Claus Von Bulow, John De Lorean, T. Cullen Davis, and other celebrated defendants who were said to have "walked" because they were wealthy.

Of course, if Steven had had access to his inheritance he would have been a rich man. But his mother's will hadn't been probated.

Carol Lynn, however, had her own pressing financial needs, and this forced Westman into an awkward position. He could not favor one beneficiary over another. If he tried to disperse money to Carol Lynn, he knew Steven would file a legal motion to block any release of funds until his criminal and/or civil guilt had been decided. That could take years. Meanwhile, Carol Lynn's medical bills and living expenses were piling up.

After some research and pondering, Carl Westman came up with a potential solution. A subsection of the Florida Slayer's Statute held that for purposes of inheritance a killer was deemed to have died *before* the person he killed. In other words, "the estate of the decedent passes as if the killer had pre-deceased the decedent." If Steven was found to have killed Margaret Benson, his share of the estate would, in all likelihood, pass to his three children, as if he were dead.

This presented the possibility of a Solomonic decision. The problem was persuading Carol Lynn, who became extremely upset when she learned that Steven's children might inherit a share of her mother's fortune even if Steven was found to have killed Mrs. Benson. But gradually she recognized that there was no way her brother would permit her to receive money from the estate unless a formula was found that relieved some of his financial burdens.

Carl Westman proposed that Steven put his children under a court-appointed guardian and let them receive part of his inheritance now. There was a strict written understanding that any money distributed in this fashion would be spent on the kids, not on Steven or his defense.

Under these terms, a partial distribution of $100,000 was made to Steven's children, in care of attorney Barry Hillmyer, their court-appointed guardian. At the same time, $100,000 was released directly to Carol Lynn Kendall.

This probate arrangement did not compare in complexity to the machinations police were going through to get Steven Benson's hand prints. It would have simplified matters if they had arrested him and taken an impression of his hands. But they didn't have enough evidence to justify an arrest. Since they found no Florida precedent for taking prints before an arrest, they decided they would have to break new ground.

On August 10, Harold Young asked Graham to help him prepare an affidavit for probable cause on a search warrant. But this wasn't to be a routine procedure where police wanted to search a house or an office for something relevant to the commission of a crime. The warrant Young and Graham drafted asserted that "on the body of Steven Wayne Benson . . . there is now certain evidence, to wit: Rolled ink impressions of fingers, palms, and writer's palms of both hands."

They didn't mean that Benson carried a document that contained latent or inked prints. They literally meant that his hands were attached to his body, and his hands had fingers and palms, and if those fingers and palms were inked and rolled on paper, they would yield impressions. Young and Graham wrote that "said evidence" was "germane to a violation of a Florida statute" and since it was "being kept on the body of Steven Wayne Benson . . . I expressly find probable cause for the issuance of this Search Warrant."

In support of their cleverly contrived claim, Young and Graham compiled an eighteen-page affidavit that was reviewed and amended by the State Attorney's office. It too demonstrated considerable ingenuity.

It described Steven Benson as "approximately six (6) feet in height, approximately two hundred pounds in weight, having dark brown hair, medium complexion." Since his height and weight were listed on his driver's license, the investigators didn't have to use approximations, but they wanted to match Benson with the description given by the salesman at Hughes Supply Inc.

Jeffrey Maynes, according to the affidavit, gave this description. But he had no memory of the man who purchased end caps. It was James Link who recalled the customer being about six feet tall and two hundred pounds. Neither salesman could pick Benson from a lineup of photographs.

The affidavit did not mention this. Instead, it emphasized that Investigator Michael Koors had done a composite picture under James Link's direction. It concluded "that the composite photo is strikingly similar to Steven Wayne Benson."

But Young and Graham neglected to add that it differed in significant respects from what Link told Koors. It depicted a man with dark hair, horn-rimmed glasses, clear lenses, and close-set eyes. James Link had described the customer as wearing oval, wire-rimmed John Lennon glasses with opaque lenses. He had no more idea of the size and shape of the man's eyes than he did of his hair color and style.

According to the affidavit, Benson had told Harold Young that he had left the house for one hour and ten minutes to buy coffee and pastry. There was no mention that Wayne Kerr estimated the absence at forty-five minutes and Carol Lynn said thirty minutes or less.

The affidavit contended that Investigator Thomas Smith told Harold Young that Carol Lynn stated Steven gave Scott the car keys, then said he "had to go into the house to get a tape measure. Steven then ran toward the front entrance of the residence, as the first explosion occurred."

The transcript of Smith's interview with Carol Lynn the day of the murders contained no statement that Steven "ran" anywhere. Carol Lynn said, "Steven had gone inside" and the explosion occurred while "He was still in the house," not while he was running toward the front entrance.

The affidavit synopsized the incident a few years ago in Lancaster when Tom Schelling allegedly saw Steven Benson detonating a pipe bomb with a remote control device. But it did not refer to Mr. Schelling's criminal record for forgery and assault. It also failed to correct a chronological error which would prove fatal.

The State Attorney's office had subpoenaed the bank records and accounts of Margaret Benson, Steven Benson, Meridian Securities Network, and Meridian Marketing and turned them over to Diana Galloway, a senior auditor with ATF. In a preliminary report, Ms. Galloway indicated that Steven had taken funds from his mother's Dean Witter account and placed them in his personal checking account and in the Meridian Security Network account. There was no mention that Steven and Margaret were in business together, that they served as officers in the same corporations, that Steven had legal access to his mother's Dean Witter account and received a consulting fee from Mrs. Benson.

Carol Lynn Kendall's interrogation constituted the centerpiece of the affidavit. Harold Young wrote that he had received a verbal report from Lieutenant Graham and Agent Nowicki and had read a transcript of the interview. The affidavit offered selected "excerpts from the transcribed statement."

Considering the seriousness of the crime and the precedent-breaking nature of what the police were trying to achieve, it would seem to have been of the utmost importance to present an accurate account of Carol Lynn's testimony. Yet the affidavit contained nine and a half single-spaced pages that amounted to a pastiche of misquotes and misleading comments, badly compounded by shoddy proofreading and a pattern of editing that suggested the conscious elimination of inconvenient or embarrassing facts. Although it may be that some of Carol Lynn's sentence fragments, repetitive phrases, and digressions were deleted to make the narrative easier to follow, this doesn't explain why substantive passages were dropped.

In some cases, brainless mistakes distorted the excerpts. In one laughable instance, Carol Lynn is quoted as saying about her sunglasses, "the darkest pair I guess was the ones that I had, I keep the Blair House."

Apparently, it did not bother anybody at the Collier County Sheriff's Department or the State Attorney's office that this made no sense. A glance at the transcript shows that she actually said, "The darkest pair I guess were the ones I had so I could keep the glare out."

Other errors were more troubling than amusing. For example: "There had been, mother had this company that, that, Steven had kind of stripped. But it was always mother's money that was used."

This sounded like evidence of Steven's pilfering—i.e., "stripping"—funds from a company financed by Mrs. Benson. But a comparison with the notarized "true and accurate transcription" reveals that Carol Lynn said, "Mother had this company at—that—that Steven had kind of *started*," not stripped.

Just as significant as those instances where the affidavit misrepresented what Carol Lynn had said are those where it omitted her unsubstantiated accusations, intemperate remarks, and irrational analyses of events. About 30 percent of the interview consisted of allegations about Debbie Benson and various family employees. But Debbie is barely mentioned, and her alleged crimes, along with the duplicitous acts of family employees, are ignored. Thus there is no context within which to weigh the credibility of Carol Lynn's accusations against Steven.

All of Carol Lynn's quips and wisecracks have been cut out, as have Graham and Nowicki's fits of laughter. Also deleted were Rick Cirace's requests to go off the record and confer with his client.

In some cases, an effort was made to show where material was deleted. A dark horizontal line across the page occasionally signaled a change of subject or a jump in sequence. Thinner lines within the text sometimes indicated breaks and new paragraphs.

But this wasn't consistent. Quite often there was nothing to show a deletion. Unless one had read the whole transcript and remembered it in detail, it was impossible to judge how drastically the affidavit changed Carol Lynn's testimony. Questions were yoked with the wrong answers. Sentences and paragraphs were run together, sometimes altering their meaning, sometimes rendering them meaningless. Quotation marks were added, and phrases and sentences were invented willy-nilly.

This arbitrary editing was so pervasive, it would take a computer to collate all the differences between the transcript and the excerpts. But one passage from the affidavit demonstrated just how far Collier County police and prosecutors were willing to go to shape sworn testimony to their purposes:

GEORGE NOWICKI: Could I ask you if your mother at any time expressed any fears to you about her own safety in regard to anybody in recent weeks?

CAROL BENSON KENDALL: My mother also, when she was in Lancaster, we were talking about, it wasn't exactly that my mother said "I think Steven would kill me." It wasn't that kind of statement but we were talking about the property that she was thinking of buying and she said something, "Steven would certainly prefer that I did it because it would be more money for him if I were dead."

I can't remember exactly but she did indicate, my mother did indicate to me that perhaps she would not put it past my brother to do away with her.

GEORGE NOWICKI: How long ago did she tell you this?

CAROL BENSON KENDALL: One evening when I was still in Boston, about three weeks ago.

The transcript reveals that Nowicki's question did not immediately prompt Carol Lynn to mention her mother's fear of Steven. Instead, she spent half a page discussing Mrs. Benson's fear of Debbie who "hated my mother and . . . wanted everything that was my mother's." Then she described Mrs. Benson's fear of Scott and his "wild and violent temper." She explained that he sometimes went off the deep end "because when he was younger he had—had smoked some pot and—some—and sniffed that gas stuff," meaning nitrous oxide. Just recently, on a trip to Europe, Mrs. Benson had been frightened of Scott.

In the transcript, when Carol Lynn finally got around to Steven, and what Margaret supposedly said about him, there are no quotation marks around *I think Steven would kill me* or around *Steven would certainly prefer that I did* buy property. In fact, the transcript indicates that Carol Lynn remembered her mother saying Steven *would certainly prefer it if I didn't* buy property. And when Mrs. Benson allegedly went on to add "it would be more money for him if I were dead," the affidavit neglected to add Carol Lynn's instant response, "Mother, that's ridiculous."

The affidavit also failed to point out that Carol Lynn made three different comments about Steven's purported feelings about his mother's buying property. From page to page she could not remember whether he was for it or against it.

When Nowicki asked when her mother had expressed these fears, the affidavit has Carol Lynn answer, "One evening when I was still in Boston, about three weeks ago." The transcript shows that she actually said, "When we were in Lancaster about—in, I'm sorry, in Boston about three weeks ago." But neither Carol Lynn nor her mother was in Boston three weeks before she made this comment. They were in Naples. Any confusion about places or times was eliminated.

With Graham and Nowicki, it took Carol Lynn forty-three pages and several hours of questioning to get around to her mother's fear of Steven. In her statement to Officer Smith when asked about threats to the family or strife within it, she said nothing about Steven. Now the finger of suspicion was pointed exclusively at him.

Although Harold Young had been present during Wayne Kerr's statement and heard the lawyer swear there had been no coffee, only instant Sanka, in the Benson house, he quoted Carol Lynn as saying, "I guess it was strange for him to go out and get coffee...for us because he could have walked into the kitchen and gotten coffee."

On August 14 and 15, while Harold Young and Wayne Graham continued working on the affidavit for a search warrant and the State Attorney's office reviewed their rough drafts, Steven Benson was kept under surveillance. Police wanted to make sure he stayed in the area. If he left town, they had orders to follow him. If he hopped on a plane, they had to hope there was another seat available. They still didn't feel they had sufficient evidence to arrest him.

Graham later claimed he cautioned his men not to interfere with Benson's "normal activities." But they maintained surveillance for eighteen and twenty hours a day and didn't try to conceal themselves.

They drove right up to his address and followed him everywhere. No one in the neighborhood could mistake their stripped-down blue Ford LTDs for anything except unmarked police cars.

On Friday, August 16, they submitted the affidavit and search warrant to Judge Ted Brousseau, who had no reason to doubt the facts set forth. Lieutenant Harold Young, the chief investigating officer, swore to them. Judge Brousseau signed both documents, and by 11 A.M. they were ready to be served.

Although the Collier County Sheriff's Department denied it had employed electronic surveillance, it somehow knew Steven Benson was headed from Fort Myers to the Naples office of Attorney Thomas Biggs. In his own automobile, Barry Hillmyer, the children's court-appointed guardian, accompanied Steven to Naples. Wayne Graham ordered a team of three cars from his Special Response Unit to follow Benson. He himself proceeded with four men to Biggs's office. They were armed with 9mm automatics and carried AR-15s in the trunks of their cars. If Steven refused to cooperate with the search warrant, their orders were to take him into custody.

As the caravan of cars headed south, Corporal Crain radioed Graham for instructions. He said Barry Hillmyer was trying to block the units tailing Steven Benson. He kept pulling his car between Benson and the surveillance teams. Graham told Crain that if trouble continued, he should pull Hillmyer over and give him a ticket.

When Graham reached the law office on 9th Street, Benson had already arrived along with his wife and Hillmyer. Harold Young was waiting for them with the search warrant.

Graham asked Hillmyer what he had been trying to pull, but the attorney laughed at him. Then Thomas Biggs came outside, and Mike McDonnell showed up with his partner, Jerry Berry. Harold Young said, "I've never seen so many attorneys in a homicide case in my life. It was like you lifted up a rock and they all ran out."

Lieutenant Jack Gant, a burly man with a baby face and a pompadour hair style, came along with his fingerprinting equipment. A colorful character, Gant liked to keep things light. He described this crucial scene by saying, "I held hands with Steven Benson for half an hour."

Apparently, Gant's merry irreverence extended to certain forensic procedures. He was familiar with the FBI's suggested guidelines for taking fingerprints, but didn't follow them.

Outside, Wayne Graham waited with his men. A woman from a nearby shop tried to sell the SRU team a trip on a cruise ship. But her sales pitch got cut short. Suddenly, Harold Young and Jack Gant came out of the law office. They had what they wanted—inked impressions of Steven Benson's prints.

That afternoon, ATF agent George Nowicki caught a flight to Atlanta and delivered the prints to Frank Kendall. On Monday, August 19, the Collier County Sheriff's Department learned that Benson's left writer's palm, the fleshy pad at the edge of the hand, matched the latent prints found on the receipts for galvanized pipes and end caps at Hughes Supply Co.

One would have assumed this cinched the matter. The police believed Benson had a motive—he'd been stealing from his mother and she decided to "pull the plug"; a means—his knowledge of electronic circuitry and his experience with explosives; and an opportunity—during his trip to buy coffee he could have planted the pipe bombs. Now they had his prints on receipts for material similar to the bomb's components. If their case was half as strong as they claimed in the affidavit, one would have expected them to pounce.

But they didn't. They kept Benson under surveillance and took their time drafting an arrest warrant. They declined when Michael McDonnell suggested that if Steven's arrest was imminent, he "would voluntarily submit himself to judicial process."

In another curious move, after laboring so diligently to get Benson's fingerprints, they left them out of the final arrest warrant. They had included them in earlier drafts prepared by Graham and Young, but then deleted them after a discussion between Lieutenant Harold Young and State Attorney Jerry Brock. Young could not, or would not, explain why. But one can't avoid the question. If they had sufficient evidence to arrest Steven Benson without the prints, why didn't they do it? On the other hand, if the prints were the conclusive piece of evidence they appeared to be, why weren't they mentioned in the arrest warrant? Was it possible the prosecutors had had second thoughts about the legality of forcing a suspect to give his prints before his arrest?

Whatever their doubts, they didn't deter investigators long. They held a last meeting on Wednesday, August 21, then went to Judge Hayes at 9:00 A.M. on the twenty-second to have the arrest warrant signed.

Steven Benson was in Barry Hillmyer's office in Fort Myers when Lee County and Collier County police swooped down on him. He offered no resistance. He barely offered any reaction, and this bothered the cops.

After booking him in Lee County, Harold Young, Wayne Graham, and George Nowicki transported the prisoner to Naples in Young's automobile. Like so many mundane aspects of the case, the reality of Young's car didn't satisfy the press. So they upgraded it and wrote that he drove a classic pink 1957 Thunderbird. In fact, he owned a 1984 beige Thunderbird.

Nowicki and Young rode up front. After complaining about the tight squeeze, Benson sat in back with Wayne Graham and said nothing. Graham didn't get it. Why didn't the guy protest his innocence? "If I was accused of killing my mother," Graham recalled, "I'd be screaming and jumping up and down denying it."

Trying to get a rise out of Benson, Harold Young talked about his mother and his family, laying it on thick, saying how much he cared about them. But Benson didn't take the bait. He leaned back in the seat and appeared to fall asleep. The three officers were convinced they had apprehended a cold, callous killer.

At the Collier County jail, a mob of reporters and TV cameramen was waiting when Steven stepped out of the car and, staring straight ahead, strode through the crowd. Hands cuffed in front of him, dressed in dark blue trousers and a light gray shirt, he kept his small pursed mouth pressed shut and let Harold Young lead him along. They were an incongruous pair, the small feisty detective and the large, fleshy murder suspect who looked as lugubrious as a St. Bernard.

One couldn't blame him for being hang-dog. He was charged with two counts of first degree murder, a single count of attempted murder, and several counts of setting off explosives and endangering human lives.

At a pretrial hearing in front of Judge Thomas Trettis, Steven was asked if he understood the charges against him. He said he did. Judge Trettis jailed him without bond. He was issued orange coveralls and remanded to the maximum security cellblock.

Although Steven had little to say, the police more than filled the silence. At a press conference held jointly by federal and local law enforcement agents, Sheriff Aubrey Rogers spoke for the Collier County police, Dan Conroy represented Alcohol, Tobacco and Firearms, and State Attorney Joseph P. D'Alessandro spoke for the prosecutors' office. While ATF announced it would continue its investigation and perhaps press federal charges later, D'Alessandro said he preferred to prosecute the case under Florida law. "Under the federal statutes, you don't have the death penalty."

Few journalists could resist commenting on the irony that Benson, the "electronics whiz," might end up in the electric chair. Since 1976, Florida juries had sentenced three hundred and fifty people to death row.

Although the matching palm prints had not made it into the arrest warrant, newspapers from Naples to Boston obtained confirmation from unnamed investigators that Steven Benson's writer's palm had been found on the Hughes Supply receipts. In an affidavit filed in Collier County Circuit Court, Harold Young claimed that witnesses had told him Margaret Benson summoned Wayne Kerr from Philadelphia to remove Steven from participation in the Meridian corporations and to draft a will that excluded him from her estate. According to Young, Mrs. Benson decided to disinherit her son when she discovered he had stolen $2 million from her stock account.

This story had such a catchy ring to it—Rich Heir Kills Mom, Feared Being Cut Out of Will—nothing that anybody subsequently said could dissuade newspapers and TV reporters from repeating it over and over again. From start to finish it affected the course of the case.

Chapter 12

The next day, defense attorney Michael McDonnell filed a written plea of not guilty for all charges and requested that reasonable bail be set. "Steven Benson announced today," McDonnell said, "that he unequivocally and categorically denies the charges for which he has been arrested."

Harry Hitchcock reacted to the arrest saying, "I am shocked. I speak for the whole family." But he soon embellished his initial remarks and produced regular homilies, all of which expressed deep Christian concern, none of which suggested that he intended to throw his personal and practical support to Steven.

He did say he knew of no ill will between Margaret and Steven. "She loved him and he loved her, so that's the reason this is a puzzle to me. There's nothing in the past to explain this."

Still, he added, he wasn't surprised by Steven's arrest. "It was the evidence, that circumstantial evidence, that was damning."

"I kept praying this wouldn't happen, it wouldn't be Steven," Hitchcock said. "It was a calamity on top of a calamity." Then he added, "I'd give everything I own in this world if I could just undo what has been done. I read about these things happening to other people. I'm eighty-eight years old and I've never had anything approaching a disaster like this in my lifetime."

But as a veteran of decades of Prayer Breakfasts, he waxed philosophical, citing one of his favorite aphorisms. "I have a saying, storms make good sailors. This was more of a storm than I've ever expected." Yet he left no doubt he would weather it.

Carol Lynn Kendall also started off expressing astonishment at Steven's arrest. Despite the fact that her statement played a major part in indicting him, her attorney, Richard Cirace, told the press, "She had no idea it was coming. It's another in a series of tragedies that has befallen the family. She will need a few days to regroup."

Apparently these days of regrouping were beneficial. On August 27, the Lancaster *New Era* ran a story with the headline HITCHCOCK GETS GOOD NEWS: GRANDDAUGHTER 'SPIRITUALLY REBORN.' Hitchcock recalled the exact words Carol Lynn used to explain how she had become "born again." "Papa, I have been close to the Lord and I recognize it."

As for Steven, Hitchcock said the evidence was mounting against him. He did not specify what this evidence was or how it had increased. But he stressed that he held out hope for his grandson. "He's innocent until proven guilty. I pray and pray that he's innocent."

While he explained that poor health prevented him from visiting Steven, he announced he was willing to talk to him by telephone. When asked whether he would provide bail money, he replied, "That's a bridge that I wouldn't try to cross until the bridge is there."

Within two weeks the bridge was there and during Judge Hugh D. Hayes's deliberations whether to grant bond, Harry Hitchcock sent a letter imploring him to keep Steven in jail. He wrote that he was "concerned and alarmed" and "afraid for my own safety." After all, "anyone capable of murdering his mother for money is capable of murdering his grandfather for the same reason." Since Steven stood to inherit "a substantial sum" upon Hitchcock's death, he felt he had good reason to be fearful. He also expressed fear for Carol Lynn's safety.

Janet Lee Murphy joined her father in his appeal to the judge. "I beg you not to set bail," she wrote.

Judge Hayes claimed these letters had no effect on him. But once printed in newspapers around the country, they had a devastating impact on the public's view of Steven Benson. What possible conclusion could people, and especially prospective jurors, draw except the obvious? If his family felt he wasn't worth defending, how could an outsider assume Benson was innocent?

Less than a week after the arrest, the Boston *Herald* reported that Carol Lynn Kendall claimed Mrs. Benson had not intended to cut

Steven out of her will. She planned to reduce his share of the inheritance by $2 million, the amount he allegedly stole from her.

"I'm just wondering," defense attorney Jerry Berry said, "if next week we'll be here explaining that the fingerprint doesn't exist."

His partner, Michael McDonnell, released a statement from Steven Benson. "This is a terrible ordeal for my family and me but I am confident we have the strength to make it through. I feel overwhelming grief over the loss of my mother and brother and for the suffering of my sister. I am frustrated and angry that I am under arrest for a crime I did not commit. I am anguished for the suffering of my children and my wife and wish desperately that I might soon be reunited with them."

Meanwhile he remained in jail awaiting a grand jury hearing and the judge's ruling on his request for bail. At 5 A.M. every morning his cell door clanged open and half an hour later the breakfast cart rolled by. Benson once asked for poached eggs, which gave the guards a good laugh. Otherwise he was an unremarkable prisoner. He was quiet and kept his cell neat, stacking copies of the *Wall Street Journal* in chronological order. Three times a week, he got to exercise in the yard, and because he was tall, he did reasonably well at basketball. He did better at chess, which he played with an accused drug smuggler. Chubby all his life, he might have been expected to put on pounds because of the starchy diet and his sedentary life. But he began to lose weight.

While Benson may have taken heart that his sister admitted he wasn't being cut out of the will, investigators emphasized that it didn't change their opinion. Deputy Chief Ray Barnett said the will was just one subsection in a six-page affidavit. "It doesn't excite us that much." Barnett felt the threat of losing $2 million in a rewritten will was ample motive for murder.

Besides, investigators couldn't be certain that Margaret Benson had told Carol Lynn her plans. "The only person who can answer that," Barnett said, "is Wayne Kerr."

2

Investigators didn't have to wait long. On September 3, Judge Hayes ruled that Kerr could not claim attorney-client privilege on behalf of a dead person. He had to answer questions about Margaret Benson and her business interests so long as they didn't involve private communications with Steven Benson.

At 9:10 A.M. on the same day, Kerr and his lawyer, William Blackwell, met Lee Hollander, Jerry Brock, and Lieutenant Harold Young. Kerr was sworn in and the prosecutors quickly established that in late June Mrs. Benson had summoned him to Naples. She was anxious about some MasterCard bills Steven had charged to her Dean Witter Active Assets Account. She was also upset that he had bought a new house; she suspected he had used her money. She felt it was urgent for her lawyer to review these matters.

But Kerr told prosecutors, "That... is not unusual because the same events occurred in February..." when Mrs. Benson called him down to monitor Steven's miserable bookkeeping. "Basically, at that point, there was no concern of appropriation of funds. It was just merely a more—more of an accounting."

Margaret often worried that she was pouring capital into Meridian Security Network with no prospect of a turnaround, no chance the company would soon support itself. Kerr felt she didn't comprehend "start up" costs and how long it took to get an operation out of the red. They had been incorporated for less than a year.

Mark Nelson, the vice-president of Meridian Security Network, agreed with Kerr and groused about the corporation's being undercapitalized. Nelson "didn't feel," Kerr said, "as if Margaret had given total commitment to the company in terms of financial resources."

When he came to review the accounts in February, Kerr found "utter chaos." If Steven Benson was embezzling money, he certainly wasn't employing some slick subterfuge. "There were many checks that... the stub of the check was never filled in. There had been no bank reconciliation prepared for me after the meeting. Checks were continually bouncing... We noticed some discrepancies taking place in intercompany transfers."

In one case, a check for $25,000 had been transferred from Meridian Security Network to Steven's account at the Hamilton Bank in Lancaster. Kerr urged Mrs. Benson to get photocopies of the bank statement and check. As so often, however, Margaret "was a great procrastinator." Despite her concern about Steven's sloppy accounting, despite the fact that in February she had learned about Meridian Marketing and wondered whether her son was diverting funds to it, she did nothing. "When I was there," Kerr said, "the interest was hot and everything was getting done, but as soon as I left, it cooled and went into other diversions."

Far from taking action against Steven, she continued to depend on him, and although Kerr didn't remind the prosecutors of this, shortly before his arrival in February, Mrs. Benson had secretly changed her will, cutting out Kerr, not Steven. Just this past June, she had entrusted Steven to write a $25,000 check to cover her estimated quarterly taxes. In the rush of flying off to Europe to watch Scott play tennis, she had forgotten to pay the IRS.

Carol Lynn claimed Steven's new house was "the straw that broke the camel's back," and her mother meant to slap a lien on it, close down the Meridian corporations, and reduce her brother's share of the estate. But while Kerr granted that she was a "loving daughter," he cautioned prosecutors that Carol Lynn "knew very little about Margaret's financial affairs. She would like to have known more, but Margaret, you know, basically did not disclose, to my knowledge, that much to Carol Lynn."

Referring to the telephone conversation when Margaret summoned Kerr to Naples, Lee Hollander asked, "Did she talk to you at all about either cutting Steven out of the will completely or adjusting his share of the take under the will? Was there supposed to be any probate matters discussed?"

KERR: Not in that call or prior to arriving in Naples.
HOLLANDER: Aside from the MasterCard were there any other improprieties?
KERR: No. This was—I guess this was what you call a hunt of sorts. Basically, there was suspicion there and she wanted to find out exactly what the story was.

Jerry Brock asked whether he had ever prepared any gift tax returns for Margaret. The lawyer explained that while he hadn't done any returns, he had advised his client that she needed to conform to a new IRS statute which prevented parents from giving large amounts of money to their children, then writing these gifts off as loans. Mrs. Benson had done this for years.

Lee Hollander asked whether Margaret characterized the funds that flowed to her children as loans because she wanted to avoid taxes or because she simply didn't care to give them anything outright. Kerr slid off the question. "It was essentially, it was—that was her position. She felt that she wanted [to be] repaid." But it was difficult to see how she had any reasonable expectation of being reimbursed when she was virtually their sole source of income.

Jerry Brock burrowed in, asking if there were outstanding loans to Steven. Kerr replied that Margaret kept a schedule of loans that she had floated to all three kids. He said he "had worked on the matter concerning Scott due to some legal problems that arose."

Neither Brock nor Hollander inquired about these "legal problems." Perhaps they already knew what he was referring to. A couple of years back, Scott had hired a lawyer and threatened to sue Margaret, ironically enough, for the same offense she suspected Steven of committing—misappropriation of funds. Scott felt his adopted mother was diverting money from his trust to her personal use. Her defense was that she had skimmed off less than she had given him. The problem was, she had no contracts or written terms for the loans, and she could not legally grab his money just because she had showered expensive gifts on him.

Incapable of comprehending the level of fiscal unreality that existed in the Benson family, the prosecutors continued to search for a rational dollars-and-cents motive.

BROCK: What was the total amount of loans that were represented on that schedule to Steven?

KERR: I don't recall a number.

BROCK: Do you recall approximately?

KERR: Certainly not the two million the papers are quoting.

This had to have stung, since it was the investigators and prosecutors who had force-fed the press Carol Lynn's claim about $2 million.

Kerr went on to say it was difficult to estimate what Steven owed his mother since "I think that some of that, in all fairness, should not have been attributed to him." In other words, while Steven arrogated her money to his purposes, Mrs. Benson sometimes recorded legitimate business losses as personal loans to her son.

Kerr conceded that he had advised Margaret to obtain notes on the loans she had extended to Steven. They had talked about this as late as July 7. But "I think she was frustrated in putting all these numbers down on paper and seeing what amounts were there." He assured Brock that Steven was not present during this discussion.

Then the attorney described driving to Fort Myers with Margaret and visiting the Meridian Marketing office. Her principal concern, he said, was whether her money was bankrolling a company she didn't own. "She ended up being responsible for a lot of these obligations that were entered into by her children, and she didn't want this to happen in this case."

Her feelings about Steven's new house were even more emphatic. Having glimpsed it from the Porsche, she angrily wondered where he had gotten the down payment. She thought it had to be her money and insisted Kerr do something to recover it. But he explained it wasn't unusual for Margaret to "go off uncocked." "You have to understand that Margaret gets into tirades. She is very eccentric and she goes hot and cold very easily and she was making statements that basically she wanted to own that house. She wanted me to prepare whatever documents were necessary to place liens or, in fact, maybe a second mortgage against the mortgage to cover the debts that she felt Steven owed her."

HOLLANDER: How did she know that any of her money went into the house?
KERR: She didn't know it.

Jerry Brock observed, "She was giving you instructions to do things that you didn't know exactly how you were going to go about accomplishing?"

KERR: That's right, and quite frankly, I—I didn't really—I listened to her—it is the typical client. They have their moments and then you listen to them and they go back and do something else anyway. I was playing a good listener.
HOLLANDER: Was there any discussion about anything else she wanted done besides putting a lien on the house?
KERR: She made statements to me concerning some will provisions...
Well, our discussion was, basically, in her tirade of anger, she had made the statement to me that she had changed her thinking concerning Steven with regard to the will and that maybe he wasn't treating her as a mother. And basically, she would never get to see the grandchildren because Steven's wife sorta kept them away and she said her thinking was changing concerning—I think in a moment of anger she said she was thinking of disinheriting him and then, of course, I said, "Well,

maybe the better route would be to get an accounting for these loans and treat those as an advancement against his share and that would be a more equitable way of handling it."

She just really didn't say anything, but I knew she was thinking and there was no final decision made, but certainly it was part of our conversation.

Hollander then brought up the De Loach will. He wanted Kerr's opinion of how and why the second will altered the first. But perhaps misunderstanding the question or presuming they knew more than they did, the fidgety attorney mentioned a third will.

KERR: She had asked me to draft a will in December of '84, had changed some provisions from the will that you saw, or the first will.

HOLLANDER: The first will that you had done?

KERR: Right. And basically, they were concerning issues pertaining to spreading out payments with regard to Steven and also with regard to Scott.

HOLLANDER: Why them and not Carol Lynn?

KERR: I don't know. I think it was just that she thought Carol Lynn was maybe a better money manager.

HOLLANDER: Did you ever draft that, the requested changes?

KERR: Yes, I have.

HOLLANDER: Was that ever formally signed?

KERR: Not to my knowledge. I had it sent down to her and she had read it and—in fact, it was I would say sometime in December and I had questioned her in June and she said, well, she had reviewed it and her mind wasn't made up as to what she wanted to do and as a result she didn't want to do anything at that point.

This third, unsigned will would later prove explosive. But even back on September 3, it showed that Margaret Benson was a volatile and eccentric lady prone to make snap decisions that she came to regret or forget. If Steven was "a CPA's nightmare," Mrs. Benson was a lawyer's nightmare, a client who couldn't make up her mind.

Having been told that no conclusion had been reached about disinheriting Steven, Hollander pressed the other point that Harold Young had emphasized in the affidavit for the arrest warrant.

HOLLANDER: Was there any question about either shutting down Meridian Security and/or any of the other companies and/or removing Steven Benson from those companies?

KERR: Yes. There were discussions in terms of what the alternatives were.

Kerr had outlined three options for his client—close the business; replace Steven with Vice-President Mark Nelson; or bring in a new man to head up the operation. But he repeated that these "were alternatives and it is important to note that no decision had been made."

Hollander tried to cut to the heart of the matter.

HOLLANDER: To your sense of where she was, did she feel that Steven was ripping her off, for lack of a better term?

KERR: Well I think she felt somewhat that. I think she had those feelings. I don't think they were—but I think she had that sense about all her children too.

Harold Young tried to pin Kerr down. "Your own professional opinion, reviewing the accounting of the books and stuff, do you think he was ripping her off?"

KERR: Well, quite frankly, I did not really get into the—the last time I had been down I really didn't have an opportunity to . . . determine whether or not that was occurring.

Part of the problem, he explained, was that Steven had the books and when Kerr finally got a look at them, there were still checks missing and no deposits listed and he said, "I can't work with this." Margaret demanded that Steven put the books in order and bring them down early the next morning, July 9.

As Kerr described the birthday dinner, he indicated that Carol Lynn's protective attitude toward her mother did not preclude her having interests of her own.

Hollander asked whether Mrs. Benson, in discussing the alternatives for her business, had sought Carol Lynn's advice.

KERR: No, but I think Carol Lynn injected her advice.

HOLLANDER: What was her advice?

KERR: If I recall this—well, I think Carol Lynn was quite upset by the fact that Steven had a nice house, tennis courts, swimming pool. I mean, to the point of being almost envious, that is.

And in terms of the business, I think she was expressing concern of putting it in the hands of Mark Nelson... This was about it. I think she was more angry about the fact that Steven had this nice big house and she didn't.

.   .   .   .

HOLLANDER: Did Margaret at that dinner repeat her alternative of disinheriting.
KERR: No. She did not.

Summarizing the discussions, Kerr again stressed "a lot of this was preliminary and I think she was waiting to see what my investigation would reveal." To date, they had spotted "symptoms of a problem; we never really determined a problem."

Hollander posed a question that had been put to Kerr during the first interrogation. Did Carol Lynn receive a phone call the night before the murders? The answer was the same as last time.

KERR: I don't recall a telephone call. I know that she was there with us and then went somewhere and—but I don't recall a specific phone call.
HOLLANDER: Do you recall her coming in and saying, "Guess who just called," or any discussion about going to stake out the area the next day?
KERR: I don't recall that. I really don't.

Without confirmation from Kerr, the prosecutors had only Carol Lynn's word that there had been a call. They had no way of verifying that Steven had volunteered to help her and that he wanted Scott to come too. For all they could prove, this had been a long-standing plan arranged by Margaret. Steven could even turn around and claim that Carol Lynn had called him to set it up. Or he could claim that Scott insisted on coming along.

Wayne Kerr's interview contained much that might have given the State Attorney's office a long pause. Instead, they took their case to the grand jury just two days later. Although the proceedings were secret, the Naples *Daily News* offered a synopsis of the evidence. "Investigators claim Kerr had been summoned to Naples by Margaret Benson after she learned Steven Benson had taken some $2 million from her accounts without her permission. Margaret Benson intended to cut Steven out of her will and to remove him from positions in companies she owned, according to detectives."

On Friday, September 6, Carol Lynn Kendall, escorted by Mike Koors, drove up to the courthouse in an unmarked sheriff's car. Looking elegant and self-possessed despite the livid burns on the right side of her face and the bandage over her right ear, she swept past the press wearing a blue dress, a broad-brimmed white hat, and a single strand of pearls. She entered the jury room at 8:55 A.M. and emerged at 9:35 A.M. still refusing to speak to reporters.

Two hours later, the grand jury returned a nine-count indictment against her brother. Nothing revealed to the public suggested that a shred of evidence against Benson had changed since his arrest on August 22.

On September 9, there was a hearing at which his defense attorneys petitioned the court to grant bond for Steven. The prosecutors urged that it be denied, and to buttress their case they filed more affidavits, including a transcript of Carol Lynn's interview. There was no mention that some of her statements had since been contradicted by Kerr.

Another affidavit maintained that ATF agents believed the bombs had been made of foot-long segments of nipple pipe filled with smokeless black powder set off by an electronic firing device. The detonator was "a circuit-type board (which) appeared to be of a type used in alarm systems." The affidavit pointed out that Benson's business was installing burglar alarms.

In fact, ATF explosives specialist Albert Gleason did not know what had triggered the bombs and although he later gave an opinion, he admitted in two sworn statements and again at the trial that he could not say with certainty what had served as the initiating device.

Michael McDonnell argued that the affidavits submitted by the prosecution were no more than hearsay and did not meet Florida Supreme Court standards for denying bond. Citing a precedent set in 1916, he claimed a defendant couldn't be held without bail unless the State had more evidence than needed to convict him. He emphasized that any alleged purchase of pipe by Benson did not directly link him to the bombs.

Judge Hayes responded, "It would appear on first blush" there was evidence linking Benson to the murders. But before he issued a ruling he wanted to study the affidavits, review the law, and read a background report on the defendant.

While the judge deliberated, Steven Benson was arraigned and pleaded not guilty to all charges. The trial was scheduled for November 13, but everybody expected a postponement.

On September 13, Judge Hugh Hayes denied bail for Steven Benson. He ruled that a 1980 case, while not specifically overturning the 1916 precedent, indicated a defendant could be held if the State showed that the "proof of guilt is evident and the presumption of guilt great." Hayes found that the prosecution had met its burden.

The press seemed to agree. The Lancaster *Intelligencer-Journal* went so far as to run an editorial praising Judge Hayes for keeping the defendant behind bars.

Chapter 13

For the next ten months, the law firm of McDonnell and Berry filed motions and scrambled to find money to mount an investigation, locate witnesses, and take depositions. Twice Michael McDonnell appealed Judge Hayes's decision not to allow bail and twice a higher court upheld Hayes.

Then, in late October, he filed a motion stating that the prosecution did not have enough evidence to hold Benson. "Virtually all the allegations of the affidavit in support of the arrest warrant and in support of the search warrant are false or misleading."

The same day he filed a second motion asking for a preliminary hearing to force the prosecutors to produce the evidence they claimed they had against Benson. "The defendant is currently incarcerated without conditions for pre-trial release because there is purportedly sufficient evidence to hold him," McDonnell told Judge Hayes. "If there is sufficient evidence, then the state should present it and make it available for inspection. If not, this defendant should be discharged from custody."

Prosecutors replied that much evidence was still in the hands of ATF agents in Atlanta and Washington. Judge Hayes denied both of McDonnell's motions.

In November Wayne Kerr gave an interview to the Lancaster *New Era* in which he took pains to explain that he had agonized over his initial refusal to answer investigators' questions. But he believed that professional ethics prevented him from divulging private communications with Mrs. Benson before he was ordered to do so by the court. "If I had been completely frank with police, I would have been sued and probably lost my license."

He went on to deny unequivocally that Mrs. Benson summoned

him to Naples to write Steven out of the will. "If I was, wouldn't you think a person would bring the will with him?"

He also doubted Carol Lynn's charge that her brother had embezzled over $2 million. "If it is true, someone has information that I didn't have."

In an interview given to a local magazine, *Neapolitan*, shortly after the murders, but not published for more than a year, Kerr took stronger exception to Carol Lynn's claim that he or Mrs. Benson had discovered Steven was stealing. "I handled her books for several years and never saw any evidence of him stealing from her. So I don't know how she [Carol Lynn] could have found out about something like that on her own."

On September 20, Carol Lynn met Steven face to face for the first time since the murders. Subpoenaed by the defense, she arrived at the State Attorney's office to give a deposition and, entering a conference room, discovered that her brother was going to be present during the interview. Two policemen stood guard over him.

As Rich Cirace described the scene, Steven never spoke to his sister, never expressed sorrow at what had happened, never asked to go off the record and declare his innocence to her. His lack of emotion, Cirace said, left Carol Lynn feeling extremely uncomfortable.

But even a more demonstrative and extroverted person than Steven would have found it difficult to know what to say under the circumstances to a woman who had spent hours spilling out accusations against him and his wife—accusations that could put him in the electric chair.

Early in the deposition, Michael McDonnell inquired about times in her life when Carol Lynn had been hospitalized. He knew she was Scott's mother and wanted to see if she would admit it. Naturally, if she didn't, he would have used this to impeach her credibility at the trial. But she said she had gone to Mercy Hospital in Baltimore when she gave birth to Scott. McDonnell didn't press the issue further.

Yet after she acknowledged Scott was her child, she continued to call him "my brother." Not once did she refer to him as "my son." This made for some jarring exchanges. McDonnell asked, "Had you learned of your . . . son's death at that time?" She replied, "When I saw my brother's body, there was something about it that I just knew that he was dead." At the trial, she unfailingly referred to Scott as "my son."

Unlike her long and, at times, bantering responses with Graham and Nowicki, she was curt with McDonnell. She volunteered nothing, answered in monosyllables whenever possible, and suddenly developed a mania for definitions.

McDONNELL: On each of these trips [to Naples], have you spoken to the police about the case?

CAROL LYNN: Would you please define what you mean by spoken about?

McDONNELL: Discussed the facts. Not the procedure, the facts.

CAROL LYNN: Would you define discuss, please?

McDONNELL: Yes, ma'am, be happy to. Wherein you made any verbal comments regarding the facts of the case as you know them.

CAROL LYNN: Are you saying they asked a question and I gave an answer?

McDONNELL: Either that or where you volunteered statements without being asked a question.

CAROL LYNN: Well, I want either/or.

McDONNELL: Either one, please.

CAROL LYNN: No, could you—

McDONNELL: Either one, ma'am. Did either one of these things happen?

CAROL LYNN: Yes.

McDONNELL: Which one?

CAROL LYNN: I was asked a question and I gave an answer.

McDONNELL: On each visit to Florida did that occur?

CAROL LYNN: Yes.

McDONNELL: Who asked questions?

CAROL LYNN: Various people.

It took five more pages of this teeth-pulling to establish which officers interviewed her.

In spite of the succinctness of her replies, there were conflicts between this and her previous statements.

After she described throwing herself out of the Suburban and rolling on the ground to extinguish the flames, McDonnell asked what she did when she saw Steven. She said, "I called for help."

But she had not been so sure of this before. She told Graham and Nowicki, "I think before I even saw him I was yelling for help." Then she added, "I think I called for him to help me." Now she claimed to be positive.

While she was calling for help, she told McDonnell, Steven "was standing perfectly still, faced in the direction of myself and the auto-mobile." After a brief interval, "Steven suddenly reacted and his body moved and his eyes opened up and his mouth kind of went open. And he said 'Oh my God, my God,' and turned around to-wards his left and headed back for the direction of where the front door is." At most, she would grant that Steven uttered "Oh my God, oh my God in a slightly raised tone of voice."

This differed drastically from her vivid evocation of the scene two months ago when she said, "I saw Steven come out of the house and stop on the driveway, and he was—he looked just terrified. And—and it was almost like he was going mad."

Memory of the incident back then had made her so emotional the investigators had to break off the interview. When they resumed, over an hour later, she had again said, "Steven just had a look of absolute horror on his face, like the...the...the world had just blown up." And he hadn't "headed" toward the direction of the front door. She told Graham and Nowicki "he ran back into the house." He went there "to get help," she added.

But with McDonnell she minimized every gesture, muted every sound.

She did acknowledge, however, that when she next noticed Ste-ven he was running around in "an agitated manner...throwing his arms about and his body." She said she had known people to act this way only on television "when you see pictures of other bombings or war scenes." Pictures, for example, of "Viet Nam or things from Beirut, when you see people around disaster."

On another matter her memory dramatically improved and she described an incident which she had not mentioned to Officer Smith the day of the murders or to Graham and Nowicki during her 136-page interview. Ten weeks after the fact, she claimed that during Kerr's visit to the Naples Community Hospital, the attorney "asked me if I thought the things that happened in the morning [of July 9] were strange, and he asked me—I can't phrase this exactly word for word, but he asked me if in view of the strange things that went on in the morning, had it possibly occurred to me that my brother might be involved."

"Did he say what he meant by strange things?" McDonnell asked.

"I don't remember if he elaborated," she said. "I remember knowing, though—I think he did say regarding his being gone so long. I don't remember exactly whether he delineated everything. I do remember that I started thinking myself about—and then, later on, I don't really remember what else we discussed."

Wayne Kerr had a diametrically opposed memory of this episode. In a personal interview, he said it was Carol Lynn, not he, who had raised the question about her brother's involvement. Kerr said Carol Lynn bluntly asked, "Do you think Steven did it?"

According to Kerr, he responded, "I think there were a lot of strange things going on, but I'm not sure what they add up to."

Kerr said Carol Lynn then declared, "Even if he did do it, I don't think I would testify against him."

Contrary to her earlier statement, Carol Lynn now recalled clearly what Steven had done with the keys to the Suburban. "He handed Scott the keys in through the window." She had twice conceded to Graham and Nowicki that she wasn't positive about this; he might have passed them from the backseat to the front.

But regarding Steven's trip to the convenience store she was vague about the length of time he was gone. She couldn't offer any better estimate than, "Longer than five or ten minutes."

2

There was no better proof of the pervasiveness of rumors and erroneous press reports than the frequency with which Benson family acquaintances and potential witnesses repeated to the police unsupported allegations that the police themselves had leaked.

In Lancaster, Ed West, a hairdresser and father of Tom West, who was later killed, gave a statement which didn't differ much from dozens of others that set off a deafening echo around the case. Although West's testimony was a little livelier and more loquacious, it demonstrated the same quality of evidence that was recycled everywhere from grocery store tabloids to the *New York Times*.

Of Margaret Benson, West said: "... she was like a princess. She was on my style. She liked to talk, very conservative, and we chatted back and forth...And when Margaret came in, she always had a long fur coat on."

Q. And this is to your beauty shop that you—
A. Yeah, Rosa Beauty Salon.
Q. Do you still own that?

A. No, I had to get out of that. Hairspray is the worst thing for my lungs. So the doctor said "Get the hell out," and I did.

Q. What time period are we talking about, when she would come in and you'd—

A. Oh, it'd be in the morning, afternoon, never was—it was never a set date.

Q. What year are we talking about here?

A. Oh, speaking of '82, '83.

Q. When did you sell the shop?

A. I just sold it a year and three months, and the guy burnt it down and then committed suicide after a year and three months . . . They all knew I dated her . . . I used to take her to Host Farm, which you could see a show and we'd have dinner . . .

. . . .

Well, anyway, every time Margaret would come out—I'm speaking of Margaret Benson when I say Margaret, 'cause I called her Margaret. She called me Ed. I took her to Host Farm. I took her to the Corral, and I took her to Stokley's one time . . .

But mostly at the Host—I introduced her to the maitre d' at the Host Farm and the food and beverage man. And she said, "Ed, you know a lot of people." And I said, "Well, this is the only place I hang out," if you want class, you eat in class. And this is what we did. And we just talked and nothin'. I mean she'd have maybe one wine and that was it and we had dinner. And we just chat, chat, chat.

. . . .

Q. How many times did you date Margaret?

A. Four.

Q. Four times?

A. Four times. It wasn't regular . . . She had nobody to fall back on. You know, you can't fall back on card-club people, the exotic women you know. I mean who was going to protect her?

The only thing she had in protection was Steve which she was afraid of—I mean now, let's face it. He'd keep on her . . . Jesus, mother of John, how much money can you give this kid? Everything he touched he—he just blew it. He figured, what the hell, he's the only son; I could bleed her to death.

Q. What makes you believe she was afraid of him?

A. Well, the simple reason is, in my case I'm alone, right? I've got a son who'd rob me blind. Long as I give him money, he's all right. Soon as I don't, he'll forge checks on me.

In fact, he's moving out. I got a two bedroom—I told him to move out. I got diamonds. I got watches, and I've got a hundred suits. And you know I was a well-dressed man. I mean I'm not a pauper or nothing else. I got enough money to live on, and I was one of the best-dressed men in Lancaster. I don't care what anybody says, and I had the cleanest car in town.

Everybody said that when West is down . . . to Host Farm his car was immaculate. Nobody smokes, uses my ashtray. And I figured Margaret didn't smoke. So the last meeting we had she always was busy, busy, busy.

I said, "Margaret, before you shut that Caddy off," I said, "give me the keys. I'll run it over to the car wash. I'll get it washed. Time you get your hair done, the car will be clean. How about a sandwich, you buyin'?" She said, "Yeah." So she'd drive me over to Treadway. We had a sandwich and a cup of coffee. And she was a little bit on the shaky side . . . So, sittin' there at the Treadway, and I can recall Earl Hess was with his wife. And I introduced Earl Hess to Mrs. Benson.

And he said, "Tomorrow I'm going to get a pacemaker put in my heart," he said. And by Jesus Christ, didn't he die the next day. That's how I can remember the day we were there because Hess's, Earl Hess is in the egg business. I couldn't believe he died. Sons took over the business.

·　·　·　·　·　·　·　·　·　·　·　·

So the last time I had her at the Treadway we had a sandwich, and she was little on the nervous side. "Margaret," I said—she said, "Ed would you come down," [to Naples] she said. "Here's my address; I'll be in the phone book." I said, "I'd be glad to."

The Lord punished me and I got sick and I wound up down in Mercy General Hospital. And I had prostate trouble at that time, I didn't know what the hell I had. So, I never did get hold of her because I was sick, and I'm still sick. I quit smokin', sex; and everything else went wrong. I gave up all this stuff. I said it's better I should have smoked, I wasn't sick at all. But now that I quit everything, I'm layin' in the hospital all the time.

So, she—she put her hand on mine and she said, "Ed, I'm just afraid." I said, "What," I said—she says, "If I don't give it"—she's talkin' about givin' Steve money for the houses and this and that. She said, "I'm afraid." I said, "Afraid of what, Steve?" And, yeah, she says, "If I don't give it to him, I don't know what will happen."

I said, "Margaret, don't feel that bad." I said, "If I get down there," I said, "you need is a back-up, you need is a man, somebody that 'ya could fall back instead of a woman." What the hell could a woman do? A man, you know, she's got a man around, and you know I'm no pushover. And she said, "Would you please come down?"

·　·　·　·　·　·　·　·　·　·　·　·

So when all this happened [the murders] I couldn't write—shit, I couldn't write for prunes. I sent a card to Naples, and I also sent another card to Boston's Burn Hospital to Carol which she was a princess too.

She was beautiful, I mean no gettin' away. She's a little on the nervous side 'cause runnin' back to Boston and here and seein' her mother, and I think she was a little afraid of Steve too.

Q. When Margaret said she was afraid, did she say what she meant by that?

A. Well, she meant that—you know, she don't give him any money, what would he do?

.   .   .   .

Q. Did she say that?

A. No, she didn't say that, but this is what I was thinkin' because suppose I cut you—like I cut my son off, he got no more use for me, right? I fear the kid.

Q. But Margaret didn't specifically say why she feared or what she—

A. She just feared that if she didn't give him any money, somethin' may happen to her she don't know.

Q. Did she say that, something may happen to her?

A. Yeah, she said she—I don't know, what would I do if I don't give him any money. I'm just afraid something would happen, because Christ Almighty, he's taken two million dollars, taken her—

.   .   .   .

Q. Did, ah, but—but she didn't say anything specifically?

A. She—the only thing she said, she was afraid of him.

.   .   .   .

And then I went to the funeral here, and all the pallbearers thought he did it. He sat in front of his mother's casket which cost eight thousand four hundred, and Scott—well, Scott received—I believe Scott received a Lotus on his twenty-first birthday.

Now Steve didn't have anything. Everything he—went into that burglar alarm system. He just, well, wanted to be the boss. And Margaret says, "No way." I said to Margaret, "If he wants to go in there, hold the reins." I told her "just be the president. Give him his money; maybe he can make it." Blew it. After he killed her everything folded.

.   .   .   .

Now, I followed this story from end to end. And I predicted everybody said it here, I said, "How can an attorney walk into Reynolds and say, "Give me a million dollars worth of negotiable securities" because he already told Steve, "You're out of the will." Right?

Now this—

Q. How do you know he told Steve he was out of the will?

A. It was in the paper.

Q. Oh, okay.

A. Right?

Q. You don't have any personal knowledge of that?

A. No, I but mean, common sense, an attorney doesn't walk in and say,

"Give me a million dollars worth of," and Reynolds says, "Wait a minute, this case is not even solved, it's a murder"—

Q. Did Margaret ever indicate that she was going to cut him off or—

A. No, she just said, "What can I do?" I said, "Just cut him off," I said. She said, "Ed, I'm afraid." I said, "Margaret, you're spending money like it's water," and I didn't think she had that kind of money, so help me God.

She had big diamonds. I mean she had big rubies, I mean gems. She was well-dressed, and I'm well-dressed too. I mean, I'm no piker. I've got a hundred suits, and I can show you them right here. I don't know when the hell I'm gonna' wear them. But I was well-dressed, and she was well-dressed, and we just clicked.

.   .   .   .

I mean Carol said that she believes he is guilty and he was—and she was afraid of him. I told the Atlantic paper that when I laid in the hospital.

I said, "There's no way in hell," when he walked out of the funeral parlor. He had his head stuck between his legs. I said, "Buddy, I'll bet you a thousand to one, and I'm not a gambler, that if you didn't kill your mother"—all indications, the caps, the trailer, Kerr was at the—they confiscated all the books and everything else; maybe he jockeyed the books. I don't know, but he had a lot of control of her money and everything else.

.   .   .   .

Q. Was—there's no other information that you have from talking to Margaret specifically that would go to the point that she was afraid of him?

A. She was afraid of him. She was absolutely afraid of him. She touched my hand, she said, "Ed, I know how you feel," she said, "I have nobody to stand behind me, a man. I can't depend on the"—

Q. Other than that one time when she actually verbally acknowledged that—

A. Only told me that at the Treadway.

.   .   .   .

Q. Did you ever meet Steven?

A. No, I never met him until I seen him at the, ah—

Q. At the funeral?

A. But I even said to her, I said, "What does Steven do for you? He don't cut the grass. He don't do this; he don't do that. What the hell does he do?" I mean you got an only son and your mother's rich, you know; you gotta help her.

Hell, he never did a damn thing. He wouldn't—hell, the damn grass was from here to there to get up them seven steps at that warehouse. Why, we had to cut that sucker down to find the steps. But Steve never did nothin'. And I still say, and I'll be a God-damn witness to the fact because he was a nut as far as I was concerned.

3

Carl Westman, the personal representative of the Benson estate, filed a motion to force Kim Beegle to return Buck, the mixed breed Bouvier and German shepherd she had taken home with her the day of the murders.

Pleading that the big bristly-haired attack dog was like Scott's and her baby, Kim pleaded to keep it. But Carol Lynn claimed Scott had promised the dog to her son Travis.

When Kim Beegle refused to relinquish the dog, the estate asked the court to put Buck under a $5,000 bond pending a resolution of the matter. Having already incurred $300 in lawyer's bills, Kim couldn't afford to post bond or continue to fight to keep the dog.

The family took Buck and left him with Ruby Caston, the black maid. He escaped and ran back to Kim. But Carol Lynn demanded he be returned.

Meanwhile, Carol Lynn was receiving offers for the exclusive rights to her story, which the Boston *Herald* characterized as "too hot to cool down." In an article entitled BENSON HEIRESS MULLS SELLING "HOT" BIO-FLICK, the *Herald* reported that Rick Cirace had been contacted by I.S.I. Productions of London, the group that did *Sophie's Choice* and *The Elephant Man*. Cirace said that Carol Lynn, identified once again as heiress to the Benson & Hedges fortune, was considering the deal. "We're in the process of negotiation."

"She's had a remarkable recovery," Cirace added. "Her spirits are very good." She was said to be shopping for a new house in Chestnut Hill.

"Nothing," the Boston *Herald* concluded, "absolutely nothing has stirred the retirement community [of Naples] like this since the threat to cut Social Security."

Cirace kept in touch with producers, directors, and writers who had expressed an interest, and he sent updated memos about the case to theatrical agencies. But he found it hard to control this "hot bio-flick" and fend off people who didn't care to pay for his client's participation. Eliot Geisinger, who produced the movie *The Amityville Horror*, began to package an independent project based on the Benson pipe bomb murders.

• • •

As courthouse insiders predicted, the trial was postponed from November 13 until January 19. The prosecution had subpoenaed a total of eighty-three witnesses, and the defense needed time to depose them. It also needed to examine the evidence, much of which the State had still not made available. More than anything, however, the defense needed money.

Although Benson's wife and children lived on the proceeds of the $100,000 trust arranged through the estate, Steven had substantial personal debts. He owed over $60,000 to four lawyers who had handled civil litigation in Pennsylvania and Florida. This did not include costs he had incurred fighting the criminal charges.

Michael McDonnell and Jerry Berry were working on a contingency basis, and their only hope of payment was to win the case and have Steven declared innocent of all criminal and civil charges. But that figured to be an uphill battle lasting several years. Meanwhile, they couldn't pay private investigators, court reporters, expert witnesses, typists, and consultants out of their own pockets.

With Mrs. Benson's fortune frozen and the interests of all other claimants upon the estate fiercely protected by a phalanx of lawyers —Steven's children and Scott's "possible" children had been assigned court-appointed representatives—Steven had one last recourse, Harry Hitchcock.

Although his grandfather had not had any direct contact with him since his arrest, the silver-haired patriarch had sent emissaries. Several evangelists visited the jail, claiming they came at Hitchcock's suggestion. They asked if Benson accepted Jesus Christ as his personal savior. Shortly thereafter, a doctor showed up and explained he was a family friend who had retired to Naples. Harry had asked him to check on Steven.

Benson and his attorneys viewed these events with mixed emotions. While they got the impression these people wanted Steven to confess and beg for mercy, they thought this might also signal a willingness on Hitchcock's part to listen to another side of the story. McDonnell took a chance and telephoned Lancaster and explained that if Harry were truly concerned about his grandson he should consider helping him.

It was hard to read any reaction long distance, but at least Hitchcock hadn't cut off the conversation. Sufficiently encouraged, McDonnell wrote a letter.

Dear Mr. Hitchcock,

I very much appreciate having had the opportunity to speak with you on the phone. Please accept my deepest sympathies for the tragedy that has befallen you and your family.

I wish, if I may, to follow up on some of the subjects we discussed on the phone. Of prime importance, is the fact that we are attempting to exonerate Steven with both hands tied behind our backs. We have little or no resources available to investigate the matter, nor to analyze scientifically the available data.

In our conversation, you indicated that the evidence was overwhelming against Steven. Mr. Hitchcock, let me assure you that in my 15 years as a trial lawyer I have never seen a weaker case. If we were to assume that everything in the newspapers were true, then, indeed, we might conclude that the evidence was overwhelming. But the newspaper accounts are false. One of the most formidable tasks ahead of me is to cut through the rumor and innuendo that has been generated by unthinking people and the media.

If you wish to see the true, so-called, evidence that the prosecutor claims involves Steven in this crime, I will be happy to share it with you. I will also be happy to share with you certain results of our investigations that we have so far, which refute the prosecutor's contentions.

I do not wish to detail all of these matters in this letter for obvious reasons. However, I am anxious to come to Lancaster and meet with you and discuss any aspect of the case you would care to discuss.

It seems to me, Mr. Hitchcock, that this is a two part tragedy. We cannot erase the loss of your family members or the injuries to Carol Lynn. On the other hand, it is within our power to establish Steven's innocence and thereby eliminate the greatest irony and the second part of the tragedy. To that end, I am reiterating my request to you for assistance in Steven's defense. I am not asking you for a penny in attorney's fees. What I desperately need are monies to finance investigation. If you would consider helping us, I feel the following benefits will result to you:

1. You will be helping in eliminating uncertainty. If Steven were convicted because we did not have the resources in the face of unlimited resources of the prosecutor, you and I will never know for certain if the conviction was a just one.

2. If Steven's innocence is established, as I expect it to be, then you will have the comforting knowledge that you stood by him during his time of need.

3. You will have been instrumental in establishing that these acts were committed by a third person and, perhaps, even instrumental in bringing that person to justice.

I am not asking you to side with Steven against your loved ones. Rather, I am asking you to remain neutral. The entire power of federal agencies and the State of Florida is being brought to bear on this case. They need no further assistance in their attempts to convict Steven.

It seems to me that a fair and impartial jury will decide these facts, but that God must and will be the ultimate judge of this case. Indeed, it seems that God will judge us all in the way we handle ourselves and I cannot help but feel that He would approve of your lending assistance in the manner requested. If Steven is innocent, as I believe he is, then we will all have to face our consciences if we do not help him.

I am reminded of Job 22:13. "How doth God know? Can He judge through the dark cloud?" There has been a dark cloud cast over Steven in this case and it is my job to dispel it. To do that, I need your help.

I hope you will read Chapter 37 of Genesis telling the story of Joseph and his coat of many colors. There is a clear message there warning of the unreliability of appearance and circumstance. I will await your response and hope that you will meet with me at the earliest possible time.

McDonnell waited more than a month and when Harry Hitchcock was unwilling to donate or loan any funds for his grandson's defense, the attorney filed a motion stating Steven Benson to be "indigent and insolvent in that he is unable to pay for costs of investigation, discovery or trial preparation." He asked Judge Hayes to order the county to pay Benson's legal expenses.

A few days later, McDonnell filed another motion requesting a change of venue. Claiming that extensive media coverage had ruined any chance of a fair trial in Naples, he asked that it be moved to a different circuit in the state.

On December 2, Judge Hayes ruled that Steven Benson was "partially" indigent and that the county should start paying for his defense. At the same time, he ruled against a change of venue, declaring that the trial would be held in Collier County unless it proved to be impossible to seat an impartial jury.

When McDonnell and Berry submitted a list of expenses, county officials protested. While they didn't deny that Benson was cut off from his mother's millions and couldn't very well earn money in jail, they raised a number of technical objections about receipts and proper documentation, and asserted that they shouldn't be held for any bills incurred before Steven had been declared indigent.

Regardless of how framed their objections, the unavoidable inference was that public opinion simply wouldn't permit the county to pick up the tab for a murder suspect who was said to have stolen $2 million and who stood to inherit millions more if found innocent. Any elected official who ruled in Benson's favor was apt to find himself out of a job the next time the voters went to the polls.

Judge Hayes scheduled a hearing on the matter for January 13, a day before the trial was due to start. McDonnell requested another delay. Prosecutors joined in the request. It was granted.

Judge Hayes, who from the first had reserved the right to reverse himself, then ruled that Steven wasn't indigent. Or rather, Hayes declared that Benson hadn't been indigent before December 2 and he wouldn't be indigent after January 13. Collier County would assume responsibility only for expenses incurred during a six-week period.

The judge based his ruling on the $100,000 distribution from the estate in August. Although signed documents indicated that Benson couldn't use the money for his defense and that Carl Westman agreed to the arrangement only on the strict understanding that it go to Steven's children, Hayes decreed that it was an asset to Benson. It "did go and does belong to Mr. Benson. The money is and was his." Thus, the judge concluded, he was not indigent.

Furthermore, Hayes said that application of the Florida Slayer's Statute was premature. Since Steven hadn't been found guilty in any criminal or civil action, he couldn't be shut off from his inheritance. As far as the judge was concerned, Benson was free to spend the $100,000 as he pleased and likewise free to request further advances from the estate.

Theoretically, this solved his problems. But practically speaking, nothing changed. Caught in a Catch-22 concocted by Franz Kafka, Steven Benson was still penniless, still unable to pay for his defense, yet also unable to obtain funds from the county. Carl Westman respectfully but firmly disagreed with the judge's reading of the law and refused to release money to Steven.

Others weren't gracious enough to grant that Hayes had misread the law. They believed he had reversed his decision for political reasons. The judge, they said, had ambitions and wasn't about to jeopardize them with an unpopular decision. In the cynical climate of opinion that was building around the Benson case everybody was assumed to have ulterior motives.

On January 20, Michael McDonnell moved that the murder charges against his client be dropped. Under the United States judicial system a defendant had a right to a lawyer and, according to Supreme Court decisions, if he couldn't afford to hire legal representation, the state had to provide it. Since Steven couldn't afford a defense and the State wouldn't pay for it, he should be freed.

Judge Hayes again told Benson's lawyers to file a petition for a partial distribution from Mrs. Benson's estate. Shortly thereafter, Hayes issued a gag order, instructing attorneys for the defense and the prosecution to quit talking about the case with journalists. He specifically forbade them to discuss plea bargaining, confessions, evidence, the identity of witnesses and their character or criminal records.

Considering how little investigative reporting had been done about the Benson murders, it was surprising that journalists became so exercised over the judge's order. They protested, they ran commentaries about the First Amendment and freedom of the press, and they filed motions in the Second District Court of Appeals to strike down the gag rule. Then they recycled the same stories, full of the same false and misleading information, which they had been running for months.

Meanwhile, Steven Benson petitioned Carl Westman to pay over to him $244,974.39, to be charged against his share of his inheritance. He attached an Amended Schedule which reflected his current debts and the costs of trial preparation. The anticipated bills for his defense totaled $105,000, and the bulk of this was for investigators, experts, and analysts.

On March 4, Judge Hayes ruled in probate court that Benson had a right to the money. He stated that if representatives of the Benson estate had wanted to stop Steven from gaining access to his mother's fortune, they should have brought civil action against him.

The decision unleashed a blizzard of paper. Within two days letters, appeals for a rehearing, petitions for instructions and for a stay piled up on Hayes's desk. Carl Westman pointed out that he had to "preserve estate assets for those persons ultimately determined to be estate beneficiaries and to distribute the estate assets to them in accordance with Florida law."

If the judge's interpretation of the Slayer's Statute meant that a beneficiary charged with the murders could invade estate assets so long as no other interested party took civil action, then Steven Benson should be denied the money. Carol Lynn Kendall had now taken such action.

If, on the other hand, Hayes meant a defendant charged with murder was entitled to money up to the time he was convicted in criminal or civil court, then Westman asked the judge to reconsider his decision. Under such an interpretation, a man charged with murder could dissipate a substantial portion of an estate before his criminal and civil trials were completed. This would not only deprive rightful beneficiaries of their shares, but contradict Florida law that stated that a killer "is not entitled to any benefits."

Westman proposed what sounded like a reasonable solution. Hayes could declare Benson indigent and order Collier County to pick up his trial expenses with the clear and secure agreement that the county would be repaid if Steven were ultimately found innocent. But the judge didn't buy this. He stuck by his ruling.

Three weeks before the rescheduled trial was supposed to start, defense attorneys and county officials, Steven and Carol Lynn, Judge Hayes and Carl Westman remained at loggerheads. For a while, it looked as though the impasse might have to be resolved by a higher court. But at the eleventh hour, the logjam broke and Carol Lynn and Steven reached a compromise agreement which Carl Westman and Judge Hayes approved. It seemed to have been based less on law than on expediency. Carol Lynn needed money too, and if she hoped to get some from the estate, she had to grant Steven the same right.

In return for a written guarantee that he would not seek more funds during criminal or civil proceedings or appeals, Steven got $105,000 for his defense. At the same time, $139,974.79 was distributed to Barry Hillmyer, the guardian of Steven Benson's children. With this, Hillmyer paid various debts and obligations, including a $35,000 tax bill which the IRS levied on the transaction.

The Naples *News* characterized this as a riches to rags, rags back to riches tale. The national press continued to portray Benson as a millionaire who was rumored to be considering hiring Melvin Belli or Racehorse Haynes to handle his case. But from the day of his arrest until the end of his trial, he had less than $135,000 to pay for his defense. By almost any yardstick, except that of the US legal system, this was a lot of money. Yet it was hardly the fortune the public imagined and it was not nearly enough to choreograph the kind of glitzy courthouse melodrama Americans have come to expect from celebrated murder defendants.

In contrast, the Collier County prosecutors were presented as understaffed and underfinanced, fighting a desperate rearguard action against a team of hired guns. Michael McDonnell and Jerry Berry managed to keep a sense of humor about this. When McDonnell was asked by a reporter whether the case wasn't great publicity for him and his firm, he smiled and said it sure was. "And every time I go to the store, I pay for my groceries with publicity."

BOOK TWO

Private
Voices

Chapter 1

I

In late March I left Italy where it was early spring, landed in New York, where it was still winter, then flew to Naples, where it was already summer. Snowbirds, those tourists and retirees who had spent the season in southwest Florida, were heading north in a migratory pattern that took them up the Tamiami Trail to Tampa and from there to Michigan, Ohio, Pennsylvania, and New York. While some drove campers with witty bumper stickers, or pulled Airstream trailers that glinted in the sun, many swept along in their sedans, as serene behind their tinted windows as any doge in his gondola on the Grand Canal.

On either side of the Tamiami Trail, parked perpendicular to the road, luxury automobiles appeared to form an honor guard ushering the snowbirds out of town. There were stretch limos, Mercedes, Jaguars, Corvettes, and Cadillac Sevilles, each with a For Sale sign on the windshield. This struck me as a strange way to sell cars, especially high-priced models. But when I asked about it at a gas station, the fellow who filled my tank said, "Happens every year. Old folks drive down for the winter. Then they get too sick to face the drive back home, or else they die and the survivors sell them off. Check 'em out. Got some real good bargains."

Houses and condos were on the market for the same reason. In Quail Creek, Margaret Benson's Spanish Provincial had an asking price of $355,000. The murders had diminished its value. Prospective buyers felt queasy about moving into a place where for months the gravel drive showed a scorch mark and the front lawn was studded with shrapnel.

When I called the real estate agent handling the house and said I wanted to see it, she asked so politely whether I "qualified," I didn't realize at first that she was asking about my credit rating. I told her I was doing a book. She said she had instructions not to show the place to journalists. If I had questions, I should call Carl Westman, the personal representative of the estate.

In the first few months after the murders the firm of Frost and Jacobs, where Westman worked, received so many calls about the Bensons, they had to hire a media coordinator to deal with the press. The "coordination" consisted of repeating a single phrase over and over, "No comment." Carl Westman would not grant interviews or respond to questions from the reporters and TV commentators who tried to bushwhack him outside his office or on his way into or out of the Collier County Courthouse.

By the time I arrived, Westman would, however, make a brief announcement to anybody who expressed an interest in doing a book or movie based on the Benson pipe bomb murders. Referring to a Florida statute, Westman said that the family did not intend to allow its name to be exploited for commercial purposes without its permission and participation. Carol Lynn Benson Kendall insisted on reviewing all manuscripts before publication.

When I pointed out that the case had been heavily covered by the press, and Ms. Kendall had given over three hundred pages of sworn statements, Westman cautioned me that the public record was riddled with errors. Those who depended on it did so at their jeopardy. He referred me to Richard Cirace, Ms. Kendall's Boston attorney.

I telephoned Cirace on March 24, and he repeated Westman's caveat. He added that the family preferred an "authorized version" of the case. He had no reluctance to tell me the names of writers, producers, directors, and agents he had dealt with to date. He mentioned John Greenya, an author he had met some years ago when Greenya coauthored a book for F. Lee Bailey. But he assured me that no decision had been made. He and his client remained open-minded and the right financial arrangement would guarantee me exclusive access.

I said I had qualms about paying for interviews, especially before a case had been tried. I would have to speak to my publisher and would also have to have a clearer idea of what his client was offering and what she expected. Since the trial was scheduled to start on April 2, I suggested the three of us meet when they came down to Florida.

Instead, Cirace phoned twice the next day and said he had enjoyed our conversation. Maybe it was due to our cordial dealings, he said, or to the fact that he was Italian and I lived in Italy, but he wanted me to do the book. It was just a matter of working out the deal.

Again, I demurred. I couldn't make any decision until I met his client and learned whether we could work together and what she expected.

Cirace replied that Carol Lynn wanted 50 percent of all revenue generated by a book and 80 percent of the film rights. Since she was a graduate student in film production, she also wanted to be involved in making the movie. She viewed this as an opportunity to break into the business.

When I explained that he and his client had unrealistic expectations, he said Ms. Kendall faced huge medical expenses and years of litigation. She intended to fight the paternity suit against Scott and move to prevent Steven's children from inheriting his share of the estate. Cirace felt it was a bad legal precedent to let a murderer's heirs benefit by his crime.

Regardless of future litigation, I said, Carol Lynn stood to inherit $3 million. She couldn't expect to get anything remotely approaching that from a book or movie deal. I suggested he also consider whether it was in his client's best interest to market her story. Whatever the financial gain, it might not be worth the criticism it could bring upon her. And, more important, it might become an issue at the trial. Steven's lawyers could charge that Carol Lynn had a financial motive for wanting her brother convicted.

Cirace didn't follow this. So I spelled it out for him. His client's version of events had currency only if her brother was convicted. If he was acquitted, Steven's story, not hers, would grow in value. If Carol Lynn auctioned off her rights now, she risked being accused during the trial of slanting her testimony to protect a book and movie deal.

Cirace said we should talk again and meet at the trial.

Meanwhile, I went to see Judge Hugh D. Hayes. Because of the gag rule and the general inclination of members of the judiciary to hold the press at arm's length, I didn't expect to do more than introduce myself. But Judge Hayes, as I learned, was seldom predictable and, to the occasional consternation of his clerks, he was quite gregarious.

Hayes was thirty-eight and looked younger. Of medium height, he was well built and a meticulous dresser, with spit-shined loafers, a tweed jacket, and a monogrammed shirt. His blue eyes invited comparison with Paul Newman's or Robert Redford's—a comparison

Hayes encouraged with his joking remarks that he wanted Newman or Redford to play him in the movie. Although his collar was buttoned and his tie knotted, a gold neck chain was visible under his shirt.

With the Collier County Courthouse undergoing renovation, Hayes's office had been switched to a trailer much like the one Steven Benson had worked out of when he directed the affairs of his fragile Meridian empire. The judge invited me into a tiny cubicle that could barely contain a desk and two chairs.

Hayes would later come under criticism from prosecutors and defense attorneys who accused him of public posturing, playing to the press. It was said that he had ambitions to get bumped to a higher court or to run for political office. But from the start he struck me as too outspoken to be a politician, and much too complicated to be pigeonholed. Many journalists, especially those from outside of Florida, tended to regard Hayes as a cliché character, the sort of Sunbelt right-winger who had hidden his red-neck prejudices behind a polished, smiling mask. But that harsh judgment did not do justice to his character.

A native of Durham, North Carolina, he had the same birthday as Robert E. Lee and was proud of it. He had gone to Lanier Military School in Macon, Georgia, then to the University of Georgia, where he was in ROTC. Deferring Army service until after he finished a law degree at the University of Florida, he eventually became a second lieutenant in military intelligence. But then "I lost my desire to make the military my career after the infamous *Pueblo* incident."

The idea of Americans held captive, of the country humiliated, offended him personally as well as politically. "That's never going to be me," he said. "I'm never going to be a hostage. I'd rather take a bullet. For one thing, you take a round, you've still got at least a fifty-fifty chance of surviving."

He advised deputies that if he were ever taken hostage in the courtroom, he didn't want some punk laying down conditions, he didn't want any negotiations. He wanted the deputies to "do like the Israelis. Break down the door and crash on in. Because I won't wait long before I take action on my own. That's why I learned Tae Kwan Do."

Yet although he practiced the martial arts, jogged, lifted weights, and drove a Jeep Renegade with a National Rifle Association sticker on the rear window and a bald eagle painted on the spare tire, he was no Rambo who believed that solutions, like political power, grew from a gun barrel. He was, for instance, adamantly against sending drug enforcement agents and the Army into Bolivia and Colombia to crack down on drug smugglers. "How can we blame poor people for selling cocaine? We have to cut off the market, change our values, not try to cut off the supply by military intervention."

In his circuit, abortion was a big issue. Hayes was against it, which sounded predictable until he explained his position. "I used to be in favor of it. But then I adopted two children. I can't very well be for it when I have two beautiful kids because a woman decided not to have an abortion."

In his last campaign, he refused the endorsement of the local pro-life group because they were against sex education. In his opinion, abortion represented "a poor excuse for birth control. The public has not yet taken a reasonable approach to the subject of birth control. We need to be much better educated on the whole matter."

He was in favor of capital punishment. "I don't give a shit about deterrence. I just know one guy who won't kill again." But early in our discussion, he assured me he would abide by the jury's decision. If they convicted Steven Benson and gave him life in prison, Hayes had the right to overrule them and send him to death row. But he said, "I don't have to prove I have big *cajones* by going against the jury and giving him the chair."

He felt the best solution to the death penalty was to reduce the number of murders and take action to rehabilitate offenders *before* arresting them. He had established the Substance Abuse Program for First Time Drug Offenders, a counseling program for people convicted of petty theft, a small claims night court, the Collier County Citizens Dispute Settlement Program, and a rape crisis center.

A devout Presbyterian, Judge Hayes was quick to point out that the greatest influence on his life was a Jew, an attorney named Ed Friedberg. Hayes lived with the Friedbergs for a while when he was a boy and their children became like brothers and sisters. He went to temple with them, even wore a *yarmulke*, and every evening sat with the family at the dinner table and listened to his surrogate father conduct a post mortem on the day's cases. He would press the kids to offer an opinion, to match wits with a trial lawyer.

Hayes must have been good at it. Friedberg took to calling him the *maven*, which Hayes understood to be a Yiddish expression meaning "wise guy" or "smart ass."

• • •

Judge Hayes said the defense claimed publicly it was ready to proceed, but he sensed they would ask for a delay and that the prosecution wouldn't object. Neither side seemed prepared.

The judge didn't appreciate postponements. He had the "best disposal rate in the county" and meant to keep it that way. He didn't like defense or prosecution attorneys attempting to dictate the schedule or how the system operated.

He had instituted the gag rule, he explained, to prevent both sides from trying their cases in the media. After the De Lorean and Von Bulow trials, he said every judge had become increasingly sensitive to this strategy. "When you don't have the evidence on your side, you try the case on law. When you don't have law on your side, you try it on the evidence. When you don't have either, you try it in the newspapers and on TV."

I mentioned that the media coverage made the evidence against Benson sound overwhelming. Had there been any movement toward a plea bargain? Had anybody proposed a life sentence in return for a confession of guilt?

Hayes shook his head. Not a hair fell out of place. The evidence, he said, far from being conclusive, was entirely circumstantial. He could not remember a case where it had been a closer call whether the facts justified bringing a defendant to trial. Usually when the evidence was this circumstantial, a case didn't make it to court or, if it did, the State lost. Having gone over the issues in his own mind, he had reached the point where "I can live with a not-guilty verdict."

There was, in his opinion, another thing preventing a plea bargain. "A case like this has a lot to do with ambition. We're talking about a lot of bucks."

For a defense attorney, it was a chance for priceless publicity, a chance to become a "rainmaker" who attracted high-paying clients to his firm. For a prosecutor, a conviction would open a myriad of options—promotion, political office, a switch to private practice with an enhanced reputation. With more to be gained by stretching out the case, keeping their names and faces in the news, there was no practical reason for the defense to cop a plea or the State to offer one.

Anticipating my next question, Hayes acknowledged he had his own ambitions. People told him this was the case of a lifetime, the perfect platform from which to leap to the court of appeals. But he claimed to find it uninteresting. "If this had happened to an Hispanic family in Immokalee, nobody would think twice."

He just wanted to wade through the motions and countermotions, put all the prologues behind him and get the trial underway. But he told me not to expect this to happen soon. "Plan on spending the summer in Florida. July sounds about right to me. That'll have given everybody a year to get ready."

2

At the Collier County Courthouse, I stopped in the offices of the prosecution team and asked for an interview.

Lee Hollander, a pleasant, bespectacled fellow, considered himself utterly bound by the gag rule and didn't care to discuss anything related to the case. I was ushered into and out of his office in a matter of minutes.

Jerry Brock, age thirty-eight, was not nearly so close-mouthed. Tilted back almost horizontal in a chair, his feet up on a desk littered with law books and legal briefs, he talked for over an hour, speaking slowly and languidly, with long pauses that sometimes left me wondering whether he had drifted off to sleep. His accent was thick as pine sap, and he seemed to exaggerate it for effect, as if to downplay his intelligence and create an impression of country bumpkin earnestness. Yet despite the lengthy silences and the way that syntax and grammar sometimes eluded him—"He done..." "He seen..." "There's six facts..."—he never lost track of his thought and never let a word slip that he hadn't mulled over.

With his pale washed-out skin, perpetually quizzical expression, his drab three-piece suits and lank hair, Jerry Brock came across as a down-to-earth guy who happened to blunder onto a movie set. His every clumsy gesture and awkward phrase suggested that he was without artifice; he wasn't playing a role; he was too absorbed by the search for the truth to be worried about anything so silly as his image.

Yet by any objective standard, Brock was a masterful performer. He was such a good actor, he made other people look like amateurs or, worse, like phonies. He had so much self-confidence, he wasn't afraid to be unlikable when the situation called for it. He even dared to run the ultimate risk and bore spectators. As one lawyer said of

Brock, "Jerry'll bore you all right. He'll bore you right into the electric chair."

Brock told me he hailed from the Florida Panhandle, north of Panama City, from a place named Vernon. His father had been the town postmaster. His mother started off as a teacher, then took over as postmaster when his dad retired.

He described his father as a frustrated lawyer, a man who believed our legal system always provided the answer. But Brock had long since learned there is no black and white in the law, just shades of gray.

Describing the type of town Vernon was, he said that some newspapers in north Florida called it Nub City. Whenever there were hard times and unemployment, the local people loaded their guns and hiked off into the woods. No, they weren't exactly hunting, but they were doing what was necessary to put food on the table. An uncommonly large number of them came back minus a finger or a hand. Then they collected on their insurance and waited for the economy to improve and their nubs to heal.

Brock left Nub City and went off to Florida State University. He called F.S.U. "Half Ass U. Home of the Semi-Holes. Where the women are women and so are the men."

If this makes Brock sound like a lively cornpone comedian, it must be reemphasized that these lines were delivered from a nearly supine position and in an uninflected voice. When we discussed the Benson case, he showed surprise at the extent of the interest the murders generated. "I suppose it's just the money."

Was he aware, I asked, that Carol Lynn Kendall was marketing the print and film rights to her story? And did he see this as a potential problem?

Brock shrugged off the question like a sleeper stirring, then resettling. He drowsily disputed any assumption that it served Carol Lynn's interests to have Steven found guilty in criminal court. If he was convicted of killing Mrs. Benson, his share of the estate would pass directly to his lineal descendants as if he were already dead, and Carol Lynn couldn't recover the money.

But if Steven was found not guilty in this trial, Brock said, and inherited his millions, his sister could sue him for damages in civil court for assault on her and for the wrongful deaths of her son and mother. It was easier to get a conviction in civil court where a plaintiff didn't have to prove his case beyond a reasonable doubt; he needed only a preponderance of evidence in his favor.

I would have found Brock's remarks more convincing if I hadn't just spoken to Richard Cirace, who said that regardless of the verdict in the criminal trial, his client was considering legal action to prevent Steven's inheritance from flowing to his children.

Brock brushed off any possibility that his ambitions might be advanced by the Benson case. He said he intended to stay right where he was. "You're not going to get rich doing this. But you have lots of friends. You get personal satisfaction, and I was brought up thinking that you had to contribute to society."

When I asked why the defense hadn't tried to cop a plea to keep Benson out of the electric chair, Brock, unlike Judge Hayes, mentioned nothing about the evidence being circumstantial or its being a close call whether to bring the case to trial. He said the crime was so heinous, it was difficult for a defendant to admit it. It was like certain sex murders where a suspect confessed to the killing, but refused to discuss the sexual assault.

Jerry Brock said he couldn't talk to me during the trial. For one thing, he'd be hard pressed for time. For another thing, he was understandably reluctant to have an outsider staring over his shoulder. Although he didn't say it, he had no way of knowing I wasn't spying for the defense or wouldn't let something leak out that could cause a mistrial or create an appealable issue. Of course, I had no way of knowing whether he'd make use of information I had revealed to him.

3

The firm of McDonnell and Berry had a suite of offices in a building called The Commons, a tall structure of poured concrete that surrounded an atrium full of tropical plants. Riding in the glass elevators, one had the sensation of traveling through a terrarium. Since I had just driven over from the institutional modules at the Collier County Courthouse, I had the feeling I had made a trip from Nub City to Fat City.

To say that Michael McDonnell and Jerry Brock had contrasting styles was to state a truth that reporters, trial spectators, and even Judge Hayes would remark upon over and over again. Describing the differences between the two men, some fell back on the fable of the tortoise and the hare; others observed that while Brock was a character from "The Beverly Hillbillies," McDonnell stepped out of "Miami Vice." Where the press secretly referred to McDonnell and his partner, Jerry Berry, as "Batman and Robin," they called Jerry Brock and his brother Dwight "The Snooze Brothers."

Whatever these nicknames might seem to suggest, there was grudging admiration and a perverse sort of affection for Brock, while for McDonnell there was an equally perverse resentment. Although the media constantly sought him out for interviews, shoving mikes and mini-cams into his handsome face, they accused him of being a publicity hound, a hot dog, the lawyer's equivalent of a carnival barker.

During our first meeting, although he never struck me as unctuous or overly eager to please, his glamour and glibness and charm set off automatic warning bells. It was a journalist's variation on the Groucho Marx syndrome; anybody willing to answer my questions can't be worth talking to; anyone who freely volunteers information can't be giving good value. But ultimately I concluded McDonnell was no more of a showboat and certainly no more self-serving than anybody else in the Benson case. In fact, he seemed to be the one most likely to come out on the short end in his dealings with the media. He might have been better served if he had shown a bit more distrust of reporters. Instead, he told me, "I think the press is like a spirited horse. You have to let them know where you stand. Then you can both have an enjoyable ride." He had no idea what a rough ride he was in for.

Wearing an Izod knit shirt, a pair of gray slacks, and loafers without socks, he showed me into a conference room and we sat at a long table. Like Judge Hayes, he stressed that the evidence was entirely circumstantial. What's more, he said, it had been selectively gathered and interpreted in a way that was invariably favorable to the prosecution. Any leads that might have exonerated his client were ignored. Even now, evidence littered the crime scene, and potential suspects, particularly Scott's drug connections, hadn't been questioned. He, Jerry Berry, and a team of private investigators were trying to track people down, but they were fighting against the clock with limited funds.

Money, he admitted, wasn't the only limitation. Because of the gag rule, he could do nothing to correct the dozens of errors and misrepresentations that had been leaked to the press. Was this why he had fought two years in Viet Nam, he asked, gesturing expansively with his hands? So that he could come back to America and have his freedom of speech restricted?

Although they were at odds on this issue and many others, Mi-

chael McDonnell had a great deal in common with Judge Hugh
Hayes. Both had come to the law after considering careers in the
Army. McDonnell had attended Culver Military Academy, then gone
to West Point and graduated in time to ship out to Viet Nam. On his
first tour of duty in 1964 he was assigned to the Delta with a mixed
group of Americans and ARVNs on a Huey gunship. On his second
tour, he was dispatched to Pleiku and worked in reconnaissance with
the 25th Infantry and a team of Montagnard tribesmen.

After that, he had had enough. "I love the Army," he explained.
"I didn't like what Johnson and McNamara had done. I wanted to
become a senator and try to do something."

But his interest in politics soon took second place to his aspirations as a performer. He worked his way through Stetson Law School
playing the guitar and singing in a club called the Down and Under
in St. Petersburg. After he got his degree and had practiced a few
years, he still had an itch to be up on the stage, and so he took off,
started the Good Time Boogie Band and, traveling by van, played in
joints as far north as Kentucky, as far west as Texas. His third wife,
Nina, a tall, beautiful, tawny-haired lady sixteen years his junior,
went with him and ran the sound board.

"Everything I did was tongue in cheek," he said. "The point was
to have fun and make fun of yourself."

He wrote an unpublished book and some poetry and songs. Then
he produced a record, and while one side was a frivolous ditty entitled "The Nightie from Frederick's Catalogue," the other side was
"The Last Burro," a melancholy folk song which Cleveland Amory's
Fund for Animals chose as its theme.

He cut a second record, a ballad called "The Assassin." It was
about a woman done wrong who hunted down her ex-lover and emas-
culated him. The lyrics would come to seem oddly conincidental
during the Benson trial.

When Nina was pregnant with their first child—McDonnell had
two sons by previous marriages—he decided he had better go back to
practicing law. But he didn't view this as a total break with his career
as a performer. "There are common components. I love acting.
There is a conveyance of ideas in an understandable form. There is a
common thread with law, sales, acting, teaching—any form of communications."

Unlike Jerry Brock and Judge Hayes, McDonnell found the Benson case fascinating and full of legal challenges. Although he professed to be no more than a small-town lawyer content to go on living

and working in Naples, he didn't deny that he relished the opportunity to try a big case. "This is what I love to do," he announced in a newspaper. "It's like playing in the Super Bowl."

Outside on the parking lot in McDonnell's reserved place, I had noticed a white Jaguar XJ 12 with a digital phone. The license plates started with the letters AMB. I asked if this was an abbreviation for Ambitious. McDonnell laughed. "No. It stands for Ambulance Chaser."

The cast for the trial seemed nearly complete. There was a judge in the clean-cut heroic mode, a flamboyant defense attorney with a self-deprecating sense of humor, a beautiful lady with a murky past, and an idiosyncratic cracker-barrel prosecutor. But what about the central figure? What about Steven Benson? After eight months in jail, he had said nothing to the press and not much more in his occasional court appearances.

McDonnell would not comment about his client except to assert that he was convinced of his innocence. But he urged me to come back on Bastille Day. Judge Hayes, rumor had it, would reschedule the trial for July 14. McDonnell promised plenty of surprises and fireworks.

When the judge did postpone the trial, I telephoned Richard Cirace and suggested I meet him and his client in Boston. But Cirace suddenly sounded cautious. After calling me twice to propose financial terms, he now urged me to forget we had spoken. He said he had gotten some static from Naples and had decided that marketing his client's literary rights might cause trouble for her at the trial. There was a chance that he himself might be subpoenaed as a witness. Under the circumstances, he thought it best to wait and reopen negotiations after the verdict.

4

It had been a painful winter for Carol Lynn Kendall. Continuing therapy for her burns, she had worked to recover mobility in her right hand and arm. The skin grafts had undergone normal shrinkage and it was hard for her to fold her arm or flex her fingers. "I have to do exercises all day long," she told an interviewer from a Lancaster newspaper. She demonstrated how she forced herself to swivel her neck. She never gave in and turned her whole body to escape the pain.

Since she had put off more reconstructive surgery until after the trial, every time she glanced in a mirror she was reminded of how abruptly her life had broken in two. Before that instant when the bomb exploded, she had been a beauty queen, always described as "a princess," "a Dresden doll." Now people wondered what would become of her.

Edward West, the beauty shop owner who had dated Mrs. Benson, said of Carol Lynn, "She wanted to go up in the world, which I hope and pray to God that she does." But he added, "I don't know how her face turned out."

To complicate her sadness at her mother and son's death, she had the lonely responsibility of raising her teenage boys. Kurt, the older one, was quiet and bookish. But Travis skipped so many days of class during his sophomore year, he had no chance of advancing to his junior year. Soon he quit going to school altogether.

Carol Lynn bought the sixteen year old dropout a Maserati. Travis drove the high-precision Italian machine to Rockport on the Massachusetts coast and wound up dropping the transmission. The Maserati had to be hauled back to Boston on a flatbed truck. Family friends and employees couldn't help recalling how many cars and trucks Travis's half-brother Scott had ruined.

On May 22, 1986, Michael McDonnell subpoenaed Ms. Kendall to Naples for another deposition. After prefatory questions about the Benson family and Carol Lynn's childhood relationship with Steven, McDonnell pressed her about her brother's financial malfeasances. When he asked for precise figures, she could not provide them. She didn't recall how much her mother or Wayne Kerr or Diana Galloway, the ATF auditor, claimed had been diverted by Steven to Meridian Marketing.

McDONNELL: Well, how much money was allegedly stolen?

CAROL LYNN: When?

McDONNELL: You're the one who has told me that your mother said Steven stole money.

CAROL LYNN: Correct.

McDONNELL: That's what I'm asking about. How much did she say he stole?

CAROL LYNN: At what time?

McDONNELL: At any time.

CAROL LYNN: I can't say she gave me a specific amount of money that Steven stole.

McDONNELL: Did she ever mention two and a half million dollars that he stole as a general, not a specific, figure?

CAROL LYNN: No.

McDONNELL: Did she ever mention a general figure of what he stole?

CAROL LYNN: No.

Still, she accused Steven of saddling his mother with debts, charging personal bills to her account as business expenses, kiting checks, using her credit cards, and pocketing money that was meant to pay for the company's insurance plan. She could not say what Mrs. Benson had decided to do about all this except remove him from his position with the Meridian corporations.

McDONNELL: Did your mother discuss this with Steven?

CAROL LYNN: No, she intentionally had not said anything to Steven about it yet.

McDONNELL: Why is that?

CAROL LYNN: Because she wanted to get all the information in black and white about all the money that he had taken from her before she confronted him with it.

McDONNELL: So to your knowledge there had been no confrontation with Steven?

CAROL LYNN: I know there hadn't been any.

She hastened to add that just because her mother had not confronted Steven didn't mean that he was ignorant of her intentions. She had been "told by numerous people they feel as though someone else informed Steven." She specified. "My grandfather, my aunt and my children and the State attorney's office" all felt Wayne Kerr had alerted Steven that Mrs. Benson "was planning to make some changes at Meridian." Except for Jerry Brock she couldn't recall the names of the prosecutors and policemen who told her they suspected Kerr passed this information to Steven, but she remembered the essence of what they said, "Wayne Kerr had to be involved."

McDONNELL: What do you mean involved?

CAROL LYNN: Well, that Wayne had to have told Steven something.

Wayne Kerr had denied under oath on several occasions that he told Steven any of the options Mrs. Benson was considering. Later, in a personal interview, he reemphasized that he had not violated his client's confidential communications.

"I can't believe Carol Lynn's saying that. I don't even know what I was supposed to have tipped Steven to. I'm not sure what Mrs. Benson had in mind. She hadn't come to any decision.

"If I was really culpable," he asked, "why wouldn't the police have pursued me? Why didn't the Brocks pursue it?"

Kerr pointed out that he had been Carol Lynn's lawyer, as well as Margaret, Scott, and Steven's. "I arranged for the air ambulance to transport her to Boston. I took care of her kids. To have her make these kinds of accusations, these utterly unsupported charges, really disappoints and hurts me."

Carol Lynn said Mrs. Benson had discussed her will and talked about reducing Scott and Steven's share to reflect the sizable sums they had already spent. Her mother referred to this as "an equitable distribution. And she used to keep what you call a little black book which was credits or, you know, debits on the account."

Steven had gone through so much money, Carol Lynn claimed, her mother wanted him to sign a promissory note and make arrangements to repay her. "She wanted Wayne to write something up, and Wayne just kept putting it off and putting it off even though she kept asking for it."

Once again, her recollection of events conflicted with Kerr's. Under oath, he told Hollander and Brock that he had suggested Mrs. Benson obtain promissory notes on the loans to all three children, but she, not he, procrastinated. In a personal interview, he said, "Why would I delay drawing up a promissory note?" Then he added, "I don't think Mrs. Benson had any great hope of recovering her loans."

This was certainly true if Steven owed as much as Carol Lynn claimed. She maintained her mother "said that he had gone through two or two and a half million dollars of her money." This supposedly included everything she had loaned him, all the bad debts, and all the money he had allegedly diverted to his personal use or embezzled. But, curiously, the "little black book" in which Mrs. Benson meticulously kept records showed that Steven owed $268,000. While a substantial lump of money, this wasn't far out of line with what the other children owed. Scott's debt was $263,000 and Carol Lynn's was $118,000.

MCDONNELL: Did she ever say she was going to disinherit Steven, cut him out of the will?
CAROL LYNN: Oh, no.

When McDonnell said, "I'd like you to tell us in your own words the history of the relationship with Debra," Carol Lynn reported, "Do you have a week?" Then she launched into an eighteen-page diatribe, repeating that her sister-in-law had tried to poison Steven, had tried to attack Mrs. Benson, was slovenly and sluttish, drank heavily, didn't love her husband, belittled him in public and berated him in private.

McDonnell ended by asking Carol Lynn whether she or her representatives had been contacted by a company that wanted to make a movie about the murders. She said she had had no personal contact with the film people, but her representatives had.

MCDONNELL: And what is it that they want, these movie people?
CAROL LYNN: I don't know. I haven't dealt with them at all.
MCDONNELL: What have you been told they want?
CAROL LYNN: They're interested in making a movie.
MCDONNELL: Okay. And has there been some negotiations regarding the movie rights by your representatives?
CAROL LYNN: Not that I know of.

This appeared to contradict the article in the November 18, 1985, Boston *Herald*, whose headline read, BENSON HEIRESS MULLS SELLING "HOT" BIO-FLICK. It quoted Richard Cirace, "We're in the process of negotiation," and stated that Ms. Kendall was considering a deal from I.S.I. Productions of London.

On May 28, 1986, six days after Ms. Kendall's deposition, Richard Cirace sent a letter to the William Morris Agency in New York City.

Re: Benson Case
In accordance with my promise of keeping you up to date regarding the above-entitled case, enclosed please find a copy of an article which appeared in last week's *Miami Herald*.
The Criminal Trial is scheduled for July 14th, 1986 and "60 Minutes" is planning a story on the Benson Family to air this fall.

5

Quite apart from the fact that Cirace dispatched it to the William Morris Agency, the front-page article in the Miami *Herald* was significant in its own right. Along with a piece that ran the same week in *People* magazine, it signaled a sudden renewal of interest in the case by the national press, apparently prompted by a May 15 Second District Court of Appeals decision that struck down Judge Hayes's gag order. Journalists were now free to interview witnesses, attorneys, members of the Benson family, and even Steven if he would agree to it. They could read the reams of sworn statements taken by the prosecutors, then compare them to the misleading quotations and charges contained in the search and arrest warrants.

Instead, *People* magazine recycled hearsay that had long been denied or refuted. It stated Steven learned that his mother had not only "decided to turn off the cash, she was about to cut him out of the will." It asserted that Mrs. Benson "asked her attorney to redraft her will, excluding Steven and cutting him off from the companies held in her name," and it claimed "$2 million of Margaret Benson's money found its way into the [Meridian] businesses." But most damaging, it was implied that Steven had waited until after both bombs exploded before going to tell Kerr to call an ambulance—a significant misimpression with which to leave readers.

The Miami *Herald* ran a puckish article that read like a screen treatment. The headline—SCHEMING CLAN TURNS LIFE INTO SOAP OPERA—made the grisly double murders sound no more serious than a parody of "Dallas" or "Dynasty." Playing for laughs, the story reassembled the stock footage, yet the plot remained exactly the same. As always there was mention of a misappropriated $2 or $2.5 million, and of Mrs. Benson's fear that Steven wanted her dead. As usual, there was talk of Steven's being disinherited, but no acknowledgment that Kerr and Carol Lynn had long since sworn this wasn't true.

Since these points were repeated so often by the local, state, and national press, it is hard to see how potential jurors anywhere in southwest Florida could avoid making prejudgments about the Benson case.

6

Carl Westman, the personal representative of the Benson estate, had no choice but to remain central to the case. Yet whenever possible, he stayed in the background, out of the public eye. It wasn't a question of keeping a low profile. He wanted no profile. He distrusted ego, his own as well as other people's. While a cast of quirky and colorful characters shouldered their way forward to tell the world what they knew—usually very little—about the Benson family, Westman, who was learning more every day, retreated to his office and pondered what he should do as new and potentially explosive material was discovered among Mrs. Benson's papers and personal effects.

Westman belonged to the same Presbyterian church as Judge Hugh Hayes, but felt religious impulses that weren't limited to a single denomination. He had something close to an Eastern mystical belief in the connectedness of all life, and in the importance of outreach groups and links between individuals. Personally and professionally he resisted the forces that encourage men to "separate, differentiate, compartmentalize, etc." He wanted to find a way of achieving an integrated existence.

A tall, slim man with auburn hair combed close to his head and a clipped reddish mustache, he stooped slightly at the shoulders, not as if bowed by age—Westman was in his early forties—but rather as if he were leaning forward to listen closer. Although he had a Frost and Jacobs business card, he passed out a personal card as well. The word Endurance was embossed in red letters on one side and a quotation from Edwin Hubbel Chapin on the other: "Not in the achievement, but in the endurance of the human soul, does it show its divine grandeur, and its alliance with the infinite God."

Endurance was the name of Westman's boat. It also referred to the fact that he jogged fifteen or twenty miles a week. In conjunction with the Naples Community Hospital, he had helped found an organization called the Wellness Community, whose goal was to develop awareness of the unity of body, mind, and spirit, to promote self-respect and mutual respect, and to establish connections between individuals.

There was always the question of how Westman could apply his beliefs to his profession as an attorney dealing in trusts and estates. Although money was a medium of exchange, even, at times, a bond between people, it could also drive them apart. He had seen families rent by greed and distrust, sons and daughters set against their parents, fathers and mothers determined to rule from the grave. Still, he strived to see things whole and to convey his attitude to clients whenever possible.

Westman was determined to keep his distance from the swirl of emotions and acrimonious legal debate. He made it his practice to turn over to the prosecution and defense anything from the estate that touched upon the case, no matter whether it helped prove or disprove Steven Benson's guilt.

What troubled him, however, was that the State Attorney's office didn't seem to understand his position or appreciate his effort to bring relevant evidence into the open. Early on, he had come across Scott's handwritten account of his turbulent affair with Tracy Mullins. Because it alleged that Mullins had made death threats and, due to the paternity suit, had a possible motive for wanting the Bensons murdered, Westman believed the prosecutors should see it. But it took weeks to get anybody from the Collier County Sheriff's Department to pick up a copy, and even then he never knew whether the police checked out Tracy Mullins.

Later, he discovered another document, the December 14, 1984, "third will," which Wayne Kerr had drafted according to Mrs. Benson's instructions. She died seven months later without having signed it. Because it had not been executed, it had no bearing on how the estate was to be divided, and when Kerr mentioned it during his interrogation by Lee Hollander and Jerry Brock, neither man seemed terribly curious about it.

But after reviewing its terms, Westman thought it might be a valuable piece of evidence. The third will placed severe restrictions on Scott and Steven. Their shares of the fortune, unlike Carol Lynn's, were to be administered under a trust arrangement that would have drastically limited the money available to them for the next twenty-five years. They would have been old men before they came into their full inheritance and could spend with the same profligacy as they had since they were teenagers.

Because the third will had been found in Margaret Benson's bureau, Steven might have seen it. If he noticed it hadn't been signed, he might have considered it a sword of Damocles dangling over his head and decided to murder his mother before she put him under the control of an executor.

Westman called Jerry Brock and suggested he have the third will dusted for fingerprints. If Steven's prints were on it, that might go a long way toward proving he had a financial motive for wanting to see her dead.

Yet again the State Attorney's office showed little interest. Eventually, someone picked up the third will. Westman assumed the prosecutors would have it dusted for prints and then share the results with the defense. But months passed and he heard nothing.

In May 1986, George Gramling, a young associate at Frost and Jacobs, found something among Mrs. Benson's belongings and didn't know what to make of it. He left it with Carl Westman and let him decide what to do.

There was an envelope with a name and a date written on the front. The name was of a Naples police officer, William Lanyisera, the date was September 12, 1983. The envelope contained a micro-cassette tape cartridge. The tape was outside the broken plastic cassette, but still on its spools. Gramling had rewound it and encased it in a new cassette so that it could be played on a recorder.

Westman sat at his desk in an office carpeted in beige pile and furnished with plush leather chairs. When he switched on the recorder an alien voice entered the room, one completely out of keeping with the family photographs, the personal memorabilia, the polished bookshelves full of dry legal language. The words on the tape weren't altogether logical or coherent, yet there was no mistaking their menace. They ended with a woman screaming, "Get your hands off—"

Westman rewound it and listened again. While George Gramling had not realized the momentousness of what he had heard, Westman immediately recognized what this microcassette with its two minutes of tormented and murderous talk might do. Through its sheer emotional weight it could obliterate the State's case. For months defense attorneys had argued that the murders were drug-related. Now they had a hook to hang their case on. The tape might not alter or expand the facts, but it was bound to change the way they were interpreted, the way Steven was perceived, the way the Benson family was regarded.

The last point was by no means unimportant. The family had had a great deal to do with the direction of the case. It wasn't just that Carol Lynn's testimony constituted a major portion of the evidence against Steven. By cutting off Steven's trust fund, refusing to support his defense, and writing a letter to Judge Hayes, Harry Hitchcock had created a strong presumption of guilt. Yet now Carl Westman had in his possession a tape that would displease the family and perhaps help persuade a jury to acquit Steven.

On June 3, he called Jerry Brock and told him about the tape. Brock came to his office, listened to it, concealed his reaction with country-boy wit, and left. He didn't take the tape or ask for a copy.

By June 20, when Westman had not heard back from the prosecutors and had no way of knowing whether they had shared the information with the defense attorneys, he called McDonnell and Berry, who were considerably more animated than Jerry Brock. They believed it was the breakthrough they needed.

7

On July 2, Naples police arrested Guido Dal Molin and charged him with first degree murder. The twenty-one-year-old electronics genius and computer expert was accused of shooting Vernon Stewart. Dal Molin drove the victim around in a pickup, police said, until he bled to death. Then he abandoned the truck and Stewart's corpse south of Alligator Alley.

Dal Molin had been questioned early in the Benson case because, Lieutenant Harold Young said, his "name came up as someone who was capable of making bombs." In fact, he had been caught with a convincing facsimile of a nuclear bomb which had all the components except fissionable material. Like Steven, he ran a burglar alarm business and had supposedly experimented with pipe bombs.

"He came in on his own to talk to us about it," Lieutenant Young said. "We could never find any reason to think he was involved."

Yet Young didn't provide any of the specifics of his interrogation of Dal Molin nor did he explain how Guido had been eliminated as a suspect.

Defense attorneys announced that Dal Molin was a potential witness at the Benson trial. According to Jerry Berry, Guido "supposedly has information concerning Scott. We want to talk to him about that and any other information he has concerning the incident."

On Thursday, July 10, just four days before the trial was due to start, McDonnell and Berry filed a motion to suppress the palm print evidence obtained with the search warrant on August 16, 1985. They also moved that the indictment that resulted from this "unlawful" evidence be dismissed.

Although Judge Hugh Hayes thought the motion was "a good

one, professionally prepared," it burned him up that McDonnell and Berry waited until the eleventh hour to file it. He scheduled a hearing on Saturday, July 12.

To add to everybody's irritation at having to work on a weekend, the air conditioning in the courthouse had broken down, and with the outdoor temperature hovering in the mid-nineties, every room in the building was sweltering. Some of the exchanges between the attorneys became so heated and obstreperous, Hayes said, "Hold it, guys. I'm going to tie you down pretty damn tight when I get you in front of a jury."

The motion to suppress argued that "Because he did not have probable cause to arrest and because Florida does not have a statute establishing non-voluntary, pre-arrest identification procedures, Lt. [Harold] Young pursued the novel procedure of requesting a search warrant for the 'body of white male Steven Wayne Benson.'"

But, the motion pointed out, search warrants authorize the seizure of "property or things," not persons. "Not since the days of slavery has the law of this country allowed a living human being to constitute 'property.'" The "thing" sought by the warrant, namely rolled ink impressions of Steven Benson's hands, did not exist. What the police actually wanted was for Benson "to submit to procedures which themselves create evidence." But this could not be accomplished by a search warrant.

"Not only does Lt. Young's affidavit fail to establish probable cause on its face, it suffers the additional deficiency that it contains statements that are factually untrue. A search warrant is invalid if it is based on an affidavit which contains false or erroneous information included by the Affiant with knowledge that it is incorrect or with reckless disregard for the truth, if the false or erroneous information is necessary to a finding of probable cause."

Besides the inclusion of false information, the affidavit excluded information which would have mitigated against a finding of a probable cause. "The affidavit tells the court that the composite description of the buyer of the pipe matched the defendant. It omitted the highly relevant exculpatory information that the sellers of the pipe had been unable to identify a photograph of the defendant as the buyer of the pipe."

Judge Hayes viewed matters differently. He cited a Supreme Court ruling that police may briefly detain a person for purposes of taking his fingerprints if they have cause to suspect he was involved in a crime they are investigating. What's more, he did not accept that the spirit and intention of Florida law precluded the issuance of a search warrrant for prints prior to an arrest.

Hayes ruled against three other motions filed by McDonnell and Berry. He refused to allow defense attorneys to question potential jurors in private about their exposure to pretrial publicity and their position on the death penalty; he refused to forbid close-up photographs and film footage of the jury entering and leaving the courtroom; and he refused to increase from ten to forty the number of potential jurors the defense could challenge.

Afterward Jerry Berry professed not to be disappointed by Judge Hayes's decision to allow the fingerprints into evidence. "It doesn't change anything at all." But he was candid enough to concede, "Had he ruled in our favor, the case would have been over with." As it was, they had to be ready for trial on Monday morning.

Chapter 2

The trial had been moved to Fort Myers, forty miles up the coast from Naples. Strictly speaking this did not amount to a change of venue. Collier and Lee counties were in the same circuit, and both had been bombarded by coverage of the case. But Fort Myers boasted a larger year-round population, and Judge Hayes believed that with a deeper pool of people to draw on, there would be a better chance of finding impartial jurors. He assured the defense that if they could not seat a jury in a week, he would consider switching the trial out of southwest Florida.

A few years before Naples claimed the title, Fort Myers had been the fastest growing metropolitan area in America. Even off season in mid-July, traffic was backed up bumper to bumper during the morning and evening rush hours. But the city center, down along the Caloosahatchee River, had retained the look and feel of a small sleepy town. The buildings on First Street bore faint traces of Mediterranean influence—whitewashed walls, crenellated roofs, and red tiles. The waterfront was palm lined, and gazebos and shuffleboard courts, abandoned during the torpor of summer, awaited the return of the winter people. Spanish moss bearded the live oaks in front of the old courthouse and a banyan tree with dozens of trunks spread leafy shade over the benches where no one sat.

Crowds streamed toward the new cream-colored Lee County Justice Center across the street. On the fifth floor, the halls were cluttered with sound and camera equipment, and signs in English and Spanish warned people to watch their step. Since Florida permits TV coverage of criminal trials and allows journalists to conduct interviews virtually anywhere—many states insist that the media keep its lights and cameras and questions and tape recorders out of the courthouse altogether—several reporters were always poised at the double doors to Courtroom A, ready for impromptu press conferences.

In addition to local papers and TV and radio stations, the Benson trial attracted all three national networks and CNN, *Time, Newsweek,* the *New York Times,* Washington *Post, Associated Press, United Press International,* and reporters from newspapers in Pittsburgh, Philadelphia, Tampa, Miami, Fort Lauderdale, and Lancaster and York, Pennsylvania. *Penthouse* and *Vanity Fair* had commissioned articles; five authors intended to write books; a soap opera writer showed up with her assistant and announced that she meant to build a mini-series around the Benson family; and Eliot Geisinger, producer of *The Amityville Horror,* sent someone to the trial every day to take notes.

Since there were long slow periods, and many out-of-town reporters arrived knowing little or nothing about the case, the press began to feed on itself like a bottle full of tapeworms. Most of this was chummy and collegial as journalists shared their notes and passed along rumors and tips. But there were some bristly confrontations. TV commentators took to jabbing mikes at print reporters and demanding, "Aren't you concerned that you're exploiting a tragedy to get a headline?"

Newspaper writers hit back with articles accusing TV commentators of creating a carnival atmosphere and reducing the chances of seating an unprejudiced jury.

Everybody began asking book authors what they had been paid and whether they had cut a deal with Carol Lynn or Steven.

A stringer from *Newsweek* flew over from Miami one afternoon, pretended to be with *USA Today,* and said he was doing a piece on journalists covering the Benson trial. Interviewing book authors, reporters, and local TV anchormen, he gleaned a few basic story points from each. Then he caught the evening plane home and filed a background article on the case.

The antics of the press, entertaining though they were, couldn't compare with the high drama, low burlesque, and occasional tragedy that transpired in Courtroom A. Wood-paneled, carpeted in dull bronze, furnished with rows of comfortably upholstered chairs, the room resembled a conference hall or a plush theater for art films. Despite the hubbub and the heat of the camera lights in the hall, it was cool in here, and one heard only the faint hum of the air conditioning and the fainter chimes of the carillon at St. Francis Xavier Catholic Church.

The defense team launched its first surprise attack by seizing the right-hand table, the one closer to the jury, where the State usually sat. Jerry Brock and his brother Dwight protested, but Judge Hayes said it was "first come, first served."

Michael McDonnell told the press he chose the right side because "that's the side of the angels." But there were earthly advantages. It was easier to watch the witnesses as they testified, and there was a better chance of establishing rapport with the jury if only by proximity.

During the voir dire process, the defense table was as crowded as the celebrity dais at a campaign dinner. In addition to McDonnell, Benson, and Jerry Berry, there was a Fort Myers attorney, Wilbur "Billy" Smith; a burly, freckled investigator, Bob Laws; and a woman with a porcelain complexion and wavy blond hair that brushed the shoulders of her conservatively cut suit. Margaret Covington, a jury consultant, attracted attention now because of her beauty and expertise. Later in the trial, sensational allegations about her past would create a furor.

The purpose of the voir dire is to see whether potential jurors are capable of judging impartially and making decisions based on courtroom evidence, not on what they've picked up as hearsay or learned from newspapers and TV. Of the first group of twenty-five people, only two said they had read or heard so much that they could not give Benson a fair trial. They were dismissed by Judge Hayes. Of the remaining twenty-three, all except one admitted they had been exposed to information about the case, but they claimed that pretrial publicity wouldn't prejudice them.

One woman explained that she was allergic to the printer's ink and never followed any story very closely. A man charged that newspapers were biased and magazines were controlled by advertisers. He restricted his reading to the sport section and want ads.

Just one person, a woman, expressed serious reservations about the death penalty. She was excused.

The others declared they "believed" in the death penalty. The way they said it, it sounded like an article of faith. Polls show that 80 percent of Floridians are in favor of capital punishment.

Members of the jury pool had a couple of other common characteristics: they were deeply tanned and casually dressed. Where Steven Benson, his attorneys, the prosecutors, and court clerks wore suits and ties, the potential jurors looked as if they had wandered in from a golf course, the beach, a boat, or strenuous outdoor labor. Not a single man wore a suit or jacket.

But they were not clones of one another. About equally divided between men and women, they ranged in age from late teens to late seventies. There were nurses, housewives, shop girls, construction workers, salesmen, a retired Army intelligence agent, a fashion coordinator, and a gospel singer. A small business owner asked to be excused because he was being sued and couldn't concentrate on this case while worrying about his own. A lady pleaded to be excused because three days ago she had rescued a woman from drowning and "I keep having flashbacks of myself and that lady."

A man of seventy-seven was dismissed when he regretfully admitted he was hard of hearing. "This thing is going nationwide. I would like to have stayed on."

During a break, when Judge Hayes said everybody could stand and stretch, a fellow named John Henry Todd limbered up by touching his toes. Then balancing on one foot like an egret, he lifted his other leg and tucked that foot behind his head. It turned out Mr. Todd was a martial arts instructor. The attorneys couldn't decide whether to put him on the jury or in the circus.

After the break and the yoga exhibition, a prospective juror identified himself as a retired explosives expert. In monumental understatement, Michael McDonnell mused, "I think that's ironic."

A lady listed her profession as "belly dancer." Margaret Covington told me a belly dancer didn't fit the profile the defense was searching for. "After all, she's an entertainer. She likes to please and might go whichever way she's swayed by the others."

The swiftest dismissal occurred when a gum-chewing, jut-jawed man said of Steven Benson, "I've already tried him in my own mind." Or as the entire defense team heard it, "I've already *fried* him in my own mind." Whichever, that guy was gone.

Jerry Brock, whose first name was Delano, and his brother Dwight were named after former presidents, but resembled a couple of meek accountants. During cross-examination they would become as aggressive as mongooses. Now, however, Jerry started off by apologizing for not being able to pronounce any name more complicated than Jones or Smith. He explained that he hailed from north Florida and his pronunciation problems were the "result of my heritage, of which I am very proud."

He also apologized for probing into their private lives and beliefs. Yet he kept at it, digging slowly and apparently without guile for the information he needed.

"Can you tell me one thing in life you know to an absolute certainty?" he asked a lady.

"No sir."

"Well, I can think of one," Brock said. "We all know to an absolute certainty that we are going to die. Now, you wouldn't make me prove the defendant's guilt to that degree of certainty, would you?"

"No sir."

He asked if any of them believed in ESP or in setting off on spur-of-the-moment vacations. While nobody admitted to believing in ESP, several said they took sudden vacations.

People who believe in ESP supposedly don't favor capital punishment. Those who carefully plan their vacations are reputed to be more inclined toward doling out the death penalty.

Repeatedly, he pointed at Steven Benson and asked, "Can you look at that defendant"—Brock pronounced it "dee-fen-dant," with the accent on the last syllable—"and say he's guilty of murder?"

They all assured him they could.

Before going into private practice, Jerry Berry worked with Brock as a prosecutor in the State Attorney's office. He told of a murder trial in La Belle, Florida, where Brock was plodding through his typical, tedious voir dire questions when the defendant jumped to his feet and shouted a guilty plea.

"You understand what you're saying?" the judge asked. "I could sentence you to the death penalty."

"Yeah, I know," the man said. "But I'd rather get the chair than listen to Jerry Brock any longer."

It was a standard, double-edged Brock story. His accent, his style, his mangled grammar, his hypnotically slow delivery, they were always good for a laugh. But they were also good for a conviction.

That evening Judge Hayes reminded prospective jurors not to read newspapers or watch television reports about the case. He didn't want them discussing it among themselves or with their families or friends. Although he wouldn't sequester the jury, he would issue the same warning every day.

2

On the second day of jury selection, defense attorneys left Steven Benson alone at the table, and he sat there in a dark gray suit, his eyes downcast. The Washington *Post* later spoke of Benson's "grim and almost affectless bearing," and it quoted an unnamed source who said he looked "brain-dead." He had lost twenty-two pounds, his complexion had turned paler, and the silver-dollar-size patch of gray in his hair had sent flecks out in all directions.

Because he had said nothing to the press since his arrest and refused to respond to the occasional question flung in his direction as the bailiff led him in and out of the courtroom, journalists studied him as if they were astronomers staring at a black hole at the edge of the universe. Just as nature hates a vacuum, the media cannot abide a blank, quiet space. So they struggled to fill it with speculation or with a catalog of minute random particulars. Now that Benson was trapped every day for eight or ten hours in the unblinking eye of the television camera, his every gesture and expression was examined as though it, like the tip of an iceberg, concealed tons of lethal subsurface ice.

"He has a very thin lower lip," the Miami *Herald* remarked. "He smirks, kind of. He chuckles impishly sometimes...Sometimes he wraps his hand around the thigh of his left leg. About four times a day he brushes lint off his jacket. Frequently, he rubs his left thumb cuticle with his right index finger."

Others attempted to define him by his daily routine. Or they wrote about the size of his cell and reported that his jailers called him "Boom Boom."

Few could resist mentioning that Debra Benson never came to court. She and the three kids were off in Wisconsin.

Steven's relatives sat in reserved seats behind the prosecutors' table. Richard Cirace, Carol Lynn's Boston attorney, also sat on the prosecutors' side, as did Carl Westman.

The reserved seats behind Benson were occupied, according to the Miami *Herald*, by "a surrogate family" composed of secretaries, wives, and friends of McDonnell and Berry. McDonnell's mother-in-law, Mafalda Gray, a lady with a handsome shock of white hair, showed up every day and was the one person Steven spoke to at length. Although Mrs. Gray had played a role in his defense, the Miami *Herald* dubbed her "Rent-a-mom" and suggested she was no more than window dressing, just a warm body and a maternal face meant to prove that Benson, abandoned by his own family, had a few people who believed in his innocence.

But during the morning break on the second day, the seats behind Benson were empty, and I was tired of peering at him from a distance. I went up, offered my hand, and introduced myself. Surprised, Steven shook my hand, but kept his eyes averted. As I explained that I was doing a book, he nodded and said nothing.

He didn't radiate hostility or rage. He didn't exude a forbidding chill. He gave off no essence, no temperature at all.

Policemen and prosecutors assured me that Benson's zoned-out appearance proved he was a cold, psychopathic killer. I was not convinced. A murderer he may be, but his nonreaction didn't remind me of criminal psychopaths I've met. Some killers can be bubbly, talkative and, on the surface, about as threatening as a glass of Perrier. Instead, Benson struck me as an introvert who had been at the center of so much attention he now wanted nothing more than to avoid all intrusions into his life. If this meant making himself colorless, motionless, and speechless, it didn't matter as long as people left him alone.

As I was about to retreat, Benson's attorneys returned and I stepped to one side with Michael McDonnell and said I'd like to interview his client, like to have access to him on a regular basis throughout the trial.

He said he would talk it over with Steven and let me know.

I didn't have long to wait. McDonnell went to Benson and, after a few minutes, told me I could sit in on a conference while they discussed strategy for the voir dire. He took me to Steven and introduced us, and we shook hands for a second time.

He gave my hand a firmer grip now and met my gaze. His face had come into focus and he smiled. He admitted being wary of the press. If he had a choice, he'd prefer to say nothing, to remain a private person. But he realized he had lost control over that part of his life.

We moved into the unoccupied jury room, a cramped space with a table, fourteen tubular chrome chairs, and a water cooler. Two toilets marked LADIES and MEN opened off the room.

McDonnell sat at the head of the table. Jerry Berry, Billy Smith,

The remains of the Benson family car, after the two pipe bomb explosions
(AP/WIDE WORLD PHOTOS)

Steven Benson, seated third from left, with his wife, Debbie, second from left with hat, and his grandfather, Harry Hitchcock, during graveside services for Margaret and Scott Benson in Lancaster, Pennsylvania   (AP/WIDE WORLD PHOTOS)

Steven and Debbie Benson leave St. James
Episcopal Church after the funeral services.
(AP/WIDE WORLD PHOTOS)

Margaret Benson, in approximately 1975   (AP/WIDE
WORLD PHOTOS)

Scott Benson, in approximately
1980   (AP/WIDE WORLD
PHOTOS)

Carol Lynn Kendall in a photo
from approximately 1975
(AP/WIDE WORLD
PHOTOS)

Carol Lynn Kendall arrives at
Logan Airport in Boston en route
to Massachusetts General Hospital.
(AP/WIDE WORLD PHOTOS)

Margaret Benson's home in
Quail Creek, Florida
(MARC WIEGAND)

Quail Creek Tennis Club, where
Scott Benson "trained for the U.S.
Open" (MARC WIEGAND)

Michael McDonnell greets client Steven Benson just before opening arguments. (AP/WIDE WORLD PHOTOS)

Prosecutors Dwight Brock, left, and his brother, Jerry Brock, confer while Judge Hugh D. Hayes looks on. (THOMAS A. PRICE, *Ft. Myers News-Press*)

Circuit Judge Hugh Hayes   (LAURA ELLIOTT, *Ft. Myers News-Press*)

Left to right: Jerry Berry, Margaret Covington, Michael McDonnell, and Steven
Benson, seated, early in the trial, during the jury selection process   (THOMAS A. PRICE,
Ft. Myers News-Press)

Steven Benson, as court prepares for final arguments   (AP/WIDE WORLD PHOTOS)

Carol Lynn Kendall awaits the results of the jury's deliberations.
(AP/WIDE WORLD PHOTOS)

Prosecutor Jerry Brock strains to hear Defense Attorney Michael McDonnell's closing arguments. (THOMAS A. PRICE, *Ft. Myers News-Press*)

Lead prosecuting attorney for the State, Jerry Brock, gives his closing arguments. (AP/WIDE WORLD PHOTOS)

Steven Benson leaves the L[...] County Justice Center in ch[...] following the conclusion of [...] trial. That morning, jurors l[...] recommended life in prison.
(AP/WIDE WORLD PHOTOS)

and I were on his left. Across from us, Benson sat between Margaret Covington and Bob Laws. Every member of the defense team, except Laws, had a yellow legal pad. Steven's pad was covered with notes. he was, McDonnell had told me, playing an active role in his defense.

Laws, who snacked on Lifesavers throughout the day, offered one to Steven. If it made them uneasy to be in the room where twelve people would eventually decide whether Benson lived or died, they didn't show it.

"Let's draw up a list," McDonnell said, "of who we definitely want to get off this jury."

"How about three lists," Margaret Covington suggested. "Yes, no, and maybe."

For the next five minutes, as they debated the merits of the men and women in the jury pool, Billy Smith watched me, not McDonnell.

Smith said, "I'm sorry. I've got a problem with him being here. Is he a lawyer?"

McDonnell told him I was doing a book.

"Is he going to be part of the defense team?"

I said I was not.

In Smith's opinion, any conversation between Benson and his attorneys that took place in front of a third party was not confidential. The State could subpoena me and force me to testify about what I heard.

I said I'd leave.

McDonnell told me to stay. He said they were discussing "procedures, not the facts of the case. As soon as we start discussing facts, he'll go."

Five minutes later, I went and never again had a chance to speak to Benson. All future communications with him passed through McDonnell. Our brief conversation at the defense table, followed by ten minutes in the jury room, constituted the total extent of his contact with the press. Since he seemed capable of projecting warmth and of expressing himself articulately, I doubt he served his best interests by remaining silent.

When the jury selection resumed, Jerry Brock began to refer to himself as the representative of the victims. "They will not be in the courtroom," he said. They were dead and buried.

Every time Brock repeated this, which was often, McDonnell

climbed to his feet, said, "May we approach the bench, Your Honor," and objected that Brock did not represent the Bensons. He represented the State Attorney's office. No more, no less.

Because of the angry outbursts between attorneys this past weekend during the hearing to suppress the palm prints, the judge had decided that Brock and McDonnell should register all their objections at the bench in quiet voices. He didn't want the jury to be influenced by injudicious comments or histrionic posturing.

In contrast to Brock's plodding style, Michael McDonnell conducted his voir dire with all the aplomb of a game-show host. By turns, he sounded paternal, brotherly, avuncular, or pastoral. He was especially good with older ladies.

Turning the prosecutor's questions against him, he asked, "Can you look my good friend Jerry Brock in the face and tell him that Steven Benson is not guilty?" Everyone swore they could.

He asked whether they believed drugs contributed to the nation's crime rate. (They did.) He wondered if they would hold it against Benson if he, McDonnell, decided there was no need for him to testify. (They vowed they wouldn't.)

He hammered at the nature of circumstantial evidence. "There's nothing wrong with it. The judge'll tell you that. So long as the circumstantial evidence offered by the State excludes every reasonable theory of innocence."

3

At lunch, I ate with Margaret Covington. A native of North Carolina, she worked out of Texas, living with her husband, also a lawyer, and her four-year-old son in Sweetwater, and flying off on assignments around the country. In a southern accent as sweet and thick as saltwater taffy, she said she had a law degree and a Ph.D. in psychology, from Baylor University. Her minor was in mathematics with emphasis on statistics.

She was thirty-six years old, but might have been a cheerleader or a homecoming queen. She had worked with Richard "Racehorse" Haynes on some of the most celebrated murder trials in the last decade and she referred to them by book titles.

"I served as consultant on the *Blood and Money* case," she said, meaning the murder trial of John Hill in Houston, about which Tommy Thompson wrote a best-seller. "Then I was a consultant on the *Blood Will Tell* case." The book was by Gary Cartwright, and it involved the trial of T. Cullen Davis, a Fort Worth millionaire accused of killing his wife's lover and his stepdaughter, and hiring a hit man to murder the judge in his divorce.

She had also done a great deal of civil litigation, in some instances helping to win damage settlements as high as $30 million.

She had worked with Michael McDonnell on another murder case in which a woman named Bonnie Kelly gunned down a prosecutor at her front door. Since there had been an eyewitness, it was generally agreed that McDonnell, with an assist from Covington, had done a miraculous job in getting Kelly a life sentence.

She told me in her sleepy voice that she had hoped to teach psychology at the university level. But she realized she'd have problems working for a male chairman—"some yoyo who'd get all the grants and the glory and the power and the money."

So she had gone into law. Since she thought most firms hired women as a token gesture, she preferred to work as a free-lancer, calling on her knowledge of psychology and statistics to redress the imbalance she felt existed between the prosecution and the defense.

When I asked whether her physical appearance was a help or a hindrance, she said it was mostly a distraction. Neither her greenish-blue eyes nor her voice betrayed much emotion on the subject, but there was a slightly downcast turn to her mouth. It didn't matter how she dressed—in court she always wore tailored suits—or whether she had on makeup or pinned her hair up or left it long, some reporter or prosecutor or even a judge would make a corny joke.

Deflecting the conversation from herself, she said her appearance was like Steven Benson's wealth. Or at least the public's perception of his wealth. Most people resented the rich and enjoyed cutting them down. One of the delights of watching "Dallas" and "Dynasty" was to see the rich suffer while simultaneously indulging in the vicarious pleasure of sharing their lives.

The dilemma the defense faced was finding jurors who wouldn't be confounded by the bizarre finances of the Benson family. He was on trial for murder, not for sponging off his mother. But people might be blinded by the blizzard of numbers and bank statements the prosecution would introduce and decide to punish Steven.

Wealth, however, was the least of Steven Benson's problems. "In most cases," Covington declared, "the State just has to show up and the jury will convict. They feel that's their job—to convict defendants—and they actually need an excuse not to." She cited the case of John De Lorean, who was acquitted of cocaine dealing because his lawyers managed to persuade jurors that he was the victim of police entrapment.

In a case like this, which had received extensive media coverage, jurors felt greater pressure to convict. They feared press and community criticism if they failed to bring in a guilty verdict. They didn't want their neighbors nagging them for letting a murderer walk. Where reports of a case had been slanted and had found the defendant guilty before his trial, it was virtually impossible to expect a jury to serve as a court of appeals and overturn a verdict.

During the voir dire, Margaret Covington said, everybody claimed to be fair and impartial. They denied they had read or heard much and insisted nothing had prejudiced them. One and all, they believed in our judicial system and swore that a man is innocent until proven guilty. If he chose not to testify, that was his right and it shouldn't be held against him.

But the reality rarely matched the ideal. A case of this kind created immense excitement, and people wanted in on it. This was a chance for them to be on TV every day, to accumulate a lifetime supply of anecdotes, to participate in a dramatic event. Under the circumstances, many people would not admit what they really felt.

Since a defense attorney could not count on getting a straight answer to a straight question, he needed another method of gaining insight into potential jurors. That's where consultants like Covington came in.

According to her research, nine out of ten people believed that if a man was arrested, he must be guilty. Otherwise, the police wouldn't bother him. Since the great majority saw fine qualities in policemen and prosecutors, and dubious ones in defense attorneys, it was foolish for a defendant to go into court laboring under the delusion that he was presumed innocent. This was particularly true of Benson, who had been in jail for a year without bond.

Although, in public, people allowed that a defendant had a constitutional right to remain silent, in private, responding to Margaret Covington's survey, eight out of ten thought a man who refused to testify was guilty.

With all this in mind, she had spent three weeks accumulating information and conducting interviews to come up with a profile of the ideal juror. Assisted by Mafalda Gray, she analyzed the lives of 250 local citizens who had been called for jury duty and might wind up on the Benson case. She concentrated on where they worked, where they lived, what they paid for their homes, when they bought them, whether they had been involved in lawsuits, and whether they paid their taxes and bills on time. She and Mafalda then photographed each prospective juror's house.

If the property was clean and well maintained, it suggested the owner was conscientious and would devote close attention to the trial. A carelss housekeeper might be a careless juror, indifferent to details or subtle nuances.

A person who paid his bills promptly was likely to be alert and diligent. If he neglected his responsibilities, he might drift through the trial with a nonchalant attitude.

Ironically, in view of Margaret Covington's feeling that people of modest means resent and envy the rich, she wanted to avoid wealthy jurors. She thought they would be even less sympathetic to Steven.

She was also wary of people who had deep roots in the community. Such jurors would find it harder to acquit Steven for fear of criticism from neighbors.

Covington believed that jurors approached a case with preconceived notions and reached a verdict by the end of the opening arguments. They spent the remainder of the trial searching for evidence to support their conclusions. Out of twelve people, three or four always led the way. The rest followed the more intelligent, verbal, and better-educated jury members.

The ideal juror for this case, she decided, was a woman of average economic means. Although women are more inclined to convict men, they are also more sympathetic and less likely to impose the death penalty.

After helping to select the jury, Margaret Covington planned to hire six people whose opinions and demographic profiles mirrored the people who would pass judgment on Benson. These six shadow jurors would sit anonymously in the gallery and take notes if they cared to. Like the real jury, they would be instructed not to discuss the case among themselves and not to follow the press coverage.

Covington would speak to them every night and, in interviews of an hour or more, ask for feedback based strictly on what they heard and saw in the courtroom. She was convinced that a good shadow jury would not simply tell her what they thought she wanted to hear. They would present an accurate reflection of how the real jury was processing evidence and responding to testimony.

Nearly 20% of the defense budget went toward jury selection.

Margaret Covington received a $10,000 fee. The shadow jurors, discussion groups, and surveys cost an additional $15,000.

4

That night, Jerry Berry gave me a ride from Fort Meyers to Naples, and we stopped for Italian food at Nino's restaurant, where we rendezvoused with private investigator Bob Laws. Although the press concentrated on the contrasting styles of Michael McDonnell and Jerry Brock, there were almost as many differences between McDonnell and his partner.

Berry was a short, compact fellow with a youthful face—he was only thirty-two—a high-pitched nasal voice, and a nervous laugh. The Miami *Herald* said he looked like Beaver Cleaver. But with murder trials he had as much experience as McDonnell, if not more. When he worked in the State Attorney's office, he had successfully prosecuted a sensational case in which members of what Berry dubbed "disorganized crime" ripped off a drug dealer. The dealer was forced to dig his own grave, then was killed and covered with lye.

Berry's time as a prosecutor had left him with few illusions about human nature or the legal system. In some wys he was a perfect counterbalance to McDonnell. While he lacked his partner's commanding courtroom presence, he had a good grasp of the practical and a wealth of knowledge about the opposition.

Berry told me Brock rarely had a case where there was much doubt about the defendant's guilt. He was used to dealing with petty crooks or career criminals who had been caught red-handed.

Still, you couldn't underestimate the man. He was like a bulldog. Once he clamped his teeth on a witness, he didn't let go until he had shaken every last dime out of the guy's pockets. "He doesn't care about dazzling a jury or the gallery. He just does his job, and he has the ego or the confidence to follow the course he sets for himself even if people start laughing at him, which I've heard them do. He won't let Mike or me hurry him into mistakes."

I asked if Steven Benson would take the stand.

Berry said they hadn't decided. McDonnell was against it. But as a prosecutor, Berry said, he had won every case where the defendant failed to testify. He told of a time between college and law school when he had been called for jury duty and the defendant didn't take the stand. "The first thing we all said when we got into the jury room was, 'If he's innocent, why didn't he testify?'"

McDonnell knew his feelings, and they were debating the matter.

At Nino's, talking between bites of spaghetti and meatballs, Bob Laws offered his theory of why Buck didn't bark the night before the murders. The dog had been in the Suburban all day, cooped up with Kim and Scott and a cloud of marijuana. Buck had been zonked and was sleeping off a high.

And what if the person who planted the bombs wasn't Steven, but wasn't a stranger to Buck either? Like one of Scott's druggie friends? Or what about Scott himself? One plausible scenario was that Scott, heavily in debt to a drug dealer and desperately afraid his mother wouldn't give him more money, planned to blow up the family and accelerate his inheritance. But he fouled up the wiring or a timer, and the bombs exploded before he got out of the Suburban.

Scott's motive didn't have to be a drug debt, Laws said. He had reason to feel resentful of Mrs. Benson, and there was no love lost between Carol Lynn and him. What if he decided to blow up his adopted mother and biological mother and take himself out with them?

A big beefy man with ham-sized fists that felt like they were wrapped in sandpaper, Bob Laws had twenty-seven years of investigative experience, most of it with the Dade County Public Safety Department. Rising through the ranks to assistant chief of police, he had retired as supervisor in the Criminal Investigation Division. In his opinion the Collier County Police and the ATF had done a terrible job on the Benson case.

He hoped the State would attempt to introduce evidence that Quail Creek was a secure community. This past April 16, in broad daylight, a two-man team from his company, decked out in camouflage uniforms and toting a replica of a pipe bomb, had infiltrated the subdivision, advancing out of the woods and onto the Benson property. One man brandished the bomb while the other recorded the invasion on videotape. McDonnell and Berry referred to the film as "Rambo III" and they were raring to show it in court.

5

After a three-day voir dire, a jury and two alternates were chosen. It consisted of ten women, two men, and two female alternates. The average age was over sixty. Three of the jurors were in their seventies. In addition to two nurses and a nurse's aide, several of the women did volunteer work with cancer patients, and mentally retarded, and unwed mothers. Showing the hallmarks of Margaret Covington's research, it appeared to be a warm, caring, maternal group. They had thirty children among them.

McDonnell made a renewed motion that the jurors be sequestered. But Judge Hayes denied it. In this circuit juries were rarely sequestered even during final deliberation. It was costly and caused great inconvenience to the people on the panel. Hayes scheduled opening statements for the next morning and sent the jury home for the night.

The defense team repaired to the Veranda lugging briefcases and folders full of depositions as thick as the Manhattan phone book. The Veranda was a piano bar and restaurant around the corner from the Justice Center. A nineteenth-century Victorian structure, painted pale green and surrounded by palms and banana plants, it had a courtyard with wrought-iron tables and chairs. But in this season no one sat outside. The chairs were hot enough to leave a brand on your behind and the air was humid enough to wilt the best-starched collar.

For the duration of the trial the defense team had reserved a corner table on the air-conditioned porch. They gathered here at noon for lunch, then again in the evening for a postmortem. When I asked Jerry and Dwight Brock where they ate lunch, they said they grabbed a Coke and a bag of potato chips and huddled in the State Attorney's office.

"I did the same when I was a prosecutor," said Jerry Berry. "Just brought a soft drink and a snack."

"That's all you could afford," Bob Laws kidded him.

"No, it wasn't that." Berry explained that the State was under pressure while they presented their case. Next week the defense would feel the strain.

McDonnell removed his suit coat, rolled his shirt sleeves, and loosened his tie. He said he was exhausted from being on his feet for three straight days questioning prospective jurors. He woke at 6 A.M. every morning, ran two miles, then swam a quarter of a mile to get in shape for a trial. But he didn't believe in working through lunch or late into the night.

"There comes a point when you have to step back and get some perspective." He compared it to preparing for an exam. It didn't make sense to keep cramming and stay awake all night studying. "I never did that." Then he laughed. "Maybe that's why I got such lousy grades."

Despite his fatigue, he was in high spirits. He recognized that his self-deprecating jokes sometimes put him in a less than flattering light, but he didn't mind. "Some people just don't have a sense of humor."

He ordered oysters and said, "They're supposed to be an aphrodisiac. I'm not convinced of that. I once ate three dozen and only thirty worked."

McDonnell was like a coach keeping his team loose before the big game. He told them Brock was on the defensive. He ended the pep talk by clapping his hands. "Now let's move for a mistrial."

I asked how he felt about pleading a case to ten women. He said he had tried a civil case in front of twelve women and won in a walk.

Jerry Berry said he, too, had experience with an all-female jury. When they retired to deliberate a verdict, they argued for hours. You could hear them through the closed door. It sounded like they were in tears, close to bloodshed. The judge finally told the bailiff to ask if they needed him to clarify some issue of law. They sent back word that they were still voting to see who would serve as foreman.

When the laughter subsided, Nina McDonnell said she was worried how the women would react when Brock introduced photographs of Scott and Margaret Benson lying mangled beside the Suburban.

Right now the women probably imagined the next few weeks would be like living in a daytime soap opera. But when they saw those pictures, they were going to think they had been trapped in a horror show. Worse, a snuff film.

Margaret Covington was less concerned about the ten women than the two men. She saw big trouble with both of them. The older one, Fred Kruger, was of German extraction. Covington said Teutonic types tended to be judgmental and disciplinarians. Kruger had stated that he charged his own kids rent, so he wasn't likely to be lenient about Steven's lackadaisical financial dealings with his mother.

The other man, Ernest Henning, also had the earmarks of a hardball juror. He wasn't as bad as some of those the defense had struck; it was a matter of choosing the lesser evil. Still, Henning was a construction inspector, a supervisory type. Such men were accustomed to making decisions, to hiring and firing people. They had fewer reservations about voting for the death penalty.

Bob Laws thought the defense might have problems long before the verdict. He had spotted some tough-looking characters in the courtroom. One guy wore dirty jeans and a T-shirt, and had a spider tattooed on his arm. The lawyers came to call him the Pirate. He showed up every day, and was heard muttering about McDonnell and Nina and Steven Benson. Maybe he was one of Scott's drug connections. Maybe he was just crazy. Laws said McDonnell should start carrying a gun.

McDonnell laughed and shook his head no. "Maybe I'll hire that guy who wrapped his leg around his neck, the Karate Kid, as my personal bodyguard."

Chapter 3

I

During his opening statement, Jerry Brock stood at a lectern staring down at a legal pad of notes. He spoke in what the Miami *Herald* characterized as a "banjo twang" voice, but that may be granting it more animation than it had. Perhaps his deadpan delivery was what German dramatists call an "alienation effect," the purpose being to force listeners to concentrate on what he said, not how he said it.

There were no stylistic flourishes to distract the jury. At most, he stepped to one side or raised both hands and skinned back his thin blond hair.

He started off by trying to draw an analogy, but immediately stumbled and lost his way. "My purpose is only to give you—and I'd like you to look at it in terms of a picture puzzle on a crossword puzzle. Whenever you buy a crossword puzzle, it comes in a box. You always have a picture of how the puzzle is going to look once you put all the pieces together. So that is my purpose for making an opening statement."

He then read the charges against Steven Benson. ". . . the defendant is charged that he did unlawfully from a premeditated design effect the death of a human being, kill and murder Margaret H. Benson, a human being, by the use of an explosive device in violation of Florida Statute 782.04."

After eight more charges, he introduced the cast of characters and gave a synopsis of events that could have been lifted from any of a hundred newspaper stories that had appeared in the last year.

"Now, Mrs. Benson had suspected for a period of time that the defendant"—pronounced, as always, dee-fen-*dant*—"had been taking money from her businesses that she had been putting into these businesses to finance his own venture and to finance some personal matters. So Wayne Kerr was asked to come down to go over the bank books to try to gleam [*sic*] a financial picture of what was transpiring."

After visiting Meridian Marketing, then seeing Steven's new house, "Mrs. Benson is in an outrage . . . She also discusses with the attorney about disinheriting the defendant."

This was the only reference, not just in the opening statement, but in the entire trial, to the often repeated accusation that Mrs. Benson planned to write Steven out of her will.

As the prosecutor described the events of July 8 and 9, 1985, he didn't forget to mention Buck. "Now, they [Scott and Kim] had also taken with them a dog, which there will probably be some testimony about; propensities of this particular dog."

Even as he reached the explosions, Brock refused to indulge in any melodramatics. Reading from his notes, he ticked off each point as he made it, and went back and slowly checked the page before turning to the next.

He summarized the investigation and the discovery that two four-inch end caps and two four-inch galvanized nipple pipes had been purchased at Hughes Supply. The receipts contained prints and, as Brock explained in a single breath, "they got a court order allowing them to get prints from the defendant." The prints on the receipt, he said, matched Benson's prints.

"I also anticipate that we will hear some testimony concerning the defendant's prior knowledge and possession of improvised explosive devices."

With that he thanked the ladies and gentlemen and turned the lectern over to the defense.

From Michael McDonnell jurors got no "alienating effects," no dry recitation of dates and names and facts. He gave a full-fledged performance, inviting them to participate, to become bit-part players in the drama. "We've heard an interesting story this morning, and I suggest to you that the evidence as it unfolds in this trial will not establish this story."

Instead, "the evidence will show that Steven Benson was the loving son of Margaret Benson, the peacemaker in the family, the man who took over for the family when he lost his father, the only one who did not fight physically tooth and nail, drawing blood."

Although "Mr. Brock found it necessary to read to you these redundant and cumulative charges," McDonnell emphasized that they all related to one incident. Leaving the lectern, he stood close to Benson, putting an arm around his shoulder. "I'd like you to look at this man. My friend, Steven Benson." The State, he said, his voice rising in disbelief, claimed that Steven, who never fought and never got angry, tried to destroy his whole family—and for no good reason. That's what all the charges and legalese boiled down to.

Steven took off his glasses and wiped tears from his eyes.

While it was impossible to tell whether the jury was persuaded, one person in the gallery left no doubt she didn't buy this story. Brenda Murphy, Janet Lee Murphy's daughter, sat behind the prosecutor's table. A tall, modishly dressed woman, she stuck a finger into her mouth and pretended to gag herself, pantomiming nausea at McDonnell's characterization of her cousin as a loving family man. The defense attorneys asked the bailiff to caution Ms. Murphy not to act up again.

McDonnell reminded the jury that when the State arrested Benson they said he murdered his mother because he had stolen two and a half million dollars from her. "But you won't hear that in this courtroom because it wasn't true."

The evidence would show that Steven and his mother were business partners, and while Margaret was concerned that the corporations were not yet profitable, she was also frustrated "that she had been giving Carol Lynn hundreds of thousands of dollars with no return," and doing the same for Scott. Since his mother was already investing in his businesses and he was due to inherit from other sources, McDonnell said Steven had no financial motive to murder Mrs. Benson.

"We don't know who committed this crime now. I suggest to you when all of the evidence is in, you will still not know who committed this crime. I have tried. I have not been able to solve it."

He primed the jury for what his witnesses would establish. Contrary to Mr. Brock's claims, Steven had been gone from the house for thirty minutes, not an hour. Furthermore, he came around the Suburban to help his sister climb into the car, "just as he had helped her and helped Scottie all his life. And he handed poor Scottie the keys to the car and the bomb went off. And you know where Steven was? Right beside the vehicle. And you will hear that from the evidence and from witnesses who have no axes to grind."

After accusing the State of ignoring inconvenient facts, McDonnell rounded off a few rough corners himself. "Steven was not badly injured," he said. In fact, there was no evidence he had been injured at all.

Despite his sympathy for the Benson family and his desire not to speak ill of the dead, McDonnell said, "the facts will be clear. Scottie was off in the wrong direction." He used, sold, and smuggled drugs. Any number of people might have had a motive for murdering Margaret and him.

McDonnell reminded jurors that they had sworn they presumed his client innocent. The State's case would not change that. "When all the evidence is in, and all is said and done, you'll be able to look at Mr. Brock and say 'Steven is an innocent man.'"

A dozen or more attorneys sat in the gallery. Some had a vested interest in the case. Others showed up in the same spirit as a musician might attend a concert or an actor might watch a new play. They wanted to study their colleagues and competitors in action. While the majority agreed that McDonnell had been more effective during his opening statement, Brock hadn't made any promises he couldn't keep and hadn't set any dazzling standard he couldn't equal or surpass in the days ahead. He was like a steady baseline tennis player. Content to put the ball in play, confident in his stamina, he let his opponent force the action and make the mistakes.

They felt McDonnell had committed himself to a more hazardous course. By starting off at a high pitch, he had built expectations he might not be able to satisfy. He had also linked himself closely to Steven, which allowed him little room to maneuver. He had called Steven his friend when perhaps it would have been better to maintain a professional distance, so that he could admit Steven had his flaws and might have skimmed some money from his mother's account, might even have been a less than admirable son, but that didn't make him a murderer.

2

The State started off by putting sixteen sheriff's deputies on the stand as if to prove by sheer weight of numbers that the crime scene had been secure and the evidence gathering proper. But McDonnell suggested that they had failed to implement sensible procedures. A police aerial photographer admitted that as he flew over Quail Creek shortly after the bombings, he had not searched the surrounding countryside for assailants fleeing on foot or in vehicles.

Sergeant Ray Williams, the first officer on the scene, conceded he had not ordered any roads blocked. He had set up one perimeter around the Suburban with yellow plastic tape, but later moved it. He could not explain why the search area had been widened—which permitted McDonnell to imply that metal fragments from nearby construction sites might have gotten mixed in with shrapnel from the bombs.

An auxiliary deputy named Ronald McNew said he had discovered someone inside the perimeter, decided he had no business there, took his name, address, and car tag number, and turned the information over to investigator Mike Koors. But McNew couldn't say whether the intruder had ever been questioned.

McDonnell observed that at some point officers from the narcotics unit arrived at the Benson house. He wondered what had prompted their appearance. Was it possibly related to the "visitor who had picked up Kim Beegle" after the murders?

Popping a mint into his mouth, Jerry Brock moved the candy from cheek to cheek, sucking at the sweetness and going about his business like a man building a castle with pea-sized stones. He suggested officers from the narcotics unit might simply have responded to the general call for support.

During a break at 3 P.M., as I stood in the gallery talking to the judge's wife, Nancy, Hugh Hayes shed his robes and joined us. "So far," he said, "it's a C+ to a B− trial." Like his wife, a high school history teacher, Hayes graded with letters.

The State's witnesses struck him as ill prepared. "They've had a long time to get ready, to review their notes. But they don't seem to have done it." He gave the defense the advantage on its opening statement, more for style than content.

He admitted it was tough to sit through hours of forensic testimony. But that was where his martial arts training in Tae-Kwon-Do helped. Whenever he felt his body sag and his mind slide toward inattention, he remembered the motto of Master Lee: "See straight." He said the phrase released the same focused energy that you used when breaking boards with your hands.

· · ·

Late that afternoon Jerry Brock called on the manager of a hardware store. Sauntering across to a table where the evidence was kept, he came back carrying a paper bag which he plunked down in front of the witness. The witness removed from it a six-battery flashlight. But before it could be introduced into evidence, McDonnell objected that its relevance had not been established. So the flashlight went back in the bag, Brock sauntered to the evidence table, then, after a long whispered conversation with his brother Dwight, he told the judge he had no further questions and no further witnesses today.

Journalists asked Brock when he intended to call Carol Lynn Kendall. He smiled wanly. "Sometime before the end of the trial."

Chapter 4

The second day started with Michael McDonnell renewing his motion that the jury be sequestered. The previous evening he had noticed a juror waiting for forty-five minutes in front of the Justice Center for her husband to pick her up. This, he maintained, exposed "her to courtroom talk, the circuslike atmosphere, the media." Local newspapers had printed the names of jurors and details about their personal lives. "Every time the jurors leave" the court, McDonnell complained, "the lights go on and the [TV] cameras hit them." Under the circumstances, they couldn't avoid being influenced and perhaps prejudiced.

The judge denied the motion, pointing out that no jurors had complained. But since newspapers with inflammatory headlines were available in dispensers all around the Justice Center, he said McDonnell could provide daily copies for the record in case of an appeal.

Kimberly Dawn Beegle wore a pink dress, white high heels, and a baggy white jacket with the sleeves rolled, and she spoke in such a faint voice, TV coverage of her testimony ran on the evening news with subtitles. Although the press portrayed her as a glamorous sexpot who had dropped out of high school to move in with a millionaire's son, she looked and acted like somebody's cute kid sister. With her strong jaw, dark tan, and sun-streaked hair, she bore an uncanny resemblance to tennis star Chris Evert.

Questioned by Jerry Brock, she described herself as Scott's fiancée and said they had discussed marriage plans the night before his death. When she referred to Scott as "a professional tennis player," Brock tried to cue the response he wanted, but wound up having to rephrase his question three times before Kim got the message.

BROCK: Well, had any events occurred that was important to Scott from his tennis activity standpoint?

KIM: He was accepted to the U.S. Open. That was very important.

She claimed this had happened in early July, and Scott "was very happy. Skipping around the house. He was acting like a little kid."

On Friday, July 5, Kim had cleaned the Suburban, vacuuming under the seats and in the console. She saw no bombs. The console, she said, had contained a fishing knife with a wooden handle, a manila envelope full of credit card receipts, and a large flashlight. Brock showed her a flashlight which she identified as looking "like the one that was in the truck." For a second day in a row, Brock seemed to be building toward some conclusion—perhaps the flashlight served as the detonator, maybe it had been removed to make room for the bomb—but during the rest of the trial he never tied up this loose end.

On Monday morning, July 8, Kim recounted, she and Scott drove to Fort Myers and spent the day looking at used cars and shopping at the Thomas Edison Mall. That evening they drove back to Naples and cruised from club to club. Buck went with them; whenever they left the Suburban, the dog remained in the car.

When Brock asked whether Scott discussed what he planned to do the next day, McDonnell objected that the State was offering hearsay, not evidence. It was suggesting that members of the Benson family had had other plans and that Steven coerced them into the Suburban, then blew them up. McDonnell protested that testimony about intentions, especially intentions which had never been carried out, was inadmissable. But the judge overruled.

Brock repeated his question about Scott's plans, then added, "Was there a rush to get home?"

"Yes," Kim said. "He wanted to get up early and play tennis."

Despite the rush, they reached home around midnight and Kim removed her purse from the console. Again she saw no pipes.

Buck slept in the bedroom with Scott and Kim. She didn't hear him bark during the night. But she was a heavy sleeper. Scott got out of bed twice the next morning without waking her. The first twenty-six-pound bomb didn't rouse her either. She woke up with the second blast.

As she described her actions after the explosions, she had to choke back sobs, and the jury and spectators strained to hear her small shaking words. She looked out the bedroom window, she said, and saw the Suburban "engulfed in flames." She dressed and dashed outside and "the first person I noticed was Carol Lynn, and she was standing across the street and she had blood, she had, she had blood—" Kim broke down.

"Just take your time," Brock soothed her.

"She had blood all over her. And I seen Steven was sitting on the steps and he had his hands on his head and his head in his hands. And I went to Scott and I seen Scott. It was obvious that he was dead."

"So then you went back into the house?"

"Well, I had stopped and told Steven Scott was dead, and he didn't even look at me nor did he even say anything."

Brock showed her "State's Exhibit Number 68 for identification. If you would take a look at it and tell me if you recognize the individual in the photograph."

She broke down and cried again. It was Scott. Out in the gallery spectators cried along with Kim. Brenda Murphy, Scott's cousin, dabbed a Kleenex at her eyes. The Judge called a ten-minute recess before cross examination.

While the State had depicted an idyllic relationship ruined by a hideous crime, the defense attempted to present a different picture of the young couple by going back to 1981, when Kim, age fifteen, started sleeping over at the Benson house in Port Royal. But Brock objected that McDonnell was exceeding the scope of direct examination. The judge agreed that if he wanted to go beyond the time frame established by the prosecution, he should recall Kim Beegle as a defense witness.

McDonnell confined his questions to more recent events, and Kim described moving from place to place, spending nights with Scott at his mother's house, at her parent's house, and at her brother David's house.

She described the July 8 drive to Fort Myers and said Buck "was like a little kid to us." They took him everywhere. That evening they ate dinner at Shallows and had ordered a bottle of wine, but Scott drank only a sip because he was in training and didn't want to do anything to harm his physical condition.

When they returned to Quail Creek, she repeated that she took her purse out of the console.

MCDONNELL: Did you take the marijuana out of the console at that time?
KIM: I don't remember.

She admitted she had put a bag of marijuana back into the console after rolling a joint for Scott during the day. She said he had smoked half of it. She herself hadn't smoked it at all. She used to smoke marijuana, but had quit.

When Brock objected that this line of questioning was irrelevant, McDonnell maintained that it had a bearing on the witness's credibility and her ability to remember and interpret events. The judge let the defense continue. But Kim swore she had stopped smoking marijuana long before July 8, 1985. When Scott finished half the joint, she put what was left into "a clear plastic bag," like the kind "you pack your lunch for a little boy or a little girl."

Confronted by a copy of her statement to the police, Kim acknowledged after lengthy argument that the Suburban was left unlocked with the keys in it. She, Scott, and Buck went into Scott's bedroom, and while she was in the bathroom removing her makeup, Scott let the dog out, using the door that opened directly to the yard. She estimated that Scott and Buck were outside for five minutes. And the defense planted the tiniest seed of suggestion that he could have put the bombs in the Suburban during that time.

After Scott and the dog came back in, he bolted the door behind him and stepped over to the dresser. Once he had changed into a pair of shorts, they climbed into bed, switched off the lights, watched TV for a short time, then fell asleep.

Inevitably, the question of Buck's barking came up. Throughout the trial there was debate whether he had been trained to bark or trained *not* to bark in the house. While the State contended Buck invariably barked when anybody approached the house, the defense claimed that sometimes he barked and sometimes he didn't. When I suggested that McDonnell bring Buck to court and put him on the stand, he grinned and said, "A smart lawyer never asks a question he doesn't know the answer to. How do I know he wouldn't bark?"

What interested him more at the moment was Buck's attack training. "Did Scott perceive the need for an attack dog?" he asked Kim.

"He never used him, if that's what you are trying to say."

"I'm not trying to say anything but what I'm saying," he sternly lied. "Did he or did he not perceive a need for an attack dog?"

Brock approached the bench and objected that the question called for a witness to testify about Scott's perceptions. This might have been a good time for McDonnell to bring up the death threats Tracy Mullins allegedly made. Kim had discussed these in previous statements to the police and they appeared to be related to Scott's desire to have an attack dog. But Tracy Mullins and her threats were never mentioned during the trial.

McDonnell rephrased his question and got Kim to agree that Scott "went everywhere with Buck that he could." Then he circled back to the marijuana, asking whether she saw it the next day, after the murders, in Scott's dresser drawers. She said she wasn't sure it was the same marijuana, but acknowledged that it was the same kind of clear plastic bag and, as far as she knew, Scott had just one stash of pot. In a deposition she had responded "Right," when McDonnell said Scott "had to get it from the truck to the dresser drawer." This suggested he had gone out to the Suburban sometime during the night and could have put bombs in the Suburban then.

But Kim claimed she had been confused during the deposition. "I was very nervous at the time because Steven was in the room." Now she was more relaxed. She conceded someone from the State Attorney's office had talked to her a couple of weeks ago about the bag of marijuana.

When McDonnell asked whether Scott used cocaine on July 8, it provoked a long bench conference. The question, Brock argued, implied that because Scott used cocaine, it wasn't "as bad he got killed."

McDonnell said, "I assure you I don't think that's justification for killing anybody." The defense believed Kim used cocaine on a regular basis with Scott and was still using it. If she had done so the night before, or the day of the explosions, "that affects her ability to perceive events." What's more "we have hard and direct evidence that Scott was involved directly in 'cocaine smuggling, selling, financing and use. That is a reasonable hypothesis of innocence in this case and one we need to develop." The State "opened the door" to the subject of Scott's drug use and the defense felt they should be free to explore it.

Brock protested, "I didn't even mention anything about the marijuana." As for Scott's involvement with cocaine, he said, "So what? It has absolutely no relevancy at this point in time. They haven't shown any way, even assuming they could bring that up in the case in chief, there is any evidence connecting Scott with the bombing."

McDonnell said "the State developed on the direct examination that Scott was an athlete, accepted at the U.S. Open, and was getting in shape for that. The witness has testified that he wouldn't drink because he was getting in shape. The issue of cocaine is directly related to that."

The Judge disagreed and sustained the State's objection. So McDonnell approached the subject obliquely, asking Kim about Scott's training program. She said he had cut down on drinking and marijuana. "Was there nothing else he did that was harmful to his body?"

"Well, he had, only time I'ver ever witnessed Scott doing cocaine was once or twice. But I wouldn't consider him a heavy user of any drug."

"Did you ever see him use nitrous oxide?"

This brought the prosecutor back to the bench. "He is attempting to impeach the witness on matters which are totally collateral to any issue in this particular case."

To the contrary, McDonnell contended, they were impeaching the picture the State had painted of a pro tennis player in training for the U.S. Open. "In truth and fact, Judge, we have a young man who wasn't all that good, who was financed and carried through by his mom, who was heavily into drugs."

Jerry Berry chimed in that "another matter goes to credibility." Kim Beegle was on record three times denying Scott used cocaine— once under oath in court, twice to the police. Now she conceded to seeing him do coke on a couple of occasions.

While the judge again cautioned the defense to keep within the scope of direct examination, he let them ask whether Kim had seen Scott use nitrous oxide in 1985. She said no. She acknowledged, however, that she had misled the police about Scott's use of cocaine.

She also acknowledged that the manila envelope of receipts covered the entire bottom of the console. She hadn't looked under it the night of July 8.

After establishing that the air conditioning in the Suburban hadn't worked for a month, McDonnell indicated Kim's perceptions had changed between the time of the murders and now. Today she testified that she "told Steven Scott was dead, and he didn't even look at me nor did he even say anything." But she had said something different in July of 1985.

She had told investigators that Steven "was sitting there crying." Wayne Kerr had urged him to calm down. At first, Kim testified she didn't remember why Kerr said this, then she admitted it was because Steven was moaning. When McDonnell asked her to demonstrate the sound, she gave a low weak moan. She granted the sound she had made when demonstrating for the police "was a little louder." McDonnell asked her to do it the same way now and, with obvious embarrassment, she imitated Steven's moans.

Minutes later, McDonnell again asked what Steven did when she told him Scott was dead, and once more she replied, "He didn't do anything." So the attorney, who had already complained at the bench that the witness had been coached by the state, confronted her with a deposition in which she said that when told of Scott's death, Steven "started screaming, sort of like oh, my God, I don't believe it. He was very upset."

Now she maintained she didn't remember him saying "Oh my God" and she didn't remember him crying.

So McDonnell referred her to another page, another line. "Remember this question and answer? 'Did Steven say anything when you said that? Answer: He started crying, moaning.'"

"I didn't see any tears come out of his eyes," Kim insisted, "and that to me is crying." Still, she didn't deny she had previously made these statements.

2

After the lunch break, Carol Lynn Benson Kendall took the stand. Local TV stations and national networks arrived in force. WINK-TV preempted its normal schedule of programs to carry live coverage of Carol Lynn's testimony.

The courtroom was crowded with spectators who had gravitated from throughout the building. In addition to the regular trial junkies, shadow jurors, lawyers, and family members, there were courthouse secretaries, cooks and charwomen from the cafeteria, off-duty detectives, and meter maids carrying the chalk-tipped batons they used to mark the tires of illegally parked cars. Even some people who had been dismissed from jury duty returned for the long anticipated pay-off scene—scarred surviving sister confronts accused-murderer brother; handsome defense attorney takes on former beauty queen.

John Henry Todd, the Karate Kid, cornered me in the hall, then slipped into the press room behind me. As the TV monitor showed Carol Lynn's face in close-up, he said that years of practicing Tae-Kwon-Do had taught him "the power of internal telegraphing." He could look into anyone's eyes and know whether he was lying. Although Judge Hayes took Tae-Kwon-Do, Todd doubted he had progressed to where he possessed "the power of internal telegraphing." Hayes was only a blue belt. But he—

"Shut the fuck up," a TV technician screamed. Carol Lynn had started to testify.

Those who had seen a decade-old photograph of her modeling a slinky sequined gown or who had conjured up an image of the sort of wealthy, high-strung heiress who inhabits the sound stage of evening soaps were disappointed. While still an attractive woman at the age of forty-one, Carol Lynn looked demure rather than seductive in a tan suit with matching pumps and purse. Her rinsed blond hair was parted down the middle, and although she had applied mascara and eyeliner, she left her face bare of makeup. Tender pink scar tissue flowed like molten wax from her right cheekbone down to the collar of her blouse. One had the sense of watching a personal injury case in which a plaintiff wanted the world to see exactly what had happened to her.

At first, she was tense, subdued. Reporters wondered whether she might be under medication—on some kind of painkiller or tranquilizer.

As Jerry Brock asked what her relationship was to Scott, a TV producer whispered fiercely to the pool cameraman, "Get in tighter. Get her face."

"Scott was my son," she said.

In more than 400 pages of statements and depositions during a period of over ten months Carol Lynn never once referred to Scott as her son, yet during the trial she never called him anything else. Clearly she had been coached.

Brock directed her attention to the events of May and June 1985, when Margaret accompanied Scott to a series of tennis tournaments. Carol Lynn explained that the trip to Europe got cut short when Scott "wanted to come back and practice, because he had gotten an invitation to play in the U.S. Open."

It was the same curious claim Kim Beegle had made—Scott was

working hard because he had received an invitation to play in the U.S. Open. This contradicted two previous statements by Carol Lynn. On July 9, 1985, she told Officer Smith the European trip ended sooner than planned because "Mother was so sick." On July 28, 1985, she told Graham and Nowicki, "They were supposed to stay longer, but Scott got in his head that he was coming home. And so he went and changed all the reservations."

Earlier statements aside, the assertion that Scott had been invited to play in the U.S. Open was absurd. One doesn't get an invitation to participate in the country's premier tennis event. One gains entry on the basis of his performance at tournaments during the past year. A computerized ranking of men around the world appears every week, and is published by the Association of Tennis Professionals (ATP), the players' union. A call to ATP headquarters in Texas revealed that during June 1985 Scott Benson did not rank in the top one thousand players. The U.S. Open admits the top 128 players. The ATP saw no way that Scott could have gotten in except as a spectator.

Still, I double-checked with U.S. Open officials in New York, who assured me there was no scenario under which Scott Benson could have been "invited." As they pointed out, if he was losing in minor satellite tournaments in Norway, how could he compete at a Grand Slam event? And how could he know by mid-June that he would play the U.S. Open in late August? The list of participating players wasn't drawn up until a week after his death.

Perhaps in his fogged and unstable mind, Scott imagined he was invited to play in the U.S. Open. Or maybe to convince Mrs. Benson to continue financing tens of thousands of dollars in lessons, travel, and equipment, he lied. Or else, the family, wanting to think nothing but good of the dead boy, invented a consoling story. However and wherever it originated, this palpable fiction was repeated by the State whenever it suited their purposes.

Carol Lynn went on to recount that she and her mother flew to Naples together in early July. Wayne Kerr arrived on the seventh. The next day, while Mrs. Benson and Kerr drove to the Meridian office, Carol Lynn stayed home and worked on plans for the new house. About noon Steven telephoned. Mrs. Benson and Kerr had been to the office, then left. "So he was calling to see if I knew where they were."

BROCK: And did you tell him?
CAROL LYNN: No, I did not.
BROCK: Did you know where they were?
CAROL LYNN: Yes, I did.
BROCK: Why did you not tell him?
CAROL LYNN: Because my mother had instructed me not to tell him.

With a few phrases, she had put a new spin on the story. In her statement to Graham and Nowicki, she hadn't said her mother instructed her not to divulge her whereabouts to Steven. There had been no hint she had even been informed that Mrs. Benson and Kerr were going to Fort Myers. Carol Lynn had only inferred as much. She told Nowicki, "I mean, I figured I knew where they went, but I played dumb."

Brock asked when Steven called the second time that day, and she said, "Around 5:00, 5:30, 6:00."

In her statement to Graham and Nowicki, she had not been sure of this. She started off saying the call came "around dinnertime." But when pressed whether it had been before or after her birthday dinner, she admitted, "I don't remember."

This was the phone conversation when Steven supposedly volunteered to help stake out the lots and said Scott should come along. Brock asked, "Whenever your brother was explaining that, what was your mental impression of Scott going along?"

Before she could respond, Michael McDonnell approached the bench and objected to the admission of testimony about mental impressions. He characterized them as "pure speculation" that was neither material nor relevant.

"May not be material," Judge Hayes said, "but I think it is going to be relevant."

McDONNELL: If it's immaterial, Your Honor, isn't it inadmissible?
HAYES: Not just because it's immaterial. May be immaterial to the issue but it's not irrelevant.
McDONNELL: Yes sir. But if it's immaterial to issues in the case, I don't see how it could be admissible. That's my point.

Hayes urged McDonnell to "look at the code, 90.402." He overruled the objection.

As the proceedings resumed, Jerry Brock gave a subtly different shading to his question, asking for her mental impression "whenever your brother insisted that Scott go along."

McDonnell objected that the witness never said Steven "insisted" Scott come along. Brock agreed to rephrase the question, but when he did so, there was no instruction to the jury that they should forget the word "insisted."

This was the great flaw of these sotto voce meetings at the bench. Although they made for an orderly, decorous trial and prevented attorneys from shouting prejudicial objections, they didn't keep them from broadcasting prejudicial testimony. And there was no mechanism for announcing which objections had been sustained and which testimony should be disregarded.

Carol Lynn said she thought it was silly to drag Scott out in the morning, "when he had to practice and he would have been tired because he often got in late." She added that it wasn't a job that required three people.

She gave the impression she hoped to discourage Steven. "I thought, well, if he . . . knew what time I was going he probably wouldn't come over, because that wasn't an hour that he was usually up."

But with Graham and Nowicki she had sounded pleased, even mischievously delighted. "I thought that that was a good thing that he had called and—and offered to come over and do that. And we all kind of got a little chuckle about the fact that Steven was going to come over early in the morning and get poor Scott up and everything."

If her "mental impressions" were admissible evidence, the question was how and why they had changed in the past year. It's possible that in retrospect all of Steven's actions and remarks struck her as suspicious. But at the trial she purported to be describing her reactions and state of mind around the time of the murders, and these simply didn't match the answers she had previously given to investigators.

She said that after the telephone call, "I turned to Wayne and my mother and I said, 'You're never going to believe who that was,' and I related the conversation."

In two statements, Kerr swore he had no recollection of this phone call or of Carol Lynn's summary of the conversation.

BROCK: Approximately what time did y'all return home [from dinner]?
CAROL LYNN: We got home at about quarter of nine. The reason I remember is because I remember what was on television.

McDonnell bounded to his feet and over to the bench. "Request the witness be instructed to respond to the question. She's not being responsive. The question was what time, and she started going into reasoning. That's my first request.

"Second request, I want to renew my objection to that prior testimony and move for a mistrial based upon the admission of her state of mind, of her mental impression.

"Referring to Professor Ehrhardt's text, I quote: 'Included within the definition of relevancy is the concept of materiality. The evidence must tend to prove or disprove a material fact. When evidence is offered to prove a fact which is not a matter in issue, it is said to be immaterial.'"

Judge Hayes denied both motions, and Brock repeated the question.

BROCK: What time was it that you returned home from dinner.
CAROL LYNN: It was about quarter to nine.
BROCK: How do you know it was about that time?
CAROL LYNN: Because we turned on the television set and I remember what was on. Because it was something that I didn't want to watch, so I went ahead and went to bed.
BROCK: Okay. Whenever you went to bed was there anyone else that was up?
CAROL LYNN: Wayne and my mother were up.
BROCK: Had Scotty returned home?
CAROL LYNN: No, he wasn't home at that time.

This recall of specific times and facts was in marked contrast to her statement to Graham and Nowicki. Less than three weeks after the murders, her memory failed when the detectives questioned her about the evening of July 8. Nowicki asked what time Scott left to pick up Kim Beegle. Carol Lynn said he usually left at 10:30 P.M.

NOWICKI: Do you think were you awake on that particular night [July 8]? Do you recall if you were awake enough and knew if he left to get her?
CAROL LYNN: Oh, boy. I really don't remember. Ummm, whether—whether we all stayed up that late or whether we were tired, I really don't remember. It was my birthday.

NOWICKI: Uh-huh.

CAROL LYNN: And we had gone out to eat that night. I—I don't think we all stayed up very late. Umm, but then Scott kind of came and went.

Two days later, the detectives doubled back, trying to get Carol Lynn to recall when people in the Benson house had gone to bed on July 8.

NOWICKI: How about how late—uhh—how late was the household that —until you went to bed? How late was that the night before, Monday night?

CAROL LYNN: I think we all went to bed pretty early.

NOWICKI: Okay.

CAROL LYNN: Because I know I was tired and—umm—I don't think we watched any television; I don't remember.

Now, a year later, she remembered precisely what time they returned from the restaurant and when she went to bed; she remembered that they had watched TV and she knew which program; and she remembered Scott wasn't home.

A similar change occurred regarding the exact time her mother woke up. On the day of the murders, she told Officer Smith that her mother was up before her, having been wakened by a mosquito. On September 20, in her deposition to McDonnell, she said she didn't know. Now she maintained, "My mother got up right after I did." While some of these changing recollections didn't concern crucial matters, others definitely did and they all called into question her credibility.

When Brock asked her to step down and indicate on an enlarged color photograph where Steven's van had been parked, she appeared reluctant to look at the crime scene with its scorched and twisted reminders. But she did as asked, then returned to her seat and primly put her purse in her lap.

Standing off to one side, Brock continued his questioning, sometimes lifting a hand and squeezing the flesh along his lean jawline. To anyone who knew nothing about the variance between her previous statements and her present answers, she was a compelling witness as she narrated the story of Steven's arrival, then his departure to buy the coffee and Danish.

BROCK: Was your mother dressed at this particular point in time in clothes to go out in, as opposed to her housecoat or—
CAROL LYNN: Yes, she was dressed.

This conflicted with Wayne Kerr's recollection that both Mrs. Benson and Carol Lynn were in their nightclothes when Steven arrived.

Carol Lynn stated she had had no discussion with Scott about staking out the property.

BROCK: Did you hear anyone else discuss that with him?
CAROL LYNN: No, I didn't.
BROCK: Did you hear your mother make some statement to him in regard to that?
CAROL LYNN: No, I didn't.

For all she could say then, Scott decided to go to the lots of his own accord. This trip to the property might have been organized days in advance, not at the last moment at Steven's instigation.

Carol Lynn said she had heard her mother conversing with Scott. Indeed, Mrs. Benson had more than one conversation with him.

BROCK: Okay. Well, the first conversation, were you privy to that conversation?
CAROL LYNN: I don't know the first time [which] my mother told Scott. It's possible she could have told him the night before, but I don't know.

McDonnell was up and at the bench again.

Object, move to strike, unresponsive, speculation. Not even hearsay, just speculation. Request the witness be instructed just to answer the question. We'd stay out of all this coming back and forth if she'll just answer the question. And I know counsel is not trying to do that.
HAYES: All right. Be specific as to your question. The answer was unresponsive.
BROCK: What about if we do this. Take a short recess and let me talk to her.

After the break, Brock established that Steven had asked "Is Scott up yet?" and Mrs. Benson went and woke him. Carol Lynn heard her tell Scott that Steven wanted to speak to him about the Lotuses.

Eventually, Steven told Mrs. Benson he wanted her to come to the lots too. Her mother showed surprise, Carol Lynn said. "She wasn't dressed for it. I hadn't heard anything about her going along before. My mother said to Steven, 'Oh well, Steven, I'm going down to the office with Wayne.'" But Steven repeated that he wanted her to go to the property.

In this case, interestingly, Brock didn't ask for Carol Lynn's "mental impression." She had told Graham and Nowicki she had initially been in favor of her mother going along. "I wanted her to look and see if she was happy with the view..." But then the secretary, Marty Taylor, reminded Margaret that a pool man was supposed to arrive to give an estimate.

McDonnell objected that this was hearsay. If the State wanted to establish a fact about an appointment with a pool man, they should do so through Marty Taylor. Brock said they didn't intend "to prove the truth that there was in fact a pool man," just that Marty had said there was one and that arrangements had to be made. McDonnell reiterated that this was hearsay.

Judge Hayes advised the prosecution to rephrase his question.

Brock had Carol Lynn explain why the pool man was expected, what he was supposed to do, and what arrangements were prepared for his arrival. These preparations sounded extensive, but Wayne didn't remember them as prolonged nor did he recall any great resistance on Mrs. Benson's part.

For a mother who supposedly had been "in an outrage" yesterday at her son for diverting money, she seemed amazingly good-natured and cooperative today. While the State described the morning of July 9 as a tense showdown with Steven under pressure to produce the books, Mrs. Benson didn't register any strong objection when he said he was going for coffee—in fact, she ordered a cup—or when he urged her to come over to the property. She didn't even suggest that he haul the boxes of records into the house so Wayne Kerr could begin his audit.

Margaret, Steven, and Scott went to the Suburban while Carol Lynn gathered up her belongings and followed them moments later. When she stepped outside, she said, she saw her mother in the front passenger seat, Scott behind the steering wheel, and Steven standing beside the open door to the seat behind Mrs. Benson.

BROCK: As you were walking to the—from the front door of the house to the Suburban, did anybody close any of the doors?

CAROL LYNN: No, they didn't.

BROCK: So at the point that you exited the house, your mother's door on the passenger side is open. Is that correct?

CAROL LYNN: No, that is not correct.

BROCK: Is it closed?

CAROL LYNN: My mother's door was closed. Scotty's door was closed. It was only the door where Steven was standing that was open.

This testimony, delivered in an authoritative manner, contradicted several of her previous statements. On July 9, 1985, she stated to Officer Smith that once they were all out at the Suburban, "I told Scott to get in." When Steven handed him the key, "I'm not sure whether Scott's door was even closed."

On July 26, 1985, she told Graham and Nowicki that as she came outside, "I have in my mind that he [Steven] had helped her [Mrs. Benson] in and was—as I was walking out he had—helped her in and shut her door."

On September 20, 1985, in her deposition, she had the following exchange with Michael McDonnell.

McDONNELL: What happened just before the point in time that Steven was standing by the right rear passenger door?

CAROL LYNN: He finished closing my mother's door and stepped around—I'm sorry. Repeat your question a minute.

McDONNELL: What happened just before the point in time that Steven was standing by the right rear passenger door?

CAROL LYNN: All right. He completed closing my mother's door and stepped around the open right-hand rear passenger door . . .

These earlier versions suggested considerably less certainty on her part and indicated that the scene she observed had not been static.

BROCK: As you looked out and you surveyed the particular things, did you have any mental impressions at that point in time?

CAROL LYNN: A couple. One, I thought it awfully strange that Scott was driving.

McDONNELL: Objection, Your Honor. May we approach the bench? (Then, out of hearing of the jury.) I object to any questions as to a general mental impression from the witness on the same grounds I cited before.

HAYES: Overruled.

Carol Lynn proceeded to say it was strange to see Scott behind the steering wheel because "he didn't particularly like to drive" and "Steven, being the eldest son, he usually drove if we were together."

Elaborating on other mental impressions, she said, "I was conscious of my mother sitting in the front seat because I got carsick, so I usually sat in the front seat, and my mother doesn't like the air conditioning blowing on her. She usually sits in the back."

Newspaper reports before and during the trial maintained that Steven had positioned members of his family in specific seats. But if Carol Lynn, Scott, and Mrs. Benson had switched seats in any possible permutation, that would not have changed the fact that all three of them were targeted for death.

The question was whether Steven was meant to be murdered too, or whether he was the murderer. But neither his position nor anybody else's in the Suburban offered any hard evidence about that. This would become all the more obvious when the State's expert witness testified that in his opinion the bombs had not been detonated by the ignition. Since Steven could easily have started off behind the steering wheel, set a timer, and gone into the house, or else gone into the house and triggered the bombs by remote control, the State did nothing but create a prejudicial smoke screen by stressing how strange it was that Scott was in the driver's seat, and Carol Lynn and her mother were out of their accustomed spots.

Carol Lynn recounted that her mother asked, "Who has the keys?" Steven indicated he did, came around, and boosted his sister up onto the backseat.

BROCK: Then what happened?
CAROL LYNN: He started to close my car door, and I told him that I wanted to leave the car door open.

In earlier statements, she had not mentioned Steven trying to close her door. This suggested he was attempting to shut her in. If the door hadn't been open, the effects of the first blast might have been even more devastating, making it impossible for her to escape.

She said he handed Scott the keys, mentioned he had forgotten something, and "headed toward the house." She didn't claim that he "dashed" or "ran" as the affidavit for the search warrant and several news reports, including an article in *Newsweek*, claimed.

Carol Lynn took eighteen minutes to describe the explosions and their aftermath from the moment Scott leaned to his right, as if to insert the key in the ignition. Her voice faltered as she told of being surrounded by an orange malevolent light and pressed back in the seat, feeling she had been electrocuted. When she opened her eyes, "I could see the body of my son lying out on the ground, he just looked so—I knew something was wrong."

Then she saw "tons of flames coming up around the front seat," and realized she had to get out of the vehicle. But she looked down and her hands weren't there. "And I thought: 'Oh, my God, my hands are burnt off.'" Still, she threw herself out of the open door and rolled on the ground to smother the flames, peeled off her burning shirt and threw it away. "The next thing that I remember is sitting up partially and seeing my brother Steven standing on the walk."

.   .   .   .

BROCK: And where was it that you observed Steven?
CAROL LYNN: He was standing on the walk.
BROCK: Do you specifically recall that he was standing on the walk?
CAROL LYNN: Yes.

Once again her memory had become more precise. In her interview with Graham and Nowicki she alternately placed Steven on the driveway, the porch, or the walk. Now suddenly she was sure it had been the walk, and although she couldn't see her hands at arm's length, she noticed other details.

BROCK: Do you recall what he was doing?
CAROL LYNN: He was just staring straight ahead.
BROCK: What did you do after you became aware of his presence on the walk?
CAROL LYNN: I couldn't understand why he wasn't coming over to help me.
BROCK: After you—was that a—I guess that was an impression you had. Did you say anything?
CAROL LYNN: No, I didn't.
BROCK: What is the next thing you recall happening after you observed Steven standing on the walk?

CAROL LYNN: Steven's eyes opened really wide and he seemed to react. He had been standing real still. Not moving at all. Just staring straight ahead. And suddenly his eyes opened and his mouth dropped and he turned around and raced towards the house or moved in a hurry; kind of ran back towards the house.

What Carol Lynn said was already damaging—Steven stood and stared, didn't help, didn't speak, didn't react at all until just before he turned and hurried into the house. But the way the scene was perceived by the public and presumably by the jury was even more devastating. Courtroom spectators reacted with frowns of disbelief and journalists revealed their views in stories that seemed to compete in presenting the defendant as callous.

Newsweek reported that Carol Lynn was "in flames, screaming as her brother stood and watched." *Time* took it a step further and claimed Steven "kept his back to her as she screamed for help." Piling error on top of error, the Washington *Post* said, "While she was being helped by [a] golfer, Carol Lynn Benson Kendall's brother Steven stood and watched the carnage. 'I couldn't understand why he wasn't coming over to help me.'"

Although press reports diverged from Carol Lynn's trial testimony, they did not differ nearly as much as that testimony differed from her statement to Graham and Nowicki.

Less than three weeks after the murders, she had said, "about this time I saw Steven come out of the house and stop on the driveway, and he was—he looked just terrified. And—and it was almost like he was going mad. And he just had—it was—he was—"

ATF Agent Nowicki cut in and said, "we better just stop right now."

But after a break, she had swerved back to Steven's reaction. "When I first saw Steven of course I was pretty—uhh—hysterical at that point and I—I think before I even saw him I was yelling for help, for someone to come and help me. And then I saw Steven out on the porch and Steven just had a look of absolute horror on his face, like the—the—the world had just blown up or something."

There was no mention that he had stared blankly, then reacted only by opening his eyes and letting his jaw drop. From the first instant she spotted him, he had been frantic and upset, and she hadn't assumed he was abandoning her.

And I think I called for him to help me, and he turned around, and he ran back into the house. And then I can remember wondering why he didn't come help me, but someone—I've been told later he ran in to get help, the police or the fire or—and that he tried to call.

Indeed, the facts showed that the first thing Steven did in the house was shout for Wayne Kerr to call an ambulance. Those weren't facts that Brock presented to the jury.

Instead, he asked what Carol Lynn recalled after Steven disappeared and she said some men in work clothes came to help her. She didn't remember the golfer, Charles Meyer, who dragged her away from the wreckage. She didn't remember the second bomb exploding, Meyer being wounded, falling on top of her, then stumbling off bleeding.

Yet Brock had based much of his case on her recollections of everything before and after that memory gap.

He ended by asking her to describe the burns and shrapnel wounds she had sustained. She characterized the injuries as on "primarily the right side and my back."

Since the first blast pressed her back into the seat, it was puzzling that she had burns from her shoulders to her spine.

During a break before cross-examination, the press room buzzed with debate, not about what Carol Lynn had said, but rather that she hadn't been asked a single question about her family's finances. For the past year accusations of stealing, embezzlement, and misappropriation of funds had dominated accounts of the case. Fear of being cut out of the will would continue to be cited by the press as the reason Benson killed his mother. Yet Brock had not touched on any of these subjects.

Some journalists predicted the State would let Wayne Kerr and the ATF accountant establish Steven's financial motive. Then Carol Lynn would return later in the trial and corroborate their testimony.

Out in the hall, I buttonholed Jerry Berry, who said the State hadn't mentioned the financial motive for a very simple reason. Little or nothing Carol Lynn had said in previous statements would stand up in court. "We'd have blown her out of the water."

While he had noticed dozens of contradictions between today's testimony and her statements, it was hard to decide whether to press her on every one. If the jury, particularly the ten women, got the impression the defense was badgering her, it wouldn't help Steven. It would just create sympathy for his sister.

Berry also questioned how much information jurors could assimilate. Educators and entertainers claimed that audiences had an attention span of about twenty minutes. But the defense had to hope this jury could concentrate for twenty days. It might be too much to expect.

Several other factors shaped the defense's cross-examination strategy. The prosecution had made it clear to the judge they intended to keep their questions within a narrow scope. If McDonnell wanted to exceed it, he would have to recall Carol Lynn. The Brocks weren't about to sit still and let the defense make its case during the State's time.

Those who had watched McDonnell and Carol Lynn lock horns during two long depositions felt he would have all he could handle even within the limits set by the prosecution. She was quick-witted and combative, and appeared to feel particular animosity toward the type of man she imagined McDonnell to be. Although when angry she might get riled, skid off the rails, and make ill-considered remarks, she was just as likely to hurt the defense as the State.

After the break, Michael McDonnell said, "I don't have too many questions to ask you, but I do have a few, Ms. Kendall." He sounded polite, almost courtly.

McDONNELL: Monday night after returning from dinner, you mentioned that there was a television program you didn't care for. What was that program?

CAROL LYNN: "Kate and Allie."

McDONNELL: Had the program started?

CAROL LYNN: No, it hadn't.

McDONNELL: What did you see so that you knew that "Kate and Allie" was coming on?

CAROL LYNN: There was a program going off, then there were commercials, and then the beginning of the program where it runs what the title of the show is.

McDONNELL: Do you recall what program was going off?

CAROL LYNN: "Scarecrow and Mrs. King."

McDonnell didn't challenge this daunting display by contrasting it with her inability to remember anything of the sort when she gave her statement to Graham and Nowicki.

Instead, he suggested that since she hadn't lived in her mother's house in Naples she wasn't familiar with the daily routine or with how long it took to drive to the Shop 'N Go. She also wasn't privy to every communication between her mother and Scott, and her mother and Steven. There were, Carol Lynn conceded, opportunities for them to talk without her knowledge.

Although much had been made about how odd it was that Steven volunteered to help stake out the lots, she admitted he had helped measure the property the Saturday before the murders. And he had been to the lots with Mrs. Benson on at least two other occasions.

Questioning the reliability of her "mental impression" of the seating arrangement in the car, he asked, "Were you aware that the air conditioning was not operable in the Suburban on July 9?"

CAROL LYNN: On July 9th it was not in my mind that the air conditioning was not working.

McDONNELL: Did you ride in the Suburban prior to that date during your July visit?

CAROL LYNN: Yes.

McDONNELL: Did you ever recall the air conditioning working?

CAROL LYNN: I remember a comment being made that the air conditioning was not working. I do not remember who exactly said the air conditioning wasn't working.

McDONNELL: Did there ever come a time during your July visit when your mother said she didn't want to ride in front because the air conditioning would blow on her in the Suburban?

CAROL LYNN: No, I don't remember that.

McDONNELL: When you went out the morning of the ninth, did you ask your mother to change places with you? Did you ask her not to sit in front?

CAROL LYNN: No, I did not.

The timbre of her voice had changed and become querulous, sarcastic. Color suffused her fair skin, darkening her scars as she described climbing into the Suburban and Steven coming around to her side.

McDONNELL: And it is at that time that Steven helped you up?

CAROL LYNN: I would be partially in the automobile when Steven put his hand on my posterior and gave me a little boost into the car.

. . . .

McDONNELL: Do you know whether Steven came around the vehicle to assist you?

CAROL LYNN: I don't know what was in Steven's mind. He wasn't in the habit of helping me into the car.

She inserted this last comment as McDonnell was pausing between questions.

Then she described Steven heading toward the house. When he was almost at the walk, she said, she glanced down to pick up a plastic glass of Diet Pepsi. When she looked up, Steven was not in sight. "I wasn't looking specifically for anything; but I was conscious of what I saw. I could see it in my mind right now. I can see them [Scott and Mrs. Benson] sitting in the automobile and I could see that empty walkway."

. . . .

McDONNELL: Is it a fair statement, is it not, Ms. Kendall, because of this tragic thing that happened to you and because of the physical nature of it, you don't remember everything that happened to you?

CAROL LYNN: I don't really understand your question.

McDONNELL: For instance, you don't remember the second explosion, I believe you said?

CAROL LYNN: No, I do not.

McDONNELL: So, therefore, you don't remember all of the events necessarily of that morning?

CAROL LYNN: Could you be more specific, please?

Given the force of the two blasts, the extent of her injuries, and the fact that she had already admitted to lapses in memory, McDonnell had an open invitation to do as she suggested—be more specific about those incidents that didn't hang together. How could she be so certain of what Steven had done during her fleeting glimmers of consciousness in the fifty-five seconds between explosions?

Instead, he changed the subject.

McDONNELL: Between the time you saw Steven on the walk and the blast were your eyes continually on him or the area where he was?

CAROL LYNN: No, I looked down towards the seat.

McDONNELL: You are certain of that?

CAROL LYNN: Yes, I am.

McDONNELL: All right. You were not certain of that when I took your deposition on September 20th, were you?

CAROL LYNN: As far as I know I was.

McDONNELL: Do you remember this question and this answer at that deposition: "Question: And between the time you saw him on the walk, as you have described, and the time of the blast, your eyes were continually on the walk; in that area? Answer: I couldn't say." Did you say that?

CAROL LYNN: That's not the same question.

.   .   .   .

McDONNELL: Did you make that answer to that question?

CAROL LYNN: If that's what you have down there, I have to assume that's correct. But that question is almost completely the opposite of the one you asked me first.

Once again McDonnell changed the subject and didn't ask her to explain how she imagined the questions differed. Perhaps he believed he had made his point. But it seemed just as possible that by letting Carol Lynn have the last word, he left jurors with the impression she was right; the present question was "completely the opposite" of the earlier one and he had been trying to trick her.

By now, Carol Lynn was prickly with anger. He scored some points, but she made him pay a price for each—and at times that price was a bit of McDonnell's aplomb. They fell into a bristling exchange over whether Steven was ever sitting in the Suburban.

CAROL LYNN: His body was partially in the automobile. He was not what one would classify as sitting in the automobile. If the car had driven off, he probably would have fallen out.

McDONNELL: Was his posterior resting on the seat at that time?

CAROL LYNN: At least some of it, yes.

McDONNELL: And you don't feel that is sitting in the car?

CAROL LYNN: No, I don't.

Brock objected that the defense was being argumentative, and the judge admonished McDonnell to make his point.

Going back to the witness, he asked, "After the explosion, did you hear Steven say anything?" When she responded, "No, I did not," McDonnell pinned down the time he was talking about—the instant when Steven had been standing on the sidewalk, before he turned to hurry into the house.

McDONNELL: At that point in time he said nothing?
CAROL LYNN: No, he did not.

She hesitated, then corrected herself. "I am sorry, yes, he did." She added a qualification as if to explain why she failed to mention this before. "But he did not say it to me. He said when he became— he had been very still and then just suddenly he opened his eyes and said: 'Oh, my God, my God.'"

This grudging concession did not evoke anything comparable to the vivid scene she described to Graham and Nowicki. Back then, the anguish and terror she saw on her brother's face had been deeply etched in her mind. "It was almost like he was going mad." "Steven just had a look of absolute horror on his face, like the world had just blown up." Now all she granted was that he opened his eyes wider and said, "Oh, my God, my God."

McDonnell would have been wise to ask why this episode had lost its impact. How had a terror-stricken expression turned into a blank stare?

But he moved on to Steven's trip to the Shop 'N Go.

McDONNELL: How long was Steven gone?
CAROL LYNN: I can't say specifically to the minute how long he was gone. All I do know, it was an inordinate amount of time for where he had indicated that he was going to go.
McDONNELL: Did you not tell me at your deposition it was thirty minutes?
CAROL LYNN: I don't remember that I gave you a specific time unless you asked me: Was it about thirty minutes and I might have answered, yes. But I did not specifically say because I had a recollection that it was thirty minutes.
McDONNELL: That is an estimate?

Brock called out for the page and line, and when McDonnell replied, "I am not referring to a page and line yet, Counsel," Carol Lynn cut in sharply, "I just told you that I do not specifically know how long he was gone." Brock asked to approach the bench, but the witness snapped, "It could have been," before he lodged his objection.

BROCK: If Mr. McDonnell's going to attempt to impeach the witness, he should read the exact question and the exact answer which the witness gave. I am opposed to the manner in which he is attempting to do it.

McDONNELL: I don't believe it is necessary. She agrees she estimated thirty minutes. There is no need to impeach her. That's what her testimony is. That's what she had in the deposition.

HAYES: The objection is a valid objection. The State is entitled to know where you are coming from on those type of questions if it has to do with prior testimony.

When McDonnell came back to Carol Lynn, he asked, "It is your testimony that it could have been thirty minutes?" She said, "It is a possibility."

McDONNELL: Ms. Kendall, is it true you are not sure at what point Steven gave Scott the keys?

CAROL LYNN: No, that is not true.

McDONNELL: Did you not tell Agent Nowicki that on July 26th, 1985; that you were not sure at what point Steven handed Scott the keys?

CAROL LYNN: I don't remember either the question or the answer. Steven handed Scott the keys through the window of the automobile.

Once more McDonnell let her have the last word. Wrestling with the thick binders full of statements and depositions, he appeared to have lost his place.

The question of when and where Steven handed Scott the keys was potentially very important. It related to the reliability of the witness's memory and to Steven's intentions in the moments before the explosion.

Carol Lynn had, indeed, admitted to Nowicki that she couldn't say whether Steven "handed Scott the keys already when he was inside of the car, or whether he went around the car and handed the keys in to Scott through the window . . . My mind wasn't on that at the time." Two days later when the detectives returned to this subject, she still wasn't sure if Steven passed the keys from the backseat or held on to them until he walked around to Scott's window.

If Steven handed Scott the keys from the backseat, it suggested the bombs weren't triggered by the ignition, since he surely wouldn't have taken a chance on Scott's starting the Suburban before he was far away. And if the keys had nothing to do with the bombs, then the suspicion that the State and Carol Lynn had raised about Scott's being at the steering wheel was without foundation. What's more, if Steven had already passed the keys to Scott, he had no reason to come around to the other side of the car except to help Carol Lynn. And why would he do that if he was about to kill her?

But the defense didn't follow up on its questions. McDonnell was still searching for pages so that he could confront her with quotes, and as he searched, she fought back, interrupting his questions, inserting comments.

McDONNELL: Didn't you also tell Agent Nowicki—excuse me—

CAROL LYNN: Mr. McDonnell, I don't have that in front of me and I can't—

McDONNELL: Just a moment, please. If you'd like to read it, I will be happy to give you a copy with the permission of the Court.

Didn't you tell Investigator Smith on the day of the bombing that Steven got out of the car and came around because you hadn't gotten in yet, and he kind of gave you a boost?

CAROL LYNN: I have no recollection of what any questions were that the man asked me or my answer. I was under sedation in the hospital in critical condition at the time.

Rather than confront her with her statement to Officer Smith, McDonnell moved over to the defense table and whispered to Jerry Berry. The jury might well have assumed that there had been no substance to his question, or that her remarks the day of the murders were invalid because of her medical condition.

When McDonnell turned back to the witness, he tried a new line of inquiry without concluding the one left dangling.

McDONNELL: Ms. Kendall, isn't it true that you observed Steven attempt to pull your mother from the vicinity of the car?

CAROL LYNN: I can't say that. At that point I didn't even know where my mother was. In fact, I was terrified that my mother had been stuck in the burning automobile and had been burned up.

. . . .

McDONNELL: Do you recall telling Agent Nowicki on July 17th that at one point Steven started to go into the car—"I guess after my mother." Do you remember that?

CAROL LYNN: No, Mr. McDonnell, I don't even know if that's what it says because I don't have it in front of me.

McDONNELL: Would you like to read it?

Brock objected that the question was different than the one in her statement and that the witness had been guessing when she answered Nowicki. McDonnell retorted that the Court had permitted Carol Lynn's testimony about other mental impressions.

BROCK: We might as well let the witness come in and testify to guesses and conclusions and everything else.

McDONNELL: Well, that is what she has been doing, Your Honor.

HAYES: If you want to have the witness see the statements and ask her if she made any statement, you can do it that way.

McDonnell asked Carol Lynn if she'd like to read the passage in question.

"Would I like to?" she repeated testily. "Yes, I would like to see it. I have no way of knowing whether I did say these things, whether that actually was in the transcript or if it's to make the jury think that's what is in the transcript."

McDONNELL: Let's clear that up right now, okay? For the record, this is the statement of July 26th and July 27th and July 28th to Agent George Nowicki, page 38 . . . Would you please read that portion out loud at this point?

BROCK: Objection, Your Honor.

CAROL LYNN: Well, you have to read what is in front of it. That's taking it out of context.

McDONNELL: Would you do that then?

Brock objected that the witness should not be allowed to publish the statement to the jury. The judge said she should read it to herself.

McDonnell then resumed, "I ask you if you made that statement that is reflected there? Read as much as you want."

CAROL LYNN: Before answering the question I have to say at the time that I made—

McDONNELL: Your Honor, I would like you to instruct the witness to answer the question, please.

CAROL LYNN: I am answering the question. I am not going to have you distort my answers by not allowing me to answer the question completely.

HAYES: I will just advise the witness she does have to answer the question at this point. If she wants to explain the answer, she can explain the answer.

Steaming mad, Carol Lynn distinguished between the day of the murders and the day of her statement to Graham and Nowicki. The day of the murders she didn't know what Steven was doing when he ran around the blazing Suburban. The day of her statement, "I was making the assumption with the knowledge that [my mother] was outside of the car that he was going around to that side of the automobile to my mother."

This wasn't just jesuitical hairsplitting. Carol Lynn had distorted the passage in question, which read: "I think he [Steven] tried to move my brother [Scott], and at one point he started to go *into* the car, I guess after my mother." He wasn't simply going around to the other side. He appeared to be going *into* the Suburban. There was nothing in her statement about Mrs. Benson being outside the automobile. In fact, according to Wayne Graham's deposition, he and Nowicki didn't tell Carol Lynn until after her statement that her mother had been blown out of the Suburban.

But McDonnell did not catch her misinterpretation of the passage. Instead, he said, "And at that time Steven was screaming?"

She quibbled and equivocated and contradicted the description she gave Graham and Nowicki. Back then, she had sounded obsessed by this scene, returning to it several times, saying Steven was "totally hysterical," "frantic," "like an insane person," "so upset" he had to be restrained. She mentioned twice that he was screaming. But she told McDonnell:

"I could not hear him. He was giving the—there was noise. I could not hear anything specifically that he said but it sounded as though he were making [a] lamenting type of sound. His body was extremely agitated and I couldn't discern any specific words."

McDONNELL: Was he screaming?
CAROL LYNN: Yes, I would say you could term it that way.
McDONNELL: He was almost pulling at his hair?
CAROL LYNN: Yes, he was.
McDONNELL: Was he crying?
CAROL LYNN: He reminded me of those women you see in the newsreel when they are screaming and throwing themselves on the coffin. That's the kind of agitated movement. And the way he was swinging his arms, that's what it reminded me of.

After prying this out of her and getting her to describe Steven racing toward the burning car and being dragged back, McDonnell thanked her and turned Carol Lynn Kendall over to Jerry Brock for redirect examination. The defense attorney looked slightly bedraggled, like someone who'd had a run-in with a very feisty porcupine.

Since the defense had sought to impeach the witness by highlighting the conflicts between her previous statements and her present testimony, Jerry Brock responded with a peculiar strategy. Although the police and the prosecution had depended heavily on Carol Lynn's interview with Graham and Nowicki—neither the search warrant nor the arrest warrant could have been executed without it—Brock suggested that she—and by extension, he and his case—could not be held accountable for what she had sworn to last July.

Her first statement, Brock established, was taken by Officer Smith in Naples Community Hospital when Carol Lynn was on pain medication. The interview with Graham and Nowicki, she assured him, also occurred in a hospital. "I had just been out of the intensive care for several days, and I was still taking medication and they were only allowing—my condition was such that my doctor only would allow them in the room for fifteen minutes at a time, then I had to rest for an hour."

In point of fact, although doctors recommended she not talk for more than fifteen minutes, she exceeded that limit during every stage of the interrogation. Often she ran on for more than an hour.

Brock encouraged the witness to review page 119 of her deposition to McDonnell. He wanted to show that she had never said her brother was absent only thirty minutes during his trip to the Shop 'N Go. Speaking for the defense, Jerry Berry objected that McDonnell had not cited a passage and Carol Lynn conceded that Steven could have been gone for thirty minutes. But Brock maintained, "I am trying to publish the statement that was being misrepresented." He and his brother Dwight insisted there was no line in Carol Lynn's deposition where she claimed that Steven had been gone for thirty minutes. Judge Hayes agreed that McDonnell "couldn't find it."

HAYES: That's all you have to bring out—the true fact of the statement—because it was never made in the deposition.
BROCK: Your Honor, just for the record, we would like the entire deposition at that particular point referring to the context published.

BERRY: Your Honor, they are impeaching their own witness with a deposition.

HAYES: I can't agree. I don't know where Mr. McDonnell was coming from. He didn't specify where he was. He didn't know where he was. If, in fact, it applies, he could use it.

After the bench conference, Brock said, "Ms. Kendall, after having an opportunity to read the deposition that Mr. McDonnell was referring to about thirty minutes, is there anything in that particular portion of the deposition that says that the defendant was gone for thirty minutes?" Carol Lynn assured him that there was not.

This exchange misled the jury on a couple of counts. The State was referring the witness to the wrong deposition. Carol Lynn's comment about thirty minutes was in her deposition of May 22, 1986, not September 20, 1985.

Yet although her first deposition did not mention thirty minutes, she offered an even shorter estimate of Steven's absence. On page 118, then again on page 119—the very page Brock urged her to read—she conceded she could not say that he had been gone more than five or ten minutes. Neither the prosecutor nor the witness advertised this information to the jury, and the defense appeared to be unaware of it.

On recross, McDonnell demanded, "Did you read the entire statement?" Before she answered, Brock objected that McDonnell needed permission to do recross. The judge said he wouldn't permit a recross unless the defense was covering a subject the State had raised on redirect.

McDONNELL: The medication issue is a totally new issue. I have to ask her about that and I have to ask her about reading the deposition.

HAYES: Okay, clearly, as to the deposition, the defense created this problem. They are stuck with it. We are not going back on the deposition. Mr. McDonnell first asked her questions, for example, about time without referring to a page or line number. That's his problem. When pressed by the State, he could not identify where he was coming from. That's his problem. So you are stuck with what you did. If you can show on the deposition where she talked about thirty minutes—

McDONNELL: I can, Judge. Just give me five minutes.

HAYES: Fine.

McDONNELL: Take a stretch break and let me look for it.

HAYES: You can go to medication.

McDONNELL: I don't think—the medication is just a couple of questions. That doesn't give me enough time. Basically, Judge, I have lost my place.

HAYES: I agree. You are stuck with it. If I let you do that, I have to let him [Brock] reread anything in that deposition they want to which is hearsay, then you are going to object to it.

McDONNELL: All I want, Judge, is a reasonable time in defending a man on a first degree murder charge to review the deposition so I can find it. It's there.

HAYES: I suggest in a first degree murder charge that if you are going to ask the witness the question, you know where the line and page is.

McDONNELL: Mea culpa, Your Honor. Out of all these thousands of pages of testimony, I have lost my place once here.

Judge Hayes suggested McDonnell proceed with his questions while Berry searched for the reference to thirty minutes. McDonnell wanted the record to reflect that he had asked for five minutes. He said his questions about medication would take only thirty seconds.

He asked Carol Lynn, "Is it your contention that the statement is invalid because of your medication?" And she snarled, "I never said anything of the kind." Then she turned to the Judge, "Can I say something?"

"You have to ask the State or the Defense first."

But after a word with Brock, she didn't get to say whatever she had in mind. She stepped down from the stand and, clutching her purse, strode purposefully out of the courtroom. Hayes was about to adjourn for the weekend when McDonnell requested that Ms. Kendall be brought back.

Face slightly flushed, obviously angry, she returned to the stand.

Directing her attention to her brother's trip to the Shop 'N Go, McDonnell asked, "Did you say that it was a half an hour sort of time length that Steven was gone?"

"No," she said. "I would say it seemed like more time than that."

He read a line he had finally found in her second deposition. " 'It was like the feeling of like it being a half an hour sort of time length.' "

"If that's what's printed on that sheet, then that's what I said."

This concession notwithstanding, it had been a dreadful day for the defense. Glistening with sweat, his white shirt sticking to his broad damp chest, McDonnell was subdued and curt with the press.

Weighted down by briefcases and cardboard boxes full of bound statements and depositions, he and his entourage descended to the lobby, then lingered there while Bob Laws went outside ahead of them. They had gotten wind of a death threat against McDonnell and his wife. A convicted drug dealer was said to have been spotted in the courtroom.

The tattooed, mustachioed character called the Pirate lurked on the sidewalk. Bob Laws moved next to him and stood staring him down. When Jerry Berry left the building and passed by with no problem, McDonnell gave Nina his briefcase, rearranged an armful of boxes, and said, "I guess it's safe for us too." Reminding everybody to be in the office on Saturday for a conference, he led Nina toward his white Jaguar, leaving Laws and the Pirate locked eyeball to eyeball. The Pirate looked less menacing then bemused.

Over the weekend, the defense team began to regard Friday in a more favorable light. Granted, things hadn't gone smoothly. McDonnell had hit some very rough patches of ground, and it had proved impossible to correct all the errors, inconsistencies, and misleading impressions. But how much had Carol Lynn actually hurt Steven?

By the time I spoke to Jerry Berry on Sunday evening, the general consensus was that she hadn't done any great harm to their case. The State might recall her later or bring her back on rebuttal. But Berry said he and McDonnell had to weigh the pros and cons before deciding whether to call her as a defense witness. There was always the danger she would widen the area of discussion and make rash charges that would take the rest of the trial to correct.

He again mentioned the risk of creating sympathy for her and antipathy toward Steven. "You probably noticed Mike went easy on her."

When I remarked that she hadn't gone easy on McDonnell, Berry insisted no irreparable damage had been done. I got the distinct feeling the defense had no stomach for locking horns with Carol Lynn Kendall again.

Curious what Margaret Covington thought, I phoned Sweetwater, Texas, where she had returned to her husband and son. She was keeping in touch with her shadow jurors by long distance. They had found Carol Lynn an excellent witness for the prosecution. True, some people had misgivings about her. They didn't understand why she had put Scott up for adoption and let Mrs. Benson raise him.

They believed she had enough money to keep her baby regardless of public opinion. They also wondered whether Scott had known the truth about their relationship. And how did this affect the family? But their overall impression was that Carol Lynn had produced damaging evidence. They were especially struck by Steven's failure to help her, and his callous behavior after the murders.

Margaret Covington agreed that Ms. Kendall had been an effective witness. Carol Lynn had a nimble mind and an actress's skill at modulating her voice and conveying suggestions. When, for instance, she had parried with McDonnell—"I am not going to have you distort my answers by not allowing me to answer the question completely"—it implied that the witness was honest and the defense attorney was a liar.

The way to handle such a witness was to attack her character—if her character was susceptible to attack—and question her credibility. But Margaret Covington stressed that she served strictly in an advisory capacity. She did her research, conducted interviews, and made suggestions. It was up to the attorneys whether they wanted to accept her advice.

What advice had she given in the case of Carol Lynn? I asked.

"Put her back on the stand and destroy her," Covington said.

Chapter 5

Michael McDonnell arrived at the courtroom Monday looking refreshed. He'd had a haircut over the weekend and played a few rounds of golf. Now he was eager to get back to business. But the day's first witness looked like he was ready to tee off.

Charles Meyer, the golfer who had dragged Carol Lynn clear of the Suburban, wore white trousers, an open-collar shirt, and a blue and white check sport coat. A thickset, ruddy-faced retired publisher, he told of standing on the green behind Margaret Benson's house and hearing an explosion. When he saw the smoke, he raced off the tee. "The minute I rounded the corner of the house, I could see the car. The car was completely skeletonized, an inferno, a mass of flames."

As he circled the Suburban, he gave Mrs. Benson a glance. "I knew that person was gone." He had no doubt Scott was dead too. He found Carol Lynn curled on her side in a fetal position, screaming, "I'm hot, I'm hot." This was immediately after she had supposedly been propped up on one arm, looking at Steven on the sidewalk. Now she was oblivious to Meyer's presence.

When the second bomb exploded, shrapnel sliced through Meyer's arm and pierced his chest. Another piece clipped off part of his nose. He fell on Carol Lynn, then staggered away, bleeding profusely. She remembered none of this.

Meyer recalled Steven after the second blast sitting on the steps of the house saying, "Oh my God, oh my God." Meyer never saw anybody move Scott or Mrs. Benson.

Yet on the other side of the Suburban, Fred Merrill, his golf partner, had dragged away Mrs. Benson and he had the scars to prove it.

On cross-examination, McDonnell established that Meyer had

concentrated on saving Carol Lynn's life, not on looking at what other people were doing.

The second witness was Lieutenant Harold Young, who said he arrived on the scene at 9:52 A.M. and started interviewing people. Steven told him his mother had only decaffeinated coffee, "so he decided to go to the Shop 'N Go and get some coffee. While at the Shop 'N Go he met some people from Sand Castle Construction that he'd had business with in the past and he was talking about future business and this caused him to be late in returning."

Steven could not remember the names of the Sand Castle Construction employees. "I met him at least three other times during the day and each time I asked him if he could recall the names and he told me 'No,' " Young said.

Benson claimed he drove the Suburban to get coffee because his van was low on gas. Young checked the fuel gauge and it registered a quarter full.

An hour after the murders, Steven struck Young as "relatively calm, considering what had happened." Benson "seemed interested in the [business] records in the house and taking care of those. He asked me if he could look through the records."

The one moment of drama in Young's fifteen minutes of testimony came when Brock asked if he saw Steven Benson in the courtroom. The "short detective" extended his arm and aimed his index finger at the defendant as if it were a .357 Magnum.

Michael McDonnell had no questions.

ATF Agent Terry Hopkins came on next, and the State took terrific pains to prove through this witness that the crime scene had been thoroughly searched and the evidence carefully preserved. Jerry Brock brought over two plastic bins and, as Hopkins pawed through dozens of exhibits, the prosecutor asked him to identify each. This became so paralyzingly boring even Jerry Brock began to yawn.

Hopkins testified that he had gone with Mike Koors to Hughes Supply and spoken to Jerry Maynes and James Link. Maynes sold two end caps on July 5. Link sold two galvanized nipple pipes on July 8. The two end caps, Hopkins said, were the same type used in one of the bombs. Neither Maynes nor Link could identify the customer from the six photographs shown to them. Steven Benson's was one of the six.

On cross-examination McDonnell carried a yellow pad and as he asked Hopkins a question and got the answer he wanted, he crossed off the question with a flourish of his pen.

Although Hopkins had testified that the guiding principle of the crime scene search was to "look for anything that didn't grow," he admitted certain car parts and other items weren't kept. He said Albert Gleason would have to explain why metal detectors, magnifiying glasses, and electronic and X-ray devices were not used.

After suggesting again that material from three nearby construction sites might have been mixed in with the bomb debris, McDonnell had Hopkins repeat that James Link could not identify Steven as the customer who purchased pipe on July 8. He also got the ATF agent to acknowledge that the two end caps sold by Hughes Supply were "similar" to, not the "same" as, those found at the scene.

2

During lunch, Michael McDonnell, Jerry Berry, and Bob Laws wondered whom Brock would call next. The prosecution had had problems with witness management and had to coordinate with ATF, putting on agents whenever they were available to fly in from Miami, Atlanta, and Washington. That meant there would probably be no set pattern, just a lot of jumping around from finance witnesses to forensic experts to policemen.

Jerry Berry said it wasn't simply a problem of witness management. "Brock doesn't think like other people. He doesn't care whether he's consecutive. He has an overall idea and seems to be able to hold it in mind."

Berry observed that "a court case, especially a trial like this, is like writing a play or rather improvising a play where the scenes change, the lines are spontaneous, and the ending is unknown."

Led back from lunch by a bailiff, the twelve jurors and two alternates wore large tags and looked like a tour group, giddy and self-conscious as they followed a guide over foreign terrain.

Captain Curtis Mills came on and told Jerry Brock he spoke to Benson the morning of the murders and "He was fairly well composed. He was able to talk to us in a normal voice." Because Steven claimed to have been close to the exploding Suburban—three feet or three steps or three yards away, according to which witness one believed—Mills felt his clothes should show signs of the same substances that were found on objects around the vehicle. The Captain asked him to surrender his clothes, and he did so.

McDonnell suggested that someone in front of the Suburban would not catch the full brunt of the blast because the engine block would shield him. Mills acknowledged he couldn't say whether the condition of Steven's clothes was different from those worn by other people close to the explosions. He also couldn't say that Steven had been any more or less composed than other people at the Benson house.

On redirect, Brock remained silent a few seconds and plucked at his bottom lip. Then he asked questions that reiterated that the side of Steven's tan van had been spackled with blood and body matter. The van, however, had not been parked in front of the Suburban.

Jeffrey Maynes, the plumbing manager from Hughes Supply, testified that a customer called asking for eight four-inch end caps. Maynes told him that he had just two in stock. At 3:25 P.M. on July 5, a man came in, paid cash, signed an illegible signature, and left with the Union brand caps. The entire transaction took five minutes, and Maynes had no memory of the customer's appearance.

On cross-examination, McDonnell asked Maynes if Steven Benson was the customer. Maynes repeated that he couldn't remember a thing about the man.

Maynes explained that Grinnell end caps were formerly stamped with the letter G. But for the last eight years they had been marked with a double diamond. Fragments of two G caps had been found at the scene of the murders.

On redirect, Brock pushed Maynes hard, but he was unbudgeable. He could not describe the end-cap purchaser in any way.

James Link had handled the sale of pipe on July 8 at 4:58 P.M.. Once again, the customer paid cash and signed an unreadable signature. A small man himself, Link described the customer as about six feet tall and about two hundred pounds. He had on a dark baseball-type cap and what Link called "John Lennon" glasses with small, oval, opaque lenses.

Investigators had shown him an array of photographs, including a picture of Benson, but Link said "they just didn't resemble the person who bought" the two nipple pipes. Pressed by both the prosecution and the defense to define what he meant, Link said the people in the photographs "all seemed a lot thinner" in the face than the man he recalled.

Investigators put together a composite supposedly based on the description Link gave them, but he told McDonnell the portrait didn't resemble the customer in several crucial respects. The glasses were large and the lenses were clear, showing the shape of the eyes. Link didn't know anything about the man's hair color or the length of his sideburns. Still, the State got this flawed composite into evidence, and it was, indeed, a dead ringer for Steven Benson.

During a break, several women around me mumbled about one of the jurors, an old woman who nodded off all afternoon. During dull testimony, her head fell forward and she seemed in danger of tumbling out of her chair.

The women in the gallery were scandalized, but they soon digressed to other subjects. This was the most exciting week of the summer. One of them gushed, "I got Caroline Kennedy married over the weekend, I've got this trial every day and, at the same time, I've got to get Fergie married off to Prince Andrew."

Lieutenant Jack Gant testified that he was a Certified Police Instructor for taking prints. Pursuant to a search warrant, he had taken rolled ink impressions of Benson's hands on August 16, 1985.

On cross-examination, McDonnell asked, "Do you recognize the Federal Bureau of Investigation as an authority?"

"Yes sir I do."

"When you took these inked prints did you take the palm on a cylindrical object?"

"No I didn't." Gant knew this procedure was recommended by the FBI, but said, "It's a guideline for fingerprint men at the beginning of the science. I've been in it twenty years and developed my way."

"So you feel that this is not necessary?"

"It's not necessary."

"Have you communicated that to the FBI?" McDonnell asked, getting a laugh from the jury and waking up the sleeping juror.

Late that afternoon Frank Kendall, an ATF fingerprint expert, now retired, took the stand, and the defense team promptly asked to approach the bench, where they objected to the introduction of evidence obtained with the controversial search warrant. The objections ran on at such length that the jury retired to its chamber and Frank Kendall sat staring meditatively into space, his gray-bearded face motionless as if he were posing for a portrait of the artist as a mature man.

When Judge Hayes ruled that Frank Kendall could testify and the jury returned, Brock introduced State's exhibits 96 and 97, which were photo enlargements of the palm prints from the Hughes Supply receipts and from Steven Benson.

Descending from the witness stand, knocking over a microphone in the process, Kendall set these visual aids on an easel in front of the jury. Although to the eye of a nonexpert, the prints didn't appear to be identical, Mr. Kendall stated that there were sixty points of comparison. The writer's palm impression from Steven Benson and the prints on the receipts were, he said, "made by one and the same person."

During McDonnell's brief cross-examination, Frank Kendall conceded there had been one usable fingerprint on the receipts that did not match Steven Benson's. He could not say whom it belonged to. He had not examined the prints of anyone else in the case for purposes of comparison.

Asked if he had studied the receipts to make sure that no one had tampered with them, Frank Kendall said he had seen no reason to do so.

When the judge recessed the trial till the next morning, the press pounced on McDonnell. "Are you still convinced your client will be acquitted?" some shouted.

"I never said I was confident he'd be acquitted. I said he was innocent." He added that the defense would show that Benson was elsewhere when the pipe and end caps were bought. "There's no question in our mind that Steven didn't buy that pipe."

But were those Benson's prints on the receipts?

"That I don't know. Nobody knows that. Whether they were put on there by somebody else or what, I don't know."

Asked who would have put Benson's prints on the receipts, McDonnell said, "I don't know. I don't have any answers, I only have doubts."

3

I lingered in the courtroom until the judge changed from his robes into a crisp blue seersucker suit.

"The testimony of the print expert brings the trial up to a B +," Hayes said. "That's classic circumstantial evidence." Still, he added as he had several times in our talks, "I don't think I've seen one this close brought to trial."

Partly, he explained, it was a question of economics. No prosecutor wanted to take a case to court unless he thought he had a good chance of winning. It was a waste of time, energy, and the taxpayers' money. Of course, Hayes said, "Law is never cost-efficient. The only really cost-efficient justice is via the Smith & Wesson—a one-shot verdict. No one wants to go back to that."

The subject of law and economics was much on his mind these days since he was due to attend a special seminar in August at the National Judicial College in Reno, Nevada. One of four Florida judges accepted into the two-week seminar, he had already had to postpone attending this past spring because of the Benson case, and he didn't care to cancel again. Law and Economics was one of several of the minicourses he could enroll in.

Chapter 6

By the fourth day of the trial, with more technical experts due to testify, the courtroom was uncrowded and the media coverage had cooled. Now only the faithful attended—the Pirate, the Karate Kid, Janet Lee Murphy, teenyboppers who rated the witnesses (He's gross. He's cute), a man who showed up every day and sat with a wooden duck decoy in his lap, and the Ladies of the Club, all those women of a certain age who knitted or filed their nails or read magazines during dull stretches. At such times you could hear the Brock brothers shake cough drops out of a box or rattle Tic-Tacs from a plastic container. They sucked on sweets all day or else chewed gum and made tiny airplanes out of the wrappers.

Michael Gideon, a sheriff's deputy who photographed the crime scene, described seeing blood, fatty tissue, and "hunks of meat" that had been blown from the Suburban. Mrs. Benson's Porsche 928S, parked some distance away, had had its windshield cracked. The State was stressing again that Steven could not have stood anywhere near the blast without being hit by something.

Five photographs had been published to the jury. Two were of the blood-splattered side of Steven's van. Three others served to locate the bodies in relation to the Suburban. Seen from a distance, Mrs. Benson lay on her stomach, and little damage was visible except to her legs. One shot of Scott on his back showed a smatter of blood on his face, but in the other photo he had been rolled over, revealing the raw, torn flesh on his right side and an oozing pink mass of internal organs.

Wayne Graham didn't have the flat, uninflected voice of other investigators. With his cherubic face and friendly drawl, he was cordial with defense and State attorneys alike.

He described searching the Benson house for explosives and bumping into Debra as she came out of the bathroom. When she heard what they were doing, she said, "Here I was sitting on the pot and I could have been blown up." Graham said Steven and Wayne Kerr laughed and joked with police as they went on with their search. Benson "didn't break down or become despondent. There was joviality."

Later, Graham had seen Steven sitting in a lawn chair while his mother and adopted brother lay dead nearby. He conceded that Kerr was consoling Steven, but insisted that the lawyer was also joking with him.

Graham told Jerry Brock that the Meridian Security Network office on Domestic Avenue was no more than two or three blocks from Hughes Supply, just a minute and a half away by car.

Michael McDonnell started off being every bit as genial as Graham, but then he said, "We've shared many laughs over the years, but this isn't a laughing matter, is it?"

"No sir."

Stern now, he asked if the "short detective" had ever studied the psychological reasons why people laugh.

"No sir, but I've enjoyed forty years of doing it." McDonnell had met his match in bonhomie.

When McDonnell tried to get Graham to describe how Steven had laughed, he pushed so long and hard, he prompted a few giggles from the gallery, and Graham gave a nervous chuckle, proving that people do tend to laugh at inappropriate and unexpected times. But it was doubtful the jury caught this.

Because Brock had not raised the subject on direct examination, McDonnell couldn't ask Graham about his interrogation of Carol Lynn Kendall, which had been full of mood swings, with her laughing one moment and crying the next.

As Collier County Medical Examiner Dr. Heinrich Schmid was sworn in, a woman entered the courtroom with a little girl and took a seat. The girl was carrying a Barbie doll dressed in a pink princess outfit. The woman and the girl wore pink too. If they were upset by the autopsy report, they didn't show it.

After Dr. Schmid described the location of the wounds and the pattern of streaking and stippling on the two bodies, he said Scott and Mrs. Benson "died of multiple overwhelming injuries."

The only surprise came when Dr. Schmid said he had tested and found no traces of drugs or alcohol in Scott's system. Kim Beegle had testified that Scott smoked marijuana the afternoon before his death.

Over the protests of the defense, eleven more photographs were introduced and passed to the jury. Several members of the panel compressed their lips and labored to control their breathing. Color flooded the faces of a few of the older women. Others turned ashen. One lady clapped a hand to her mouth and shook her head. The twenty-one-year-old alternate put her arms under a loose sweater and hugged her chest. One woman didn't want to look. She held each photo in her lap, glanced down quickly, winced, and jerked her head to the side as if slapped.

The color snapshots, some in close-up, showed what might have been corpses in an anatomy textbook with the skin peeled back to display the bone, muscle, and internal organs. Scott's skull was shattered and a wooden stake had been driven into his thorax. Laid out on an autopsy table, Margaret had little left of her face. Her empty eye sockets gaped in hideous shock at what had happened to her. Her left hand was missing, which had prompted reports that her gold ring with its spindle-shaped aquamarine, surrounded by six smaller diamonds, was somewhere on the lawn at 13002 White Violet Drive. Police had combed the grass, only to learn later that she had not been wearing the ring. Still, rumors persisted that Steven had found it, ghoulishly removed it from a severed finger, then wiped the blood on the seat of his pants.

Jerry Brock apologized for having to ask the question, but it was a legal requirement. "Was Margaret Benson a human being?"

Dr. Schmid answered that she was.

"Was Scott Benson a human being?"

Dr. Schmid said he was.

The defense didn't ask the medical examiner any questions. They were understandably eager to end this macabre scene. But it might have helped to establish why no drugs showed up in Scott's system.

Judge Hayes called a lunch break, not that anybody felt like eating. The press asked Brock why he had insisted on showing the jurors such explicit—and so many—photographs.

"I think they were necessary for the jury to fully comprehend the severity of the crime that was committed here."

McDonnell said, "There's no reason why people should be subjected to that sort of thing. The pictures are just to stir up the jury, play on their emotions. But this jury's too smart."

Steven was broken up, his attorney said, and had had a tough time controlling his emotions.

Back in the press room, a reporter joked about his lead: "Steven Benson's emotions ran the gamut from A to B today as the State introduced autopsy pictures."

McDonnell later told me that it wasn't without foresight that the defense had selected three women with nursing experience. He figured they wouldn't be so upset by the pictures that they'd lose sight of the facts.

That afternoon, the State presented evidence from Theodore Toth, a bearded metallurgist with twenty-nine years of experience. Toth told Jerry Brock that the pipe fragments found at the crime scene had the same composition as the pipes reflected on the Hughes Supply receipt. They were galvanized steel. The fragments came from at least two, but possibly more, foot-length pipes that could have been four or five inches in diameter. He had measured one of the end caps and determined it was four inches in diameter. If his measurements and deductions were correct, the cap matched those purchased at Hughes Supply and would have fit on the pipes purchased at the same place.

Toth had also analyzed a particle of zinc about half the size of the tip of a ballpoint pen. It had been found on Benson's pants. Toth said it could have come from handling galvanized pipe. Since the particle didn't appear to have been subjected to extreme heat, he doubted it had been blown onto Benson by the explosion.

But on cross-examination, Toth conceded that he had to make certain assumptions about industry standards and uniform specifications to reach his conclusions. Since he did not know whether the pipe fragments he studied were made in America and he couldn't be sure what standards applied in other countries, he couldn't say with scientific certainty that his assumptions were correct. Even when it came to determining the diameter of the end caps, he acknowledged he made the assumption the caps were screwed onto the pipes. But there was nothing to prove this and therefore nothing to prove the diameter of the pipes. Their thickness, he stated again, was consistent with five-inch, as well as four-inch, pipe.

He also admitted his testimony about the length of the pipe was predicated on unproved assumptions. No fragment found at the scene was a foot long.

As for the tiny particle of zinc on Benson's pants, Toth could not swear that it had not come from the explosion. There were any number of ways a particle could be dislodged from a pipe, and he couldn't verify one to the exclusion of any other.

McDonnell ended by asking, "Are you able to tell this jury that the pipes reflected on the invoice are one and the same with those pipes [found at the crime scene]?"

"No, sir."

At the end of the day, I stood at the rail behind the defense table with Nina, McDonnell's willowy, twenty-nine-year-old wife. She and Mike were smiling and saying "Good night" to the jurors as they filed out. "About half and half is the way I figure it," Nina whispered to me. "About six are still with us. The rest won't even meet your eyes."

I asked McDonnell when he had mastered metallurgy.

"No mastery," he insisted with a broad grin. "Just Irish blarney."

On the sidewalk next to the Justice Center, Judge Hugh Hayes stood in the wilting heat and talked to me and Richard Fitzhugh, a free-lancer from California who had driven east and was covering the trial for *Penthouse* while living in his camper. He also worked as a stringer for Associated Press and the *New York Times*.

There had been a tropical downpour earlier in the day, and rush hour traffic splashed through puddles on the street. A few raindrops fell now, splotching Hayes's white shirt and the gray jacket he carried over his arm. Dapper as always, his blue eyes alert after a long day in court, he seemed undaunted by the humidity.

Hayes said he had been impressed by McDonnell's cross-examination of the metallurgist. "The problem is how much the jury is taking in, how much it's following the facts and inferences. That's always the question with circumstantial evidence."

The judge mused that if Carol Lynn hadn't survived, if the palm prints didn't exist, "it would have been a hell of a piece of work, a perfect crime." He wondered whether Wayne Kerr would have come forward on his own and volunteered information about the family's finances and feuds.

Hayes still had hopes that the trial would proceed on schedule so he could make it to the seminar in Reno. But he hastened to add that that was secondary. With ten women and two men on the jury, he anticipated prolonged debate before a verdict was reached. In fact, he feared there might not be a verdict unless the group had a strong leader. He expected the jury to be out for at least two days.

Leaping ahead to that time, Judge Hayes said that regardless of how the trial ended, there would be lingering doubts and unanswered questions about the Benson pipe bomb murders. It wasn't the kind of case where a verdict came down and you closed the book.

Chapter 7

Because he was an accountant as well as an attorney, Dwight Brock questioned witnesses about financial matters. Shorter and sturdier than his older brother, Dwight had a mustache and horn-rimmed glasses, and spoke in a brisk animated manner, with a pronounced Panhandle accent.

Through the records custodian at First Federal Savings and Loan at Fort Myers, he established that Benson had been denied a loan to buy a new van. Later when his mother agreed to guarantee the loan, it was approved. Early on, Steven wrote a payment check that bounced. Margaret Benson made three payments on the loan before she died.

Carl Westman came out of the gallery, and identified ledgers and files that were in his custody as personal representative of the estate. Brock was at pains to emphasize that Westman kept these records in a perfectly professional and secure manner. Then Westman returned to his seat behind the State's table and sat watching the proceedings with the thumb of his right hand under his chin and his index finger against his cheek. He looked a little detached as if his proximity to the prosecutors and to the Benson family lawyers didn't necessarily mean he was with them.

Marlin "Marty" Taylor was sworn in and identified herself as Margaret Benson's personal secretary at the time of the murders. She said that in May 1985, when Mrs. Benson traveled to Europe with Scott, she left two signed checks to cover unexpected household or business expenses. The checks were made out to Meridian Security Network, with the space for the amount left blank.

Taylor testified that the checks disappeared—the first not long after Mrs. Benson left, the second while Marty was out of town. When Mrs. Benson returned, she was talking to somebody on the telephone and instructed her secretary to enter figures in a ledger indicating that one check had been written in the amount of $1,000 and the other $3,000.

Dwight Brock introduced checks #247 and #248 which Mrs. Benson had left with Marty Taylor. They had been made out for $50,000 and $10,000, signed by Steven Benson, and marked on the back "For Deposit Only," with the account number of the Meridian Security Network. Taylor swore she hadn't filled in the amounts or deposited the checks.

"Are you aware of $60,000 in household or other expenses at that time?" Dwight Brock asked her.

"No."

Under cross-examination, Ms. Taylor admitted that Mrs. Benson had placed no limitations on the uses or the amounts of the checks. Although she assumed Mrs. Benson had been talking to Steven when she said to fill in the figures of $1,000 and $3,000 in the ledgerbook, Ms. Taylor conceded she didn't know for sure.

Several unasked and unanswerable questions loomed long after Marty Taylor left the courtroom. If, as Carol Lynn Kendall claimed, Mrs. Benson had known for years that Steven was "stealing her blind," if Mrs. Benson had learned about the diversion of money to Meridian Marketing long before the trip to Europe, why did she sign a note to cover the loan for his van? Why did she make three of the monthly payments? Why did she leave behind two checks made out to Meridian Security Network when Steven would have access to them and have the authorization to do with them as he wished? Why did the disappearance of the checks not prompt a call to the police?

ATF Agent Tommy Noel described finding a tape measure in the debris around the Suburban. Benson was supposed to have gone back into the house to fetch a tape measure he had forgotten.

Noel also said Benson had been calm after the murders.

On cross, McDonnell got Noel to acknowledge that Steven had been no more or less calm than anybody else at the scene. No more or less calm than Noel himself.

Brock jumped on this on redirect. "Officer, was that your mother and brother laying out there dead on the lawn?"

"No," Noel said.

* * *

Terrill Combs, manager of a General Motors truck assembly plant in Flint, Michigan, was flown in to testify to two facts. The Chevy Suburban had a console twenty-one inches long, eleven inches wide, and ten inches deep—more than adequate to accommodate a foot-long pipe bomb. The backseat was five and one-half inches to six inches off the floor. Although a tight squeeze, this too was enough space for a bomb.

Walter Mitchell, a chemist with Alcohol, Tobacco and Firearms, was a bookish man with gray hair that stood on end as if he had been caught in a laboratory explosion. He testified that the bombs in the Suburban had been charged with smokeless powder of the kind used in shotgun shells.

Sauntering back from the evidence table like a man carrying pails of milk in from the barn, Brock brought to the witness stand three cans with Povia Paints Sta-Nu labels. The cans contained the clothing worn by Scott and Mrs. Benson the day of their death. Mitchell had examined it, as well as Carol Lynn Kendall's clothing, and found a residue of burnt and unburnt smokeless powder.

In contrast, the blue jeans worn by Steven Benson contained no traces of powder. Mitchell said he did, however, discover a tiny zinc particle on one pant leg. Tests determined that the zinc resembled the coating on the galvanized pipe.

Michael McDonnell asked how far wafers of burnt and unburnt powder would travel from a blast. Mitchell didn't know. Individual wafers were feather-light and might scatter only a short distance. Since the front end of the Suburban was between Benson and the bombs, Mitchell admitted that might make it less likely the powder would reach him.

He said thirty-three pieces of galvanized pipe did not bear traces of smokeless powder. McDonnell implied it wasn't so strange then that the zinc particle didn't have powder residue on it either.

Mitchell also said the fragments of galvanized metal showed signs of oxidization, which indicated they were old. Exactly how old was a matter of debate, but McDonnell suggested that the pipe sold by Hughes Supply was too new to have reached this stage of oxidization.

. . .

During lunch at his sunlit table at the Veranda, the defense attorney learned from members of his team that one of the jurors was nodding off again during the technical testimony. McDonnell burst into laughter. "Now we got them right where we want them." The State was putting people to sleep.

With more scientific evidence due to be introduced, the defense team wondered whether the judge would replace the dozing juror. McDonnell hoped not. "I'd rather have a sleeper than one of those alternates."

When someone commented how much more forceful and lively Dwight Brock was than his brother, McDonnell agreed, but observed that Dwight's problem was that he was forceful with every witness, every question. "He's like a golfer who hits his putts the same way he hits his drives."

After some speculation about who might be called next, they discussed whether they were apt to see Carol Lynn again as a State witness. And if she were recalled, how hard should they push her? Maybe under pressure she'd start popping off about Debbie and accuse her sister-in-law of poisoning Steven.

McDonnell said, "It may be time to pull Carol Lynn's plug." Nina added, "Peel her banana."

Strolling back from lunch, the defense team appeared to have had its batteries recharged. But then Bob Laws spotted something across the street from the Justice Center, and the lively good humor turned into a red alert. A Chevy Suburban was parked at the curb.

Had the prosecutors brought it here as some sort of demonstrative evidence that the defense hadn't expected and wasn't prepared for? Berry, McDonnell, and Laws looked stricken as they crossed the street to study the vehicle for clues of the State's intentions.

Then Laws broke into loud, relieved laughter. This Suburban wasn't like the Benson's. It didn't have bucket seats up front, and there was no console.

"What a coincidence." McDonnell let out his breath. "There've been too many coincidences in this case."

2

That afternoon, Albert Gleason testified for three hours about the composition of the two "improvised explosive devices commonly known as pipe bombs." For part of the time, as McDonnell questioned the ATF explosives expert about his assumptions, the jury was out of the courtroom. But even when they were present, some of them seemed to find the proceedings less than gripping and "the sleeper" was soon nodding off again. Judge Hayes interrupted to say, "I asked the bailiff to advise one of the jurors to pay more attention. I guess that's the nicest way of putting it."

Gleason himself became irascible as Jerry Brock plodded through each stage of the investigation, then asked him to take out his log book, review his notes, and identify every piece of evidence he had examined. Flicking his fingers to brush off the soot from the pipe fragments Brock handed him, Gleason answered over and over again, "Yes, I examined it."

The bomb expert said a search of the crime scene turned up pieces of four D-cell batteries, two circuit boards, and an electronic chip which might or might not have come from either circuit board.

In the jury's absence, McDonnell objected to Gleason's estimate of the diameter of the pipes. "He's making an assumption," McDonnell insisted to Judge Hayes. The assumption was that the end caps had been screwed onto the pipes, but there was no proof of this. As a matter of law, it wasn't enough to reach an inference and maintain as Gleason had that "to make a pipe bomb, the caps have to fit on the pipe. If the cap was four inches, then the pipe had to be four inches." No complete end cap was ever located. McDonnell pointed out, and metallurgist Theodore Toth had testified that the thickness of the fragments was consistent with five-inch, as well as four-inch, pipe. The murderer could have put odd pieces of end cap into the console to confuse investigators or to serve as extra shrapnel.

Hayes ruled that common sense had to be applied. The defense, he said, had never made a prima facie case that the State didn't have the proper evidence.

Gleason went on to testify that the bomb had been triggered electronically. "You would have to set up the device so that you don't get blown up," he said. "There would have to be some type of switching or arming mechanism." Climbing down off the stand, he showed the jurors a hole that had been drilled in an end cap where a detonating device could have been placed.

But he couldn't say whether the explosions had been initiated by a remote control device, a switch, or a timer. Although he couldn't exclude the possibility, he didn't believe the bombs were triggered by the ignition.

He said the four D-cell batteries didn't seem to be related to any of the Suburban's electronic equipment. And of the two circuit board pieces recovered, one appeared to be different from anything known to be in the vehicle. These might have been involved in the blasts. But again he couldn't swear to it with scientific certainty.

Brock brought a cardboard box to the stand, and Albert Gleason lifted out a replica of a pipe bomb and plunked it down in front of him. Magnified by the microphone, the noise resounded in the quiet courtroom like an explosion. The crowd gasped at that and at the size of the thing. Empty, it weighed twenty pounds. It could have held three to six pounds of powder.

Jerry Brock lugged the replica over to the jury and passed it from person to person like a priest passing a chalice. Each juror touched it, held it, hefted it, turning it this way and that.

Then Jerry sat beside his brother Dwight at the prosecutor's table, and the two of them rocked metronomically in their chairs like a couple of old codgers on a front porch back home in Nub City. They appeared not to have a care in the world as they watched what the defense would do with the witness.

From the start, Gleason served notice he was a tough cookie and didn't intend to take any guff. Sighing and sometimes wisecracking about the questions, he gave a dazzling little lecture, advising McDonnell not to say "detonation" when he actually meant "deflagration." An improvised bomb "deflagrated" because the grains of powder ignited unevenly and incompletely. In contrast, a piece of military ordnance "detonated" because all the explosive material ignited simultaneously. If there had been fifty pounds of ordnance in the Suburban, it would not have been standing there after the explosion. Neither would most of the Benson house.

Gleason admitted the circuit boards he had referred to were too badly burned for him to say positively whether they did or did not come from the CB radio in the Suburban. And he conceded that the engine block might have shielded Benson from bomb shrapnel, but he said plenty of other debris, including glass, would have been blown off the vehicle.

When McDonnell asked about similar double pipe bomb explosions which ATF had under investigation, Brock objected and Gleason didn't answer. But the defense did establish that a timer could have been set to ignite the bombs in a matter of minutes, hours, days, or longer.

When the State called Thomas Schelling, McDonnell and Berry scrambled out of their chairs and objected. For ten minutes they crowded in front of the bench along with the Brock brothers and the court reporter and jawed away out of earshot of the jury. The only sound in the gallery was from reporters who had portable battery-powered typewriters and word processors in their laps. One could hear the clicking at the keys.

The bailiff, a beefy, bald-headed man named Val Everly, growled for the journalists to quiet down. Then he noticed three Cubans laughing and speaking Spanish. After the death threats to the defense team, the bailiffs had all been alerted. Everly shouted, "You find something so funny, you can just get out of the courtroom."

Shocked, the three Cubans shut up.

The judge ruled that the State could bring on Schelling for a voir dire proceeding with the jury out of the room. A handsome fellow with sun-streaked blond hair and a dark mustache, Schelling described the incident when he was working on the roof of the Benson home in Lancaster and saw Steven pass by down below carrying what appeared to be tubes with protruding wires.

"About five minutes later I heard an explosion, two explosions, I believe," Schelling said. "I came down off the roof, ran across the driveway through the pool area and observed Steven standing in the tennis area with what to me looked like a garage door opener."

Jerry Brock asked, "What did the explosions sound like?"

"To me it sounded like a shotgun." Schelling had previously mentioned three explosions and compared them to M-80 fireworks. Now he went on to add that he was sure this incident occurred in 1982 because it happened around the time John Hinckley attempted to assassinate President Reagan.

Judge Hayes ruled against the admission of Tom Schelling's testimony. First, it was remote. As Hayes pointed out, the assassination attempt occurred in 1981, not '82, which placed it more than five years ago. Secondly, Schelling's knowledge was too vague. He had never seen Benson detonate any explosives and couldn't connect the noise he heard with the pipes and other paraphernalia he claimed he saw Steven carrying.

The last witness discussed a topic that was never far from the Brock brothers' minds—did Buck always bark at passersby?

Afterward, as I walked with McDonnell through the lobby, he complained, "I don't get it. What are they trying to do? Send a man to the electric chair because of a barking dog?"

But he didn't pretend to be displeased by the day's events, particularly the exclusion of Schelling's testimony. "I was scared shitless," he said. "The State sandbagged me. I didn't expect to see Schelling."

At the doors he hesitated. Val Everly, the bailiff, had gone outside ahead of us. He indicated which way the Cubans went. McDonnell headed in the opposite direction.

3

I ran into Judge Hayes in the parking lot as he was about to climb into his Jeep Renegade. He said he had heard the rumor about death threats, but he didn't believe them. No one seemed to know how the rumor started or whom it involved. "I don't sense any guns in the courtroom," Hayes said. "That's why I'm not packing my piece."

As for the exclusion of Schelling's testimony, he explained that the legal concept of "remoteness" generally meant more than three years. He would have admitted a remote incident if it related to the commission of a crime. Benson had allegedly set off pipe bombs, but there was nothing criminal about that.

As a matter of fact, the judge said, he had made pipe bombs as a boy. It was no big deal. He and his friends dropped them into a pond in North Carolina to bring up fish. What they'd do, he explained, was empty shotgun shells, both pellets and powder, into a pipe, seal the ends with paraffin, then use magnesium from a flashlight and a six-cell battery to detonate it.

The mention of "detonation" brought a grin to Hayes's smooth, boyish face. He said he had been amused by the give and take between McDonnell and the ATF bomb expert. "Gleason's a typical New York cop, a big-city boy. He wasn't going to let some Florida attorney jerk him around by the ying-yang. At a certain point he was going to say 'Fuck you, Jack,' and hit back, make Mike dance."

Still, he acknowledged Gleason's testimony might be the source of an appeal if Benson were convicted. McDonnell could claim it was a reversible error that the judge had let Gleason testify that the end caps were screwed onto the pipes. Then again, Hayes said, maybe Mike was just trying to sucker him into saying he personally believed the State had to prove the caps were screwed onto the pipes. Every court case was a constant cat and mouse game.

Hayes didn't believe he had committed any single error serious enough to cause an appellate court to grant a new trial. But he said he had to worry about cumulative errors. If Benson got a life sentence, the appeal would go to the District Court where there was a judge who had once been burned by some police and prosecutors and was very hard on the State. If there was a death penalty, that meant an automatic appeal to the State Supreme Court, where there was a judge who didn't believe in capital punishment.

Standing in the thick warm air of a Florida summer evening, and speaking unprompted by questions from me, Judge Hayes admitted that one possible ground for an appeal really worried him. He had allowed the State to show the jury a picture of Margaret Benson on the autopsy table.

The State had the right to introduce recognizable photographs of a murder victim at a crime scene. But in all the snapshots of Mrs. Benson near the Suburban, she had been lying face down, and there was no way of identifying her. The only photograph that showed what was left of her face was the one on the autopsy table. So he let it in even though technically it should have been a picture from the crime scene.

When I asked how he thought the jury had reacted to the grisly photographs, he expressed the hope that they would return with a verdict based on facts, not feelings. He said he was as sensitive as the next guy, but he had forced himself to go hunting and kill deer, then gut and dress them. He had done this to harden himself so that when he saw pictures of murder victims he didn't get too upset to render objective judgments.

At times when I later heard Judge Hayes talk Rambo-tough, I wondered how much of it was a way of protecting himself against deeper feeling. What he seemed anxious to conceal were actually his best qualities. It was as though he feared people would take him for what he appeared to be——a boyish, blue-eyed, polite and thoughtful fellow.

As for his alphabetical evaluation of the trial, he said, "We may be locked into a permanent B." He characterized Jerry Brock as a "B" prosecutor, but one who won a lot of cases because he recognized his limits and worked right up to them. "He'll always give you a 'B' performance," and Hayes meant this as praise, not disparagement.

Michael McDonnell was a much more complex equation. Hayes felt he could have been the best trial attorney in southwest Florida, a multimillionaire, and a national celebrity. "Edward Bennett Williams, F. Lee Bailey, Percy Foreman, Melvin Belli, they've got nothing on Mike. But, but . . ." The judge groped for the answer. "But he has a flaw."

He couldn't put his finger on what it was. Maybe McDonnell didn't prepare enough. Maybe he'd been dragged down by the weak local competition. Perhaps he got carried away by his invincible aura of charm and cheerfulness. Whatever, this trial would go a long way, Hayes thought, toward showing what McDonnell and everybody else were made of. In a phrase he often used, it was going to give a lot of people "a window on their souls."

Then he hopped into his Jeep Renegade and pulled out of the parking lot. As I started my rental car, I saw Jerry and Dwight Brock crossing the heat-warped macadam, weighted down by boxes of evidence, looking as weary as a couple of lonely traveling salesmen after weeks on the road. They climbed into a drab, stripped-down state car and started the forty-mile drive south to Naples. Hungry and thirsty as I was at the moment, I hoped they had had more than Coke and potato chips for lunch today.

Chapter 8

Tall and disheveled, Wayne Kerr hunched forward to speak into the microphone. Occasionally he jabbed a finger at his glasses, shoving them back up his nose. Although the courtroom was refrigerator cool, he pulled out a handkerchief and swabbed his brow.

Dwight Brock conducted the direct examination, and Michael McDonnell objected from the start that he was leading the witness. Explaining that the defense expected "evidentiary problems" with Kerr, McDonnell asked Judge Hayes to remind him "of the hearsay rule and ask him not to blurt out hearsay things."

Although Kerr had served as a corporate officer in Meridian Security Network and as a personal attorney for Steven, Scott, Carol Lynn, and Mrs. Benson, Brock said that he was no different from any other witness. Still, Judge Hayes urged Dwight to be more careful in framing his questions.

After many objections and heated discussions of attorney-client privilege, Kerr recounted that he had come to Florida in February 1985 to start Margaret Benson's tax preparations and "to do some research into this entity, so called Meridian Marketing." Reviewing Meridian Security Network records, he found a rat's nest of unbalanced books, missing bank statements, missing checks, and befuddling transactions.

"Did this cause any suspicions in your mind?" Brock asked.

"Well," Kerr said, "initially I thought it was just sloppy bookkeeping."

McDonnell darted from the defense table like a Thoroughbred from a starting gate. "Your Honor, suspicion in the mind doesn't even rise to the dignity of a lay opinion. If he's formed a professional opinion, I think he's probably qualified to give one. But suspicions are not competent evidence."

Hayes instructed Dwight that "Probably the better way to put it is what did you think, therefore what did you do? A matter of phrasing the question."

So Brock established that Kerr "thought" he had found sloppy accounting procedures. And what he "did" was to continue his investigation. Yet even after the lawyer-accountant discovered financial discrepancies and learned that Steven was lying and denying his connection with Meridian Marketing, neither Kerr nor Mrs. Benson acted on this information. While as an attorney Kerr could do no more than advise his client and let her decide what Steven could do with her money, as a corporate vice-president he theoretically had an obligation to see that funds weren't misused.

But the State stayed away from that. Strictly interested in Steven's wrongdoing, it displayed complete indifference to repeated indications that his financial delinquencies had long been disregarded, if not condoned. And it ignored all signs that the Meridian companies were a seat-of-the-pants operation run out of Margaret Benson's hip pocket for purposes that were as unfathomable as her filigreed mind.

The one thing that came through clearly, however, was that she had extravagant personal expectations when she backed Steven's ill-conceived ventures. As Kerr put it, "Margaret certainly had a burning desire to be a businesswoman, to run a business, to have a business, and it was, I can't say that it ranked up there with designing homes, but certainly it was a priority in life that she wanted to hold herself out as a businesswoman, have her own business cards and say that she is an owner of various companies."

For someone obsessed with appearances—reality always took a backseat in Mrs. Benson's life—the crucial point was her image in other people's eyes. She had little patience and less talent for playing a productive role in business. She knew nothing about making decisions, managing employees, or handling money. She was too busy planning her dream house, playing golf and tennis, and dancing at a club called Exclusively Singles, an establishment run by a lady who referred to herself as Countess Rosine.

But Dwight Brock continued to question Kerr as if the lawyer represented General Motors, not some Rube Goldberg outfit operated out of a trailer on a vacant lot. And he kept inquiring about his suspicions and Mrs. Benson's intentions as if they were a couple of hard-nosed corporate executives who had discovered a colleague with his hand in the till.

When Margaret Benson returned from Europe and learned that Steven had bought a house and was moving Meridian Marketing to a larger office, the State wanted the jury to believe that that was the last straw. She was ready to take action. Yet, as Michael McDonnell objected, "What we're talking about is the state of mind perhaps of Margaret Benson, but not the defendant's state of mind." Since there was no evidence that Steven knew she had discussed putting a lien on his house, it wasn't relevant to his alleged motive.

But the judge ruled it was relevant to the heated conversation Mrs. Benson and Kerr had with Steven when they returned from Fort Myers and told him they had seen his new house and they had seen his Datsun 280Z that was supposed to have served as the down payment. The testimony was damaging to the defense, and the damaged doubled when Kerr said that Steven claimed he had sold the Datsun.

After an hour and a half, Kerr said, he had asked, "Can I start taking a look at the checkbooks?" and Steven brought them, and the attorney tried "to determine the degree of completeness of the records." At one point he had had a question and went looking for Steven in the other rooms of the trailer, but couldn't find him. "Apparently," Kerr said, "he had just run out for something. And I came back and I basically told Margaret that the books were in no better condition than they were in February."

When Steven returned, they said the records were in no shape to be audited. Although they had planned to work late, Steven had a "prior social engagement," and so Mrs. Benson "indicated that Steven was to update the books by the next day." Then they went home, Kerr and Mrs. Benson to Quail Creek, Steven to Fort Myers. How they expected him to accomplish overnight a task he had shirked for the past five months was never explained.

Dwight showed Kerr some checkbooks and Dean Witter account registers that the lawyer had inspected on July 8. Brock asked if these records were different from when he last saw them. Kerr said that they had been incomplete before. Now figures were scribbled on the check stub register. Kerr said he hadn't made these entries. The handwriting appeared to be Steven Benson's. The suggestion was that the defendant had done this the night before the murders or in the following weeks when he realized the documents would be audited by law enforcement officials.

Then Brock introduced "a 1984 Form 1099 which is remitted to the Internal Revenue Service for non-employees for Margaret Benson." It listed Steven as a non-employee receiving $36,000 a year as a consultant. The prosecutor asked whether Steven was receiving any other funds as compensation for running the Meridian corporations. Kerr said, "Not to my knowledge."

Brock showed him three quarterly reports for Meridian World Group, Inc. "Is Steven Benson listed on these as an employee?" Kerr said, "No, he is not."

When asked to describe the events of the morning of the murders, Kerr related the by now familiar story. The only surprise during his testimony was that Brock never inquired about Margaret Benson's will or her plans to disinherit Steven.

But the press disregarded this and continued to print the same mistake, often maintaining that the subject had come up during the trial. *Time* and *Newsweek* ran stories stating that Steven feared disinheritance and that his mother planned to write him out of her will. The Washington *Post* and the *New York Times* would recycle the same error during and after the trial. Trade publications announcing books about the Benson case would repeat this misinformation more than a year after it had been corrected.

2

On the way to lunch, McDonnell smiled and said, "I'm reminded of that old Elvis Presley song, 'Suspicious Mind.' But I go back to Billy Joel's 'Innocent Man.'" Both songs were in his repertoire, and both came to mind because he had never before known a court to accept testimony about a witness's suspicions. Facts, not suspicions, were supposed to be what a jury considered. As far as he was concerned, this alone was enough to overturn a guilty verdict. He said he'd noticed five other reversible errors. "But who wants to think about appeals? We're going to win."

At the Veranda, waiting for his stir-fried shrimp, McDonnell made a phone call and discovered that a witness, an optometrist who had examined Steven Benson's eyes, wanted to back out of testifying. Her husband didn't like the idea of her helping to defend an accused murderer. But McDonnell handled this in stride. He'd been through it before. Just the other day a secretary in the courthouse sidled up to him and hissed that she thought that lawyers should be jailed along with their clients. "It's always refreshing to find that people don't believe in the Constitution," McDonnell said.

• • •

"Afternoon, Wayne." McDonnell started off first-name friendly during cross-examination.

"Afternoon," Kerr replied.

"I don't think I want you to look at my checkbook." In an amiable, easygoing tone, he established that Kerr wasn't aware of all the conversations between Steven and Mrs. Benson, primarily because Kerr lived up north, not in Naples. Although he had advised Mrs. Benson to stop acting as a bank for her children, he couldn't say that she had done so.

MCDONNELL: Now, you mentioned that Steven was not an employee of any of the corporations.

KERR: That is my understanding.

MCDONNELL: All right, sir. What are we really talking about? Are we talking about a classification for tax purposes?

KERR: I think that's correct.

MCDONNELL: Steven was president of one of the companies, wasn't he?

KERR: Yes.

MCDONNELL: Now, I don't practice corporate law, but isn't it true, Mr. Kerr, the president is usually an employee of the corporation in fact?"

KERR: Yes.

By listing Steven as a consultant, not as an employee, his mother saved the money she would have had to pay to match his Social Security contribution.

Directing Kerr's attention to the evening before the murders when Mrs. Benson told Steven to update the books, McDonnell asked, "Is it consistent with her instructions that further entries were made in the checkbook?"

KERR: Yes it is.

MCDONNELL: Were you familiar with Steven's general accounting habits and practice?

KERR: Yes.

MCDONNELL: How would you characterize it?

KERR: Shoddy.

MCDONNELL: You don't have to pull any punches, they were atrocious, weren't they?

Kerr said they were, and added "Steven was a very creative person, good idea person. But detail was always missing."

To end the cross-examination, McDonnell addressed Kerr's suspicions and invited him to remind the jury what they were. Kerr said, "One, that it was shoddy bookkeeping and two, that it could be basically misappropriation of funds." But the attorney admitted that to this day he could not substantiate that any money had been misappropriated.

On redirect Dwight Brock tried to get Kerr to say Mrs. Benson had confirmed that Steven had misappropriated funds. But while he acknowledged that he had seen evidence of transfers to Steven's personal accounts, he had not reviewed all the pertinent documents.

Approaching the subject from a new direction, Brock asked whether Kerr had attempted to curb Mrs. Benson's spending, and this opened areas that the prosecution would have preferred to ignore.

Kerr described a memo he drafted advising Mrs. Benson that during a recent eleven-month period she had run through a million and a half dollars. Although Margaret worried about the sums she was pouring into the Meridian companies, they amounted to approximately $250,000 or less than a fifth of what she had squandered on expenditures which offered neither the hope of a return nor a tax write-off.

By asking about the repayment of loans which Mrs. Benson expected of her children, Brock allowed Kerr to mention "one matter pertaining to Scott Benson [for which] we had to have an accounting done."

On re-cross, McDonnell zeroed in on "this matter pertaining to Scott Benson," and Kerr explained that in 1983 Margaret had sold some securities that belonged to Scott and kept the money. Scott hired an attorney and accused his mother of misappropriating his funds. An accounting was prepared, Kerr said, "to show him that even if that is the case...there were no damages in the sense that those funds were disbursed to satisfy obligations of Scott R. Benson."

Whether this would have held up in court or not, it demonstrated again the casualness with which money moved from pocket to pocket in the Benson household, and it underlined the misunderstanding

and strife provoked by their bizarre way of handling financial matters.

After getting Kerr to describe "start-up problems in a business"
and establishing that it wasn't uncommon for a company to take
three years to make money—the Meridian Security Network had
been in operation for nine months—McDonnell asked if he knew
"why the Meridian Security monies that you mentioned were placed
in the personal account of Steven?"

"No, I have no idea," Kerr said.

The next witness, Steven Hawkins, had run the Meridian Marketing office in Fort Myers and spent eight hectic months dealing
with Benson's absorption in detail and indifference to the larger picture. Hawkins wasn't without sympathy for his boss. He later told
the Philadelphia *Inquirer* that Benson was so incompetent, so oblivious to basic business concepts it "made you want to help the guy."

Hawkins said Benson told him Meridian Marketing had to be
kept a secret. Although the company did promotional work for Meridian Security Network, Benson urged him never to come to the
Naples office.

On July 8, Benson telephoned Fort Myers, said his mother and
Wayne Kerr were on the way, and asked Hawkins to hide the computer where Kerr wouldn't see it. Although fed up with these subter-
fuges, Hawkins stashed it in his car.

That evening, around 6:30 P.M., Benson called again and invited
Hawkins over to his house for dinner. There had been no prior engagement. If it escaped any juror's attention that Kerr had testified
that Benson left the office early because of a "prior social engagement," Dwight Brock repeated his question with sufficient incredu-
lity to remind them.

Hawkins stayed at Benson's house from seven till eleven or eleven
thirty, and left as Benson was heading for bed.

"Did you ever see Steven Benson working on any checkbooks
that night?" Brock asked. Hawkins said he hadn't.

Next day, Hawkins drove Debbie to Quail Creek. They arrived at
11 A.M., less than two hours after the murders and "Steven asked me
if I had gotten any money in that day. It struck me as a little unusual."

Indeed, it was so odd that it seemed to some people in the courtroom to suggest that Benson was in shock. As one observer, a lawyer

with no ties to the State or defense camp asked, "If he just killed his family to get his share of a $10 million estate, why would he be worried about the day's receipts?"

According to Hawkins, Debbie asked him to move the blue Datsun 280Z from their house to the Meridian office. Although he wasn't crazy about starting any car that belonged to the Benson family, he did as Debbie requested.

The judge called a ten-minute recess, and when he returned attorneys for the State and defense clustered around him. Then three ladies—two teenagers and a woman—were summoned from the gallery and brought up to the bench. The jury was in its chamber, and one could hear their laughter more distinctly than anything said in front of Judge Hayes.

After several minutes of discussion, the ladies returned to their seats and soon left the courtroom looking badly rattled. They refused to give their names to the press or to explain what had happened.

Jerry Brock told reporters that the women had overheard two witnesses talking during a recess and believed they had violated the rule against discussing the case outside of court. This explanation was accurate as far as it went, but it didn't come close to telling the whole truth.

Diana Galloway, an ATF auditor, appeared at 4 P.M., and after the defense did a voir dire, there was a long break followed by an announcement from the judge that the testimony would run late tonight.

Ms. Galloway had such a low, caramel-coated southern accent and such an abundance of material to explain, it was easy to believe we'd be here for the rest of the summer. Dwight Brock settled her at a desk directly in front of the jury, and the frowns of concentration from jurors, the riffling of pages, the general torpor and confusion in the courtroom were all reminiscent of the first day of school.

A double major in math and accounting, Ms. Galloway had a luxuriant mane of ash blond hair, a slightly flustered demeanor, and a disconcerting habit of mispronouncing words. She consistently referred to Mrs. Benson's "Dean Whittier account." But she had drawn up a daunting set of charts full of arrows that tracked the flow of cash back and forth among ten accounts held by Steven Benson, his mother, the companies she owned, and Steven's lone independent enterprise, Meridian Marketing.

In fourteen months from May 1984 until Mrs. Benson's death on July 9, 1985, Steven, according to the charts, received $247,000 from his mother and her business accounts. Some of that was legitimate compensation, Ms. Galloway said. Subtracting $36,000 for Steven's annual consultant's fee, and $25,000 for paying Mrs. Benson's estimated quarterly income taxes, the ATF agent arrived at a figure of $179,000 which represented transfers to Benson that were difficult to account for.

Still, she tried her level best to do just that—account for it all, show where every dime and dollar came from and went to. Long before she finished, however, Judge Hayes called a truce in the barrage of figures and announced a dinner break.

3

Deputy Clerk of Court Sharon Telly and summer law intern Paula Kelley were waiting to be seated at the Veranda when Michael McDonnell, Bob Laws, and I arrived. McDonnell asked the ladies to share a table with us. I expected them to view the defense as the enemy and say no thanks. After all, they sat on the prosecutor's side of the courtroom, where Sharon Telly swore in witnesses and kept track of the evidence. A third-year law student at the University of Florida, Paula Kelley did research for Judge Hayes and had to be ready to find an opinion whenever he asked.

But Sharon and Paula surprised me by saying they'd be glad to join us, and after we had ordered, they surprised me again by volunteering their reactions to the trial. A lively, funny woman in her forties, Sharon Telly said there was something she couldn't understand. If Meridian Marketing was supposed to be such a secret, if Steven didn't want his mother to find out about it, why did he give it that name? Why not call it anything but Meridian? And why let it do PR work for Meridian Security Network?

There were other things that didn't add up, the ladies said, as McDonnell sat quietly and listened. It didn't strike them as logical that Steven would drive up in front of his mother's house at that hour of the morning, when neighbors were leaving for work, and lug two twenty-six-pound bombs from his van and load them into the Suburban. Then he had to stop someplace—but where?—en route to the

Shop 'N Go and run wire under the floor mat, arm the bombs, and set a timer or detonator to trigger the explosives. Then he still had to go to the convenience store and buy coffee and pastry. Sharon laughed and shook her long wavy hair. That must have been one very hectic, nerve-racking trip. Had anybody here ever been to the Shop 'N Go during morning rush hour? Even in low season, that was the busiest time of day, with people pulling in to get self-service gas or grab cigarettes and something for breakfast.

Paula Kelley was a slight young lady given to wearing severely cut suits and ties. Tonight, however, she wore a bright green jacket and looked like she was dressed for St. Patrick's Day. During the long break before Diana Galloway came on, the prosecutors, defense attorneys, and Benson had gathered in the judge's chambers to discuss how late they'd run tonight. She and Sharon were snacking on Oreo cookies when Paula heard Steven's stomach rumble with hunger. Her instinct had been to offer him one. But she hadn't and now was ashamed at her failure to do the natural thing, the human thing, for fear of what the judge and the prosecutors might think. She asked if she could leave some cookies with McDonnell and have him pass them along to Benson. He said he'd be happy to.

Sharon said she was having a hard time keeping track of the evidence. The State had introduced over one hundred exhibits. She had complained to the Brocks, and Jerry said, "You can't be expected to look after the whole world." Just when she was about to give up and tell him she was not going to wheel the files and court records around on a luggage caddy any longer, the prosecutor showed up with a grocery cart and smiled like a possum as he pushed it down the courtroom aisle chock-full of evidence. "Coming through," Brock called, "butter, eggs, milk."

That got a good laugh from everybody, but soon we were back to more serious talk about the trial. Paula said the judge asked every night if the State had proved its case yet. The young law clerk had her doubts. So did Sharon Telly.

"Once the State rests," McDonnell said, "I'm going to make a strong motion for a directed verdict." Since he didn't believe the State had made a convincing case, he would ask Hayes to acquit Benson. Although such pro forma motions are generally dismissed in minutes, he noted that the judge had set aside an hour to consider the issue. McDonnell thought his chances were good.

If he was fishing for a sign of how the judge was leaning, he got it. Paula said Hayes had had her do research on directed verdicts, and she concluded that circumstantial evidence cases were almost invariably sent on for the jury to decide.

McDonnell didn't show any disappointment, didn't react at all.

As we finished our meal and called for the bill, he squeezed in a few more comments that amounted, I thought, to messages he hoped the two ladies would carry back to the opposition. He believed the judge had committed a reversible error when he let the State introduce Diana Galloway's charts. Only one of them had been submitted in time for the defense to review. The rest had sailed in from the blind side.

"But hey," said McDonnell again as he did quite often these days, "why talk about appeals? We're going to win."

The ladies left first. Then while McDonnell went to make a phone call, Bob Laws and I walked back to the Justice Center. When I asked him what had happened when the womn and two teenagers had been summoned from the gallery, the private investigator broke into a big smile. With his freckles and a toothpick that looked like a straw stuck in the corner of his mouth, he resembled an oversized Huck Finn.

The teenyboppers and the woman, Laws explained, had overheard Steven Hawkins talking with Jack Gant, the Collier County police fingerprint expert. One of the two witnesses—it was unclear which—had told the other, "I know what they want me to say; I just don't know how to say it."

To the three women this suggested the State's witnesses were rehearsing during the recess. So they got word to McDonnell, and the defense complained to the judge.

To all outward appearances, it was a case of concerned citizens stepping forward to insist that the prosecution play by the rules. But Laws allowed as how outward appearances, particularly in a murder trial of this magnitude, often concealed more than they revealed. What transpired in the courtroom was a kind of ritual competition. The real gut-fighting took place behind the scenes.

Bob Laws said the older woman, the mother of one of the teenyboppers, was on the defense payroll. She and a friend of hers had been hired to hang around and keep their eyes open. They got lucky today and heard something that shook up the State—which delighted Laws, who suspected the prosecution had its own people lurking around the courtroom and halls picking up rumors and planting them. "It's all part of the game," he said, tossing aside the toothpick as we stepped onto the elevator.

4

When the judge entered the courtroom after dinner the bailiff asked, "Are you ready, Your Honor?" Hayes chuckled. "Not really." But presumably he repeated Master Lee's motto "See straight" and managed to stay awake for the next few hours. Others let their eyes and minds and bodies drift, and before long spectators in the gallery had fallen fast asleep.

Remarkably, the jurors, even the lady who tended to nod off, seemed riveted by the reams of information that Dwight Brock introduced via Diana Galloway. The witness spent hours explaining what she said were over fifty suspicious transactions.

But, in truth, the transactions seemed less suspicious than screwball and crack-brained. Tracing one of the signed checks Mrs. Benson had left to cover expenses during her trip to Europe, Ms. Galloway showed that it had been made out for $50,000 and deposited on June 11 in the Meridian Security Network account. On the same day, Steven wrote himself a check for $23,000 and used it to buy a cashier's check that he put as a down payment on his new house. The ledger from which this check came indicated it had been for $3,000, not $50,000.

If this was embezzlement or misappropriation of funds, it was fiscal crime at a submoronic level. So was another example cited by Galloway, this one a $5,300 check that flowed from the Meridian Security Network to Steven's personal account, but was logged in the ledger as a $50 check to Radio Shack.

Ms. Galloway also described how Steven had obtained a bank loan for a Chevy van in March 1985. His mother had co-signed the loan. When the check came through for $25,000, Benson deposited it in his own account, then wrote a check to Meridian Marketing for $15,000.

Since Mrs. Benson had floated Steven a personal loan of $25,000 to pay for the van, and since the auditor and the prosecutor assumed the bank loan had been meant to repay Mrs. Benson, this was viewed as more money Steven had diverted from his mother. There was no explanation of why Mrs. Benson hadn't complained about this between March and July and why, in fact, she had covered three of the monthly payments for the bank loan.

The bottom line, the State contended, was that during a fourteen-month period Steven had diverted $26,600 from his mother and her companies to Meridian Marketing. During the same period, from the same sources, he had diverted $85,692.43 to his personal use. For those spectators and reporters who stayed awake until the end, this moment was fraught with a sense of thunderous anticlimax. After a year-long investigation, a federal audit that lasted months, and six hours of Ms. Galloway's testimony, it seemed the State had been straining at a gnat.

If one accepted that Benson was guilty of every single financial infraction the prosecution suggested, that meant he had stolen little more than $112,000. While that was a substantial piece of change, it fell way short of the two and a half million dollars Carol Lynn had accused her brother of ripping off. And, in the context of the Benson family's haphazard handling of wealth, it didn't amount to a credible motive for murder.

Shortly before 10 P.M. the judge asked the defense whether they wanted to start cross-examination.

"I want to go home," McDonnell said.

"The truth of it is," Dwight Brock wearily admitted, "so do I."

After praising the jury for its staying power, the judge adjourned until the next morning. Then he took the elevator to the lobby where he nearly blundered into Harry Hitchcock and Carol Lynn Kendall who stood frozen in a tableau of grief and confusion. Frail and looking lost in his own clothes, the old, white-haired man consoling his granddaughter, who was crying.

As Judge Hayes later described the scene, he was tempted to tell Hitchcock, "You blew it." He had read somewhere that the family patriarch believed that love of money was the root of all evil. From what Hayes had seen as a judge, "poverty is the root of all evil. But if you don't use your money wisely, of course you've got a problem."

Chapter 9

On Friday, July 25, the final day for the prosecution, rumor spread that the State would put Carol Lynn back on the stand while Harry Hitchcock sat in the courtoom lending moral support. TV networks considered this a great photo opportunity and returned with full crews to the Justice Center.

McDonnell's cross-examination of Diana Galloway seemed to be regarded as little more than a delay of the grand drama to come. But it too had its threatrical moments and startling role reversals. Whereas the ATF auditor had been the schoolmarm last night, the defense attorney now played the part of formidable professor.

He pointed out that her charts represented records from radically dissimilar time periods. Some of them differed by as much as six months. Didn't she feel this was like comparing apples and oranges?

Ms. Galloway replied that she depended on the documents provided by the State. She had no independent knowledge of the case or the Benson family's finances.

Could Ms. Galloway explain to the jury what a "corporate resolution" was? No, she couldn't. Although she had audited a number of Benson corporations, she had little knowledge of how they were constituted or how a "resolution" extended certain powers to officers. She had no idea what Steven Benson's corporate powers were nor whether he owned any of the corporations in question, including Meridian Marketing. Although Mrs. Benson and her children were involved in over a dozen corporations, Ms. Galloway acknowledged that she had analyzed only five of them.

She said that she assumed Steven's compensation as a consultant was the same in 1985 as in 1984. But she admitted she had no proof. He might have been receiving much more. She couldn't say whether some of the funds that she classified as "diverted" hadn't been earned by Steven.

Likewise, since no documents existed for the $25,000 personal loan Steven had used to buy the van, Ms. Galloway couldn't say how, when, or whether Mrs. Benson expected to be paid back. She also could not state that Steven had no right to use the van as collateral to obtain a bank loan for $25,000. McDonnell argued that that amount should be deducted from the total the auditor claimed had been misappropriated.

Angrily flapping his notes at the lectern, dramatizing his disgust at Diana Galloway's "shoddy accounting procedures," McDonnell demanded, "You're not saying that Steven Benson stole this money?"

"I can't make that statement," she said.

"Are you telling us that Steven Benson blew up his mother, his brother, and his sister for $85,000?"

"I can't make that determination."

"Are you telling us he did it for $60,000?"

"I can't make that determination."

McDonnell stalked away from the lectern.

That afternoon, Jerry Brock put on a few witnesses to tie up loose ends. The only one whose testimony packed a wallop was Stephen Dancsec, a former employee of Meridian Security Network, who swore that he had overheard a conversation at Pittman Funeral Home two days after the murders. Brenda Turnbull, the company secretary, told Benson that police had asked her whether he knew how to make bombs.

According to Dancsec, Benson replied that when he was younger he had constructed pipe bombs. Benson described filling copper tubes with powder, sealing the ends, and detonating them.

Michael McDonnell asked Dancsec, "Now you remember that phone call you made to me, don't you? Didn't you tell me that unless you were paid your wages you were going to have a press conference and really hurt Steven?"

Dancsec admitted he made the call, but said he had done so out of frustration when he had helped keep Meridian Security Network in business after the murders, but never received his salary. "I just felt we were being dealt a raw deal."

On redirect, Brock asked, "Do you hold any animosity toward the defendant today?"

Stephen Danscec swore that he didn't.

Minutes later, when the State rested, disappointed spectators and angry journalists, some of whom had flown in just for the afternoon, spilled into the halls babbling, "What happened? Why didn't she testify? Where's Carol Lynn? Where's the old man?" It was as if they had paid a fortune to see a Broadway show, and the stars had canceled.

Jerry Brock told reporters Carol Lynn was at the Justice Center. But he claimed it had never been the State's plan to recall her.

When the defense team came out, McDonnell was asked to rate the State's case on a scale from 1 to 10. "I'd give Jerry Brock an eleven for professionalism. But zero for evidence and facts."

Since the next day, July 26, was Steven Benson's thirty-fifth birthday, journalists asked whether the defense had anything planned. McDonnell said, "I'd like to give him a special present." He didn't explain what he had in mind.

"Will Steven take the stand?"

McDonnell said he hadn't decided. "One question is whether there's anything left for him to say."

"Do you think the testimony about Steven making bombs hurt?"

Not much, he said. After all, lots of boys fool around with explosives. He himself had made bombs as a kid.

"What! When? Tell us!"

McDonnell laughed. "Hey, you're not going to pin this on me, are you?" He excused himself to go in and move for a directed verdict.

Steven Benson smiled now that he had heard all the evidence against him. The Brock brothers looked relaxed, too, as they sat and rocked in their chairs and chewed gum. The jury had been sent home before McDonnell made his motion.

Citing Florida Supreme Court decisions, he contended that a case based on circumstantial evidence shouldn't be sent to a jury unless it is consistent with only one theory of guilt. The evidence presented by the State "does not exclude every reasonable hypothesis of innocence," McDonnell said. "We ask you, Your Honor, to make a diffi-

cult and courageous decision and enter a judgment of acquittal for
Steven Benson."

Judge Hayes rejected the motion, just as Paula Kelley had predicted he would. "There is sufficient evidence for the jury to conclude that there is guilt." That didn't mean Steven was guilty, but
that the jury would have to decide.

Afterward, McDonnell said he wasn't surprised or disappointed.
"These things are settled at the appellate level."

All during the trial Jerry Brock kept his distance from the press
and would do no more than drawl a few bland remarks as he came
out of the courtroom. But I found a member of the prosecution team
who, when guaranteed anonymity, explained why Carol Lynn Kendall hadn't been recalled. Despite Jerry Brock's public protestations
to the contrary, the State had planned to have its star witness testify
again. But as she waited, Carol Lynn became increasingly agitated.
The pressure built, and she began crying and carrying on in a loud
voice. Finally, her emotional state was such that the prosecutors decided it was too risky to put her on the stand. They knew what she
was capable of saying when upset.

As another source close to the events told me, "It was like a 747
coming in for a landing, then being waved off at the last minute."

2

I sat with Judge Hayes in the lounge of the Ramada Inn overlooking the Caloosahatchee River, where power boats ripped white seams
in the dark waters as they sped past. Grace Buonpane, a secretary
from his office, had a drink with us.

The judge praised McDonnell's cross-examination of Diana Galloway, but didn't believe he had completely impeached her testimony. Although she hadn't known what a corporate resolution was,
Hayes felt Galloway had been effective with the jury because she was
a woman, as were ten of them; she was a southerner, and Fort Myers
was much more a southern city than Naples; and Brock had seated
her at a desk at their level.

The judge expressed great respect for this jury. He couldn't say
whether as individuals they were bright or came from superior back-
grounds, but they had a collective energy. He marveled at how atten-
tive they had been last night. At the end of the session his admiration

was so immense he had been tempted to stand and bow to them as he would to an opponent in Tae-Kwon-Do.

But he didn't get the sense that they had the death penalty in them. They weren't a hanging jury. Maybe that was because of the care Margaret Covington took in selecting them. Maybe, he said, that had been the defense's primary goal—to seat a panel that wouldn't impose capital punishment.

But in the end, this struck Hayes as pointless speculation. He was willing to bet the jury would acquit Steven Benson.

Grace Buonpane piped up in agreement. "I think he'll walk."

If anything surprised me more than their openness, it was their belief that the jury was not convinced of Benson's guilt. I had yet to meet anyone else outside the defense camp who shared this sentiment. Of the dozens of journalists who covered the trial, only one— Denes Husty of the Fort Myers *News Press*—admitted there was a remote chance the defendant would be acquitted. Yet the judge reemphasized the narrowly circumstantial nature of the case, conceding the possibility that a guilty verdict might be overturned because of the single piece of hard evidence the State had—the palm prints —and offering his opinion that at this point the prosecution hadn't proved Benson's guilt.

Judge Hayes went on to mention an audacious tactic the defense might try. If his hunch was right and the jury hadn't already reached a decision, McDonnell might be smart to rest his case without putting on any witnesses. While this would be risky, he would run almost as many dangers by introducing evidence that Brock could pick apart on cross-examination.

What's more, once McDonnell put on witnesses, Brock not only got to question them, he got to call rebuttal witnesses and to speak first and last on final argument.

Still, Hayes said, regardless of what the defense did, he was betting on a not guilty verdict. He supposed an acquittal might be perceived as bad for him. But he repeated he could live with that. The system was the system. He did his job, the jury decided, and the rest was irrelevant.

He stressed, however, that the State could have done a much better job presenting its case. He didn't blame the Brocks. He said they hadn't had the manpower or the money. The fault lay at higher levels.

Then, too, there was the problem the Benson family presented to prosecutors. "To get equity," Hayes said, "you have to give equity."

But the State didn't respect the family and that made it harder to mount a case. How could you feel sympathy for the victims? Judge Hayes characterized them as "a coke head," "an air head," and "a bitch."

He mused that if Steven did murder his mother and brother, he must have justified it in his own mind by saying, "Maybe these people just weren't meant to live." That might explain why he didn't show more emotion or any contrition.

Hayes finished his vodka and tonic and said anybody who wasn't totally insane needed a justification before he killed a human being. If Benson got the death penalty, the judge told me, he would send him to the electric chair with the same sort of reasoning with which Steven might have justified the murders. Some people just weren't meant to live.

Chapter 10

I

While the judge was at the Ramada Inn theorizing that it might be smart for the defense to rest without calling witnesses, Michael McDonnell was at home in Naples pondering precisely that strategy. He had done this before—gone directly to final argument—and won civil cases, but it was different in a murder trial. He felt "like a football coach with a touchdown lead at halftime. I didn't want to lose by doing anything stupid. But I didn't want to be too conservative, too passive either." He concluded he had some witnesses who could offer testimony of true evidentiary value.

On Saturday morning, Nina McDonnell handed Steven a card and wished him a happy birthday. Then, as the defense was about to open its case, Judge Hayes asked the jury the routine questions—Had any of them discussed the case out of court? Had they been exposed to media coverage?

Two jurors said the Fort Myers *News Press* had called to inquire how the trial had affected their home lives. Although the journalist hadn't spoken directly to the jurors—he had asked their families for reactions—the judge was outraged and warned reporters that any repeat of this performance would result in charges of jury tampering. Still, he refused to sequester the panel.

The defense called Brenda Turnbull, the secretary at Meridian Security Network, and her testimony on direct examination must have convinced McDonnell he had made the right decision.

She described Steven as a happy, likable guy devoted to his children and considerate of his mother. His relationship with Scott was "big brother taking care of little brother."

By contrast, Carol Lynn and Mrs. Benson were "always arguing in the office. Steven never argued with his mother that I saw."

Far from being a secret operation, Meridian Marketing performed services for Meridian Security. "We all knew about it."

As for the conversation at Pittman Funeral Home where Benson allegedly admitted he made bombs, Turnbull said, "There was none."

Discussing Steven's movements on July 5 and 8 of 1985, she assured McDonnell, "I'm a clock watcher"; she kept track of people's "comings and goings." Benson was in the office at 3:25 P.M. on Friday when the end caps were purchased. She swore he was also there Monday at 4:05 P.M. when the pipes were bought. "I'm certain of that," she said.

"Do you have any doubt?" McDonnell asked.

"No, I do not."

But McDonnell's satisfaction was temporary and Brenda Turnbull's agony was about to begin. Sucking on a Luden's cough drop, Jerry Brock embarked on a cross-examination that would last over three hours. His job was to break down Brenda Turnbull's story, and that he did, reducing her to tears in the process.

Confronted by previous statements, she explained that when she spoke to investigators shortly after the murders "I was very upset, very distraught." She had had the events of July 5 and 8 reversed in her mind when she said Steven left the office on July 5 at 2:30 or 3:00 P.M.

As for her deposition to the defense in which she said Benson was gone on July 5 between 3 P.M. and 4 P.M., she maintained she realized her mistake and telephoned McDonnell an hour later to correct it.

"So you're telling us your memory's better now than a few days after the event?" Brock demanded.

"Yes."

He told her that her memory must be "like good wine that improves with time," and as she defended her recollections by saying she always kept an eye on the clock, he asked, "Whenever you got home that night did you have a crimp in your neck from looking down at your watch so much?"

Admitting that she had given contradictory statements in the past, she said it had helped her to consult her notes before the trial.

"Can we see those notes?" Brock asked.

"I don't have them with me today."

Not content to cast doubt on her memory, he questioned her objectivity, emphasizing Turnbull was the only Meridian Security Network employee who got paid after July 15, 1985. She had cut a company check for herself and carried it to Benson to get his signature.

By the time Judge Hayes called a recess, the woman looked drained and close to defeat. In part, she had been skewered by her previous statements, in part by the prosecutor's indefatigable commitment to consistency. If there were fifty, a hundred, or five hundred conflicts in a story, he didn't rest until he had forced a witness to account for each of them. It was intriguing to speculate what Brock could have done to Carol Lynn Kendall on cross-examination.

As we left for lunch word reached the Justice Center that Guido Dal Molin had escaped from the Collier County jail. The news rocketed through the crowd. "Everybody be careful before you start your cars," the judge wisecracked.

When asked how important Dal Molin was to the Benson trial, McDonnell observed, "He's becoming more and more important with every step he takes."

Bob Laws said, "Guido must have felt this case was getting close to him."

Dal Molin had picked the lock on his cell, scrambled down the hall to the security control room, and started punching buttons on an electrical panel. In a matter of seconds, he had shut the guards out and opened a door and a gate at the perimeter of the compound. "He'd never been in there before," Jail Commander Louis Gibbs said, "but he knew just what to do. You could say he outsmarted us."

While the escape made the Collier county police look like Keystone Kops, the crucial question was whether Guido had also outsmarted them last summer when he was a suspect in the Benson case, but never came under anything more than cursory questioning. As McDonnell took the opportunity to point out, this episode revealed the way the entire investigation had been conducted. "People who demonstrate the talent to make bombs and buy parts under assumed names and allegedly take human life are suspicious. We can make some assumptions." He let others say what those assumptions should be.

2

After Brock's crushing cross-examination of Brenda Turnbull, McDonnell did what he could to rehabilitate his witness on redirect.

Writing names, dates, and times on sheets of paper propped on an easel, he ran through the sequence of events with the secretary. "Is this the way it happened on Friday, July 5?" he asked.

"Yes."

"Is this the way it happened on Monday, July 8?"

"Yes."

"Is there anything in Mr. Brock's questions or statements that changes the truth of this?"

"No, sir," Turnbull said.

Despite the considerable success the State had had assaulting the credibility of this first witness, McDonnell came away convinced of one thing. While he had somebody who swore Steven was in the office when the pipes and end caps were purchased, the prosecution hadn't been able to put anybody on the stand to testify he or she had seen Benson in Hughes Supply during the times in question.

Dr. Bonny Eads, an optometrist, had examined Benson's eyes on July 11. Since the man who entered Hughes Supply had worn sunglasses, the defense wanted to show that Steven was legally blind and couldn't have handled the transactions for pipes and end caps without his glasses. And since there was no proof that Benson owned prescription sunglasses, McDonnell hoped to convince the jury the defendant wasn't the customer in the dark "John Lennon glasses."

But the Brocks objected that Dr. Eads was a last minute witness whom they hadn't had an opportunity to depose. "The advance notice we got was four days ago," Jerry complained. Brother Dwight added, "It's sort of hard to do anything when you work fourteen hour days."

In a shouting match in front of the bench, lawyers from both sides accused each other of not following the rules. While Jerry Brock stood belly to belly with McDonnell, shaking a finger in his face, Jerry Berry, no Beaver Cleaver he, snarled at Dwight, "I don't like the insinuation you're making. If you've got something, back it up."

The judge usually switched off his microphone before speaking to attorneys, but in the heat of the moment he forgot and his voice resounded through the courtroom. "I don't like anybody filing last minute witnesses. That's nothing more than bush league law. In the middle of a trial to tender a witness for deposition is—." He caught himself and realized he could be heard. "—irritating. It's time to call a recess. There's no point in making the system look ridiculous."

After the break, Hayes announced that today's session would be cut short so the State could take Dr. Ead's deposition. Meanwhile, the defense had another witness, William G. Eubanks, an FBI serologist, who had analyzed the stain on Steven's pants and confirmed that it was human blood. It had the same characteristics as Carol Lynn Kendall's blood, but Eubanks testified, "I would never be able to say it came from a particular unknown person."

The defense hoped the jury would see this as evidence that Steven had touched one or more of the victims in an attempt to help them. The State left the impression that he had brushed up against a blood splatter at the crime scene.

When Judge Hayes sent the jury home at 3 P.M., Brock told reporters the defense's tactics weren't just "bush league," they were "bush whacking."

McDonnell said Hayes "seems to be very much concerned with attending an upcoming judicial conference. I think it is very important to him and his personal career. I would hate to get in the way of his advancement."

This provoked the judge, which may have been McDonnell's intention. "School or no school, this trial comes first," he responded in the press. "I'll give this case six weeks if that's what it takes."

McDonnell shrugged off the suggestion that he shouldn't have gotten Hayes angry. "If you're a criminal case attorney and you don't make the judge mad, you're not doing your job."

Later that day, someone called emergency number 911 and reported an individual with a gun was in a house at 1291 Royal Palm Drive. When police arrived, they learned the armed man was Edward Carr, age thirty-eight. Sergeant Ken Ferrell entered with Carr's wife and was greeted by a gun barrel pointing from a bedroom. "You've got five seconds to get out of the house," Carr shouted and started counting.

Sergeant Ferrell retreated, cordoned off the area, and called in reinforcements. During the siege, Edward Carr came to the door of the house wearing shorts, a helmet, a web belt with cartridge pouches, and a T-shirt with U.S. Army stenciled across it. When not squeezing off rounds from a .22 rifle, he screamed for his wife, ignored his mother's pleas that he surrender, claimed that he was suffering flashbacks from combat in Viet Nam, and said he hoped the police didn't miss when they shot at him.

After six and a half hours, Carr spoke to a professional siege negotiator and agreed he needed help. He was taken into custody and placed in a mental health unit. Police said he had family problems and "was firing out of frustration."

In a sidebar to this story, the Naples *Daily News* said the events were unrelated, but explained that Edward Carr was the brother of Steven Carr, who was listed as a defense witness in the Benson trial. While Edward Carr had holed up in his house shooting out streetlights and flattening the tires of squad cars, Dwight Brock had been searching for information about Steven Carr, who was in the Collier County jail doing time for probation violation. This nine-month stretch followed thirteen months he had served in a Costa Rican prison for participating in a guerrilla attack with Nicaraguan "contras" against a Sandinista army outpost. Having held a number of press conferences from his cell in Costa Rica, then his cell in Naples, Steven Carr was reputed to have been invited to testify before Senate and House committees conducting hearings on aid to the contras.

What he had to say about the Benson case the defense wouldn't reveal and the Brock brothers wouldn't guess. But he had once had a serious cocaine habit and he knew Scott Benson, Kim Beegle, and her brother David. Among his distinguishing scars and marks, Steven Carr had a skull with a knife in its teeth tattooed on his left biceps. Beneath it in bold print was the motto "Death Before Dishonor."

Meanwhile, Guido Dal Molin remained on the loose and Naples police confessed they didn't know what to expect next. "I would not be surprised," said Louis Gibbs, "if he tried to break back in."

Chapter 11

On Monday morning, a threatening, oppressively humid day, the trial resumed with a conference in the judge's chambers. While Steven Benson sat alone looking even thinner than he had two weeks ago, Dwight Brock and Bob Laws came out from time to time to fetch legal books. After more than an hour, the lawyers emerged, with Jerry Brock fuming and McDonnell smiling. Judge Hayes announced there would be a half-day session. The State and the defense had to conduct "some discovery."

Then Dr. Bonny Eads was called and testified that Benson had 20/400 vision without glasses. The definition of legal blindness was 20/200 vision. But "legally blind" did not mean blind. It meant very poor vision.

On cross-examination, Jerry Brock asked, "Do you believe [Steven] could walk into a room and walk over to a counter and purchase some pipe?"

"I believe a person with vision like his could do that," Dr. Eads said.

Showing her the Hughes Supply receipts, he asked if someone with Benson's eyesight could scrawl the indecipherable letters in the signature space. Dr. Eads said he could.

Before observers could assimilate this information and attempt to understand what the defense had hoped to gain, McDonnell called John Gargiulo, Mrs. Benson's next-door neighbor. Gargiulo said the explosions on July 9, 1985, had blown a scrap of metal onto the screen enclosure over his swimming pool. He had alerted the police and the ATF about this, but ATF never responded and a Naples police officer took one look at it from down below, then left. The rusty fragment was still there.

Steven's blood-spattered van had been parked for days in Gargiulo's driveway, and a blood-smeared pair of shoes had remained in front of his house for weeks. Before he could cut the grass, Gargiulo paid $200 to have a landscaping company clear the debris from his property.

McDonnell left the jury in no doubt that valuable evidence may have been ignored.

Gargiulo then described how his work as an agricultural executive took him out at odd hours. Yet he never heard Buck barking. There were possums and raccoons in the neighborhood that ransacked garbage cans, and Buck didn't bark at them either. In fact, Buck hadn't even barked when Gargiulo loaded his .357 Magnum and went out at night and shot a raccoon and a possum.

On cross, Jerry Brock showed a droll sense of humor. "Those animals out there in Quail Creek sound pretty vicious." But he immediately dropped back into his role as Chinese water torturer and questioned every facet, no matter how minor, of the witness's testimony. How did Gargiulo know the shrapnel came from the explosion? Why did he assume it or the blood-smeared shoes were relevant evidence? What experience did he have at crime scene investigation? And, by the way, didn't Mr. McDonnell once serve as your legal representative?

Gargiulo stood up to this better than most people would. But Brock's technique, which was like getting sucked into a slow-grinding garbage disposal, had to make the defense think twice about whom they dared call to the stand. The State was getting as much, if not more, out of these witnesses as the defense.

Afterward, when the press put McDonnell through its own inquisition, he couldn't help feeling their disappointment with his performance. They had counted on fireworks, but believed they were getting fizzle.

"What's going on today?" a journalist asked.

"You tell me."

Why all these delays and last minute witnesses, they wanted to know.

McDonnell thought they were timely, not last minute.

"What about the optometrist?" a reporter demanded. "Why put her on?"

McDonnell said it was to show how implausible the State's case was. "What Brock is trying to claim is that Steven tiptoed out of the trailer, took off his glasses, stumbled in a blur to Hughes Supply, blundered inside to the sales counter, and signed a receipt he could barely see."

Of the State's labors to cobble together a scenario that could account for all the logical improbabilities, McDonnell said it reminded him "of the old joke about the guy who goes into a store to buy a jacket. He tries it on and finds one sleeve is too long, the other is too short, one shoulder is out of line and the waist is too tight." McDonnell acted this out, contorting his body. "The salesman says, 'Gret! Just lean this way a little bit, stretch out that arm, pull the other one in, lift your left shoulder, and suck in your gut.'

"Well, the guy buys the jacket and walks away hobbling. Another customer says, 'Poor man, look at his limp.' But the salesman says, 'No, no, look at that jacket. It's a perfect fit.'

"That salesman is Jerry Brock. He wants everybody to concentrate on the jacket and ignore the way he had to twist the truth to make it fit."

The joke got a good laugh, but it didn't make the papers. Journalists wrote that the defense's case was falling apart. Instead of mentioning the ill-fitting jacket Brock was trying to sell them, some remarked that McDonnell was wearing boots with inch and a half heels. They made him sound like a dwarf in elevator shoes.

2

Next morning, after another long delay for an *in camera* conference, George Gramling, the young lawyer from Frost and Jacobs, took the stand and, questioned by Jerry Berry, told how he had discovered among Margaret Benson's belongings a broken microcassette. He had pieced it back together, played it, then passed it on to Carl Westman.

On cross-examination, Jerry Brock did his standard search and destroy, casting doubt on Gramling's honesty, his handling of estate property, his knowledge of electronics—anything to suggest that the contents of the tape weren't trustworthy or that the cassette tape had been planted among Mrs. Benson's personal effects.

When Berry called Carl Westman out of the gallery, just as Brock had done, the personal representative gave a dispassionate account of how he had received the tape, listened to it, then notified the State and the defense, as was his practice when he came into possession of material bearing on the case.

In a trial brimming over with outlandish incidents, the cross-examination of Carl Westman was, in its way, one of the most bizarre for what it demonstrated about the US legal system and about Jerry Brock. While theoretically committed to uncovering the truth and determining guilt and innocence, American trials are really adversarial proceedings in which winning is all that matters. Thus, the same prosecutor who had the previous week offered testimony through the same witness, depicting him as a paragon of professionalism and probity, now did everything in his power to imply that Westman was incompetent or worse, and that the tape was tainted or manufactured evidence.

If the prosecutor subjected the personal representative to an extra measure of harassment, it may have been because the State not only objected to the relevancy of the tape, but resented Westman for passing it on to the defense. Sources close to the Brocks said they felt "raped" by Westman's willingness to help McDonnell. The personal representative continued to assert that he wasn't "helping" either side. He was simply making evidence available.

Once Carl Westman stepped down, Jerry Berry called Joyce Quinn to the stand. Now living in Massachusetts, Quinn had come to Naples in June 1983 and worked as a secretary for Margaret Benson, who at the time resided in Port Royal. Scott and Kim Beegle made it an uneasy *ménage à trois* in the house on Galleon Drive. This was the period during which Scott threatened legal action against his mother for misappropriating his money. One of Joyce Quinn's tasks during the tumultuous months she worked for Mrs. Benson was to provide an accounting of what Scott had received in the last two years. She came up with a total of $250,000 that had flowed to the nineteen-year-old boy in the form of cash, cars, furniture, and loans.

The former secretary described the morning of September 12, 1983. "This was the worst Monday I ever had." Arriving at the house at 8:30 A.M., she "heard this heavy, heavy breathing coming out of Scott's [bedroom] door. There was deep laughter, like a fun-house type laughter. It was very creepy, very eerie."

Mrs. Benson told Joyce she was upset because she had let Buck into the house over the weekend and the dog had wet the rug, leaving a stain. Suddenly "Scott came running out of the room yelling at" his adopted mother, screaming that she should leave his dog alone. If she didn't, "he could have the dog attack and kill her if he wanted to." Grabbing Mrs. Benson and shaking her violently, he repeated the threat five more times, shouting, "If you ever do this again, I will have the dog kill you."

Mrs. Benson thrust a microcassette recorder near Scott's face and for a couple of minutes the boy's delirious tirade was captured on tape. Then he tore the recorder from her hands and smashed it.

Introducing the tape into evidence, Berry stood in front of the jury holding a cassette recorder in his right hand and a microphone in his left hand. When he pushed the On switch, the courtroom fell perfectly silent, and jurors, reporters, spectators, lawyers, and the judge leaned forward and listened to the frenzied scene played out against the insipid strains of background music from a radio in the Benson house.

SCOTT: Mother, I'll give you all the respect you deserve.

MRS. BENSON: What do you mean by that, Scott?

SCOTT: The dog is Scott Benson's. The dog is Scott Benson's. Say it. Come on, say it right into the recorder because I'm gonna find—I'm gonna trap you over and over. I'm gonna point it out because I want everybody—everybody who is around here knows that you call it my dog. You hear that, Mother. Joyce was here when you said that and she is a witness and she will in fact be in court. Because this is a serious situation. That dog will not be around you because it's not yours. And you listen when I tell you to keep him the hell out of the house, can you understand that? Just because it's your house doesn't mean you can do what you want with my dog. Can you understand that, huh? Can you? Can you?

(Loud screech)

MRS. BENSON: Get your hands off—

As the tape abruptly ended, Steven Benson removed his glasses, held a handkerchief to his mouth, and cried uncontrollably.

Joyce Quinn said she called the police at Mrs. Benson's request, and the two of them waited outside until Officer William Lanyisera and his partner arrived, handcuffed Scott, and dragged him, struggling and crying, to a squad car. "Oh, Mother, look what they're doing to me," he sobbed. The cops drove him to the Naples mental health unit and confined him under the Baker Act as somebody who was a danger to himself and other people.

In the face of this testimony and Scott's maniacal chanting on the tape, cross-examination seemed irrelevant to everyone except Jerry

Brock, who perhaps believed he could blunt the edge of what the jury had heard by bludgeoning the witness into submission and numbing the nerve endings of anybody who remained in the courtroom.

He had Joyce Quinn draw a floor plan of the Benson house, then told her to indicate where each person had stood during every instant of the episode. He asked her to describe the path Scott followed to and from his bedroom. And was he walking or running? How did she define running? Where was the spot Buck had left on the rug? How could she be sure it was urine? Where had she stood in relation to the stain? Did she specifically recall Scott threatening to have Buck rip his mother to pieces?

He challenged her assumption that Scott had received $250,000 from his mother. Did Joyce Quinn have any independent knowledge of what Scott spent?

She conceded she worked with the records Mrs. Benson provided her. She had no way of knowing Mrs. Benson had not exaggerated what Scott owed her. But the very suggestion that Mrs. Benson might have overstated her adopted son's debt indicated she could have done it to Steven as well. Brock appeared to realize this and quit trying to shake the secretary from her story.

He asked just one more question. How did she know the five-foot-tall canister in Scott's bedroom contained nitrous oxide? She admitted she hadn't sampled it and couldn't be sure. Satisfied, Brock removed a wad of gum from his mouth and returned to the prosecutor's table.

3

During the lunch break I learned from the defense that they had decided to streamline their case, cutting loose some witnesses, calling on a new batch that had been subpoenaed after the trial started. Their intention was to establish an alternate scenario—namely that Scott's involvement with drugs led to his death and Mrs. Benson's murder. But there seemed to be debate whether the defense believed Scott was in debt and had been rubbed out by vengeful dealers, or whether his emotional instability and physical dependency on drugs led him for reasons unknown to plant the bombs in the Suburban.

When court reconvened, the judge and lawyers again gathered *in camera*. After an hour and twenty minutes, they returned and Hayes dismissed the jury, explaining that he and the attorneys would spend the rest of the day in discovery.

Three prospective witnesses that Jerry Berry put on the stand were currently in prison. Steven Carr testified that he had been a cocaine addict and scored much of his dope from David Beegle, Kim's brother. He had seen Scott Benson buying and using cocaine. "I guess he got it from David Beegle just like everybody else."

Asked how much dealing Beegle did, Carr said, "You could have put a revolving door on that place." He estimated Beegle cleared $1,400 to $2,800 a week. But Carr admitted Scott Benson hadn't been central to his life. "I was just over there to pick up and go. Like at a Seven Eleven."

When Brock objected, asking what this had to do with the murders, the judge told Berry to tie the testimony into the case or have it thrown out.

On cross-examination, Brock pinned Carr down about dates and places and rooms and the people in them. With other witnesses, the prosecutor's technique was like pulling teeth. But Carr put up no resistance; getting answers from him was as easy as pulling fruit out of Jell-O. He admitted he was zonked on drugs during those days, and "when you're using cocaine like I was, you don't want to be around other people." He added, "You stay awake all night and guard the windows. Then when it gets light, you get secure enough to go to sleep."

Because he snorted so much coke, Carr had lost his sense of smell and taste, and started injecting it. He conceded he had been discharged from the Navy for alcohol abuse, and at one point his family "Baker Acted" him. Still he insisted he had seen Scott buy and use cocaine, and he remembered David Beegle complaining about how much money Scott owed him.

The next witness, Stephen Fife—there were now about twenty Stevens or Stephens associated with the case—came on wearing skintight Levi's and a blue T-shirt with *Mad Dog* stenciled on the back. Muscular as a stevedore, with tattoos of the Confederate flag and a skull and crossbones, Fife was serving a year in the Collier County jail for probation violation on a forgery conviction. Ironically,

Fife's father, Thomas, a detective with the Sheriff's Department, had already testified in the Benson trial and would be a prominent figure in the news that night.

Asked by Jerry Berry if he knew Scott Benson, Fife replied, "I refuse to answer that on the grounds that it may tend to incriminate me."

Berry said, "Your Honor, knowing Scott Benson, I don't see how that can be incriminating." Then spotting an opportunity, he mused, "Maybe it can."

Without immunity, which the State refused to grant, Fife feared he could be prosecuted for any crimes or parole violations he mentioned in court. Judge Hayes instructed him that some of Berry's questions didn't incriminate him and he couldn't remain silent without running the risk of being cited for contempt.

Fife admitted knowing David Beegle, but said he had never seen Scott Benson use drugs. When asked whether he had seen Beegle sell drugs, he took the Fifth, and Jerry Brock objected to the relevancy of the question. "My mother used to sell milk. That doesn't make me a milkman."

"It may," Berry snapped.

After a bench conference, Hayes told Fife a public defender would advise him which questions he should answer. The witness climbed down and swaggered out of the courtroom like a miniature King Kong.

Daniel Gallaway (no relation to ATF auditor Diana Galloway) was doing a three-and-a-half-year stretch in state prison on charges of burglary, trespassing, and arson of a dwelling. Allegedly he had witnessed an incident in which Scott Benson agreed to put up his Lotus as collateral for a $40,000 cocaine deal. A tall man with neatly combed blond hair and a tan suit, Gallaway didn't answer a single question. The instant he hit the stand he complained that he wanted to speak to his attorney before he testified.

Judge Hayes said he could step down. If he had a lawyer and needed to consult him, the defense could question him later.

With his tousled blond hair, baggy white trousers, and maroon sweater, Edward Malone looked like he hailed from a different planet than the three cons. He told Berry he had met Scott in 1982 while playing tennis. Two years later, during a party at the Naples Bath and Tennis Club, he had seen Scott buy an ounce of cocaine from two dark-complexioned strangers from Miami.

Brock objected that this was hearsay. Although Jerry Berry was conducting the questioning, McDonnell stood up and responded to Brock, asking the judge for relief from the hearsay rule. The defense, he explained, wasn't trying to prove these rumors about Scott were necessarily true, only that they existed. McDonnell claimed they showed a reasonable hypothesis of Steven Benson's innocence, and indicated that there were avenues of investigation that the police had never pursued. He stressed that, unlike the State, the defense could not grant immunity or amnesty, nor could it compel testimony from witnesses who feared discussing Scott's drug use and dealing because it would reveal their own. This placed the defense under an especially onerous burden.

When Judge Hayes observed that this was a novel reason to justify the admission of hearsay, Dwight Brock broke into loud giggles. Nevertheless, the judge let Malone relate that he had heard in February 1985 that Scott Benson owed thousands of dollars and was in danger of losing his "fanny." A man from out of town told Malone that dealers "fronted" Scott $30,000 worth of cocaine. Malone named two men to whom Scott was said to owe vast sums of money.

Keith Goodall was a big, amiable mason with a walrus mustache, stringy hair, long sideburns, and a heavy five o'clock shadow. His brown shirt was stretched taut across his belly and hung loose outside a pair of dirty plaid pants. He said he had lived with David Beegle for three months in 1985, and Scott Benson spent much of that period there too. Each day they smoked a dozen joints and drank a dozen beers. He had seen Scott use nitrous oxide on three occasions, inhaling from a canister the size of a scuba tank. According to Goodall, Scott went through a tank in twenty minutes.

On cross, Dwight Brock sang out, "Good evening, Mr. Goodall." But Mr. Goodall didn't respond.

Asked how marijuana affected his memory, he admitted, "It doesn't help too much."

"Have you smoked so much of that marijuana that your memory has completely and totally lost you now?"

Goodall stood by his story.

"The truth of the matter is," Brock retorted, "you never saw Scott Benson smoke marijuana at all, did you?"

"I saw Scott Benson smoke marijuana."

The dialogue between the small prosecutor and the burly witness began to sound like a Laurel and Hardy skit, and before it ended, a liberal whiff of laughing gas seemed to leak into the courtroom. Even Steven Benson chuckled.

Goodall said he first met Scott Benson one night outside a bar. Scott was staggering around the parking lot lugging a scuba tank with a hose hooked to his mouth.

Brock didn't believe it. "He was out in the bar parking lot just totin' around his bottle of nitrous oxide?"

"Yes," Goodall said.

"So out there in front of God and everbody he was suckin' down this nitrous oxide?"

"Right."

4

While the courtroom in Fort Myers convulsed with laughter, Detective Thomas Fife was off duty, driving down Bayshore Drive in Naples, when he saw Guido Dal Molin cross the road and dart into an alley. Keith Graf, a construction worker, also saw Dal Molin. "I didn't think twice. I knew it was him. The guy's got black eyes—he looks like the devil. It looked like he was staring right through me."

Fife and Graf chased the accused murderer. Fife got to him first and regretted it. He came out of the scuffle with a broken toe and serious bites on both hands.

Dal Molin managed to get a grip on Fife's gun, and Graf had to pry it loose. "Kill me right here. I want to die," Dal Molin hollered. "Don't let me up or I'll kill you both." He screamed at Graf, "There's no prison in the country that can hold me. I'll kill you."

Sent back to the Collier County jail, facing additional charges of escape, resisting arrest with violence, and battery on a law officer, Dal Molin awaited his own murder trial for killing a close friend and waited to see if he'd be called as a witness in the Benson trial. Asked where he had spent his few days as a fugitive, the electronics wizard said he had wandered in the woods, passed a night on the roof of a K-mart, and hid in the shrubbery at Lieutenant Harold Young's house.

· · ·

That evening I met Judge Hayes in the Ramada Inn lounge and remarked how each day's events seemed dizzier than the last. But Hayes wasn't amused by the progress of the case. "No doubt they're in deep guano," he said of the defense. "McDonnell is throwing a lot of shit at the wall and seeing what sticks. It's all bullshit. The question is whether the jury should get a chance to hear this bullshit."

He would have to do his homework tonight and decide how much of the testimony—if any—should be admitted. He felt McDonnell and Berry were attempting to dispute circumstantial evidence with hearsay that didn't rise anywhere near the level of circumstantiality. But he acknowledged that an appellate court might feel differently, might read the transcript cold and conclude that the defense hadn't had a fair chance to make its case.

Although he repeated his opinion that the defense had fallen back on bush league tactics, he said that if they worked, that was all that mattered. Personally, he thought McDonnell and Berry were now in a position where they had to put Benson on the stand. Or they had to hire a fingerprint expert to dispute the State's evidence about the palm impression. With enough money, Hayes said, there was always a professional witness who would testify to anything.

The judge then provided information that placed tomorrow's testimony in an intriguing context. When Scott Benson was Baker Acted in 1983, he had been treated by a psychiatrist named Dr. José Lombillo. After Scott's death, the doctor-patient privilege no longer applied, and Dr. Lombillo was free to testify. But McDonnell and Berry faced a ticklish dilemma.

Late in the spring of 1985, Dr. Lombillo had been arrested and charged with sexual battery of two women. The women claimed that in separate incidents the doctor had drugged them and taken pictures of them while they were unconscious. When police searched his house, they found explicit photographs of one woman and an equally explicit video tape of the other. In both instances, Dr. Lombillo was apparently performing sexual acts with the women.

Although the women didn't deny that they had had intimate relations with Dr. Lombillo on occasions when they were conscious, they maintained that he had no right to have sex with them when they were powerless to resist, and they asserted they had not given him permission to take their pictures.

Dr. Lombillo came to trial on September 25, 1985, in front of a jury of six women. Two charges relating to one plaintiff were thrown out by the judge, who ruled that the prosecution had not been specific about the time when the alleged rapes took place.

The trial continued with the other plaintiff. But defense attorney George Vega contended that the sex acts in the photographs were only simulated, not committed. What's more, it was impossible to determine whether the woman was truly unconscious and, in some snapshots, impossible to say whether the woman depicted was, in fact, the woman pressing charges against Lombillo.

The judge ruled, "I do find the State has not met its burden for sexual battery. There is still the matter of battery to be decided by the jury."

But nine minutes after the six female jurors received their instructions, they returned with a verdict of not guilty. Dr. Lombillo expressed great gratitude and said, "I have no wounds. The past nine months have been a period of tremendous growth for me spiritually."

Less than a month later the women filed civil suit against Dr. José Lombillo. Both were represented by—Judge Hayes smiled and paused a beat—the firm of McDonnell and Berry.

Now McDonnell and Berry needed Dr. Lombillo's testimony, and Hayes wondered whether they'd get what they wanted. And would they have to give anything in return? Would Jerry Brock bring up this tantalizing issue on cross-examination, undercutting the doctor's credibility?

Judge Hayes also pointed out that George Vega, who represented Dr. Lombillo in the sexual battery case, represented Tracy Mullins in her paternity suit. Conceivably, Scott Benson had admitted to Dr. Lombillo that he had fathered a baby by Tracy. Conceivably he could be called as a witness in the paternity case. Conceivably...

5

By the time Judge Hayes and I parted company that night almost anything seemed conceivable—anything except the bit of gossip that had been passed to me by somebody from the Collier County Sheriff's Department. This source said that Margaret Covington, the beautiful blond jury consultant, had been tried and convicted of killing her ex-lover.

When I called Sweetwater, Texas, Ms. Covington fielded the question with amazing equanimity. No, she said, she hadn't killed anybody, but she had had enormous problems with a man in Corpus Christi who was the father of her son, yet had refused at first to acknowledge his paternity. The parallels with aspects of the Benson case—an illegitimate child, threats over a paternity suit, a sexual liaison in which love had turned to hate and then to something worse —seemed overpowering.

But Ms. Covington was not altogether forthcoming with salient details. The assault charge concerned an incident on November 2, 1981, when, four days after Cage Wavell refused to sign an affidavit acknowledging that he had fathered Covington's son, a couple of thugs arrived at his office, roughed him up, and left him with a bullet in the chest.

Terry Michael Noah pleaded guilty to the attack. "The second assailant was never identified," according to the Houston *Post*. "Noah testified against Covington at her trial on a state charge of burglary with intent to commit aggravated assault, saying that he was given a $500 down payment to injure and sexually incapacitate Wavell."

The events seemed to echo the lyrics of one of Michael McDonnell's songs, "The Assassin," a ballad about a woman done wrong who hunts down her ex-lover and emasculates him.

"A Corpus Christi jury found Covington guilty in December, 1985, but State District Court Judge Mike Westergren threw out the verdict and acquitted the lawyer."

Although Cage Wavell subsequently admitted he was the father and paid a reported settlement of $25,000, he "filed a civil lawsuit in Nueces County charging that Covington hired two men to assault him and that Houston attorney Richard 'Racehorse' Haynes encouraged Covington to commit the crime."

On October 31, 1986, a Houston federal grand jury indicted Margaret Covington on two counts of using interstate facilities or travel to commit a violent crime to further an alleged extortion scheme. She is now awaiting trial.

On matters pertaining to the Benson case, Ms. Covington was more expansive. From her shadow jurors she had heard that recent delays were prompting speculation about the defense and where it was headed. It was dangerous, she said, to leave a jury guessing.

As for Scott's drug abuse and his confinement after a bout of nitrous oxide inhalation, the shadow jury essentially dismissed this. They felt he couldn't have had a serious drug problem since he was such a great tennis player he had been invited to participate in the U.S. Open.

While in this instance their response was prompted by false evidence, Covington had picked up repeated indications that inadmissible information had also played a part in shaping the shadow jury's attitudes. Like the real jury, they were not supposed to discuss the case or to follow press reports of it. Yet during nightly interviews, they broached subjects that could only have come from news accounts. She felt that if the shadow jury was influenced by the media, the real jury was too.

Chapter 12

I

Anticipating another interval of discovery during which he would determine the admissibility of evidence and witnesses, Judge Hayes had instructed the jury to report at 10 A.M., not 8:30. But the first witness didn't testify in the jury's presence until 3:10 P.M.

Since some witnesses had previously provided evidence about Scott Benson but now refused to talk for fear of self-incrimination, McDonnell got the judge's permission to call Mike Schulgen, a private investigator employed by the defense. With the jury out of the courtroom, Schulgen said he had twice interviewed Daniel Gallaway in prison and learned that Scott had offered his Lotus as collateral for a $40,000 cocaine deal.

Then in an eccentric ploy, McDonnell put his partner, Jerry Berry, on the stand. Berry said Stephen Fife had told him he saw someone go into David Beegle's house with $2,000 and come out with no money and a large quantity of cocaine. Since Scott Benson was also at Beegle's house, one might infer he was dealing drugs. At least the defense hoped that inference would be drawn.

Paul Harvey, the captain of Mrs. Benson's yacht, the *Galleon Queen*, came on and described a shakedown cruise he took on May 15, 1985, with Scott and three of his pot-smoking, coke-snorting friends. These fellows discussed a drug rip-off that had taken place or was about to take place. Harvey remembered one of them with special vividness; he was about six feet tall and weighed about two hundred pounds, the same description as the customer who purchased pipes at Hughes Supply.

Dwight Brock did the cross-examination and subjected Harvey to the third degree. "Are you sure? Or do you know for a fact?" "I'm not wanting what you believe. I want what you know." "Did you take any of this joint they were passing around?" "You don't know whether Scott in fact smoked the joint or just passed it around."

Asked whether he had ever smoked pot, Harvey admitted he had tried it ten or fifteen times when he was younger.

"On any of those occasions when you smoked marijuana," Dwight said, "did you ever feel like you wanted to go out and blow somebody up?"

Harvey grinned. "Not that I remember."

Dorothy McCormick, a grandmotherly lady with white hair and glasses, had worked as a secretary for Mrs. Benson from spring of 1984 until shortly before the murders. Characterizing Steven as the family problem-solver, she said, "He was more or less a father" figure and "a pacifier" for Scott. Margaret, Scott, and Carol Lynn often turned to him for help and Carol Lynn, in particular, spent hours with him on the telephone.

On Christmas Day, 1984, on Scott's twenty-first birthday, the secretary witnessed a scene as weird as any recounted during the trial. There had been sniping and taunting between Scott and Carol Lynn, and when Carol Lynn reappeared in the living room after a shower with only a towel wrapped around her, Scott attacked her, bending her back over a couch. "Scott was beating on her face and pulling on her hair," Ms. McCormick said. "He pulled her onto the floor and her towel came off," leaving the enraged son standing and shouting at the nude woman whom he may or may not have known was his mother.

Ms. McCormick testified that Mrs. Benson feared Scott and had installed dead bolts on the outside of his bedroom door and on the inside and the outside of her own door.

While the prosecutors tried to downplay the 1983 incident when Scott was "Baker Acted"—they suggested he was soon back on the straight and narrow path that led to the U.S. Open—Dorothy McCormick established that there was an ongoing problem of pathological dimensions in the Benson house. Having assaulted and threatened to kill his adopted mother, Scott had then attacked and beaten his biological mother little more than six months before the killings. While this didn't prove he was responsible for the pipe bombings, it did raise the puzzling question of why the family pacifier came under immediate suspicion while the son who had a history of mental illness, drug abuse, and violent behavior didn't interest the police at all.

The last witness to proffer testimony in the jury's absence was Dr. José Lombillo. An elegant and urbane man in a gray suit and blue shirt with a wide, loosely knitted tie, he wore horn-rimmed glasses and gave an impressive list of academic credits—University of Havana, University of Madrid, Menninger Foundation. But he hardly seemed the professorial type. His mane of silver hair curled at his collar, and he spoke with a pronounced Spanish accent, breaking his words and sentences into stress patterns peculiar to ears habituated to American English, the southern dialect in particular.

Once the witness had been admitted as "an expert in psychiatry and human behavior," Jerry Brock approached the bench and suggested that since Carl Westman was in the gallery, it was appropriate to ask the personal representative whether the estate had waived the psychiatrist-patient privilege. McDonnell and Berry remarked that no objection had been raised by the family, so why was the prosecution bringing it up? Besides, McDonnell said, the privilege lapsed with Scott's death. The judge agreed and ruled the witness could testify.

But Lombillo asked whether the privilege had been waived only for his communications with Scott. What about other members of the Benson family? He considered them patients since they had spoken to him about intimate matters when he treated Scott.

The defense said it would confine itself to the psychiatrist's analysis of Scott.

Synopsizing his notes from the day when Scott was rushed to the mental health unit in a squad car, Dr. Lombillo said, "He have been using excessive amount of consumption of nitrous oxide since he a child. And he described to me how this evolve through his life, almost when he was in middle school he begun use." Due to an overdose the morning he attacked Mrs. Benson, Scott "developed a condition called acute psychotic organic mental disorder that make him confused and belligerent." With his mood vacillating between depression and rage, he had trouble concentrating, dealing with abstractions, and recalling the sequence of events that landed him in custody.

Considering the volume of gas he had inhaled, Scott should have suffered physical deterioration, nerve damage, and lack of coordination. But surprisingly he hadn't shown any serious neurological abnormalities. His symptoms were primarily psychological. Dr. Lombillo theorized that this was due to his extraordinary tolerance for drugs and strong physical constitution.

In answer to McDonnell's questions, the witness explained that nitrous oxide didn't in itself produce aggressive, paranoid, or violent behavior. But it reduced Scott's ability to control his moods. If he was frustrated or caught up in a turbulent environment full of pressure and conflicts, then he might react violently. Dr. Lombillo stated that if, against medical advice, he had continued using nitrous oxide and had complicated the problem by smoking pot and drinking large quantities of alcohol, then he would probably have suffered the same acute organic brain syndrome with all its related emotional symptoms.

The attack on Carol Lynn Kendall late in 1984 was, he said, consistent with Scott's 1983 attack on Mrs. Benson. It was also consistent with the strong feelings the boy had "about different members of his family." When free of drugs, he could keep these feelings suppressed, but under the influence of narcotics, he could lose control.

On cross-examination, Jerry Brock moved quickly to establish that Scott had recovered all his faculties and was symptom-free within a few days of his 1983 confinement. Then he got Dr. Lombillo to explain that "acute organic brain syndrome," which sounded so severe, was no different from the condition a person might suffer after drinking too much alcohol. Once the toxic substance passed out of his system, the condition disappeared.

BROCK: So if we assume Scott was still playing tennis and as a matter of fact had gotten an invitation to play in the U.S. Open tennis tournament, we can assume that he did not have any type of neurological change, is that correct?
LOMBILLO: That's very correct.
BROCK: So the only type of syndrome that he could be suffering from conceivably would be a temporary transitory type of syndrome.
LOMBILLO: Yes.

Suggesting that Scott's problems with nitrous oxide had been shortlived, Brock said, "You indicated that in Scott it would only take him a couple of days, or three or four days to recover."

Dr. Lombillo replied that that depended on how much he had

been inhaling. The patient had admitted to a prodigious intake and had purchased nitrous oxide on an industrial scale. Ordering tanks of it with the excuse that he was super-charging his car, he had had a dentist design a mask so that he could ingest the gas from a five-foot-tall canister beside his bed.

This was in contrast to most laughing-gas abusers, who took a few sniffs, got high, and let it go at that. "Typical situations you see," Lombillo explained to the utterly incredulous Brock, "people who go to the supermarket and usually always begin by the milk containers. And they buy the ready whipped cream. And what you do in that situation, you see any supermarkets, they get a can of whipped cream, then don't shake it up, put inside your mouth when nobody is looking, push to one side, and you get two shots, five shots of nitrous oxide in your mouth. You get an instant high."

"What's this?" Brock asked. "Not that I want to do this, but what is that from, from whipped cream?"

"Yes. The reason I am talking is because people don't know what nitrous oxide is. I feel if people know a little more, they have a better understanding of many of the issues we are talking."

As Brock faded from the picture, the suave psychiatrist took flight with an editorial, speaking directly into the cameras, advising concerned citizens that nitrous oxide was cheap and legal, yet very dangerous. Kids could buy it in kitchen supply stores. That's what Scott Benson had done in junior high school—bought cases of small nitrous oxide cartridges used in making whipped cream, then sold them to his classmates at a profit high enough to finance his own rapidly increasing habit.

"He wanted more and more," Dr. Lombillo said. "And Scott and a tank of nitrous oxide in his bedside are synonymous of anybody talk about that. So what I'm saying to you is this. He inhaled nitrous oxide probably like you might drink that Pepsi . . . sometimes it was so severe he became very violent . . . Other times he want to sleep."

On redirect, McDonnell asked the psychiatrist, "Would it be consistent with paranoia and suspicion to express fears that people wanted to kill you?"

"Yes."

"Would it be consistent to want to have a trained attack guard dog around you at all times wherever you went?"

"That would be consistent."

Dr. Lombillo explained that he had urged Scott to stop using drugs, but he had no way of knowing if the patient followed his advice since he failed to remain in therapy.

"What if, under this condition, Scott were unable to purchase drugs?" McDonnell asked. "What would happen?"

"He would become, if wants them available, he will become very restless, he will show sign of a withdrawal syndrome in which he'll become more paranoid, become more violent, it could become more irrational. And then will go to extremes in trying to obtain the drugs."

On recross, Dr. Lombillo said Scott would surely have difficulties if, on top of nitrous oxide, he drank twelve beers and smoked twelve joints a day. But he conceded to Brock that if this occurred in February or March, then ceased, it wouldn't affect him "two or three months down the road."

2

Late that afternoon, the jurors were ushered to their seats, and Steven Carr, still in the white uniform of a Collier County jail trusty, testified that he had seen Scott use cocaine two or three times and purchase it on one or two other occasions. He had also seen him smoke sinsemilla, an especially potent variety of marijuana.

Brock's brief cross-examination emphasized that what little Carr had witnessed had occurred months before the murders.

By contrast, Paul Harvey got to repeat most of what he had said this morning. The only evidence Judge Hayes excluded was the conversation between Scott and his friends about a drug rip-off.

McDonnell showed him the composite picture done by Mike Koors, and Harvey said it resembled one of the fellows who had been on the *Galleon Queen*.

On cross, when Dwight Brock challenged Harvey to demonstrate how Scott and his friends snorted white powder from a small bottle, the witness cheerfully complied. Then Dwight stumbled into the subject of the day the police and ATF agents finally responded to Harvey's request that the *Galleon Queen* be searched for bombs. This allowed McDonnell to show that detectives had been far more interested in Steven Benson than in searching the boat or in listening to the captain about Scott and his friends.

Harvey described the scene when Lieutenant Wayne Graham stood on the bridge of the *Galleon Queen* and paused, not daring to insert the key and start the engines. "I guess you had some doubt what would happen when he turned that key," McDonnell said.

"I didn't have any doubt what would happen to me," Paul Harvey responded. "I was off standing in a field three hundred feet away."

Edward Malone came on again looking like an ad for leisure wear. Today he had on tan pants and a white V-neck sweater with a club insignia. He told of seeing Scott at a party at the Naples Bath and Tennis Club and said that Scott accepted a bag of cocaine from another man.

Once more Brock kept his cross-examination brief and got Malone to acknowledge he hadn't seen Scott give the man money, hadn't heard any conversation, and hadn't seen Scott snort the cocaine. The judge ruled inadmissible Malone's story that he had heard that Scott was in debt to drug dealers and was about to "lose his fanny."

Wearing the same dirty brown shirt and check pants as the day before, Keith Goodall, the good-natured guy with the walrus mustache, gave a repeat performance, describing the period of time— vague in length, imprecise as to dates—when he and Scott Benson were housemates at David Beegle's and each smoked twelve joints and drank twelve beers a day.

Whereas other witnesses testifying about Scott's drug use were cross-examined with great dispatch by the Brocks, Dwight couldn't resist trying to get a firm grasp on Goodall's foggy memory. "Where was Scott sitting on the first occasion Scott drank twelve beers?" he demanded. "Where was Scott sitting on the next day Scott drank twelve beers? Where was Scott sitting on the last day Scott drank the last beer?"

But Goodall placidly glided over these questions, refusing to get into a sweat about details. The thing he knew for sure was how much grass and how much beer he and Scott had consumed.

When he admitted he had taken an occasional sniff of Scott's nitrous oxide, this excited Dwight to a new line of inquiry. "When you used nitrous oxide, did it make you want to go home and blow up your mother?"

"Nossir."

"How about your sister?"

"Nossir."

"How about your brother?"

"Nossir." Goodall smiled and gladly agreed.

"No further questions."

Dorothy McCormick, the grandmotherly secretary, said Scott and Mrs. Benson had "a peculiar relationship." Scott frequently demanded money and screamed until he got it. "Mrs. Benson had to control everything. She belittled her daughter. But Mrs. Benson had the money, so therefore Carol Lynn had to do what her mother said."

Mrs. McCormick remembered that Steven was often at the house when she arrived for work, which conflicted with Carol Lynn's claim that it was unusual that he volunteered to come as early as 7:30 A.M. on July 9, 1985. She also recollected that Scott left the house every day between 9:00 and 9:30 A.M. This suggested that whoever planted the bombs might have known his schedule and been aiming for him.

It was in September 1984, she said, after the move from Port Royal to Quail Creek that Mrs. Benson installed a lock on the outside of Scott's door and on the inside and outside of her bedroom door. Then she described the Christmas 1984 incident when Scott beat Carol Lynn with his fists, and she wound up on the floor naked.

Ruby Caston, Mrs. Benson's housekeeper, confirmed that Scott attacked Carol Lynn. But on cross, Jerry Brock didn't care to discuss that. He wanted to talk about Buck. Ruby testified that the dog barked every time a car pulled onto the gravel drive. Once, at her house, Buck got so worked up he jumped through a window screen.

Since Ruby corroborated what several witnesses said—that Scott and Carol Lynn argued with Mrs. Benson, but Steven would walk away from a squabble—Brock started to suggest there was something sinister about a man so quiet and controlled.

On McDonnell's redirect, Ruby Caston recalled another incident when Scott roughed up Mrs. Benson, pushing her so hard she slipped to the floor. Steven then ordered Scott to get out of the house.

· · ·

Scott's coach, Steven Vaughan, took the stand to testify not about his pupil's character or his physical and emotional condition or even about his tennis talent. Since Wayne Kerr had sworn that Steven returned from the Shop 'N Go twenty minutes before Vaughan called Scott on July 9, the defense wanted to establish that Vaughan had telephoned at 8:50 A.M. Since Steven had not left before quarter to eight—Carol Lynn stated that he hadn't *arrived* until quarter of eight—he could not have been gone an hour. The question remained, however, how long it took to plant the bombs and rig a detonating device. Neither side offered testimony on that matter.

Jerry Brock tried to chip away at Vaughan's credibility. "Wherever you made this phone call, where was the big hand pointing and where was the little hand pointing?"

Vaughan punched this away like an easy volley. "The big hand was on the ten and the little hand was between eight and nine."

But how could he be so certain, the prosecutor insisted?

"That was a pretty memorable phone call."

That evening, Jerry Brock pushed his Publix Grocery cart full of evidence into the hall and told reporters that Scott Benson was a murder victim now suffering character assassination. "Whatever his character was, he had a right to life."

McDonnell felt Scott's character was precisely the issue which the State had ignored. His unstable personality, forged in a family highly charged with conflict, might have driven him to murder or a murder/ suicide.

Suicide is "consistent with Dr. Lombillo's testimony," he told the Fort Myers *Free Press*. "If he didn't commit suicide it [the bomb] went off accidentally" and Scott became his own victim.

"Are you really going to put Guido Dal Molin on the stand?" a reporter asked. "I mean, you don't know what he's going to say."

The trouble, McDonnell laughingly admitted, was "you don't know what he's going to do."

Jubilant that Judge Hayes had admitted so much evidence about Scott, McDonnell asked me to join Nina and him for "a jar" at the Veranda. Stripping off his suit jacket, rolling up his sleeves, he said, "I don't mean to criticize the competition, but I feel that long discovery process yesterday and today gave our witnesses—and gave us—a practice session. Today the witnesses were looser and more at ease. The Brocks made a mistake."

This was the harshest criticism of the Brocks McDonnell ever made in my presence. Although he laughed at jokes about the "Snooze Brothers," he never cracked any himself and when other people put them down, he always insisted, "I like them."

Of course, it was easy to be generous on an evening when he was exultant about his own good fortune, but McDonnell acted the same when things went against him. If this was phoniness, as some trial regulars groused, I'll have to add that from my observation it was a seamless performance. Under the most trying circumstances he treated everybody with extraordinary patience and consideration.

In fact, if McDonnell had a flaw as a defense attorney, I thought it might be his friendliness, his wish to be liked even by hostile witnesses. An accomplished entertainer, an intuitive politician, he may have lacked that last ingredient—call it a killer instinct, call it indifference to other people's feelings—that sets the superstars apart.

But tonight any thought of flaws or defeat was far from Michael McDonnell's mind. He said he felt like a gambler on a roll, like a guy throwing dice and just knowing he'd make his point.

Chapter 13

I

By Thursday, July 31, the Benson trial had run over two weeks, and the defense was supposed to conclude its case the next day. With his legs shackled and his hands cuffed, Guido Dal Molin had been transferred to the Lee County jail, where he was locked in a single cell behind a solid steel door and checked by a guard every fifteen minutes. Yet while that kept Guido secure, Bob Laws didn't believe it guaranteed safety in court. He thought there should be metal detectors and X-ray machines to screen people as they filed into the room. And it didn't strike him as such a farfetched idea to bring in bomb-detecting dogs.

With the jury out of the room, Daniel Gallaway returned to the stand and even after Judge Hayes cautioned him that he had to answer nonincriminating questions, the convict refused to say whether he had seen Scott Benson snort, inject, or smoke cocaine. He admitted he had known Scott for four years, but that was all.

When Hayes warned him again, Gallaway toughed it out. "Is my attorney present?" he demanded. "Stand up please." When no one rose, Gallaway said, "I do not see my attorney. This is a violation of my constitutional rights."

He added that self-incrimination wasn't the only reason he was remaining silent. He didn't want to endanger his life and the lives of his family.

Hayes cited Gallaway for three counts of contempt and said he would sentence him later.

Still wearing his *Mad Dog* T-shirt, Stephen Fife received the same warning from Judge Hayes. But he explained that the questions asked by the defense related to a time when he had been on probation and was supposed to avoid places where drugs were sold or used. If he described drug deals he may have witnessed—forget about those he might have participated in—he felt it laid him open to problems with the parole board.

Jerry Berry said this was absurd. Fife was currently doing time for probation violation. His testimony could hardly jeopardize probation that had already been revoked.

But the judge ruled that evidence of several probation violations could result in Fife's receiving a longer sentence. Since the State would not guarantee immunity or assure Fife he wouldn't have time tacked on to his sentence, Hayes agreed he had a Fifth Amendment right to remain silent.

It was almost eleven o'clock when the jury enteed the courtroom for the first time that day, and Dr. José Lombillo repeated the testimony he had offered yesterday during discovery. In fact he provided more information about members of the Benson family and the emotional dynamics that dominated their lives.

He started off by describing Scott's "severe drug dependency." Since adolescence the boy had experimented with a cornucopia of narcotics—LSD, peyote, cocaine, amphetamines, barbiturates, and marijuana. But it was primarily the nitrous oxide that provoked his aggressive, irrational, and violent behavior. While Dr. Lombillo explained that nitrous oxide didn't produce suicidal tendencies, he added, "if you are depressed and your mood is labile and if you happen to be in a very low mood, it could develop a suicidal behavior."

McDONNELL: You mentioned, Doctor, that Scott had difficulty with his mother. Would you explain that to the jury? What were the difficulties? What was his view?

LOMBILLO: At the time he came to the hospital, in addition of the problems that he was experiencing with drugs, he was experiencing a tense situation with his mother who have to do with the finances of the family. Scott hoped at this—to have access to an unlimited amount of funds. An unlimited amount of funds was then owning condominium alone some place in Florida when you are 15 years old; and bringing a girl friend home at just 13; and buying a new super sports car at the age of 15. And on and on and on.

Scott had little notion of the value of money, but he knew he had a trust fund and it belonged to him, not Mrs. Benson, "and he just wanted to have that money. The struggle began because the mother was trying to—was concerned about Scott's excessive use of money. That she insist that Scott seek the advice of the person in the family who provided financial advice to the mother and provided support to the mother, who was his brother, Steve Benson."

As the psychiatrist stressed Scott's obsessive desire for money, he made a point which the defense had tried to promote since Steven's arrest. Benson was his mother's financial adviser and the family's emotional pillar—or perhaps lightning rod was the more appropriate term. People depended on him, but sometimes resented him when he didn't tell them what they wanted to hear.

When Steven recommended that his mother contact Wayne Kerr and place Scott under economic restraints, the boy turned belligerent. "She was trying to change completely the financial relationship with Scott," Dr. Lombillo said. "And that means she was not giving money to Scott that Scott wanted... And this created a tremendous amount of tension between both of them; and that the fight that led him to the hospital was a combination of nitrous oxide, his organic brain syndrome, and this struggle with money."

By contrast, "Steve was very patient. Scott felt closer to Steve than to the sister. Steve was more distant. Wasn't a talker. Steve was the one like a supporter at home. He described Steve as almost being like in a cloud. I mean, it was so much action and turmoil around Scott when he has young girls, cars, things. Steve was quiet, more intellectual. He have soothing influence in the family. He got along much better with Steve. He liked Steve."

Throughout his testimony, Dr. Lombillo referred to Carol Lynn as Scott's sister. Since everyone in the courtroom knew she was his mother, it raised the question of whether the psychiatrist had been aware of this when he made his diagnosis. Surely that would have had a bearing on Scott's problems and the family's conflicts. But neither the defense nor the State asked Lombillo to clarify the matter.

Later I asked Dr. Lombillo, and he said he had known the tuth about their relationship. But he would not tell me how he had learned it. Since he was legally free to talk about Scott, I inferred that he had been told by the other members of the family. This left the question of whether Scott knew the truth. Dr. Lombillo declined to speak about that.

Under oath, however, he summarized Scott's feelings about his sister/mother. "He had a great deal of competition with the sister. He felt that she was very selfish, very interested in herself, in her social life, in her extravagance." The doctor said they were like "two teenagers fighting with each other."

"I have concern about the family, because if you picture the characters ... then you add the resources, the financial sort of resources that they have, you only increase the intensity of the feeling one hundred fold. In addition to that, in some situations you have drugs, then the situation would be very, very complex." More than complex, he called it "explosive" and said he suggested Scott shouldn't live at home.

But Scott didn't move out and he didn't stop taking drugs. If he were using them on the same basis as before and were suddenly deprived of them, Dr. Lombillo said, "he will try to make steps of any type to obtain drugs."

McDonnell concluded by asking about a hypothetical situation in which somebody's mother and brother were killed and his sister badly injured. If in the hours following this catastrophe a surviving son laughed several times, "is that consistent with normal human behavior resulting from such stresses?"

Dr. Lombillo said it wouldn't be inappropriate "in some personalities who have difficulties expressing feeling ... I mean, if you don't practice, you don't know how to express feelings. Suddenly you have something so overwhelming you need to express a large amount of feelings, and then you don't know what to do."

On cross-examination Jerry Brock reiterated that whatever Scott Benson's physical and/or psychological problems might have been in September 1983, they weren't permanent and there was no proof he was suffering "acute organic brain syndrome" on July 9, 1985. He suggested that someone under the influence of nitrous oxide wouldn't have had the coordination or the mental agility to construct, plant, and detonate a couple of pipe bombs.

Brock also asked—actually it was more in the nature of a statement—whether anyone who had suffered neurological damage from nitrous oxide abuse would "be able to play tennis and receive an invitation to play in the U.S. Open?"

"Under any circumstances," Dr. Lombillo said, "no."

"They could not do that?" Brock repeated.

"They could not do that."

After the trial McDonnell explained in an interview that he had not considered it crucial to refute with specific evidence the bogus claim that Scott Benson had been invited to play at the U.S. Open. He felt the claim was so obviously false and so clearly contradicted by other testimony that he did not need to call on a U.S. Open official to deny it. He also believed that recent drug scandals in sports, including the death of basketball All-American Len Bias from a cocaine overdose, amply demonstrated that an athlete could be a star and still have a serious drug problem. But if only to emphasize the State's misrepresentation of the facts, this information should have been presented to the jury.

Brock inquired about irrational behavior, framing questions that admitted only one answer.

BROCK: So if someone were to kill their mother, to you and I that would be irrational conduct?

LOMBILLO: Yes.

BROCK: And you don't have to be under the influence of nitrous oxide to kill your mother, do you?

LOMBILLO: Of course.

.   .   .   .

BROCK: Now, everyone that has or that you would diagnose as having an organic brain syndrome, you are not saying that that individual would go out and kill mama, would you?

LOMBILLO: Oh, no.

Then the prosecutor took aim at the issue of Benson's laughter in the hours after the murders. Like Buck's barking, this was imbued with enormous significance by the State.

BROCK: . . . if witnesses testified that the defendant was laughing while his mother and brother were laying outside, you have no basis as far as an examination of the defendant, to determine why he was laughing?

LOMBILLO: No, I don't have any basis.

BROCK: And it's also true, isn't it, that people laugh because they do not have any feelings for anyone.
LOMBILLO: That is one reason. That's one reason they can laugh.

Brock went back to the subject of tennis, asking the psychiatrist to discuss Scott's ambitions, apparently hoping to show that, given his goals, Scott would have kept free of drugs. But Dr. Lombillo said, "He had distortion in his tennis potential. He wanted to be Number One but he was not."

Although this wasn't what the prosecutor wanted to hear, he nimbly recovered.

BROCK: This is nothing unusual about that type of a situation? I guess a lot of us want to be Number One and we just simply do not have the capacity to be Number One.
LOMBILLO: That is the bitter principle.

Had defense attorneys been alert to the opportunity they could have suggested that Scott Benson's aspiration to be Number One was not a wistful daydream. It was a profound refusal to accept reality. He had spent thousands of hours practicing and his mother had spent hundreds of thousands of dollars on lessons, equipment, and travel, and far from being Number One, Scott Benson wasn't Number One Thousand. The defense might have asked Dr. Lombillo whether Scott's delusion that he had been invited to the U.S. Open—assuming it wasn't his family's fabrication or the State's—indicated he was on hallucinogenic drugs before his death.

2

Chin poised on the palm of his hand, Carl Westman sat in his chair three rows behind the prosecutor's table. But since the introduction of the tape of Scott's attack on Mrs. Benson, Collier County investigators treated him like a pariah. One member of the prosecution team confronted him in the gallery and demanded, "Do you get paid from Mrs. Benson's estate to sit here all day?" When Westman declined to answer, the man jumped to his own conclusion. "That's outrageous."

Still Westman stuck to the decision he had made a year ago. He would remain neutral and reveal information that might help either side. He had, for example, given Jerry Brock the unsigned third will, the document drafted by Wayne Kerr which would have placed Steven and Scott under severe monetary restrictions until decades after their mother's death. Thinking it might contain Steven's fingerprints and thus offer evidence of a financial motive, Westman had urged the State to have it dusted. He assumed the results would be shared with the defense, as would the "will" itself.

This past Sunday, he had realized that a parallel case could be made that Scott had seen the third will and concluded that his adopted mother was about to cut off the torrent of cash that had flowed to him since he was a kid. He might then have decided to murder Mrs. Benson and the rest of the family, but wound up killing himself too. If Scott's fingerprints were on the third will, that would lend credence to this theory.

At 11 P.M. on Sunday, Westman called Jerry Brock and talked to him for an hour. The personal representative hung up convinced the prosecutor would have the document dusted for Scott's prints as well as Steven's.

But when Monday passed, then Tuesday and Wednesday, and Jerry Brock still hadn't produced a lab report from a fingerprint expert, Westman became disconcerted. It had taken investigators twenty-four hours to process the Hughes Supply receipts. Why was it taking days to do the same with the third will?

Westman's agitation increased as he listened to Dr. Lombillo describe Scott's desire for unlimited money. When his adopted mother attempted to curb his spending in 1983, he had overdosed on nitrous oxide and threatened to kill her. Who could say what he might have done if he discovered a document that put him under the thumb of an executor for the next thirty-five years?

After Dr. José Lombillo stepped down, Carl Westman realized he couldn't delay any longer. He went to the rail in front of the bench, motioned to Jerry Brock and Michael McDonnell, and asked about the third will.

It quickly became clear that McDonnell didn't know what the personal representative was talking about. The defense attorney angrily accused the State of concealing evidence. He claimed he had never received a copy of the third will.

Jerry Brock said that was nonsense. He had sent it over to McDonnell and Berry months ago.

McDonnell denied this and charged the prosecution with blindsiding him with last minute evidence that should have been shared during discovery. Regardless of how the third will read or whose fingerprints were on it, the defense had no time now to evaluate the information.

Westman kept returning to the fingerprints. Had the document been dusted? Brock said it was being worked on. The tests would be finished over the weekend.

How was that possible, McDonnell demanded? Did they have an inked impression of Scott's hands? No, he knew they didn't. Again, it would be a one-sided investigation. If Steven's prints were on the third will, the State would introduce that evidence on rebuttal. But they would sit on exculpatory evidence.

"I really don't appreciate this, Jerry." McDonnell stalked out of the courtroom.

While the Brock brothers busied themselves packing their Publix Grocery cart, Westman was left standing alone at the rail wondering what he should do with a last significant piece of information. He had been brooding over it for almost a year. Jerry Brock already knew about it. But the defense didn't and, unless Westman did something soon, neither would the jury.

3

That afternoon, Dr. Chester Grelecki, a chemist serving as a paid witness, testified that judging by the trajectory of the first explosion and the location of the shrapnel listed on the schematic chart compiled by investigators, it was possible Benson had stood nine feet from the Suburban and not been hit by metal fragments. The fireball associated with the blast would have consumed itself quickly, Grelecki said, and not have spread as far as Benson. The single, light particle of zinc, however, could have floated down onto his pants.

On cross-examination, Grelecki acknowledged that he hadn't considered glass from the windshield. Any debris not listed on the schematic chart didn't play a part in his analysis.

When Mike Schulgen took the stand, I was seated between a lady who was knitting a Christmas stocking and a lady who announced to no one in particular, "That McDonnell, first you see him smirking and swaggering and it makes you mad. But eventually you just want to take him home with you."

After offering his credentials—FBI, Dade County Sheriff's Department, and now private investigator—Schulgen described visiting the crime scene on September 7, 1985, and again on December 27. On the first occasion, he said, metal fragments remained scattered about, suggesting police and ATF agents had neglected evidence. On the second occasion, he discovered that with the windows closed and the air conditioner running in Scott's bedroom, he couldn't hear a car drive up on the gravel. Whether a dog could hear it was another question.

He had also done a couple of time and mileage checks. The drive from 13002 White Violet to the Shop 'N Go and return took 20 minutes and 53 seconds—and that was without buying coffee, capping the cups, buying pastry, or chatting with anybody. The walk from Steven Benson's office on Domestic Avenue to Hughes Supply and return took over 19 minutes. When he included a simulated purchase of pipe, the total elapsed time was 26 minutes.

McDonnell asked Schulgen to explain how Mike Koors should have done the composite picture with an Identikit. But Judge Hayes ruled that since Schulgen hadn't had the requisite course to be considered an expert in the field, he couldn't testify on this subject.

Brock then did a nuts-and-bolts cross-examination that would have flustered an astronaut. He asked questions about crime scene procedure, Schulgen's expertise in analyzing bomb fragments, his knowledge of speed limits along Immokalee Road and within Quail Creek, and the basis for his assumption that oval, wire-rimmed spectacles are called "John Lennon" glasses. This last discussion may someday be of interest to rock and roll archivists, but it put the courtroom into a coma—which was perhaps Brock's intention. No juror was likely to retain an impression of anything except great relief when the witness stepped down.

Guion De Loach had left his office across from the black housing project in Naples and driven to Fort Myers, where he was admitted as an expert in wills and probate. He wore a khaki green suit, pink shirt, and dark tie, and his wavy silver hair gleamed on the TV cameras. When Michael McDonnell showed him defense Exhibit 11, De Loach identified it as the will he had prepared for Margaret Benson on January 29, 1985.

Jerry Brock objected that the document was irrelevant and should not be published to the jury. McDonnell maintained that since the State had tried to prove that Steven Benson had a financial motive and that his mother's attitude had hardened against him, it was highly relevant that a will made out five months before her death named Steven as co-executor and left him a full share of the estate. The only person whose financial fortunes had diminished in the De Loach will was Wayne Kerr, who was eliminated as executor.

Judge Hayes overruled the State's objection. While the De Loach will was passed to the jury, Richard Cirace, Carol Lynn's attorney, came down to the rail behind the prosecutor's table and talked at length with the Brock brothers. Then Dwight moved into the gallery and carried on a whispered conversation with Carl Westman. This convocation provided a lively little melodrama in the wings while the characters on center stage went about the staid business of introducing Mrs. Benson's first will, the one prepared by Kerr.

During bench conferences the State revealed exactly how anxious it was to restrict testimony about Mrs. Benson's wills. Jerry Brock objected to the introduction of documentary evidence about what Margaret actually did as opposed to what Carol Lynn Kendall claimed her mother intended to do. He went so far as to characterize the Kerr will as "hearsay" and to contend that since Mrs. Benson's signature had never been authenticated, the will might have been forged.

Judge Hayes pointed out that both wills were public documents under the seal of the Clerk of Court. Unless Brock had proof of forgery, the will was presumed to be authentic.

Brock then objected to any testimony about the amount Wayne Kerr would have received in executor's fees if he had probated the Benson estate. McDonnell argued that "Steven's motive as alleged is not so special or unusual as to give an inference of guilt. That other people would have benefited from the death as well." But the judge sustained the objection, and De Loach did not get to give his estimate, previously published in newspapers, that Kerr stood to make between $500,000 and $750,000.

With McDonnell's next question, Brock was back at the bench objecting to any discussion of "Steven's expectations of inheritance" under the De Loach will. He said this dealt with inadmissible evidence about the defendant's state of mind. Judge Hayes joined with

McDonnell in explaining that in probate law "expectations" referred to facts, to tangible goods and money, not state of mind. Still, Brock objected that the second will's provisions were irrelevant anyway since there was no proof the defendant knew about them. But the judge let De Loach testify that Steven's expectations had changed in the sense that the will he drafted did not leave the estate to Wayne Kerr as trustee.

On cross-examination Jerry Brock asked, "Did you have knowledge of a third will that Mrs. Benson had in her possession but had not executed?" De Loach said he didn't.

As usual, Brock was more interested in what Mrs. Benson could have done than in what she did. He got De Loach to agree that she could have revoked the January 29, 1985, will "if she had gotten mad or had a falling out or found out that one of her children was stealing from her in July."

Suddenly another conversation flared up between Richard Cirace and Dwight Brock. Then Dwight crossed the courtroom to his brother and whispered in his ear. When he returned to the prosecutor's table, Cirace was still at the rail.

"One other thing," Jerry drawled. "I guess there were some other differences between the first will and the will that you drafted, besides the provisions about the trust?" Slowly and with apparent casualness, he reestablished that all three children were to be co-executors and to receive equal shares of the estate.

BROCK: So if Carol Lynn and Scott had been killed, would all of the estate have gone to the defendant?

DE LOACH: Oh yes. He would have been the survivor. It was not an alternative provision there for their shares to go anywhere. But as I say—

BROCK: So the defendant would have been the big winner in this situation?

DE LOACH: He would have been the sole survivor, yes.

Triumphant, Jerry went and sat beside his brother, with Cirace poised behind them. Carl Westman's face had flushed deep red.

There were red faces at the defense table too. After laboring so diligently with De Loach, not to mention with Wayne Kerr and ATF auditor Diana Galloway, to destroy any suggestion of a financial motive, McDonnell and Berry were now back to square one. Worse than that, as Jerry Brock would later express it with wicked glee, "McDonnell really stepped in shit." He had put De Loach on the stand to establish that Kerr, not Steven, had been cut out of the will and that Mrs. Benson had left her son's expectations undiminished. But this had opened them to Brock's counterattack that Steven had had an enormous economic incentive to murder his mother, sister, and adopted brother: he wanted the entire estate. In a matter of seconds, the State had dumped a $6.6 million motive in Benson's lap.

What made this bombshell all the more ruinous was that Guion De Loach's answer was apparently absolutely wrong. He had testified that Mrs. Benson instructed him to prepare a will that left her estate in equal shares to her surviving children.

Under Florida law if Mrs. Benson didn't want her estate to pass on to the lineal descendants of her children, the attorney had to clearly spell out this intention in her will. In the absence of any clause to the contrary, her fortune would automatically flow to her grandchildren. Notwithstanding De Loach's testimony, since the will he drafted did not specifically preclude it, the Florida anti-lapse statute (732.603) applied and Mrs. Benson's estate would pass now to her children's children.

The De Loach will, as written and introduced into evidence, did not make Steven the "big winner." But Brock was eager to have the jury believe otherwise and if this meant allowing another error to enter the record, that was the defense's problem. De Loach was their witness and they were stuck with him.

On redirect examination, McDonnell tried to correct De Loach's misinterpretation of the effect of the will. He pointed out that De Loach had put the phrase *per stirpes* into one paragraph. Generally speaking *per stirpes* refers to the distribution of an estate to succeeding generations, with each heir receiving a share of the ancestor's money on a pro rata basis. But De Loach said that in this will the phrase was meaningless. No matter how McDonnell phrased the question, De Loach kept repeating that Mrs. Benson simply didn't want to deal with the issue of the estate passing beyond her three children.

On recross, Brock pounded away at the misleading point.

BROCK: Now this particular will that you drafted for Mrs. Benson, to fulfill her expectation, was that if two of her children died, if Carol Lynn and Scott died, the defendant over here gets the whole pie, right?

DE LOACH: Yes.

By suddenly introducing a presumption of Mrs. Benson's "expectation," Jerry Brock was once again trying to convict Steven on the basis of unestablished intention.

BROCK: Okay. Now you don't know whether or not Mrs. Benson had ever told the defendant that, do you?

DE LOACH: No.

.   .   .   .

BROCK: Okay. Whenever you drafted the thing, you gave her a copy of the will for her to carry home with her.

DE LOACH: Yes.

While Brock hinted Steven might have discovered the will in his mother's house or otherwise believed that he could get "the whole pie" by killing the family, he failed to mention that Carol Lynn was the only one who had gone on record that she had known about the De Loach will. She discussed this during her interview with Graham and Nowicki.

When court recessed for the day, I asked Jerry Brock if he knew of the existence of a third, unsigned will. He claimed he didn't. He offered no explanation of why he had posed the question to De Loach.

McDonnell told reporters he knew "very little" about a third will. Then he added, "There's not a third will. There's talk about drafts that have floated around."

Carl Westman's response to the press was "No comment." He left the Justice Center heartsick at what had happened. After worrying all morning that the third will had never been dusted for prints, he had sat in court all afternoon listening to the jury get more misleading and utterly erroneous information.

After downplaying the importance of Guion De Loach's testimony, McDonnell switched gears and said he might introduce evidence tomorrow proving that under Florida law Carol Lynn's children would have inherited her share of the estate if she had died along with her mother.

Exhausted and on edge, the defense team retreated to the Veranda. Still perplexed by De Loach's testimony, McDonnell compared the experience to "putting an engineer from Ford on the stand and asking him can a car go forward and backward and having him swear it can only go backward."

Mike Schulgen, who had gone through the grinder of Jerry Brock's cross-examination, tossed down two quick drinks and said that the prosecutor's technique might provoke boredom in spectators, but it produced panic and confusion in witnesses.

"We're winning." McDonnell tried to rally his troops. "We're really winning."

McDonnell and Berry, Bob Laws, Mike Schulgen, and Nina McDonnell wondered who the State might call as rebuttal witnesses. They felt sure Brock would try to rebut Brenda Turnbull. Perhaps they'd fly in ATF explosives expert Albert Gleason to counter Chester Grelecki's testimony.

But if the defense rested tomorrow, they doubted the Brocks would be ready with rebuttal witnesses. They'd ask the Judge to give them till Monday.

When Schulgen and Laws decided to call it a night, they kicked in for their share of the bill. Everybody was on a pay-as-you-go basis. The war chest for Steven Benson's defense had long been empty. The private investigators, like the lawyers, were now working with the knowledge that a guilty verdict meant they wouldn't get paid.

"I want you guys around for the verdict," McDonnell said, "for the party."

"We'll be there," Laws said. "We'll pull my car around front and bring Steven down the steps and take off. Shall I wear a piece?"

"Why not," McDonnell said.

"Yeah, I think that's best," said Laws.

Then Jerry Berry had to leave. Alone with Nina and me, McDonnell seemed to slump a little. Perhaps it was just that he no longer needed to keep up the spirits of the others. In a more meditative mood than I had seen him in before, he said, "If we win this one, I'm not going to get much credit. They'll say I wasn't up against F. Lee Bailey. Of course, if we lose, I'll get all the credit."

Then he caught himself and said in a more assertive voice, "I really think the guy's innocent. When I read about the case in the newspapers, I didn't. But then when I got to know him, I believed him."

Chapter 14

On Friday August 1, a local TV station had taped to its monitor a quote from Thomas Jefferson. "I shall ask for the abolition of the punishment of death until I have the infallibility of human judgment demonstrated to me."

People had plenty of time to contemplate the quote since this day, supposedly the last for the defense, started as had so many others with a delay and ended in recriminations. After a conference in the judge's chamber, the Brock brothers and McDonnell and Berry approached the bench for yet another conference. Carl Westman was with them, slightly slope-shouldered as if dragged down by the weight of his briefcase. Then after an extended and animated conversation in which the personal representative did not participate, Judge Hayes announced he was recessing the trial because the State had been notified of new witnesses it wanted to depose. "All I can say," Hayes told the jury, "is that we didn't know about it until this morning... I'll see you at 9 A.M. Monday."

Jerry Brock said, "It seems like every other witness they have called has been disclosed just before the trial or during the trial. I've never encountered this in thirteen years."

Michael McDonnell assured the press he had informed the State of new witnesses as soon as he knew about them. But "I'm still trying to get evidence out of the State. I've never seen anything like this in my sixteen years as a lawyer."

He explained that the judge would have Carl Westman testify and correct the mistaken impression Guion De Loach had created. But McDonnell said, "I changed my mind. We didn't feel it was terribly important."

What he didn't mention was that Hayes would also have allowed Jerry Brock broad latitude to show that the defense was impeaching its own expert witness, and to develop on cross-examination information helpful to the State's case. Rather than risk opening new areas of inquiry, McDonnell withdrew Westman as a witness.

On August 2, I met Carl Westman at Frost and Jacobs in Naples. Since it was Saturday, we had the suite of offices to ourselves. Although he wore a pair of slacks and a sport shirt, Westman looked and acted anything but relaxed. He was distressed that the trial would end and the jury would reach a verdict without having heard a proper interpretation of Florida probate law.

He was also coming under pressure to stop his "neutral cooperation," as he expressed it. He said Carol Lynn Kendall had attempted to have him discharged as personal representative because he had shared with McDonnell the same evidence he offered the State. Now, through a third party whom he named, but asked me to keep secret, he had heard that Jerry Brock had contacted Carol Lynn and asked her to intervene and have him refrain from raising more issues.

What people forgot, Westman said, was that the court had appointed him to his position and he had a fiduciary duty not to favor one beneficiary over another. The murder trial, he maintained, could not be divorced from the question of who should inherit Mrs. Benson's estate. Any evidence that related to Steven's guilt or innocence —and therefore his rights as a beneficiary—had to be explored before the will was probated.

What evidence, other than the third will and a correct reading of the De Loach will, was he talking about?

At first he evaded the question. But finally he recounted an event that explained why he felt such anguish at the way the trial had progressed. He feared that the State—and by extension, he himself —had withheld critical evidence.

On September 9, 1985, several days after she testified to the grand jury, Carol Lynn Kendall stopped by Carl Westman's office with Richard Cirace. She was in high spirits and aksed him to send out for a bottle of champagne. He did so and the three of them moved to a cluster of chairs and tables at the far end of the room. There they sipped the champagne and discussed Carol Lynn's testimony.

A gifted narrator, she amplified the story she had told the grand jury. She managed, as Westman remembered it, to bring the day of the murders more vibrantly alive than if she had shown them a movie.

Eventually, they switched from Westman's office to a conference room, and the narrative continued. She was still describing incidents from Benson family history as background to the bombings when the last of the firm's lawyers left for the evening at 8 P.M. Skipping dinner, scarcely noting the passage of time, they stayed hour after hour at a glass-topped table that gave off a glaring reflection from lights recessed in the cork ceiling.

She said that her mother feared Scott and often fought with him. He and his girl friend inhaled nitrous oxide from the tank beside his bed, and then he was apt to strike out at anybody. Carol Lynn told of one terrifying incident when he had grabbed her by the throat. Another time, he turned Buck loose on Kim Beegle and had the attack dog pin her to the floor. There had been nights when Mrs. Benson locked herself in her bedroom to escape Scott and telephone for help.

But frightened as Margaret was of Scott, she felt a deeper fear of his friends. Carol Lynn spoke of death threats against the family and said the Naples police had been alerted and a private guard hired.

She mentioned, as she had in her interview with Graham and Nowicki, that her mother remarked that she wouldn't put it past Steven to do away with her if it meant more money for him. But in context the comment had struck Carol Lynn as a joke, not as a genuine expression of fear. Westman got no sense that she had imagined her mother was in danger.

As he understood it, it had not occurred to her that Steven might be involved until Wayne Kerr visited the Naples Community Hospital and asked if she thought her brother's behavior had been suspicious. (Kerr recalled that it was she who raised the question.)

When she described the events before, during, and after the explosions, Westman felt the tone and content were strikingly different from the story she later told at the trial. As Steven came around the rear of the Suburban, for example, Carol Lynn said he gave her a little "pat on the ass." It seemed a wildly improbable thing to do if he was about to blow her to pieces.

After listening for more than nine hours, Westman believed he had a clear image of events. Immediately after the first explosion, she remembered being outside the Suburban with an orange cloud pressing her to the ground. It sounded as if she had been blown out of the vehicle by the bomb, then showered with live sparks and burning powder. Perhaps she had not been sitting squarely on the backseat, facing straight forward, watching Steven walk toward the house. She might have been sitting sideways, he thought, which would explain how she got burns on her back.

She didn't mention seeing Scott's body on the ground or throwing herself out of the flaming vehicle. One instant she was in the Suburban; the next instant she was on the gravel with live cinders raining down; then she spotted Steven, his face etched with shock, horror, and disbelief. He was screaming, "Oh my God. Oh my God."

Memory of this scene prompted a spontaneous and emotional outburst from Carol Lynn Kendall, "He could not have done it."

Westman recalled her certainty about this. Steven simply couldn't have killed Scott and his mother. He was always quiet, the family peacemaker, the one who walked away from fights.

The marathon session ended at about 1:30 A.M. with Carol Lynn instructing her dumbstruck attorney, Richard Cirace, to call the State prosecutors tomorrow morning. Stricken with doubts, she was ready to recant her testimony.

The following day, September 10, Jerry Brock and a second man —perhaps Lieutenant Harold Young—met Carol Lynn, Cirace, and Westman at Frost and Jacobs. When she told them Steven was incapable of murder, Brock said it was perfectly understandable that she needed to deny her brother could do such a thing. She probably felt guilty for accusing him of an unimaginable crime, felt she was responsible for his arrest and indictment, felt enormous pressure at being a key witness for the prosecution.

Both Brock and his colleague assured her they weren't depending on her alone. They had a strong case against Steven. Repeatedly they emphasized to Cirace how overwhelming the evidence was against her brother.

Slowly and subtly, over a period of almost two hours, they coaxed their star witness back onto the tracks. But after swearing that they wanted an objective account of events—she wasn't testifying against Steven; she was testifying to the facts—they suggested a subjective and prejudicial interpretation of why he had screamed "Oh my God! Oh my God!" He wasn't shocked by the horror of what happened; he was shocked to discover that someone had survived.

Still, Carol Lynn wasn't completely convinced. She said the most she could do was describe what she had seen and heard. No more, no less.

Westman told me that troubling as this recantation, then rehabilitation of the State's star witness had been he could have accepted it if Carol Lynn had testified to the facts and nothing more. But during the trial, there was nothing detached about her testimony.

How could anyone, he wondered, undergo such a dramatic change—at one point giving incriminating evidence to Graham and Nowicki, then wanting to recant, then agreeing to be an impartial witness, then turning into a witness so aggressive and hostile she argued over almost every question? She wouldn't yield an inch to McDonnell, and she appeared to begrudge any evidence that might present her brother in a slightly more favorable light. What happened to the woman who in a spontaneous outburst said of Steven, "He could not have done it"?

I asked if anyone knew about Carol Lynn's recantation. Did McDonnell and Berry realize that shortly after their client's indictment, his sister had told her own attorney and the personal representative of the Benson estate a different story? Were they aware that she had repeated this story to Jerry Brock and Harold Young? In criminal cases, evidence tending to support the innocence of the defendant is supposed to be shared with his counsel. Carol Lynn's claim in front of our witnesses that her brother "could not have done it" would certainly appear to be relevant to Steven's defense.

Carl Westman doubted McDonnell had been informed. Here was yet another piece of evidence that might never be introduced. If a man ran a chance of being condemned to death because the jury didn't have all the facts . . .

His voice trailed off. He ended by telling me what might happen if he came forward with this information. He could lose his job. Frost and Jacobs could lose an account, and he might leave himself and the firm vulnerable to legal action.

2

Sunday morning, Carl Westman called to say he had made up his mind. He planned to discuss the matter with Michael McDonnell.

When I arrived at his office, Westman was dressed for business in a gray suit, white shirt, and tie. Last night and much of this morning he had worked at a word processor producing several documents that enumerated the Florida statutes in question and itemizing the issues involved—Carol Lynn's recantation and subsequent trial testimony, the State's failure to lift fingerprints from the third will or to correct the misleading information about the De Loach will.

He mentioned in passing that he had gotten word last night that the third will contained no prints of any value. He wasn't sure whether this meant no identifiable prints, no prints of known suspects, or no prints, period. Since Wayne Kerr, Mrs. Benson, George Gramling, and he had handled the document, Westman figured there should have been some prints on it.

Michael McDonnell had no idea what the personal representative wanted, but he knew from his voice that it was urgent. He drove over without changing clothes and showed up in a Lacoste shirt, a pair of shorts, and moccasins with no socks. Sitting in front of Westman's desk, he crossed his legs and sat listening with his hands at chest level, fingertips poised on fingertips. Then as Westman described Carol Lynn's recantation, consulting his records and his daily work agenda for dates and hours, McDonnell scrawled a few notes.

When he was finished, and McDonnell said nothing, Westman observed that perhaps the incident had no relevance to the trial. If so, he apologized for interrupting McDonnell on his day off. But he thought the defense should be aware of it.

McDonnell straightened in his chair and said he felt Westman had an obligation to inform the judge.

They arranged that McDonnell would go to Hayes on Monday morning, outline what had occurred, then have Westman repeat his story. If nothing else, this would show how the State had conducted its case throughout. Praising Carl Westman's courage, McDonnell said he would see him in court tomorrow.

Chapter 15

On Monday, McDonnell and Berry, the Brock brothers, Judge Hayes, and Carl Westman met *in camera*, and the personal representative said, "Your Honor, I at this point have formulated no personal opinion whatsoever as to the guilt or innocence of Steven W. Benson. I am, however, deeply troubled with the process that I see being used by the State and in the prosecution of this case."

As an example of what troubled him he mentioned an item—he didn't specify it was the third will—that he had passed to Jerry Brock which might suggest a motive for Scott as well as Steven.

"In addition, I'm troubled... with the State's resistance to accommodate some method of correcting the erroneous testimony of Mr. Guion De Loach, creating in my judgment motive where no motive existed, strictly because of inaccurate statement of the law.

"Thirdly, I am troubled by the fact that to at least some extent the State has been involved with influencing Carol Lynn Benson Kendall, who has very subtly and through indirect means, issued threats that I be removed as personal representative, primarily because of my judgment... to turn over the tape that was played and deemed by this court to be relevant to the proceedings.

"Finally, most troubling to me is the trial testimony of Carol Lynn Benson Kendall. I observed her testimony. I was shocked by the intensity of it. I noted what I deemed to be considerable variance with personal accounts that she gave me of the incident on September 9, 1985."

He described the "very touching and intense detail" of her account of "the events leading up to the explosion, after the explosion, and certain accounts regarding her family and her brothers. The bottom line conclusion," Westman said, was that Carol Lynn instructed Richard Cirace to contact Jerry Brock. They met the next day with Brock "and to the best of my recollection Harold Young." She re-

peated to the prosecutor and the investigator what she had told Westman and Cirace: "Steven could not have done this."

While Westman conceded there was nothing abusive about Brock
and Young's response, "I would characterize their actions as very
subtle" in explaining away her doubts. At the end of the meeting, she
had been at best "a neutral or very slightly prosecutorial witness. I
have not been made aware of any additional evidence which has come
to point since that night, and yet I heard her testimony in trial to be
very intense, to be very prosecutor-oriented, rather than a neutral
witness."

"Am I being accused of something?" Jerry Brock asked.

Nobody directly answered his question. Instead, for over an hour,
five lawyers and the judge debated two of the issues Westman raised.
The other two—the third will and the the threats to fire the personal
representative—got lost in the confusing adagio of clotted language
and legal opinion. Brock never explained his handling of the third
will, and nobody pointed out that any effect to influence or threaten
Westman because of evidence he had given in the past or might offer
in the future could amount to witness tampering.

The primary topic of discussion was Guion De Loach's testimony
and what, if anything, should be done about it. Carl Westman
claimed, "If the State Attorney has taken an oath to serve the ends of
justice [it] seems to me he could fashion a method and has a duty to
do so to make sure this jury does not go to that jury room with the
impression that the defendant had a six million dollar motive."

McDonnell was equally unequivocal. "Clearly what we're discussing here is the fact that on the record there is a mistake. Justice
should not accommodate such a mistake."

Inevitably, Jerry Brock disagreed. "I believe there are many,
many mistakes as far as testimony that has been offered here. But in
order to correct the mistakes, if you're going to correct the mistakes,
you have to do it in conformance with the rules of evidence."

"Seems if justice were to be served," McDonnell said, "the swiftest and easiest way to achieve that [justice] is the instruction from the
Court. This is what the legal effect of this will is [and] leave it at
that."

But Judge Hayes replied, "My problem is I'm not really sure I
can honestly tell you what the legal effect is at this point. Because I'm
also doing the probate estate, I'm not willing to...go out and tell
this jury what the law is regarding this particular will, when I
haven't even had a trial on it in the probate case."

The judge also stressed that Carl Westman might have a vested interest in stating for the record that De Loach had wrongly interpreted or wrongly drafted the will. "... it wouldn't surprise me to find Mr. Westman and Mr. De Loach as being cross parties and involved in a future lawsuit." Although Hayes was willing to let Westman testify, he said he couldn't prevent the State from pointing out that the personal representative had a possible bias.

McDonnell moved "for a mistrial on the grounds of denial of fundamental due process and fairness through surprise to the defense of the witness testifying, as though an automobile expert were testifying that a car could only go in reverse."

Hayes denied the motion. "I don't believe the evidence supports surprise... I don't think Mr. De Loach has ever taken any contrary position than what he put on at trial. It's just his understanding of the law ... may be different than ours."

That left one remaining issue, and McDonnell said, "We certainly intend to call Mr. Westman to relate these events to the jury, but would also request that because of this revelation first ... Carol Lynn Benson Kendall be recalled for continued cross-examination on these points.

"Secondly, that the court make a full inquiry into whether or not there was undue pressures brought to bear upon her to change her testimony after she had concluded that her brother couldn't be guilty..."

Furthermore "... the fact that she said that should have been disclosed to the defense in accordance with Brady versus Maryland. And we either move for a continuance to deal with this issue or for a mistrial on that basis."

Brock broke in to say that if Westman "is alleging that she made some contradictory statements, let's hear what those contradictory statements are?"

The personal representative obliged with an abbreviated list of examples, concluding "I heard her comments during the trial to be somewhat slanted." The events she described on September 9, 1985, unfolded "over a period of hours and in intimate detail that formed a very clear impression in my mind. And there was no impression in my mind as I heard her testimony at the trial that that testimony was remotely similar to the testimony that took place in my office."

"Your Honor," Brock said, "I submit the only difference between what Mr. Westman has recorded there [is] whether or not she was on the ground or in the vehicle. And you will recall that she threw herself out of the vehicle on to the ground."

But that was far from the only difference Westman described. His impression was that Carol Lynn had been blown from the Suburban, may never have been seated facing forward, and may never have seen the events she so vividly recounted on the witness stand.

The personal representative went on with what he regarded as an equally important point, "Carol Lynn's descriptions of Steven's reactions...her conclusion that led her to instruct her attorney to contact Mr. Brock and meet with him as soon as possible was her description of looking into Steven's face.

"She did not comment as she did in the trial, that his face was a blank stare. She said she focused on Steven's face and there was an expression...of shock, horror, and disbelief, and he was screaming 'Oh my God, Oh my God.'"

Westman reminded them that McDonnell had to struggle to get Carol Lynn to admit that Steven had said anything. But Brock maintained it was just a matter of perspective. "Mr. Westman's version of all this and the procedure in which it was being conveyed to him, I mean it's fine and dandy if I were to talk to two witnesses under different circumstances and at different times, I'm liable to come away with a different impression myself.

"But again, I don't see what the difference in testimony is. Maybe somebody did not ask these particular questions either in direct or on cross-examination."

In his prattling, cornpone style, Brock muddled the facts. On direct examination he himself had asked "particular questions" to establish through Carol Lynn that Steven had been "staring straight ahead" with a blank face, hadn't come to help her, had simply opened his eyes wide and run back into the house. If Brock couldn't see the difference between her trial testimony and the description Carol Lynn gave earlier of the horror, shock, and disbelief on Steven's face, then the prosecutor wasn't the meticulous detail man he pretended to be.

Furthermore, Westman had not been talking about "two witnesses under different circumstances" and he reminded the prosecutor, "I was remarkably relieved and impressed with Carol Lynn Benson Kendall's ability to restate, under very emotional circumstances, the following morning on September 10, 1985, a very similar account to the State's Attorney, Mr. Brock.

"So I don't believe it's simply a matter of my interpretation in trying to impose my judgment as to weighing of evidence...I think the State clearly had contrary information to what they have heard at the trial."

But Judge Hayes remarked, "Well, I don't know how to say this, but I can't find anything that's substantially for impeachment here." He acknowledged there had been no indication during the trial that Carol Lynn ever said "'Her brother couldn't have done it.' And, you know, that very well may be part of some testimony the defense could put on to show that that was her position."

Brock objected. "Your Honor, that would be totally irrelevant. That's a conclusion."

He made this claim as if Carol Lynn had not already drawn dozens of conclusions, as if testimony about "her mental impressions" of Steven's behavior weren't based on conclusions.

The judge added, "I'm not sure she's actually, any of her testimony has said that 'I believe Steven Benson did this.'" Although Hayes was technically correct—she had not spoken those precise words—every line of her testimony led to that assumption.

In the end Hayes ruled that since Carol Lynn had never specifically said, "Steven did this," the defense could not call on Carl Westman to testify that she had said to him, to her lawyer, the chief investigating officer, and the prosecutor, "Steven could not have done this."

The judge also denied the motion for a continuance or a mistrial that McDonnell had requested on the grounds that the State should have disclosed Carol Lynn's recantation to the defense.

Carl Westman emerged from the judge's chambers looking careworn and exhausted. He took his accustomed seat and watched the proceedings feeling that Steven Benson's fate had been sealed. Hereafter, members of the prosecutor's team referred to Westman as Judas.

2

The defense called David Humphrey, a Naples architect who had helped design the 17,000-square-foot dream house Mrs. Benson hoped to build. He had also discussed with Steven and her the feasibility of moving the Spanish Provincial from 13002 White Violet

Drive to the new lots in Quail Creek. In fact, he had spoken to Steven about this by telephone early in the afternoon of July 5 and had tried to arrange for a house mover to come to the Benson home on July 8 or 9 and give an estimate. While this demonstrated that Steven took a more active role in his mother's affairs, especially in plans for the new house, than Carol Lynn indicated, it was debatable whether McDonnell managed to convince jurors that Steven wouldn't have been consulting an architect and encouraging a house mover to stop by on the very days when he was allegedly buying bomb components and planning to murder his family.

Ralph Frederick Merrill had been driving off the third tee behind the Benson house the morning of July 9 when the first bomb blew. Following hard on the heels of Charles Meyer, he ran to the scene and saw the Suburban in flames. "It was almost like a blast furnace." While Meyer hurried to the other side to help Carol Lynn, Merrill grabbed Mrs. Benson by the ankles and was dragging her away when his heel caught on a stump and he started to fall. At that instant, the second bomb exploded and Merrill was wounded by flying shrapnel.

It was uncanny how alike Merrill and Meyer were. They were golfers and retirees, wore glasses, were thickset but seemingly healthy, were affable and articulate witnesses. Yet the State called Meyer, not Merrill. Since Jerry Brock had shown no reluctance to present redundant testimony, one wondered why he hadn't put both men on as prosecution witnesses.

At least one wondered for a minute or two. Then it became obvious that their stories varied substantially, and Merrill wouldn't help the State's case. Seconds after the first explosion, just as the smoke rose above the roofline of the house, Merrill "heard Steven cry out. I recognized his voice." And what he cried out carried an uncanny echo of what Carol Lynn recalled her brother saying, "Oh my God, come quick. Help."

As he rounded the corner of the house, "I saw Steven Benson. He . . . was near the left front fender [of the Suburban]. He was running" toward the front door of the house.

Subsequently, he saw Steven "sitting on the front steps. He was moaning and crying and rocking back and forth and shaking uncontrollably."

Describing his wounds, Merrill said he had a minor abrasion on his chest and a laceration that required six stitches. Although he spoke of the great volume of debris unleashed by the second blast, he found only one piece of metal about half the size of his little finger on his clothes. He recalled no scorch marks, no unburnt or spent powder. And he had been standing, McDonnell established, off to one side of the Suburban, eight or nine feet away, with nothing between him and the twenty-six-pound pipe bomb. The doors on the vehicle had been blown open by the first explosion.

Benson claimed to have been standing nine feet in front of the Suburban, shielded by the engine block.

On cross-examination, Jerry Brock began slowly, but soon one heard the sound of rocks and slag being ground to rubble, and realized this process wouldn't end until everything was reduced to powdery-fine dust. His unvarying method was to cast doubt on a man's ability to remember one thing, no matter how momentous unless he remembered everything, no matter how peripheral. By his logic, a description of the Pyramids was suspect unless one could describe every grain of sand in the surrounding desert. While his case, like any prosecutor's, depended upon a highly selective use of evidence that served his purposes, and an absolute indifference to anything that did not, he refused to accept the possibility that a defense witness's perceptions could be incomplete, yet still valid.

Since Brock wasn't often reined in by the judge or curbed by objections from opposing counsel, he naturally grabbed every inch of ground he could get away with. But this created an extraordinary degree of distortion when, as with Merrill, he spent over three hours exploring a period of time that lasted fifty-five seconds.

As always he asked garbled, ungrammatical, or goofy questions. ("At this point in your life and in my life and in everybody else's life, you presumed—" he prefaced one question.) Then he insisted on pinpoint precision in the answers. It wasn't enough that Merrill could remember where he was standing and what he did when the first bomb went off. Brock badgered him to describe what others did and said. Did Charles Meyer have a golf club in his hand? "Not being familiar with golf, had he put the little pin in the ground?"

Half a dozen times, in half a dozen ways, he demanded whether Merrill could see the front of the Benson house from the back. And did he hear Steven Benson's voice before he noticed the column of smoke or after? Why had he heard Steven and not Carol Lynn crying for help on the far side of the van. "Are you sure it was Steven's voice?"

Merrill, a friend of the Benson family, said, "It was a man's voice with Steven's characteristics."

"Are you sure?"

The witness, worn to a razor's edge, sighed. "At this point I'm not sure of anything."

The prosecutor pushed him hard on whether he saw Steven at the left front fender of the Suburban, heading for the house. "You're sure the person you saw was Steven?"

"Yes."

"The reason I'm asking that, Mr. Merrill, I'm going over the statement you gave police officers back on July 11, 1985." He read, "'It was my perception that I thought I saw Steven Benson going toward the front door of the house.'"

"Sometimes you get very careful with your speech," the witness replied, "and trying to be a careful person, never anything being 100 percent, I sometimes qualify my comments." Still, he insisted, "Unless . . . somebody had makeup to duplicate his facial features, that was Steven Benson."

Since Merrill was so sure he had seen Steven's face, Brock followed his standard procedure and asked whether he had seen Mrs. Benson's face. The golfer made a fatal mistake and said yes.

In the press room, reporters hooted and one shouted, "Yeah, he saw her face. It was on the side of Steven's van."

Deepening his disaster, Merrill described her normal features and stated that her left cheek had been turned to him.

Brock stepped over to Sharon Telly's table where the evidence was kept, picked up a sheaf of photographs, and shuffled them as he strolled back to the stand. He passed Merrill the snapshot of Mrs. Benson on the autopsy table. It was the picture of a woman without eyes, without half her face.

Merrill's own face blanched, then flushed. "That was not her condition when I saw her," he managed to murmur.

This was a fiendishly effective piece of courtroom theater which seemed to undercut every line of Merrill's testimony. But in reality what did it prove beyond the fact that he had manifestly not seen Mrs. Benson's face? It didn't necessarily mean he had not seen Steven or had not heard him cry out "Oh my God." Carol Lynn admitted she couldn't see her hands at arm's length, had not seen Charles Meyer as he dragged her away from the Suburban, had not heard the second bomb erupt. Yet the State based its case on the assumption that everything else she heard, saw, and remembered was completely accurate.

Brock ended his cross by asking how closely Merrill had examined his clothes for debris, powder, and microscopic particles of metal. The golfer admitted he had given only a cursory glance at his shirt and pants before throwing them away. The prosecutor scored a point by implying that Merrill should have performed a laboratory analysis on his clothes when, in fact, that was what the State should have done.

Since Merrill had been grilled for almost four hours, McDonnell kept his redirect brief. He simply got the witness to repeat that he had noticed nothing on his clothes; he had heard Steven's voice "to the best of my knowledge"; and he had seen the defendant near the Suburban, headed toward the house.

When after a lengthy recross by Brock, Fred Merrill stepped down, the press room broke into applause. It was difficult to know whether reporters were praising him for surviving or just expressing relief that it was over.

At 3:40 P.M. the defense rested, and during a recess McDonnell came out to the hall and told journalists, "I'm here because you asked me to be here. If you want me to give press conferences, don't write that I'm out trying to whip up enthusiasm for press conferences."

"Why didn't Benson testify?"

"No comment," he snapped.

"What do you see as the greatest strength of your case?"

"My strongest point is the weakness of the State's case."

Asked why he didn't put on a witness to dispute the evidence about Benson's palm prints, McDonnell said he didn't feel the need to do so since the prints were irrelevant to Steven's guilt or innocence.

Jerry Brock told the press, "We feel comfortable with our own case, especially since the defense had put on nothing other than to ... slander Scott Benson." He dismissed out of hand the relevance of Scott's drug connections. "The question is 'Who put that bomb in there?'"

Brock said there was an obvious reason why the defense had not put on a fingerprint expert. They couldn't find one anywhere who could refute ATF Agent Frank Kendall's testimony. As Brock later told me, if McDonnell had brought on a witness to attack Frank Kendall, "We'd still be in there parading experts on and off the stand to say he was full of shit."

The State called Harold Young as a rebuttal witness, and he testified that he had measured the distance from the Benson home to the Shop 'N Go as 7.2 miles. The round trip took fifteen minutes, which included the time he spent in line waiting to buy cigarettes. He had made this test run on a couple of occasions—on July 12, 1985, at 9:30 A.M. and yesterday, August 3, 1986, at noon.

During cross-examination, Young admitted he hadn't had a stopwatch. He depended on one wristwatch last year and a new one yesterday. He hadn't taken anyone with him to confirm the accuracy of his figures and, he conceded, he had made both trips on Sundays, not at rush hour on weekday mornings.

Since the State had no other witnesses ready, the judge adjourned until the next day. Walking to the parking lot, he said he was fed up with the sloppy way both sides had conducted their cases. Then he added with a sardonic smile, "The last one who talks is the one who'll lose."

The following morning, Jerry Brock announced the State would offer no more rebuttal witnesses. McDonnell renewed his motion for a directed verdict, claiming the prosecution had not eliminated all reasonable theories of Benson's innocence.

Judge Hayes said, "The evidence is sufficient for the case to go to the jury."

McDonnell moved for a mistrial on the basis of the palm prints, which he again argued were taken illegally.

Hayes denied that motion too. He told the jury to return at 8:30 A.M. and be prepared to spend the night if they failed to reach a verdict.

Chapter 16

I

In March, Michael McDonnell had told me, "I think the press is like a spirited horse. You have to let them know where you stand. Then you can both have an enjoyable ride." By the time he realized the press can be rambunctious and unbridled, he and his client had been thrown and trampled.

On the morning of his final argument McDonnell decided to unplug the press. Arriving early at the courtroom—not as early as some spectators, who started lining up for seats at 6 A.M.—he collected all the microphones and stuffed them in a closet. This cut the audio to the news room and to the local TV station that provided pool coverage to other stations and national networks.

When journalists complained, McDonnell said he didn't want a microphone in his face when he spoke to the jury. Judge Hayes granted that it was his prerogative not to have a mike on the podium, but he ordered the rest of the courtroom rewired for sound. The only microphone that worked, however, was at the judge's bench, and Hayes switched it off during conferences, then often forgot to turn it back on. Even when he did, it picked up the nervous tap of his fingers more clearly than the voices of the attorneys.

Just before bailiff Val Everly called the court to order, Harry Hitchcock, escorted by his daughter, Janet Lee Murphy, made what the media referred to as "a dramatic entrance." Dressed in a blue seersucker suit, white shirt, and blue tie with a clasp in the shape of a fish attached just beneath the Windsor knot, he walked slowly to a reserved seat behind the prosecutor's table. There he alternately listened and dozed for the next four hours, his head with its thatch of white hair nodding like a fluffy dandelion.

Steven Benson didn't glance in that direction. Looking pallid and shrunken, he sat with his hands tucked under his legs.

Each side had two hours for final arguments. The State got to speak for the first hour. Then the defense took the podium for two straight hours, followed by as much of an hour of rebuttal from the State.

As they say down home in the piny woods, Jerry Brock decided to dance "with the girl that brung him." Rather than change tactics now, he stuck with his methodical approach, piling names atop dates atop facts. "The events leading up to this horrible crime began unfolding back in January 1985."

Like a child connecting dots on a place mat and sketching a picture of a giraffe, he recapitulated the basic touchstones of his case— the purchase of pipes and end caps, the palm prints on receipts, Steven's hour-long trip to buy coffee and pastry. Anybody who had followed the trial in the daily newspapers or on television would have had no trouble anticipating the prosecutor's points.

At 10:15 Michael McDonnell wrote the word "suspicion" on a chalk board. He urged the jurors not to reach a verdict based on innuendo and suspicion. "Mr. Brock told you a story based upon evidence that has not come before this court." The story, he said, reminded him of the joke about a tailor and a customer and a suit that didn't fit. It was the same joke he had told reporters a couple of weeks back. Again it got a good laugh when he sprung the punchline, "You're being sold a suit that doesn't fit."

He characterized Carol Lynn Kendall "as a poor woman who didn't deserve to go through what she did." But "because of what she went through, her testimony is unreliable." With never a harsh word for the lady, he highlighted some of the contradictions and inconsistencies in her story and attributed them to shock. He suggested she was confused about time sequences; events blurred in her mind. Some of what she imagined she saw while she was beside the Suburban had actually occurred when she was sitting on a neighbor's lawn after the second blast.

The composite picture done by Mike Koors, he reminded them, was inaccurate and misleading. At the chalk board, he sketched the lower half of a face. The State had just half a face and half a case.

As Judge Hayes drummed his fingers on the bench, mimicking the beat of a heart, McDonnell discussed palm prints. Frank Kendall, he said, was a fingerprint expert. There was no evidence he was an expert in palm prints—a partial writer's palm print at that. But it didn't really matter because the State never proved that the pipes from Hughes Supply were in the bombs.

He pointed out that the end caps with the Grinnell logo were at least eight years old. Where did they come from? And the pipe bomb fragments, according to the State's own expert witnesses, showed heavy deposits of zinc oxide, which indicated they were old, far older than the pipes sold by Hughes Supply, he said.

As McDonnell described Scott's erratic and violent behavior, Steven removed his glasses and cried. "We have one poor, unfortunate young man running amock...He would do anything to get more drugs."

The State alleged a financial motive. But what was it? In the Benson family, large sums of cash had always flowed to all three children. Steven had no reason to kill his mother to accelerate his inheritance.

Circling back to the palm prints, he suggested there were differences between those on the receipts and the impressions of Steven's hands. He urged the jurors to ask for a magnifying glass and study the enlargements.

By now Harry Hitchcock appeared to be deeply asleep and so perhaps he didn't hear McDonnell paraphrase the biblical story of Joseph and his coat of many colors as an illustration of circumstantial evidence. It was the same story he had mentioned ten months ago in his letter to Hitchcock, appealing in vain for funds for Steven's defense.

After emphasizing to the jurors that they were "Angels of Justice," not "Angels of Vengeance," McDonnell ended by returning to the defense table and putting his hand on Steven's shoulder as he had weeks ago during his opening statement. "I'm going to give him to you now. Take good care of him."

The prosecutor started off his final fifty minutes by discussing "reasonable doubt" versus a "possible doubt or an imagined doubt." "You don't know that I didn't do it," Brock told the jury. "There's not very many of us who have an alibi for that particular day, but that is not a reasonable doubt."

More animated than at any time during the trial, he found it fascinating that the defense had spent a week of testimony on Scott's drug problems, but gave it no more than a five-minute mention in a two-hour closing argument. "Scott was involved in drugs," Brock said, his voice dripping sarcasm, "so he goes and blows mommy up.

If that is so, there are a large number of mommies out there who would be in danger."

Rolling his head, more and more incredulous, he mused, "Perhaps Scotty committed this murder. Is there any evidence of that? Absolutely not, unless the defendant was out purchasing pipe so Scotty could blow himself up."

McDonnell's criticism of the crime scene search and subsequent investigation prompted more scorn. Brock suggested that the defense wouldn't be satisfied unless the police had seized the Benson house and carried off the cars in paper bags. "Gee, give us a break," he said.

He apologized if his cross-examinations bored or annoyed anybody. He promised he didn't do it for his benefit. But he hoped the jurors got some benefit as he forced witnesses to distinguish between facts and impressions. He reminded them of Brenda Turnbull. "The truth changed in every one of her statements."

Reviewing McDonnell's remarks, he underlined each inconsistency, dubious assumption, misquote, shaky assertion, or outright inaccuracy. He pointed out that Frank Kendall's testimony about the prints were unrefuted. Palm prints, fingerprints, footprints—it was the same principle. No two were the same. If Steven Benson had put his bare toe on the receipt, Brock said, lifting his foot as if to prop it on the rail around the jury, "We'd still have him."

The jurors, he stressed, did not have the training or the experience to substitute their opinions about the palm prints for the expert's testimony.

He also urged them not to forget what Dr. José Lombillo said. If Scott was on drugs, he couldn't have gotten an invitation to the U.S. Open.

And he wanted them to recall Steven Dancsec's testimony; Steven Benson used to make bombs.

Mr. McDonnell, Brock said, striding toward the defense table, claimed to have done a lot of pondering, but he "wasn't able to determine who did this particular crime. Mr. McDonnell's problem is that he was looking everywhere else except right here at the table in front of him."

Brock banged his fist on the table between Benson and McDonnell, and McDonnell shot to his feet, standing face to face with the lanky prosecutor. Brock turned away and went to the State table where his wife leaned over the rail and hugged him.

After listening to testimony from seventy-seven witnesses and reviewing 176 exhibits—162 of them introduced by the State—the jurors heard forty minutes of instructions from Judge Hugh Hayes about the charges and the verdict options. Then, at 2:04 P.M., they retired to their chambers to begin deliberations.

2

Besieged by reporters, McDonnell was asked whether there was anything he wished he had done differently. "Yeah, run further every morning and gotten more sleep." He pushed through the mob and walked down the hall.

A sparse crowd remained in the gallery, killing time until the verdict, rating the final arguments, reading *Cosmopolitan*, *National Geographic*, and gothic romances. One woman watched a soap opera on a miniature portable TV the size of a transistor radio.

The weather, as if on cue, grew dark and brooding. In front of the old courthouse, a group of people unfurled a banner that fluttered and snapped in the wind. Obsessed for so long by the Benson case, I assumed the banner had to be related to the trial. A protest against the death penalty perhaps. Or a call for swift punishment.

When I went downstairs for a closer look, I saw it was a vigil to commemorate the bombing of Hiroshima. It was August 6, and there were larger worries in the world. As the sky lowered and unleashed a downpour, I hurried back inside and up to the fifth floor.

In the hall outside Courtroom A, cameramen, producers, reporters, and trial groupies sat on the floor, leaning against the walls. A TV commentator applied makeup, getting ready to do an update. People stood in line to use the lone pay phone. Newspapers were spread everywhere, as if at the bottom of a birdcage.

I spotted a member of the prosecutor's team who agreed to an interview as long as it was without attribution. When I told him I had a hard time believing in Benson's financial motive, he said he didn't buy it either. He wasn't sure anybody did, not with the way Mrs. Benson had thrown money at her kids.

After reminding me that the State wasn't obliged to prove any motive, he admitted that it helped to suggest a reason why a guy blew up his family. But the real motive in this case was too complicated to allow for easy explanation. Essentially it boiled down to Benson's desire for independence from his mother. Here he was in his early thirties and everything belonged to Momma. So he started skimming off money to open his own little business and buy a home.

When Mrs. Benson found out what he was doing last winter, she jerked his chain to give him fair warning. She resented his going behind her back to break away. In July she decided to give his chain another jerk, a hard one this time. Maybe she overdid it and scared him. More likely, she made him realize she was never going to let go, not while she was still alive.

But money, no, that wasn't the motive. It was an emotional thing.

One truism at murder trials is that a quick verdict generally favors the defense. It means jurors dismissed the State's case out of hand. So there was a flurry of excitement when at 4:15 the jury knocked for the bailiff.

But they hadn't reached a verdict. Ernest Henning, the younger of the two men, had been elected foreman and he said they wanted to hear Carol Lynn's testimony, starting from when she seated herself in the Suburban.

Taking the witness stand, a court reporter read the questions and answers that described Carol Lynn watching Steven walk toward the house.

Henning then requested aerial photographs of the crime scene and enlarged pictures of the palm prints and the invoices from Hughes Supply. He also asked the court reporter to read the testimony of Frank Kendall, first those passages that established his credentials as a fingerprint expert, then his answers on direct and on cross.

When the jurors retired to continue their deliberations, the courtroom cleared of all but the diehard. Outside, the storm had passed after dumping two inches of rain; banyan and palm trees gleamed in the evening sun. Michael McDonnell eased over to me and whispered, "I predict we're going to get slam-dunked in two hours. Guilty! The foreman wouldn't even look me in the eye. The whole trial he wouldn't look at me."

His big body sagged. His guard was down, his face crestfallen. He feared he had lost and that his client stood a good chance of going to the electric chair.

"The print is what killed us," he said. "What was I supposed to do? I wasn't going to go out and hire somebody to lie." Although everyone, including Judge Hayes, seemed to feel that a defense attorney could always find a professional witness who, if paid enough, would testify to anything, McDonnell declared he wouldn't put some charlatan on the stand.

3

When, by late evening, the jurors still had not reached a verdict, they were led by a bailiff to the Snack House, where they had a choice of baked chicken or liver. Meanwhile, the defense team gathered at their corner table at the Veranda, but nobody had much of an appetite. McDonnell, his wife Nina, his second son Jimmy, his mother-in-law Mafalda Gray, his partner Jerry Berry, an associate in his office, Randy Thomas, and several secretaries sat drinking and nibbling at nachos. The atmosphere was reminiscent of an Irish wake. Loud outbursts of laughter alternated with intervals of lugubrious silence. Everybody appeared to be bone-weary and tense.

"Well, they had to fight for it," McDonnell announced with no prologue. "They had to fight for every damn inch."

"What?" Nina asked.

"The conviction."

No one contradicted him, no one offered a word of false hope.

"Any second thoughts about not having Steven take the stand?" McDonnell asked.

Randy Thomas shook his head no.

Jerry Berry smiled and nodded his head yes. "You know how I feel." From the start he had said it was dangerous for Benson not to testify.

McDonnell said that if by some great good fortune Benson were found innocent, he didn't care if he had to borrow the money, they were all going on a long vacation. Of course, if there were a guilty verdict, they'd have to get right back to work. They had to pay the rent. The firm had spent more than a year on this case with little or no return.

While others at the table paired off in conversation, McDonnell turned to me. "I'm at a fork in the road." He held out a hand with the index and middle fingers spread. "If he's found guilty, I guess I'll just go on as before. But if there were an acquittal—" He shook his head and sighed. "That could change everything."

It could catapult him into that select group of trial lawyers who got the biggest, most prestigious and challenging cases. "When people are in trouble, I want them to say, 'Get me Mike McDonnell.'"

Money was not the goal that drove him to reach for the top rung. He wanted to test himself against the best. But to participate at that level, you needed a showcase and you needed financial backing. He couldn't complain. He had had the showcase of a lifetime. He just wished he had had more support—if not as much as he needed, at least as much as everybody reported he had.

He spontaneously praised Brock's final argument. "I was sitting there peeing in my pants, wondering what I'd say."

The conventional wisdom was that the longer a jury deliberated, the more likely it was that those who favored guilt would wear down the others. McDonnell said, "If that's the way it's going to be, I'd like them to be out for three days. I want to think we gave them a run for their money, gave them something to ponder."

While everybody else was drinking beer or cocktails, Jerry Berry sipped at a vanilla milkshake. This prompted a lot of razzing about the piece in the Miami *Herald* that claimed he resembled Beaver Cleaver. Mopping off a mustache of milk, Berry said that if the jury remained out overnight, that might be a good sign. Maybe they had serious doubts, and the more they discussed them, then slept on them . . . well, anything was possible.

But, Berry granted, nobody could guess what was going through a jury's mind. He remembered a time as a prosecutor when he argued a grand larceny case, certain he had a good shot at getting a conviction. If nothing else, he knew he'd get the defendant on petty larceny. It just depended on what value the jury put on the goods that had obviously been stolen.

Sure enough, after hours of deliberation, they asked for a definition of the difference between grand and petty larceny. Berry's confidence soared. But then a few minutes later, the jury came back with an acquittal on both counts. "How can you figure that? Why ask for the definition if they intended to acquit?"

Suddenly, a boisterous contingent from the prosecution team— Jerry and Dwight Brock, their wives, Harold Young, Richard Cirace and Carol Lynn Kendall—waltzed into the Veranda, and of all the tables they might have taken, they chose one next to the defense. One could view this as nose-thumbing on a grand scale—to sit next to the enemy. But it wasn't intended as such. There was a bond between the two camps. Like boxers who embrace after a bitter and bruising fight, they were linked by the intensity of the experience. Shaking hands, slapping backs, ribbing one another, relieved it was over, they acted much friendlier than anybody in the courtroom, particularly the defendant, would have imagined possible.

McDonnell worked the State's table like a wardheeler. He and Harold Young agreed to get out on the golf course soon. He squeezed and massaged Jerry Brock's shoulders. Whatever the verdict in the Benson trial, they all had to go on living together in the same small town and undoubtedly would wind up on opposing sides of a courtroom over and over again.

When McDonnell returned to his chair, I asked if he'd been angry today when Brock pounded the table between Benson and him. McDonnell laughed and said he'd have done the same. "If I were a prosecutor, I'd pound right on the defendant."

More drinks and nachos arrived, and the State table ordered the same. There were no solemn, pensive silences now. Both groups were loud and lively. Somebody shouted at McDonnell, but he couldn't hear. Cupping a hand to his ear, he responded, "In the immortal words of Buck, huh?" The room exploded with laughter.

One of the secretaries at our table said a charitable organization in Naples had requested a souvenir from the Benson trial to raffle off for some worthy cause. McDonnell suggested a pipe bomb fragment encased in plastic. Another explosion of laughter.

Yet much as McDonnell might appear lost in this levity, he was, at least in part, just keeping his colleagues loose, keeping their minds off the subject he couldn't forget. Leaning close, he whispered to me that if the verdict was guilty, he couldn't cave in with disappointment. He had to be prepared to go back to the jury and plead for Benson's life. "I'll be the only thing standing between him and old Sparky."

When a musician at the piano bar struck up a rendition of "Misty," McDonnell started to sing, but had done no more than a few verses when Richard Cirace came over and said Judge Hayes had just sent a message. The table fell silent and froze.

There was still no verdict, Cirace said. Hayes was sending the jury to the Holiday Inn, but wanted everybody back for instructions before he recessed for the night.

*   *   *

I found myself walking with the prosecution team. They joked about having to pull themselves together before they reached the courtroom. Cirace stepped off the curb and into the middle of the street, following the yellow stripe to prove he could walk a straight line. As we approached the Justice Center, a black woman in swirling green robes and a red turban—she could have been a fortune-teller or an escapee from a harem—asked for spare change.

"Hey, what are you doing?" Harold Young asked. "Working for Mike McDonnell?"

In the elevator, Carol Lynn giggled and wondered aloud whether she should come into the courtroom. She hadn't been there since the day of her testimony.

No one answered her, and she tagged along with the rest of the prosecution team, loose and jolly as everybody else. As she settled into a seat beside Cirace, Steven turned from the defense table and took a long look at his smiling sister. A camera clicked, and the moment crystallized into another icon of the case.

Judge Hayes told the jurors they would be sleeping two to a room. He instructed them not to go out tonight, not to watch television, and not to discuss the verdict. They should wait and continue their deliberations when they returned here at 9 A.M.

Chapter 17

I

On Thursday, August 7, 1986, as the jury resumed its deliberations, reporters crowded into a small room and watched "Rambo III," the amateur video of two private detectives penetrating the security perimeter of Quail Creek and marching up to the Benson house brandishing a pipe bomb. McDonnell hadn't put the movie into evidence during the trial and he didn't watch it now. He was out in the hall pacing when word spread that there had been a knock on the jury room door. It was 1:14 P.M.

"This has to be it," McDonnell said, hurrying into the courtroom with a swarm of reporters.

The bailiff brought Steven Benson from his holding cell at 1:20. His face was as gray as his suit. McDonnell met him in front of the judge's bench, shook his hand, and said, "We've got a verdict." Then they sat at the defense table with Jerry Berry and Bob Laws. Benson clasped his hands in his lap and leaned forward as if his midsection had gone hollow.

The court reporters arrived, then the Brock brothers, then Sharon Telly, the Clerk of Court, and Paula Kelley, the judge's summer assistant, and finally, at 1:30 P.M., Judge Hayes himself. Carl Westman had spent every day sitting in a reserved seat behind the prosecutor's table, but he wasn't there now. He had moved off to one side and sat in a chair provided by a bailiff.

During voir dire, Jerry Brock had asked prospective jurors if they could look Steven Benson in the face and say "He's guilty." Michael McDonnell asked if they could look Jerry Brock in the face and say "He's innocent." But when they came into the courtroom at 1:31 P.M., the jurors wouldn't look at anyone. They settled into their chairs and fixed their eyes on the floor.

Ernest Henning, the foreman, passed the verdict to the bailiff, who carried it to Judge Hayes, who, after a glance, gave it back to the bailiff, who brought it to Sharon Telly. The Clerk of Court stood up and read in a quavering voice the list of nine charges, and the verdict for each—guilty, guilty, guilty. . .

McDonnell put a hand on Benson's shoulder. Steven seemed to sigh or suck in a deep breath. That was all.

McDonnell asked that the jurors be polled individually. Benson turned his impassive face toward the panel, but no one met his eyes except Fred Kruger, a retired industrial safety engineer.

Somewhere in the gallery a woman's voice was audible. "They got him and they got him good."

But other spectators were crying; around the courtroom handkerchiefs came out.

Judge Hayes called for a conference with the opposing attorneys in his chambers, and as the crowd cleared the room, Benson stood at the table, propped against it with his hands, and watched the noisy procession with a tight little smile on his face.

After the conference, the judge announced that attorneys would spend the rest of the day reviewing aggravating and mitigating factors to present to the jury during the penalty phase. Each side would have half an hour to make its plea. Then the jury would deliberate whether to give Benson life in prison, which meant at least twenty-five years without the possibility of parole, or death in the electric chair. Sequestering jurors for the second night, Hayes recessed the trial until 9 A.M. tomorrow.

McDonnell told the press, "This is round one. I'm not through. Steven is innocent. We will continue to work for him as long as he wants us to."

He said there were numerous grounds for appeal and cited several: The palm prints should not have been admitted. The judge should have excluded testimony about the dimensions of the pipe in the bombs since there was insufficient evidence to support the State's claims. The judge should have allowed more testimony about Scott's involvement in drug dealing.

Jerry Brock was ebullient and told reporters without a trace of irony, "I think this demonstrates that the amount of money a defendant has doesn't make any difference. It doesn't buy his freedom."

After asserting that Benson, for all his wealth, couldn't escape justice, Brock seemed to see no contradiction in saying Steven "was totally supported by Margaret. The guy who did not have a penny that he was not getting from Margaret."

The prosecutor announced that he intended to consult the family before deciding how hard to push for the death penalty. "Usually, when someone kills somebody, it's not a member of that person's family. We feel that we're compelled to consult."

As Brock saw it, there were plenty of aggravating factors that justified capital punishment. While he admitted Benson wasn't your average murderer who had a long record of previous convictions, he said, "You gotta start somewhere. He started at the top."

Although the prosecutor didn't ask Kim Beegle's opinion, the press did, and Scott's girl friend wasn't shy about saying she hoped Steve got the chair.

Janet Lee Murphy seconded the motion. "I'm very happy about the verdict. As far as the death penalty is concerned, I'm all for it."

Harry Hitchcock told a reporter, "In view of the evidence, any other verdict would have been a miscarriage of justice." But he added, "My reaction was tempered by my sorrow that my flesh-and-blood grandson would have done this, and to that extent, I feel sorry for him. He must have had a sick mind."

He wouldn't take a position on whether his grandson should live or die. "I wouldn't want to be the one to make the decision."

Once she returned from the hairdresser's, Carol Lynn Kendall released word through Richard Cirace that she would meet with journalists and make a statement after she'd had time to reflect. She hadn't decided whether Steven should be spared or sent to the electric chair.

In the end, Carol Lynn never held this press conference and never revealed what she had recommended to the prosecutor.

2

Judge Hugh Hayes was one of very few people to follow the trial from start to finish and not look hollow-eyed with fatigue. His baby blues were clear, his hair immaculately combed, his smooth cheeks a healthy pink.

He felt the case hadn't been won until final arguments. Jerry Brock, he said, had done a better job of being specific and dealing with details. Hayes allowed that McDonnell may not have been as effective because he didn't have the facts on his side. The defense had three big things going against it—the palm prints, Carol Lynn's testimony, and Steven's failure to testify.

Although he didn't have any doubt that Benson qualified for the death penalty, he questioned whether he'd get it. His instinct had always been that Margaret Covington had selected jurors wisely, and this group just didn't have the death penalty in them. The delay of the penalty phase until tomorrow also worked in Benson's favor. Hayes had wanted to push on to the penalty phase today. But the prosecution had for once sided with the defense because the Brocks wanted to consult with Steven's family.

The irony, Hayes pointed out, was that while he believed the family would urge the death penalty, they were less likely to get it precisely because the prosecution had insisted on this pause to ask their advice.

When I brought up the third will, he said he wasn't certain it constituted admissible evidence. But the question had never arisen since both sides danced clear of it. While Brock had obvious fears that it would cloud his case, McDonnell was wary for a different reason. If Scott's prints, not Steven's, were on the third will, that would strengthen suspicions that the younger son had a motive, but the defense couldn't afford to emphasize the importance of prints when Steven's palm impressions were on the Hughes Supply receipts.

Hayes felt that the defense had done well to keep Benson from talking to the police and the press for the past year. That meant he came into the trial an enigma, an unknown quantity. But the defense then had to explain the enigma, fill in the blank space. This didn't necessarily entail putting him on the stand. There could simply have been more interaction between Benson and the jury, Benson and spectators, Benson and the press during the four weeks of the trial. But when he sat there woodenly, conveying little by his expression or his body language, the jurors had had nothing to go on except the circumstantial evidence, which favored the State.

I mentioned that I had spoken to a member of the prosecution team who told me that, despite claims to the contrary, money wasn't Benson's motive. Judge Hayes agreed. It seemed to him there were ample psychological motives for Steven to strike out at his family.

While he conceded he had heard that the prosecution had not recalled Carol Lynn because of her fragile emotional state, he volunteered that the Brocks might also have feared that Carl Westman had a version of events that would contradict her testimony. This was as far as he would go in discussing the day when Westman revealed that Carol Lynn had recanted and told a startingly different story to her attorney and Jerry Brock.

The judge thought McDonnell had made a mistake in not calling Carol Lynn as a defense witness and really going after her, rending her limb from limb. The defense's only hope, Hayes said, was to persuade the jury that the Bensons didn't deserve to live, that Carol Lynn didn't deserve their sympathy and couldn't be trusted, that everything she said was colored by hatred and resentment of Steven, by greed and the desire to profit by his problems.

But Hayes never claimed this would have been an easy task. Carol Lynn was a formidable lady who "could have turned around and taken a bite out of McDonnell's ass."

To end a classic circumstantial evidence case McDonnell had chosen a classic example of circumstantial evidence—Joseph and his coat of many colors. But from years of experience, both as a lawyer and as a judge, Hayes believed that anytime anybody quoted the Bible in court, "They're about to shovel shit on you."

With that, Hayes swung his briefcase into his Jeep Renegade and rumbled out of the parking lot.

On the top floor of the Justice Center two windows had signs in them. One said STEVEN WAS FRAMED. The other said FREE STEVEN.

3

The next day, Jerry Brock spoke first and made an impassioned plea that Benson be executed. As the prosecutor saw it, there were four aggravating factors that justified the death penalty.

Steven had not only killed his mother and brother—"For our purposes it makes no difference Scott wasn't his natural brother"— he badly wounded and scarred his sister and the two golfers, and endangered the lives of others.

The murders and other crimes were committed in the course of an arson, or throwing or placing a bomb.

These crimes were committed for financial gain.

The fourth and most compelling aggravating factor was that these crimes were committed in a cold, calculated, premeditated manner.

"Think in your mind what crime known to man is more reprehensible than taking the life of the person who gave him life. It's just such a shocking situation," Brock said, "it sends goose bumps down my back. Treason, betraying your country, is minuscule compared to taking the life of the person who gave birth to you."

As for premeditation, he stressed, "There's no way you can accidentally or by mistake or by any other fashion other than a cold, calculated fashion place a pipe bomb in an automobile between your mother and brother. Not to mention sit your sister on top of one of those things, twelve inches long, filled with gunpowder."

Brock asked them to think back on the Book McDonnell quoted yesterday. In the Bible "Judas sold out Jesus Christ. That was nothing compared to what this defendant did. At least the relationship between Judas and Jesus Christ was not that of a family relationship."

He suggested the jury consider the victims. "You never knew Mrs. Benson or Scott. They are not here. They are in the ground somewhere. They had a right to pursue their lives."

These factors, he felt, far outweighed any mitigating circumstances. He urged the "ultimate sanction." Brock quoted the Book again, "An eye for an eye."

McDonnell, speaking in a whisper barely audible in the back rows of the courtroom, took just eight of the thirty minutes available to him and began by agreeing with the prosecutor. He defied anyone to justify these crimes which "run contrary to everything we believe and were taught." But while the crimes were unjustifiable, he felt they were also incomprehensible. "I submit none of us will ever know why this happened."

He said he could claim Steven had no criminal record, had performed generous acts for the family the jury had just convicted him of killing, and was a good father. But this didn't change things. "So I have no choice but to simply plead for his life. I suggest to you there has been enough killing. I suggest to you we can spare three little children the horror of knowing their father was executed. Give me time. There's no appeal once he's executed."

He too concluded by referring to the Bible, the New Testament, not the Old. "As Mr. Brock spoke about Jesus I remembered his words, 'Forgive them.' I don't think that gentle man from Galilee would execute Steven Benson."

With that McDonnell sat down, and Judge Hayes reminded the jury this wasn't the same process as reaching a verdict. The vote didn't have to be unanimous. A simple majority ruled. Seven jurors could send Benson to the electric chair. In the event of a 6–6 tie, he got life.

An hour and fifteen minutes later, after sending out word asking Judge Hayes if they would be individually polled on their decision—he assured them they wouldn't—the jury returned, and Foreman Ernest Henning informed the judge that they were tied. Benson's life had been spared by a single vote.

Judge Hayes delayed the sentencing until September 2 to allow time for a probation board report.

Today it was the defense team's turn to be exuberant. "I'm delighted," McDonnell said. "It's a great victory. I've never had any [client] go to the electric chair. I don't ever intend to have that happen."

Jerry Brock said, "I never criticize a jury's decision." Still, he added, "I would have thought, under the circumstances, that the death penalty would have been appropriate."

John Greenya, who hoped to write the authorized story of the Benson case "as told by" Carol Lynn Kendall, had come to Fort Myers late in the trial and filed a couple of stories for the Washington Post. For its coverage of the penalty phase, however, the Post depended on United Press International.

The New York Times needed a wrap-up of the trial, and since their correspondent, Jon Nordheimer, had returned to Miami, they asked Richard Fitzhugh, the free-lancer from Penthouse, to write it. But Fitzhugh wanted a byline, hoping that would help him get a book contract. The Times insisted it didn't give bylines to stringers. Fitzhugh then said he wanted a dollar a word, not the stringer's fee. The Times would not meet his demands, and so it too ran the UPI story.

As a result, the two most illustrious newspapers in the nation published the same catastrophically inaccurate report. The Washington Post claimed that the jury heeded "the family's wishes that [Steven's] life be spared . . . Prosecutor Jerry Brock said he conferred with several Benson family members before asking the jurors to recommend the life sentence to Circuit Judge Hugh Hayes."

The New York Times said, "The prosecutor, Jerry Brock, surprised a packed courtroom by asking the jury to sentence [Benson] to a life term rather than the electric chair. Mr. Brock told the jurors that the Benson family wanted the life sentence."

In this instance, as in so many others, the press, like the prosecutors during the investigation, seemed to start with an inference, then work backward to justify it. If Steven Benson got a life sentence, it had to be because Jerry Brock had asked for it, and if Brock asked for it, it must have been because the family told him to.

4

I called Margaret Covington to ask how her "shadow jury" had voted. She said they had reached a guilty verdict with life in prison, predicting hours in advance what the jury would do. The turning point for her "shadowers" had come with Guion De Loach's mistaken testimony that Steven would have inherited the $10 million estate if he had succeeded in killing his whole family.

Although they had sworn that they believed in a defendant's right to remain silent, the shadow jurors admitted they resented it when Benson didn't take the stand. They wanted to hear his side of the story, they wanted him to deny the charges.

Covington repeated that her "shadowers" had given indications that they disobeyed their instructions and followed press reports during the trial. Or maybe they had misrepresented their original exposure to information about the case. Whichever, she suspected the real jurors had also reached their verdict based on "evidence" never introduced in court.

In the coming weeks, as members of the jury spoke to the press, it became clear that Covington was right. In separate interviews, Patricia Bennett, at thirty-eight the youngest juror, and Fred Kruger, at seventy-one the second oldest, mentioned Mrs. Benson's will.

In an article in the Lancaster *New Era*, a reporter said Mrs. Bennett "found Benson's misuse of his mother's money and his fears of being disinherited only unconvincing circumstantial evidence." In fact, no evidence, circumstantial or otherwise, and not a word of trial testimony, had been introduced about "disinheritance."

While Mrs. Bennett claimed not to have been swayed by this non-evidence, Fred Kruger said bluntly of Benson, "He was just a kid with too much money. His mother found out he was ripping her off and was going to disinherit him."

Chapter 18

I

The day the jury voted a life sentence for Steven Benson, I joined Jerry Brock in the State Attorney's office in the Lee County Justice Center. Now that the trial was over, he agreed to an interview. He had slumped into the same posture as I had first seen him in four months ago in Naples. Leaning back almost horizontal in a chair, his feet up on a desk, he was smoking a cigarette and sipping Coca-Cola from a can. He looked tired. His face was thin and haggard, but he was a happy man and couldn't hide it.

He called the trial "a good learning experience. If you could do three or four a year like this, you could get to be sharp as a tack. It's hard work, but you're on a high. You can go a long time on that adrenaline. It's a good feeling, and you miss it when it's all over. I know in the next few weeks I'm going to feel depressed."

While making no great claims for himself—"I just do the best according to my talent"—he felt "we put on a damn good case. We anticipated everything they did. We got tired, but we never gave up. The low point came whenever the judge decided to let that stuff in about drugs and Scott. We felt the jury might decide he deserved to get killed, and that attitude might carry over to Margaret. But we didn't give up. We kept fighting."

Brock believed the jury wanted and expected Steven to testify. "They're accusing you of killing your mother and brother. Now what the hell have you got to say about that? Benson would have been the only person we had not had a chance to talk to" before he testified. "That would have been a disadvantage. But I guarantee you we'd have showed him every check and every receipt and forced him to account for every bank transaction."

Since he had probably spent as much time around the defendant as anybody except McDonnell and the jailers, I asked for his impressions of Benson, and he wasn't reluctant to supply them. Brock characterized him as a "very cold individual...more concerned about himself than anyone else. He only thinks about number one." He was "stony-faced during a year of depositions. I never saw him express remorse over Mrs. Benson and Scott. He'd listen to all the details about the autopsy reports and never once show emotion. How the hell could you kill your mother and brother and show no conscience? How could you live with yourself?"

The prosecutor acted and sounded less down-home, less earnest and bumbling now than he had in the courtroom. When I asked if he was conscious of playing a role during a trial, he conceded he changed according to the circumstances. "Whenever I give an interview, I'm in a different role. I sound different on the telephone to my mother than I do in conversation. On TV you try to portray an appropriate image. But in court, during a trial, I'm much more natural. Whenever I do something that's not natural to me, I feel uncomfortable. People can see through you whenever you do something that's not you. Whenever you're living with them for a month, you can't fool twelve people.

"And what's so bad about being yourself," Brock asked, "unless you think there's something wrong with the way you are? I used to be conscious as a boy of my big ears. Now I couldn't care what other people think. I pay my own bills."

He was candid enough to admit his style was an advantage. Jurors believed he was natural and unrehearsed. "McDonnell," he remarked, "can seem staged—putting his hands on the defendant and so forth."

Did he view that as a flaw, McDonnell's theatricality?

No, he thought the defense attorney's flaw was his ego. He said he and his brother Dwight felt the longer the trial lasted, the more the jury would see through McDonnell.

Unfortunately, the prosecutor wasn't so blunt and forthcoming about other subjects. When I brought up the third will, he didn't deny knowing about it, as he had when I asked a few days ago, but he tried to dismiss its significance and relevance, as well as its authenticity.

"I don't even know where it came from. Guys from the estate got boxes of shit laying all around," he said as if someone might have planted it.

Wayne Kerr had mentioned this document during his statement

to Brock and Lee Hollander and could undoubtedly have identified it for the prosecutor.

The whole issue of the third will was beside the point, Brock claimed, because "it had so many prints on it, they were of no value."

He didn't explain how it was possible to reach this conclusion when no comparison prints had been taken from anybody involved in the case.

When I asked if it surprised him that McDonnell didn't do more to undercut Carol Lynn's credibility and character, Brock scowled in disbelief, as though it had never occurred to him such a thing was conceivable. "Carol Lynn is a very, very intelligent girl," he said. Although she had had an illegitimate baby, any questions along those lines would, he said, have generated sympathy for her. "There was a woman on the jury who worked with unwed mothers," he pointed out.

I told him I had heard that Carol Lynn once wanted to recant and she went so far as to say Steven couldn't have killed Scott and Mrs. Benson.

The prosecutor replied that this wasn't true. He didn't appear to be particularly excited about the subject. He dismissed it with a languid wave of his hand, saying that she had simply had some concern shortly after the murders about being a witness against her brother. "We had to explain to her she wasn't testifying against anybody. She was testifying about events and facts. She wasn't an advocate."

He went on to add that this had happened up in Boston, when Graham and Nowicki wanted to interview her. She asked to speak to a priest for moral guidance. "The priest told her it was her obligation to tell what happened."

I thanked Jerry Brock for his time, left the State Attorney's office, and ordered a document from the Official Court Reporter labeled "Transcript of Excerpt of Proceedings (Chamber Conference) Monday August 4, 1986, commencing at 8:30 A.M." These fifty-one pages contained a verbatim account of Carl Westman's description of September 9, 1985, when Carol Lynn Kendall told Richard Cirace and Westman, "Steven could not have done it." The next morning she repeated this to Jerry Brock.

At no time during the proceedings did Jerry Brock ever deny that Carol Lynn said, "Steven could not have done it." He argued instead that this evidence was inadmissible.

2

Over the weekend, people on the periphery of the Benson case shared their views with the press. Kim Beegle said, "I'm happy. Now Scotty can rest in peace. Whether Steven dies in the electric chair or rots in jail doesn't matter to me."

Janet Lee Murphy told journalists in Florida and Pennsylvania that she was "joyous" that Steven had been found guilty. Although in her deposition to defense attorneys in May she had sounded neutral on the matter, she now told the Naples *Daily News*, "Of course I thought he was guilty."

Mrs. Murphy added, "I must preface this by saying I really never had any great feelings for Steven through the years, so that's why it hasn't been bad for me. When this happened, I suspected Steven right away and I really right away kind of [considered he] was no longer a relative of mine. He was this horrible man who had murdered my sister and Scott. He wasn't the kind of person you could get close to, so it wasn't that I had to change my feelings all of a sudden having loved this wonderful nephew...

"Scotty was always the lovable, outgoing nephew. He couldn't talk to me without saying 'I love you.' He was just so affectionate and Steven was always very distant and aloof and cold."

While Carol Lynn Kendall postponed speaking to the press, her personal attorney, Richard Cirace, talked to reporters on and off the record, gave on-camera comments to local TV stations, and conferred with a producer from CBS's "60 Minutes." He told the Fort Myers *News-Press* that his client intended to request that the Collier County Probate Court declare Steven a convicted slayer. Under Florida law this would prevent him from inheriting a share of his mother's estate. Cirace remarked that it might also mean Steven's children would lose any claim to his share. "I'm not so sure that killing someone and having your family benefit is not an indirect benefit" to the slayer.

Cirace indicated that Carol Lynn would move forcefully to prevent Tracy Mullins' daughter, Nicole, from inheriting Scott's share. If both actions were successful Ms. Kendall would be the sole heir to the fortune.

Cirace met the next day with a reporter from the Naples *Daily*

News and announced that Carol Lynn would soon check back into the Massachusetts General Hospital and undergo reconstructive surgery on her face.

In a front-page story under the headline SISTER ACTUALLY HELPED STEVEN, LAWYER CLAIMS, he emphasized that Carol Lynn had been anxious to see that her brother got a fair trial and so she had delayed filing a personal injury suit until after the verdict. According to Cirace, she did this to avoid any negative influence on the jury and to allow Steven to receive $244,000 from Mrs. Benson's estate to pay his legal bills and support his children.

This goodwill gesture, Cirace mentioned, cost his client $244,000. But he based his opinion on the unproven assumption that Steven's children had no legal right to inherit.

On Monday, August 11, I went to the Edgewater Beach Club in Naples where Carol Lynn Kendall and Richard Cirace had a couple of suites overlooking the Gulf of Mexico. During the trial I had had occasional conversations with Cirace, who asked me to postpone my request for an interview with his client until after the verdict. Carol Lynn, he gave me to understand, didn't want to make any decision about cooperating on a project until she had had a chance to meet all the people who were pitching books, movies, and mini-series.

Ms. Kendall, wearing a floral pink pants suit, opened the door and stood there staring blankly, saying nothing. She appeared to be distracted, perhaps slightly puzzled. I introduced myself and asked if this was the right time and the right place. She said it was and led me into the living room where Cirace, in a pair of blue shorts and a blue T-shirt, sat at a table clipping articles about the trial out of newspapers.

While Carol Lynn sat at the far end of the table and folded her arms, Cirace passed me a sheaf of glossy color photographs. They showed Carol Lynn in the hospital shortly after the murders. There were close-ups of the gruesome burns on her face, the shrapnel wounds on her lower legs, and the charred skin on her back.

Another writer who had come asking for an interview had been shown these photographs. He bet me Cirace would start off the same way with me. Even though I was forewarned, the hideous pictures had their impact. I said it must have been a horrible experience for Carol Lynn Kendall. Her lawyer assured me it had been dreadful. She herself said nothing.

Cirace explained he wanted me to see the photographs so that I'd understand why his client was filing a personal injury suit and moving to prevent Steven's children from inheriting his share of the estate. She had suffered enormously and faced an uncertain future full of pain, emotional and physical scars, and ruinous medical expenses. If she agreed to speak to me, what could she expect in return?

I said she could expect an opportunity to express her views about the case. I would give an accurate account of whatever she told me. I would not, however, pay for an interview. I was not interested in doing an authorized version of events and did not believe it was appropriate to have a business relationship with anybody in the case.

If she decided not to cooperate with any writer, I would understand entirely. It was bound to be a painful process. There was, in my opinion, no economic inducement great enough to compensate for the agony she would experience as she relived not just the day of the murders, but the years that led up to them. What any author would want to know, I said, was how the Benson family had come to this end.

Ms. Kendall spoke up for the first time, asking what sort of influence she would exercise over the content of my book. She had heard false and slanderous stories about herself. Just yesterday a magazine writer had asked for Cirace's reaction to a rumor that Carol Lynn had some years ago appeared topless at a yachting party in Lancaster. It was an absolute lie, she told me. "I've never even been skinny-dipping." Would she have an opportunity to set the record straight?

I replied that we would do tape-recorded interviews. She could keep a copy for herself and verify that any quotes in the manuscript came from her statements. I welcomed comments on any matters pertaining to herself that she felt needed correction or clarification.

Would she be allowed to review those parts of the manuscript that didn't deal directly with her? She conceded she couldn't control people's personal impressions, but she said there had been many factual errors in the press, especially about her parents, and she wanted to correct them.

When I asked for examples, she cited three. The Miami *Herald* had referred to her mother as "a kind of Gucci-two-shoes." She said Mrs. Benson owned no Gucci shoes and was more apt to wear jogging shoes.

People had written that her father had been in the Navy instead of the Army Air Corps.

More than anything, though, she resented the Miami *Herald* for stating that Mrs. Benson had had no talent as a mother.

I assured her I was eager to correct factual errors. But it wasn't enough to assert that Mrs. Benson had been a good mother. Carol Lynn would somehow have to explain how Scott became a drug addict, playboy, and pathetic dreamer, and Steven wound up convicted of murder.

Carol Lynn bristled. Her eyes flashed, and her folded arms appeared to clench tighter across her bosom. This was precisely the sort of thing she didn't like—these accusations about Scott and her mother. They were dead and couldn't defend themselves, so she seemed to feel an obligation to do battle for them. She said that a lot of what had been written about Scott and Mrs. Benson was libelous, and if any of this got into a book she would take legal action.

Cirace tried to calm her, explaining that it wasn't possible to libel the dead. They had been through this before when she wanted him to take action against magazines which she felt had maligned members of her family. But she dismissed the soothing words of her attorney and again stressed that she didn't intend to let people criticize her dead mother and son.

This brought her back to the necessity of correcting errors. She said she wasn't going to put her name on anything unless it was accurate. I politely explained that I wasn't looking for a coauthor and didn't expect her to put her name on anything. I wanted to interview her for the very reason that was uppermost in her mind—to correct errors. Some of these, I said, were in her trial testimony. Would she be willing to go back over it and iron out all the contradictions, inconsistencies, and mistakes?

Carol Lynn bridled again and demanded what I meant.

Given her present mood, I knew it would do no good to ask about the episode in Carl Westman's office or to raise the matter of her dramatically different descriptions of Steven's reaction after the first explosion. I chose what I thought would be a neutral example less likely to inflame Ms. Kendall. I mentioned her claim that Scott had received an invitation to the U.S. Open. According to my research, that was inaccurate. Would she be willing to amend it? And did she have any idea how the mistake gained such currency that it was repeated half a dozen times during the trial?

The room turned dead still. When Carol Lynn finally spoke, her voice was icy and precise. She said she would not discuss the facts of the case unless or until she decided to grant me an interview. She would consider my request, and Mr. Cirace would contact me. Her attorney ushered me from the suite.

3

Wearing a white short-sleeve shirt and a tie, Lt. Harold Young sat at his desk with the miniature skull serving as a paperweight atop a litter of documents. Although pleased by the verdict in the Benson trial, he couldn't afford to luxuriate in glory. He had other cases to attend to.

Not wanting to take up too much of his time, I told him I was interested in knowing how the police had eliminated potential suspects and come to focus on Steven. How, for example, had they satisfied themselves that Scott wasn't involved?

Scott was an occasional cocaine user, Young explained. "There's no indication he was a smuggler or a dealer. He'd buy it and use it or give it to his friends."

But what about nitrous oxide? I asked. And how had they checked out whether he had killed himself and tried to take the rest of the family, or at least Carol Lynn and Margaret, with him?

Without providing any specifics, he said, "We considered the suicide possibility. But there was nothing there."

He believed that if dopers had been involved in the Benson pipe bomb murders, one or several of the many drug dealers or users already in jail would have come forward to trade information for freedom or a reduced sentence. It happened all the time, Young claimed. Cons were always trying to cut a deal that let them talk, then walk.

What he seemed to forget was that several prisoners in the Collier County jail had offered information—to Steven Benson's attorneys. But far from promising these cons an early parole or a sentence reduction, the prosecutors had refused to guarantee them immunity or amnesty. In fact, they refused to promise that additional charges or penalties wouldn't be imposed if these prisoners revealed, in the course of their testimony about Scott and his drug connections, evidence that could be used against them. Under the circumstances, Stephen Fife and Daniel Gallaway took the Fifth Amendment.

I asked about Tracy Mullins. She was said to have criminal contacts and she had threatened Scott and Mrs. Benson. How had she been eliminated?

Young admitted that investigators had never managed to locate, much less interrogate, Mullins. Mike Koors tried to track her down, but had no success. A used car dealer, a friend of Tracy's, supposedly sent the Bensons threats. Police telephoned the man, Young said, and were satisfied with his alibi. He wouldn't or couldn't say what that alibi was. But he believed it was irrelevant since Tracy had been in jail at the time of the murders.

This didn't really appear to resolve the issue. The Benson family had taken Tracy Mullins' alleged death threats seriously because she was said to have criminal contacts who could carry out her wishes. Where she was at the time of the murders didn't necessarily matter.

"If Tracy inherits Scott's $3 million, she can buy her own drug rehabilitation center." Young closed that subject.

"We consciously tried to eliminate Steven as a suspect," he assured me, "but he just got to be a stronger suspect every day of the investigation." Wayne Kerr, he said, had revealed Benson's financial motive very early on.

Kerr denied this repeatedly in two long statements to prosecutors, and his trial testimony provided no evidence to buttress Young's claim.

When I asked whether Carol Lynn Kendall ever wanted to recant her story, having concluded "Steven couldn't have done it," Young's recollection sounded a lot like Jerry Brock's. He vaguely remembered her having the general feeling at some imprecise time that she didn't want to be the lone witness convicting her brother. "We assured her she wouldn't be the only one," Young said. "We didn't want her to make any assumptions. Just give us the facts."

Across the highway from Lieutenant Harold Young's office lies George Vega's office. The well-known Naples attorney represented Tracy Mullins in her paternity suit against Scott Benson. When I went to verify whether his client had been in jail on July 9, 1985, he didn't dispute it. "Sounds like her," he said. "I wouldn't doubt she's seen the inside of lots of jails."

But if she had been in custody at that time, Vega pointed out, it should have been no problem for the police to find her. The fact was, though, neither the prosecution nor the defense had ever spoken to Tracy Mullins. In a case that hinged partly on Scott Benson's character, Vega thought it odd that the boy's ex-lover had never been questioned.

• • •

Three weeks after I spoke to George Vega, the failure of police to conduct a thorough investigation of Tracy Mullins became all the more curious. In fact, flabbergasting.

On September 3, 1986, Carol Lynn Kendall came to Vega's office to give a deposition relating to the paternity suit. When asked what Mrs. Benson had told her when Tracy turned up pregnant and accused Scott of being the father, Carol Lynn said Mrs. Benson "indicated that it was totally absurd, and she had a few other things to say which I really do not feel she had—she had something regarding the character of Miss Mullins that she had been previously informed of that was certainly brought up in the discussion, but I'm not sure that for my own protection I am at liberty to repeat those things."

VEGA: By protection do you mean physical, or do you mean legal protection?

CAROL LYNN: Both.

VEGA: Well, I don't want to do anything contrary to your physical well-being, but I have to ask you what did your mother say. And then you can ask your attorney if there is some overwhelming physical reason, then maybe we can work it out through some statement, you know, or something. I'm not sure how. So—

CAROL LYNN: Well, as far as my physical well-being, Miss Mullins has at previous times threatened the lives of my mother and my son, Scott. And, therefore, I have to assume that she is being the same person that she was before, that anything that I might say, and this obviously is on public record, my life could also be in danger.

VEGA: All right. How did she threaten your mother or Scott or anyone else?

CAROL LYNN: She threatened to have them murdered amongst other things, physical harm, destroying their property.

VEGA: How do you know this? They've told you, or you were there?

CAROL LYNN: Both of them told me. They were both threatened. And my mother was in fear of her life, and she consulted the authorities regarding it.

Yet, remarkably, when Scott and Mrs. Benson were murdered, these authorities did not include Tracy Mullins among those suspects it considered worth questioning. Just as remarkable, this was the fourth time Carol Lynn had expressed fear for her life or that of a relative.

During her divorce, she had accused Tom Kendall of threatening to kill her. She said she also feared Kendall would harm her son, Kurt. During the investigation of Scott and Mrs. Benson's murders, she not only claimed Mrs. Benson feared Steven might kill her, she accused Debbie of trying to poison Steven. Now she said she was so afraid Tracy Mullins might murder her, she was reluctant to answer questions. Yet police had ignored everything except her accusations against Steven.

4

When I called Wayne Kerr long distance in Philadelphia, the big disheveled lawyer expressed deep sadness for the Benson family. His only acerbic comments were aimed at Harry Hitchcock and Janet Lee Murphy, whose smiling picture had appeared in the Lancaster *New Era* looking, as a former family employee put it, "as if they had just won a lottery, not as if they learned that their relative had been convicted of murder." Several times during our conversation, Kerry said of Hitchcock and Murphy, "People who live in glass houses shouldn't throw stones."

Otherwise, he stressed his sorrow for the people involved. "If they didn't know him," Kerr said, "Steven came across as a snob, as stone-faced. Journalists got down on him for that. But he was always compassionate and very considerate with me and my wife. I hope his positive side comes out. I feel sorry for him. He doesn't have anybody. He's been utterly abandoned."

He described the night before the murders when he, Carol Lynn, and Margaret had gone out to dinner on Carol Lynn's forty-first birthday. "There was no plan for a celebration, no family involvement. It was sad. I feel sorry for Carol Lynn. Thre's a real question as to what she'll finally get financially. And now she's going to be alone, with no father, no Margaret, not even Steven to help her."

Six weeks later when I called Kerr back to let him respond to various accusations Carol Lynn had leveled against him, he again expressed more disappointment than anger. Yet he observed that the case had been characterized all along by Carol Lynn's rash charges. "Look at the original affidavit," he said, "the one that was filed to have Steven arrested. Where did all those supposed facts come from?

Where did the police get that information? Then ask yourself how much of it ever got into evidence at the trial. I mean what happened to the two million dollars Carol Lynn said Steven was supposed to have stolen?"

When I paid Wayne Graham a final visit, he had shed his courtroom suit and tie and was back in blue jeans, a polo shirt, and jogging shoes. An AR-15 semiautomatic rifle was propped in a corner by his desk and pictures of his camouflage-clad Special Response Unit hung on the wall. There was only one reminder of the trial that had just ended. Taped to the wall along with the photographs was a cartoon showing Buck, the barking or non-barking attack dog, dressed in a flak jacket, carrying a metal detector and a lunch box labeled "Benson Bomb Case."

Graham was happy as ever to talk, but garrulous as he got, he wouldn't say much about the affidavit in support of the search warrant which he and Harold Young had drafted. "It'll go all the way up to the Supreme Court," he predicted, smiling. "We're going to be a little bit of American legal history."

I told him I had it from several sources, one of them a member of the Benson family, that Scott had not been Carol Lynn Kendall's only illegitimate child. Her surviving sons, Kurt and Travis, were said to have different fathers. There were people who doubted either boy was Tom Kendall's son.

Wayne Graham confirmed that Carol Lynn had told him Kurt and Travis had different fathers. This happened when he confronted her with the fact that investigators in Naples knew Scott was her son. Since they feared the defense had the same information, they felt Carol Lynn had to admit the truth. Otherwise her credibility as a witness could be called into question during the trial. For some reason, it seemed not to matter that she had had a second and possibly a third illegitimate child.

I called Richard Cirace and advised him that if his client agreed to an interview, I would certainly expect to discuss Kurt and Travis's fathers. Even if she didn't grant an interview, I wanted to give Cirace and/or her an opportunity to respond.

Cirace sounded shell-shocked. He said he had known nothing about this. He had repeatedly cautioned his client that she had to tell him everything. He'd have to consult her now and get back to me.

While he was at it, I asked him to check out another story that was circulating in the Collier County courthouse. I had heard that Carol Lynn's younger boy, Travis, had a keen interest in explosives and had set them off in Naples and in Boston. He was alleged to have detonated a bomb in his mother's garage while she was still in the hospital in late July 1985.

Badly shaken, Cirace agreed to meet me two days later after he had had a chance to discuss things with Ms. Kendall.

It was early evening when I arrived at the Edgewater Beach Club. Carol Lynn had left town, Cirace had stayed on.

Dressed as before in a T-shirt and shorts, he had been sitting outside on the balcony, and his skin was burnished like fine mahogany. With his sharp features and his short hair pushed straight back from his forehead, he had a slightly startled appearance. But his voice was calm, and he chose his words carefully as he explained his client's response to my question about her children.

While stressing that she refused to confirm whether they had different fathers, Carol Lynn took the position, according to her attorney, that this was an intimate matter between her and the man involved. It constituted private information that was nobody's business and didn't have any bearing on the Benson case. If I wrote about it, I would be guilty of invasion of privacy and could expect his client to take legal action.

I reminded Cirace that I had gotten this information from several sources, including a relative of Carol Lynn's and now an investigating officer. It had an obvious bearing on the case, as did any information about Carol Lynn's character, credibility, and mental state. It could have become an issue at the trial. The defense might have used it to impeach her testimony by suggesting that Ms. Kendall had a history of erratic behavior and a long-established pattern of telling misleading stories about herself and her family. If she had lied to her children, and about her children, on such a basic matter as who their fathers were, Steven's attorneys might well have asked why the jury should believe her other statements.

There was also the question of whether the complicated relationships and intrigues in Carol Lynn's life provided a possible motive for the murders, or at least presented a plausible hypothesis of Steven's innocence. Investigators had asked if her mother had enemies who would like to see her dead. But what about Carol Lynn? Was there an ex-lover or the father of one of her three boys who harbored a grudge and wanted to get even? Was there anyone whom she feared?

Cirace simply repeated his client's position. Regardless of who had fathered her sons, it was a private matter. But then after threatening a lawsuit, he made a personal appeal and begged me to consider what was best for Kurt and Travis.

I asked if he had checked out Travis's interest in explosive devices. While Carol Lynn was in the hospital, had the boy packed a tennis ball can with gunpowder, rigged a fuse with a flash bulb, attached wires and run them to a battery, then planted the bomb in the garage and detonated it?

Cirace said he had no recollection of any such incident. He was sure he would have heard about it if it had occurred. And he emphasized that this episode, even if true, had no relevance to the pipe bomb murders in Naples because Travis had been in Boston on July 9, 1985.

Cirace then informed me that he didn't care to discuss Kurt and Travis any further. Since he was now their lawyer, he didn't want to violate the attorney-client privilege. He explained that two days ago, when I asked about their father, Carol Lynn hired him as their attorney as well as hers.

Cirace also said his client had reached an agreement to grant John Greenya the exclusive rights to the "story as told by" Carol Lynn Benson Kendall.

Despite the arrangement with Greenya, I voiced the hope that we could keep in touch so that I could verify information and ensure that my own book was accurate. For example, I continued to be curious how the story of Scott's invitation to the U.S. Open had gained such a grip on the prosecutors.

Cirace had no idea. He had never known Scott and couldn't say how good his tennis game was. He did volunteer, however, the information that shortly after he began to represent Carol Lynn, she, or she and her family together, tried to make a donation to the U.S. Open for an award in Scott Benson's name. Officials of the U.S. Open declined, explaining that they had never heard of Scott Benson.

This would appear to indicate that a year before the trial, it was clear Scott had not been "invited" to play at the U.S. Open. The question remains how Kim Beegle and Carol Lynn Kendall could testify that he had.

5

After the guilty verdict and the jury's recommendation of a life sentence, Judge Hugh Hayes received letters from all over the United States urging him to have Steven Benson executed. In the Lancaster *New Era*, Ad Crable quoted from these irate epistles in an amusing article. "Can a non-resident be a party to a class-action suit to persuade you to sentence him to death?" a man from North Carolina asked Hayes.

A native of Wisconsin claimed he was writing in behalf of "200 other Milwaukeeans: In cases of multiple murders, the chair within one year."

Crable concluded by putting things in perspective. "The trial also seemed to attract another element. One 14-page handwritten letter rambled incoherently except for a line that claimed, 'I am or was captain of the *Andrea Doria*.'"

On September 2, Judge Hayes abided by the jury's decision, just as he had sworn he would. He sentenced Steven Benson to life in prison, but stipulated that for two first degree murder convictions he should serve consecutive life terms. With credit for the 377 days he had already spent in jail, Benson wouldn't be eligible for parole for forty-nine years, by which time he would be eighty-four years old.

Janet Lee Murphy's response was, "Oh, great . . . I just hope he's in for life. I think life should mean just that."

Harry Hitchcock told reporters he hadn't encouraged prosecutors to push for the death penalty—"I didn't want to be the one to pull the switch"—but he said, "I'd like to see [Steven] out of circulation for the rest of his life."

Carol Lynn Kendall, in Florida to give a deposition in the paternity suit against Scott, was interviewed on WINK-TV in Fort Myers. "I'm very relieved at the judge's decision on the sentencing." She said she had been afraid Steven would receive only one life term and be eligible for parole at the age of fifty-nine when, presumably, he would still have been spry enough to make another attempt on her life.

When I reached Lancaster the day after the sentencing, the Benson case was front-page news and would keep making headlines for weeks to come. While reactions ranged from those who were convinced of Benson's guilt to those who suspected he had been framed, from citizens who believed he deserved the electric chair to those who thought a double life sentence was more than sufficient, there was one common denominator among the townspeople I interviewed. They all found something troubling and unseemly about the family's response. They didn't understand why, amid the expressions of joy and relief at Steven's conviction, Harry Hitchcock, Janet Lee Murphy, and Carol Lynn Kendall showed so little concern for Benson's children, so little interest in confronting the underlying causes of the tragedy, and so little inclination to begin groping toward forgiveness.

Some expressed consternation that Carol Lynn would try to prevent her brother's children from inheriting a share of their grandmother's estate. Why punish them? They were bound to have enough trouble for the rest of their lives.

Friends, neighbors, and fellow churchgoers wondered whether Harry Hitchcock hadn't forgotten the New Testament with its message of hope and redemption. If one assumed Steven had done exactly what he was convicted of doing, he remained a child of God. What was the point of thirty years of prayer breakfasts if Harry hadn't learned that Christ's love and grace could transform the basest sinner into a saint?

As one longtime family employee told me, "If you believe in God, then you believe only God can give and take life. Yet here's the family—some of them anyway—asking for the death penalty. If a family drove Steven to murder, why not show him some mercy and understanding now? They just had no family loyalty. Everybody was out for himself."

On September 5, 1986, I called Richard Cirace. In Lancaster, I had located several more sources who confirmed that Kurt and Travis had different fathers. In fact, the public documents pertaining to Carol Lynn's divorce contained the following sworn testimony.

Q. Are there any children born of that marriage [to Tom Kendall]?
CAROL LYNN: Yes, a son, a boy, yes.
Q. His name?
CAROL LYNN: Is Kurt Ross Kendall.

The Divorce Master, John S. May, Esquire, later set forth the facts of the case, asserting, "There was one child born of this marriage, to wit: Kurt Ross."

Cirace blandly replied that Ms. Kendall had "dealt with the situation." She had decided to tell her sons they had different fathers.

That left the question of whether either boy was by Tom Kendall. Cirace said he would have to check on this. But in subsequent calls, he never provided an answer.

He did, however, confirm that after Steven's arrest, when Carol Lynn was afraid her brother would be released on bail, her son Travis had made threats, saying he would have his uncle Steven taken care of.

6

In Lancaster, as in Naples, rumors about Scott Benson's father ranged from the sublimely ridiculous to the obscene. Like investigators from the Collier County Sheriff's Department and ATF, I continued to hear gossip about an incestuous relationship between Carol Lynn and her father, or even Carol Lynn and Steven. (This would have made Steven a father at the age of twelve.) Then I got a tip, made a telephone call, and talked to a man who admitted he had been very close to Carol Lynn twenty-five years ago. Judging by his loquacity, he had been thinking about her for almost that long and waiting for a chance to talk.

We agreed to meet in a popular nightspot in Lancaster. He warned me he might be late. He was married and had kids, but would be coming alone. I would have no trouble recognizing him, he said. "I look just like Jack Nicholson, only with blond hair."

When he arrived, I didn't catch the resemblance to Nicholson, but from photographs I thought I saw something of Scott in the set of the man's jaw and mouth, the shape of his nose and eyes. Although middle-aged and slightly paunchy, he dressed and acted a bit like a college boy headed for a party. He had an easy, engaging smile, pale blue eyes, and the sort of wry cynicism that a sophomore might affect. He drank gin and tonic, and chain-smoked cigarettes.

He told me he'd met Carol Lynn when he was nineteen and in college, and she was sixteen and a high school junior. He worked in a marina down in Maryland, on the Chesapeake Bay, where the Bensons docked their yacht *Marlynn*. The two teenagers fell in love, and he transferred colleges to be near Carol Lynn. Then he moved into the Benson home and worked for the family business, Lancaster Leaf. When Benny Benson was in town, Carol Lynn's boyfriend slept in Steven's room. He claimed he helped Steven build a Heathkit radio. But when Benny was on the road buying tobacco, he said he moved into Carol Lynn's room. Mrs. Benson knew about this and seemed to think it was cute, "because Carol Lynn was in love and that's what she wanted."

I let him run on, figuring I would eventually work the conversation around to Scott. But he got to it long before I would have asked. With no transition, he said, "A lot of people suspected I was Scott's father."

"Were you?"

"That's what Carol Lynn said. I have no reason to doubt it. But the news came at a tough time. I had just gotten married."

He explained that after a time things between them had become less than idyllic. The Bensons interfered, as they did in every aspect of their children's lives, and he felt Carol Lynn had inherited a large measure of stubbornness from her headstrong father, and a calculating instinct from her manipulative mother. By the time she graduated from high school and left for Goucher College, he had moved out of the Benson home and started dating other girls.

Describing himself as depressed and disconsolate, he had married a woman on the rebound. Two weeks after the wedding, Carol Lynn called and said she was pregnant. At a family conference, he explained that he was in no position to do more than assume financial responsibility. Benny angrily dismissed the offer and gave him to understand Carol Lynn would go away and put the baby up for adoption. But the plan changed, partly, he thought, because Benny couldn't bear to give up anything that "belonged" to the Benson family, partly because Margaret was going through menopause and wanted to raise another child.

As we talked, his face was fixed in a smile that rarely matched the events and emotions he described. The sunny expression was for the stream of people, most of them women, who stopped at our table to ask where he was headed later tonight. He said he figured to do a little barhopping with friends. Then he swung back to me and continued talking about Carol Lynn.

He next heard from her three or four years later when his marriage broke up. She called to say she wanted to see him. She brought a little boy with her and said, "Scott, this is your father."

He felt she wanted to rekindle the affair. But he told her it was too late. He assumed Scott would have a good life, materially at least. He never saw her or his son again. His work sometimes took him to Boston. He knew she had moved there, but he never tried to find her. He was married again and had other children. But he thought about her and sometimes heard news second and third hand. He asked if I had seen her. How was she doing? How badly had she been scarred?

The afternoon of July 9, 1985, he said he received a call from somebody in the Benson family—he wouldn't mention a name—and learned that Scott was dead. Still smiling, waving to friends, he spoke of the pain he felt. He said his entire experience with the Bensons had been painful except the early days with Carol Lynn.

At one point, he claimed, a prosecutor contacted him from Naples and said he would be subpoenaed for questioning. There was talk of his being a witness at the trial. But he convinced them he knew nothing and had had no contact with Carol Lynn or his son since the late sixties.

He asked me about Scott. Was he a ladies' man and a hell raiser, like the papers said? It seemed to please him that his son had that reputation.

He ordered another gin and tonic, stood up, and carrying the drink, moved unsteadily through the bar. People attached themselves to him. Several women asked if they could come along. He picked one and pressed through the crowd and out onto the sidewalk, still carrying the drink. In a limo with tinted windows, a stereo system, telephone, and television a friend waited to give him ride. He got in, and so did a few hangers-on. "Remember me to Carol Lynn," he said. "Tell her I asked for her." Then he rapped the window between the driver and him, and they pulled off down the deserted street, looking for a party.

7

My last evening in Lancaster was hot and humid enough to be reminiscent of those soggy summer days during the trial when no breeze stirred off the Gulf and the palm fronds hung limp in the dank air. With a gray sky lowering and the light dying, I drove out to the Woodward Hills Cemetery where the Benson-Hitchcock mausoleum stands on a slight rise just inside the front gate, with a commanding view of a heavily traveled street and a row of run-down houses, none of them worth as much as the $60,000 family tomb. Surrounded by shrubbery, it has a stained-glass window that lets in jeweled light on the sealed vaults of Charlotte Hitchcock, Edward Benson, Margaret, and Scott. A space has been prepared for Harry Hitchcock; his name is chiseled in stone.

The scene would have been tranquil and consoling had it not been for a couple of anomalous touches and all too obvious reminders of the family's problems.

On the sidewalk leading into the cemetery, a drug addict had dropped a bloody syringe. The needle called Scott to mind.

On the wall of the mausoleum, somebody had scrawled the word SADE in block letters. At first I assumed it was shorthand for the Marquis de Sade.

But then I realized it must refer to the beautiful black torch singer, whose ballads are a lament for lost love, dead childhood friends, Mr. Wrong, and illegitimate children. As if to ensure that this single four-letter word—SADE—would suggest the source from which the family's blessings and calamities flowed, somebody had drawn two straight lines through the S, changing it into the sign under which the Bensons lived, conquered, collapsed, and died. $.

Afterword

After Steven Benson's conviction the long knives were out for Michael McDonnell. As most spectators, interested citizens, and the press saw it, the underdog had triumphed and justice prevailed. The headline of a guest column in the Fort Myers *News-Press* crowed, "Common Sense of 12 Ordinary People Shows System Works." The writer, a local English teacher, poked fun at the defense for its pre-trial surveys and search for the ideal juror, and he claimed that McDonnell and Berry "didn't fear the Brothers Brock. After all, they had no 'mirror' jury and were just a couple country boys who couldn't even pronounce defendant." Jerry Brock "just kept coming back. In the end, those 12 ordinary Americans believed him."

In an interview with the Lancaster *New Era*, Steven's aunt, Janet Lee Murphy, said "the family feared the persuasive effect Benson's defense attorney, Michael McDonnell, would have on the jury.

"McDonnell was just so slick. He made black seem white," she said. "He would just twist the words of the witnesses. Carol Lynn was the only one who stood up to him. She told him, 'I will not have you distort my words.'"

In the same issue of the Lancaster *New Era*, John F. Pyfer, Jr., a court-appointed lawyer who represented the interests of Steven Benson's three children, was scathing in his criticism of McDonnell. "The defense was just terrible. I thought the defense lacked direction. There didn't seem to be a game plan followed, if there was a game plan."

Joseph Madenspacker, assistant district attorney for Lancaster County, said McDonnell "fought a smoke-screen kind of case...all the defense could do is keep [Benson] off the stand and create as much smoke as possible."

Jerry Brock went on a Naples TV talk show and accused McDonnell of running with the "SODDI defense—the Some Other Dude Did It defense."

Off the record, policemen, members of the prosecuting team, and journalists were more vituperative in their criticism. Some, who harbored greatly inflated ideas about the amount of money available to the defense, wondered what McDonnell had done with a quarter of a million dollars. Others, who were aware that he had had only half that amount, said he had taken the case for publicity and would now abandon Steven Benson.

A rumor circulated that the defense had put Benson through a polygraph test and, since the results were never made public, everyone assumed that Steven had failed and that McDonnell had known all along that his client was guilty.

When, in the weeks after the trial, I interviewed McDonnell he showed no inclination to blame anybody else. As he had said repeatedly since the verdict, "The result was totally my responsibility. The people around me did a super job. It's my responsibility that we lost."

He denied Steven had taken a lie detector test. "I wouldn't subject him to that. It's totally irrelevant and unreliable. Even if you pass, it's meaningless and inadmissable."

He pointed out again that he had had a budget of not much more than $100,000, all of which had gone toward trial preparation, research, consultant and private investigators' fees. He and others at his office had devoted over 4,000 hours to the case, and they weren't finished yet. They had every intention of following through with an appeal.

While he didn't care to involve himself in an endless wrangle and respond to every charge leveled by people who weren't aware of all the facts, he briefly explained that, like any trial attorney, he had had to weigh carefully the pros and cons of the decisions he made. "Every piece of evidence you put in," he said, "is a two-edge sword. Sometimes you just have to call a witness and take a chance, take the burn you're going to get, and hope it's worth it to make your point."

But in other situations, it simply isn't worth the risk. He knew there were witnesses whom people had expected him to call. These were the very witnesses who could have done more damage than any conceivable good. "They could have popped off," McDonnell said, "and put Steven in the electric chair."

In view of the State's performance during the trial and, earlier, during the investigation and discovery phase, McDonnell found it ironic that he was accused of manipulating the facts and distorting the truth. He felt that police had consistently ignored evidence that might have exculpated Benson and refused to pursue alternate theories or even to question obvious suspects. The prosecutors, along with the police, had leaked unsubstantiated, prejudiced stories to the press and had filed affidavits full of demonstrably untrue assertions. They had failed to share evidence with the defense, had resisted Carl Westman's efforts to pass important information to both sides, had neglected to tell McDonnell and Berry that Carol Lynn had once recanted, and fought any attempt to correct inaccuracies that reflected poorly on Benson. It was, McDonnell maintained, the State, not the defense, that had mounted a slick, manipulative case that depended more on smoke than substance.

Of course, this overlooks one concrete fact. Steven Benson's palm print was on the receipts for the purchase of two pipes and two end caps. It falls to a higher court to determine whether Benson was illegally forced to give police samples of his prints. The same court will have to decide whether the jury was right to infer that the pipes and caps from Hughes Supply were the ones used in the bombs. The State's own witness, metallurgist Theodore Toth, testified that they were "similar," not the "same," and neither he nor anyone else ever established where the other two caps, the smokeless powder, and the detonating device—whatever it was—came from.

Michael McDonnell has suggested that the prints on the receipts could have been "made under other circumstances." The implication is that somehow they were transferred to the receipts from another surface. ATF print expert Frank Kendall admitted that he did not examine the receipts to determine whether they had been tampered with.

The notion that anybody would manufacture evidence confounds all our beliefs about the American judicial system. But reluctant as one might be to accept the possibility that it occurred in the Benson case, the fact is that the State's performance has raised lingering and profoundly troubling questions. Having created a palpably inaccurate composite drawing and cobbled together grossly inaccurate affidavits in support of the search and arrest warrants, did the investigators and/or prosecutors go a step further and manufacture the conclusive piece of evidence?

Just as the State's conduct of the case lays it open to doubts and second guesses, Carol Lynn's testimony, with all its contradictions, inconsistencies, and alterations of earlier statements, calls into question her credibility as a witness. It is possible that everything she said about Steven and his actions on the day of the murders was true. But since so many of her other assertions are dubious one has cause to wonder. And since so much about her character and her own actions, especially her recantation, was kept secret, the jury lacked sufficient information to evaluate her testimony.

Interestingly, at this writing, Michael McDonnell's attempts to win a new trial have been stymied from the start. Although he has filed the proper motions, his client lacks the funds to mount an appeal. On November 8, 1986, Steven Benson signed an affidavit swearing that he had only $49.50 in assets. "I am insolvent, an indigent person unable to pay the costs of an appeal."

But Collier County officials have resisted all efforts to obtain public funds for his appeal. During a hearing on January 5, 1987, in front of Judge Hugh Hayes, Jerry Brock protested that Benson was not indigent and should not expect taxpayers to pick up the tab for his legal bills. In support of his case, Brock introduced a letter, written before the murders, in which Benson, when buying his house in Fort Myers, claimed that he had $288,500 in local assets and a $500,000 share of a trust fund set up by his grandmother. "There is no explanation of where these personal assets went to," Brock pleaded to Hayes.

Like the prosecutor's tactics throughout the case, this was grossly misleading. Weeks before Benson's arrest, Harry Hitchcock cut Steven off from his grandmother's trust. As for Benson's claim that he had $288,500 in local assets, Jerry Brock and his brother, Dwight, had spent days during the trial proving to the jury's satisfaction that Steven had virtually no assets.

After he got the conviction, Jerry Brock told the press "the guy did not have a penny that he was not getting from Margaret." Now he contended in front of the same Judge that the same defendant did have money of his own. This would appear to contradict the entire theory of the State's case—namely that Benson, having no other source of income, feared Margaret was about to cut off the cash flow and decided to kill her and the rest of the family to accelerate his inheritance.

The prosecutor went on to claim that Benson also could not be considered indigent because he had received an advance dispersal of $244,974.39 from his mother's estate. Carl Westman acknowledged at the January 5, 1987, hearing that he had paid over this amount, but he pointed out that he had done so only with the written guarantee, ratified by Carol Lynn Kendall and the court-appointed guardian for Steven's children, that $139,974.39 of the dispersal would be put into a trust for the kids. The remaining $105,000 was earmarked for Steven's defense, and all of it had been spent preparing for and pleading his case, during the trial.

In fact, Michael McDonnell swore that the trial had cost far more than $105,000. He and his firm had not only worked without fees, he had also spent several thousand dollars of his own money. "I just can't do it anymore." He added, "It is improper for a defendant who has no funds to be denied an appeal." He requested $15,000 in county funds to pay for a transcript of the trial and to start the appeal process.

Judge Hugh Hayes, however, ruled "the motion will have to be denied... There is lack of proof that he is indigent."

In a telephone interview, Hayes explained to me that his decision the previous spring to grant Benson $244,974.39 from his mother's estate was made without restrictions. As far as the court was concerned, Benson had access to the entire sum and could use it as he pleased. If he chose to put more than half of it into a trust for his children, that was his prerogative. But he couldn't then claim to be indigent. If the court allowed that, every defendant going on trial could place his assets in trust for his family and demand that the county or state pay for his defense.

The difference was that Benson hadn't chosen to place the money in trust for his children. The arrangement had been imposed upon him as a condition of his receiving any money at all. If he had not agreed, Carl Westman, the personal representative of the estate, and Carol Lynn Kendall, currently the only other clear beneficiary, could have filed legal appeals that would have taken years to resolve. Meanwhile, Benson would have remained in jail awaiting a trial that he could not afford and that the county refused to finance.

Although that might be so, Judge Hayes said it had no bearing on his present ruling. Steven Benson had assets which he had put into trust for his children. If he wanted to appeal his conviction, he should reclaim the money from his children.

But the fact is that to reclaim the money would itself require extensive litigation that Benson could not afford any more than he can afford an appeal. Even if he had the money, the reclaiming process would take years.

This situation has prompted the first very quiet and tentative criticism by the press of the way the case is being conducted. In an editorial on January 8, 1987, the Fort Myers *News-Press* observed of Hayes's decision to deny Steven public funds:

> But couldn't this also be a little too convenient for the judge?
> Suppose Benson is really innocent? It's possible. And what if he really can't get his hands on enough money to pay the lawyers?
> No judge likes to have errors found. No judge wants to be overturned. One would suspect that most judges would just as soon not even have their cases reviewed.
> This is not to suggest there was an ulterior motive in Hayes's ruling. But turning down Benson for indigency needlessly raises the question when all it would have cost is a measly 15 grand.

One might add that Jerry Brock's name could easily be substituted for the word "judge" throughout the editorial. Isn't this a little too convenient for the prosecutor? How eager is he to have the case reviewed or even to have the full transcript typed and made available to the public? At this point, only a handful of people know about the conference in the judge's chambers when Carl Westman came forward to say that he had heard Carol Lynn Kendall tell a markedly different version of the events surrounding the murders. She had concluded in an emotional outburst, "Steven could not have done it."

As the Fort Myers *News-Press* asks, "Suppose Benson is really innocent?" The public has a right to know. If on the basis of the whole truth, Steven Benson is convicted again, then he will at least have had the fair trial to which he is entitled. No American citizen can ask for more, and no society that professes to be just can settle for less.

Born in Washington, D.C., Michael Mewshaw graduated from the University of Maryland with a B.A. and earned a Ph.D. in literature from the University of Virginia. The author of seven critically acclaimed novels and two prize-winning books of investigative nonficton, he has received a Fulbright Fellowship, a grant from the National Endowment for the Arts, and a Guggenheim Fellowship. Mewshaw has written for the *New York Times*, the *Washington Post*, *Playboy*, the *Nation*, the *New Statesman*, and other publications in the United States and Europe. He lives in Rome with his wife and two sons.

Made in the USA
Middletown, DE
08 July 2024